CW01064402

Family and *Familia* in
Roman Law and Life

Family and *Familia* in Roman Law and Life

Jane F. Gardner

CLARENDON PRESS · OXFORD

*This book has been printed digitally and produced in a standard specification
in order to ensure its continuing availability*

OXFORD
UNIVERSITY PRESS

Great Clarendon Street, Oxford OX2 6DP

Oxford University Press is a department of the University of Oxford.
It furthers the University's objective of excellence in research, scholarship,
and education by publishing worldwide in

Oxford New York

Auckland Bangkok Buenos Aires Cape Town Chennai
Dar es Salaam Delhi Hong Kong Istanbul Karachi Kolkata
Kuala Lumpur Madrid Melbourne Mexico City Mumbai Nairobi
São Paulo Shanghai Taipei Tokyo Toronto

Oxford is a registered trade mark of Oxford University Press
in the UK and in certain other countries

Published in the United States
by Oxford University Press Inc., New York

© Jane F. Gardner 1998

The moral rights of the author have been asserted

Database right Oxford University Press (maker)

Reprinted 2004

ISBN 0-19-815217-5

Preface

This is a book about Roman law, for Roman social historians, although I hope that it will be of some interest also to social historians in other fields and to specialists in Roman law. Of necessity, much of the source material is drawn from Roman legal writings, both since relevant literary and epigraphic evidence is very limited in amount, and since legal writings are our largest single source for actual behaviour.

Juristic writings are by their nature crabbed and not easy to understand, for those unfamiliar with this sort of material. The texts are not only highly technical but also elliptical, since they tend to be concerned only with the specific points of law discussed, and usually neither provide a full description of the factual background, nor spell out all the legal implications. I have done what I can to remedy these drawbacks, both by unravelling in (I hope) fairly plain language the relevant legal points, and also by drawing attention to the actual human behaviour underlying the situations discussed and where possible making use of relevant literary and epigraphic material. I hope that the result is reasonably user-friendly.

The thinking which prompted this book originated in preparations for papers to be delivered at conferences in Paris in 1993 and in Canberra in 1994. I am grateful to the Comité National de la Recherche Scientifique, Paris, for their hospitality on the former occasion and to the British Academy for a grant towards the cost of travel. My warm thanks are also due to the Humanities Research Centre, Australian National University, Canberra, for making me a Conference Visitor, and so enabling me to participate in the third Roman Family conference held there.

Preface

I owe a special debt of gratitude to the Leverhulme Trust for the award of a research fellowship for the academic session 1995-6, during my tenure of which much of this book was written.

J.F.G.

Department of Classics, The University of Reading
December 1996

Contents

Contents

Abbreviations

Listed below are a few abbreviations for legal and epigraphic sources which may be unfamiliar to some readers.

Bruns⁷ | K. G. Bruns (rev. O. Gradenwitz), *Fontes Iuris Romani Antiqui. Leges et Negotia*, 7th edition (Tübingen, 1909).

Cod. Iust. | *Codex Iustinianus*, P. Krüger (ed.), *Corpus Iuris Civilis*, ii (Berlin, 1877).

Coll. | *Mosaicarum et Romanarum Legum Collatio*.

Cod. Theod. | *Codex Theodosianus*, Th. Mommsen and P. Krüger (edd.), 2 vols. (Berlin, 1905).

D. | *Digesta Iustiniani*, Th. Mommsen, and P. Krüger (edd.), *Corpus Iuris Civilis*, i (Berlin, 1920); also English translation, ed. A. Watson, 4 vols. (Philadelphia, 1985).

FIRA | S. Riccobono, G. Baviera, C. Ferrini, G. Furlani, and V. Arangio-Ruiz (edd.), *Fontes iuris Romani anteiustiniani*, 3 vols. (Florence, 1940–3).

Frag. Vat. | *Fragmenta iuris Romani Vaticana*.

Gaius | Gaius, *Institutiones iuris civilis commentarii quattuor*.

Gaius, *Epit.* | *Epitome Gaii* (see Schulz (1946) 302).

Honoré | (preceded by number) Reference number of rescript in the *Palingenesia*, serially numbered database in Honoré (1994).

Huschke | P. E. Huschke, *Iurisprudentia Anteiustiniana*, 4th edition (Bratislava, 1878).

Inst. | Iustinianus, *Institutiones*.

Nov. | Iustinianus, *Novellae*.

Paul. *Sent.* | Iulius Paulus, *Sententiarum ad Filium libri v*.

Tab. Herc. | *Herculaneum Tablets*, published by V. Arangio-Ruiz and G. Pugliese Carratelli in the periodical *La Parola*

	del Passato, vols. 1, 3, 8, 9, 10 (1946, 1948, 1953, 1954, 1955).
TP Sulp.	*Tabulae Pompeianae Sulpicianae*, edited by Camodeca (1992).
Ulp. *Reg.*	Domitius Ulpianus, *Liber singularis regularum reliquiae*.

Introduction: *Familia* and *Families*

According to Roman law, Roman society was made up of *familiae*; in real life, the Romans belonged to families. The two might sometimes coincide in composition, but only to a limited extent and for limited periods of time, since whereas the *familia*, being a legal construct, had a universal and unchanging, clearly defined structure and a fixed membership, with only a few variables, there were almost infinite possibilities of variation in the make-up of individual family groups, and these could also undergo considerable alterations, from the point of view of an individual, within his or her lifetime. Another difference was that the *familia* was self-contained; it not only had a very restricted membership but it was entirely separate and discrete from all other *familiae*. Families, on the other hand, overlapped with each other, and were constantly creating new overlaps, through the usual means of marital couplings and births. The main thing that the *familia* and families had in common was biological connection between the persons each contained. This was real for 'real', i.e. natural, families, while for the *familia* there was a presumption that those free persons under the control of its legal head, the *paterfamilias*, were biologically descended from him—although such descent could also be fictitiously created by the legal mechanism of adoption.

A *familia* was still a *familia* even if it consisted of only one person. Ideally, however, the notional *familia*, in the strict legal sense,[1] which provided the structural framework for Roman law consisted of: an adult male Roman, the *paterfamilias*, lawfully married, with children born to him and his wife (or successive wives), together with the children, if any, of sons (and their sons, and so on in the male line only, through as many generations as might be simultaneously alive). The

---

[1] *Iure proprio*: D. 50. 16. 195 (Ulpian). Ulpian also mentions a number of non-technical usages (such as body of slaves under a single ownership), and the word was commonly used to refer to much more extended kinship groups in the male line: Saller (1984), (1994) ch. 4.

paterfamilias was sole owner of all the property of the *familia*, both inherited and otherwise acquired. Within the *familia*, he was virtually autonomous; he had *patria potestas*, legal power, over the persons of his children and descendants—and, in early Rome mainly, usually of his wife as well. This was an authority which extended, theoretically at least, to a power of life and death over those under his legal control.[2] The right to inherit the property of the *familia* after his death vested primarily in those free persons who had been subject to his *potestas*. All valid legal relations with other *familiae* were mediated through him, and he was personally responsible for their consequences.

This notional structure provided the parameters for analysis of the legal effects of all transactions between Roman citizens, not only, but certainly including also, those relating to family matters, and so it determined the character of a certain kind of picture of Roman life and behaviour, presented in the main in Roman legal writings (or sometimes in other sources when dealing with matters where the legal rules are relevant). In this sort of account, framed in terms of the system of civil law and the rights and powers of the *paterfamilias*, actions are analysed solely in terms of their legal effects, with reference to a particular point of law at issue, and no more detail of the personal circumstances of the persons involved is supplied than what is relevant to the legal question. If one were to treat this kind of material as providing all that was relevant for a full description of Roman family life, and were to use it as a database to try to construct an image of what actual Roman families were like—not only their composition and the respective legal status of all the component members, but the moral and emotional basis of relationships between individuals within them—a very strange and distorted picture would emerge. The powers of the *paterfamilias*, it must always be remembered, were a legal construct, not the essence of Roman family life.[3]

Most of the recent work on the Roman family, therefore—once the basic statement of the legal framework is out of the way—has tended, either explicitly or implicitly, to treat *familia* and family as separate entities, and to ignore the *familia*, in favour of a variety of other approaches directed upon such evidence as may be found for actual families. There have been various studies of emotional and moral rela-

---

[2] For its exercise, and limitations placed upon it in practice, see Rabello (1979) 14ff.; Voci (1980) 50–66, 74–5; Harris (1986).
[3] See Saller (1991*b*) 144–6 for some trenchant criticisms of proponents of the opposite view.

tionships within the family group, on such topics as *pietas* (essentially untranslatable, but roughly a blend of 'affection' and 'dutifulness').[4] Adult, and particularly parental, attitudes to young children have been explored,[5] as have personal relationships between mothers and their children[6] or those between husband and wife,[7] and, more generally, the Romans' own ideal of family life.[8] There has been some investigation of the composition of certain types of 'non-standard' families, such as those of ex-slaves or mixed-status groups;[9] and of outsiders, such as foster-children or bastards.[10] The effects have been examined, for the formation of kinship relationships and for the formation and reformation of family groups through time, of factors such as divorce, mortality, and remarriage.[11] Conclusions have been drawn from demographic projections, based mainly on statistics derived from analysis of relevant funerary inscriptions, about the effects of factors such as age at marriage and life expectancies, not only on the composition of families,[12] but on consequences for the care of children and of their property.[13]

In these accounts, some use is made of legal sources, by far our largest single body of evidence for Roman behaviour, and in particular in regard to investigation of Roman practices in the transmission of property. How and to whom did Romans arrange to pass on their worldly goods when they died? Important studies have been published, copiously illustrated with examples from legal writings, showing how individual Romans, especially through the medium of wills, devised strategies tailor-made to the circumstances, so far as these could be predicted, of themselves and their own families.[14] These shed much light on the kinds of motivations which influenced the testators, and in particular on the social and emotional pressures to which they responded.

Many elements of the above will be found also in the present study,

---

[4] Saller (1991*b*) 146–51, (1994) ch. 5.

[5] Wiedemann (1989); Dixon (1988) ch. 5 and (1992) ch. 4; B. Rawson (1991).

[6] Dixon (1988) chs. 7 and 8.   [7] Treggiari (1991) chs. 6–9.   [8] Dixon (1991).

[9] Rawson (1966); Treggiari (1981*a*); van de Wiel (1992); Weaver (1986).

[10] Nielsen (1987); Rawson (1986) and (1989).

[11] Bradley (1991*a*) chs. 6 and 7; (1991*b*).

[12] Parkin (1992); Saller and Shaw (1984*a*); Shaw (1987); Bagnall and Frier (1994); Saller (1987) and (1994) chs. 2 and 3.

[13] Dixon (1988) ch. 6; Saller (1987) and (1994) ch. 8.

[14] Especially by Saller (1991*a*) and (1994) ch. 7; see also the social and cultural survey of wills by Champlin (1991).

and my debt to many of the works mentioned will be obvious. In this book, however, the starting point is the *familia* itself. The intention is to investigate the interrelationship between family and *familia*, and this will be done by considering three groups of people outside the *familia*—those removed from it (emancipated), those taken into it (adopted), and those never in it but linked by blood and affection (mothers and maternal kin).

The self-contained unit of the *familia* was not treated in practice by the Romans as something inviolable, a sacred cow—far from it. For their own private purposes they exploited in various ways the legal rules based on the *familia*. The legally-defined unit was freely disrupted by use of mechanisms such as emancipation—release of an existing member of the *familia* from *patria potestas* and so from membership of the *familia*—and adoption—taking an additional person from outside into the *familia* and under the *potestas* of its head—and the two were even sometimes used in combination (1.12 below). Socially, 'family' connections outside the *familia*—that is, the mother, and through her the relatives in the maternal line—assumed, for a variety of reasons, increasing importance during the historical period.

In each of the three areas, concerning persons taken out of the *familia*, those brought into it, and those outside it from the start, it is possible to observe an evolution in the law, the rules of the strict civil law, and in particular the law of inheritance, being modified and adapted in response to the needs and wishes of people in Roman society, who are adopting strategies that they see as being in the best interests of those emotionally and socially closest to them, their immediate families; this is particularly evident in the law relating to the transmission of property. That is, the priorities of the Roman man in the street were not bound up with preserving the *familia*, but with doing the best for his family. The legal system responded to this— even if often slowly and lagging behind events—since the purpose of the civil law was not to compel society into a predetermined mould, but to facilitate society's wants and purposes, so far as these could be identified and agreed upon, as they changed over time. Rules originally framed in terms of *familia* only were gradually altered to accommodate 'family' interests.

Some of the tensions between the emotional concerns and legal roles of mothers and their kin in relation to the family will be explored, especially in Chapter 3. The practical effects of emancipation and adoption for the individuals and the families concerned will also be examined, in Chapters 1 and 2 respectively, and both the private and the broader social reasons for the adoption of such strategies will be investigated. Especially, it will be shown how these deliberate disruptions of the *familia* influenced many of the substantial changes in Roman family law between the early Republic and the law of the *Digest. Patria potestas* and the legally-defined unit of the *familia* lasted as long as our documented knowledge of Roman law but that does not mean that they governed the Romans' conduct of their lives. They were a convenient organizational device, the price which had to be paid for some stability in society, and they could be turned to advantage for 'family' purposes.

In each of the three chapters of the book (especially in 1.8, 2.8, and 3.6 and 7), particular attention has been paid to the special circumstances of a large and important section of Roman society and the consequences of their persisting presence among the Romans, that is, freed slaves and persons of ex-slave descent. Their status created many anomalies and disparities which made adaptation to the *familia* framework difficult or even impossible for them and their families, and sometimes disadvantageous. Their presence and importance to society is reflected in several significant changes to Roman family law.

The period studied will be in the main that for which there is most legal and historical evidence, that is the last two centuries BC and the first three centuries AD, although where relevant certain earlier and later developments (such as the reform of the legal consequences of adoption under the emperor Justinian) will be considered. No comparable treatment of the subject exists, either by Roman lawyers, whose approach largely precludes synthesis and pays little or no attention to social factors, or by social historians, who tend to use legal material illustratively, rather than to analyse the legal rules and their effects in themselves. It is hoped that this study will be useful to both.

I

Out of the *Familia*: The Practice of Emancipation

1.1 INTRODUCTION

The civil law of the Romans, of which the earliest form known to us took shape, according to Roman tradition, in the middle of the fifth century BC in the law of the Twelve Tables, was constructed, so far as the law of persons and property was concerned, with reference primarily to the interests of a close-knit and exclusive group of persons, the *familia*, and its property. Both were under the legal control (*potestas*) of the head of the *familia*, the *paterfamilias*. The persons under his control—i.e. his sons, daughters, sons' children, and, at least in earlier times, his wife *in manu*, that is, also under the legal control of her husband[1]—had no property of their own, and lacked independent power of legal action. Their position had, however, certain benefits (even though in practice in early Rome it is doubtful whether much could be done to enforce them); provision of necessary maintenance was the responsibility of the *pater*, and they had the right to share his inheritance—on intestacy, at least—when his *potestas* terminated at his death.

These benefits were lost if they left the *familia*, which could be done in one of two ways, both dependent on the act of the *pater* himself. Either they were given over into the *potestas* of another *paterfamilias* by adoption (or, in the case of women, being placed at marriage into the *manus* of her husband or his *paterfamilias*), or they were released from *potestas* without passing into that of anyone else, that is they were emancipated. Those given in adoption lost the benefits of membership of their original *familia*, but immediately passed into another *familia*, and gained the corresponding benefits of being a member of that. Those emancipated, however, apparently lost one set of benefits

[1] Treggiari (1991) 16–32.

6

without being given another in its place; they were on their own. Emancipation, that is, release of an individual from paternal *potestas*, could therefore be seen, if one were to attend only to the strict letter of the civil law, as an expulsion from the *familia*, even as possibly an intentional punishment.

To suggest, however, that punishment was the *purpose* of its invention is to fall into the error of treating the letter of the Roman civil law and the powers of the *paterfamilias* as if they were the emotional and moral basis of family relationships, rather than a legal construct.[2] The idea of emancipation as punishment retains its attraction, however, for some modern commentators, for example, 'We must not therefore think of it as necessarily the conferring of a benefit; it might equally well in earlier times be a punishment, casting the son out into the world without property and without hope of inheriting any from his father.' Omitting the qualification 'in earlier times', another writer remarks: 'Becoming legally independent was scant recompense for being thrown out onto the streets without any *peculium* by an angry *paterfamilias*. Emancipation could thus be a hostile act, the threat of it used by the *paterfamilias* to control unruly children.'[3]

If these were indeed the effects, emancipation would be a daunting prospect, especially as the dependent son seems to have had little say in the matter.[4] 'Cast out' and 'thrown out onto the streets' are dra-

---

[2] Girard (1911) 190 distinguishes in point of time between the two views commonly taken of the purpose of emancipation; later, it took on the aspect of a benefit to the child, increasing his independence, but in its inception, he suggests, it was invented as a new mode of punishment, falling in a scale of severity between death or sale on the one hand and disinheritance on the other. Kaser (1971) 69 prefers to stress the aspect of independence, pointing out (n. 11) that fathers in early Rome had more drastic and effective means of punishment at their disposal. Girard's idea of deliberate provision of a 'menu' of punishments of graduated severity from which fathers might pick and choose is rather bizarre. As evidence for punitive emancipation, Thomas (1982) 554–5, cites only 'le très considérable dossier des controverses et déclamations consacrées au thème du fils *abdicatus* et exhérédé' and the treatment of Agrippa Postumus. The latter, however, was rather a special case, involving important political considerations, while the former belong to a type of writing that is manifestly rhetorical in intent and not to be taken as *reportage*: as Thomas himself goes on to say, the theme of the majority is the injustice and arbitrariness of fathers.

[3] Nicholas (1962) 80; Borkowski (1994) 107. Normally, however, Borkowski observes (with reference to the classical period), the person emancipated would be provided with funds, if possible, and might expect a legacy, or institution as heir in the father's will.

[4] Whether in classical law either emancipation or adoption required the consent of the person affected is controversial: Buckland (1963) 124 and 132. Adoption will be discussed in 2.7. As for emancipation, the apparently clear statement of Paul, *Sent.* 2. 25.

matic expressions, but need not, of course, be taken literally. Did change of legal status necessarily entail change of residence? In the later Republic at least, many adult sons *in potestate* especially if married but also some bachelors, will have lived elsewhere than in their fathers' houses; so would married daughters, emancipated or otherwise.[5]

A very different interpretation has been offered. Far from 'casting out' being the effect of emancipation, it has been suggested that the departure of sons from the family home was the original *cause* of the institution of emancipation. This diaspora, it is alleged by Voci, had two main causes, one agricultural, the other commercial.[6]

1. Sons had to move away from home because the ancestral land no longer sufficed for the family's needs. Thanks to Rome's early conquests in Italy, there was public land available for distribution, either to settlers in colonies or, mainly from the later third century, as individual tracts. However, as it was rationed, it was necessary for the sons in question to become independent heads of household; the story of C. Licinius Stolo (see below) affords some confirmation for the first half of the fourth century, though the process may have begun earlier.

2. The son chose an economic activity which kept him away from

---

[5] 'Filius familias emancipari invitus non cogitur' (A son in power is not compelled to be emancipated against his will), i.e. his implicit consent, at least, is necessary, has been suspected of being post-classical. On the other hand, Seneca, *Contr.* 2. 1. 19 appears to take it for granted that it was not in the power of the *filiusfamilias* to refuse. A son about to be emancipated by his father, for opposing being given in adoption, speaks: 'Quid enim ad amittendum patrem interest, utrum eiiciar an transferar? Si non licet recusare, cur potius abdicas me quam tradis?' (What difference does it make, to my losing my father, whether I am ejected or transferred? If refusal is not permitted, why do you renounce me rather than hand me over?). Though there is no explicit legal text in the same sense, Marcianus is very positive (*D.* 1. 7. 31) that a son in power had no means of *compelling* his father to emancipate him. See further Volterra (1966) 124ff. There are similar ambiguities in the legal evidence on consent to marriage; unfortunately, we do not have for emancipation the kind of historical evidence which shows that in contracting marriage, despite the theoretical legal authority of the *paterfamilias*, the wishes of children sometimes in practice prevailed: Treggiari (1991) 170–80.

[5] See below, 1.9. Imperial jurists conventionally dated the inception of marriage from the completion of *in domum deductio*, the formal conducting of the bride to the groom's home which was part of traditional wedding celebrations; see Corbett (1930) 92–4.

[6] Voci (1982) 392–448, esp. 408. See Cornell (1995) 301–4, 327–30, 364–8, 380–3 on the acquisition of public land and the development of colonies, and ch. 14, *passim*, for the development of relations with the southern half of Italy.

the family home and made him act independently of his *paterfamilias*. This is linked by Voci with the development of extensive relations with the cities of southern Italy, especially in the second half of the fourth century.

Concerning the first suggested reason, it is the rationing of land allotments, rather than the need for physical removal, that constitutes the most obvious motive for emancipation from *potestas*, nor does it appear that legal independence was particularly necessary in order to cope with such litigation as might occasionally arise for farmers and peasants, any more than it was needed in order to conduct commercial activities. This was certainly not true of the later Republic, when the praetor's edict (see 1.4 below) made various means of taking legal action available to *filiifamilias* engaged in business activities; even before these were introduced, however, the inconvenience of physical remoteness was not something arising from the effects of *patria potestas*, but rather from the participatory nature of Roman legal procedures and the need for litigants, whether in power or not, to travel to the nearest seat of government.[7] Physical separation from the family home does not in itself seem to have any necessary connection with the rise of the practice of emancipation.

As for the immediate implications of emancipation for the economic well-being of sons, remarks such as those of Nicholas and Borkowski quoted above are dramatic over-simplifications, based on hypothetical extreme cases of paternal hostility. As we shall see, there is some evidence that in practice fathers were concerned to make present and future provision for children released from *potestas*, while in course of time the loss of benefits was much reduced; the legal entitlements of the emancipated child were transformed, especially in relation to inheritance (and also, though admittedly to a much lesser extent, maintenance). Some of these changes affect also the legal obligations and entitlements between mothers and children, which require detailed discussion elsewhere; the present discussion will concentrate on developments affecting emancipated children.

Nor have such extreme situations of hostility much relation to the variety of motives for emancipation, and the variety of legally complex family situations, discussed in surviving texts. These texts, almost entirely legal, date mostly from the second century AD or

---

[7] Gardner (1993) 74ff.

later, though they reflect developments going back much further. Like the modifications to the civil law, they reveal a society in which, though *patria potestas* and the *familia* are still active institutions, increasing attention and consideration is paid both in law and in life to emotional and moral obligations between those closely related by blood. That is, 'family' in practice is as much regarded as *familia*—or even more so, since the *familia* was created not as an end in itself but to serve certain social purposes, both public and private, among the latter being the economic welfare of its members, who, in theory at least, and for the most part in practice, were the blood descendants (i.e. the 'family') of its head.

It is important to remember that the *familia* was entirely a legal construct, the composition of which was created both 'naturally', by blood descent within lawful marriage, and artificially, by co-opting legal outsiders (who might or might not have blood connections with the *pater*) through the medium of adoption. Releasing someone from the legal control of a *paterfamilias*, though it had certain legal consequences, and ended membership of the *familia*, cannot therefore be equated with expulsion from the *family* group. Emancipation was merely a legal mechanism (as was adoption), which created certain possibilities for the person emancipated. To represent it negatively as a punishment or deprivation is to ignore its positive aspects.

The practice of emancipation can be seen, in a sense, as the antithesis of the formation (through marriage and adoption) of the *familia*. It came into existence fairly early in the Republican period and persisted, apparently (since the law was adjusted to take account of it) in frequent use, throughout the period for which we have evidence for Roman law. The *familia*, however, showed equal durability in Roman law. Both served certain social purposes, those of emancipation essentially private and 'family' oriented, those of the *familia* both public, in the interests of social order (see n. 73 below) and private, essentially safeguarding the economic rights of individual members and the status of the family in successive generations.

1.2 THE PROCEDURE AND EFFECTS OF EMANCIPATION

A procedure for emancipation originated early in the Republic; the earliest mentioned emancipation, but probably, even if genuine, not the first, is that of the son of C. Licinius Stolo in the 360s BC. It continued in force until abolished in AD 531 by Justinian. Objecting to the complicated rigmarole (*circumductiones inextricabiles*) of the sequence of imaginary sales and manumissions of the old procedure, he instructed that in future emancipation could be effected either by imperial rescript[8] or by a simple appearance of the parties concerned in front of a competent magistrate.

The classical procedure, used both for adoption and for emancipation, is described in detail by Gaius (writing in the middle of the second century AD). The father mancipated (i.e. 'sold') his son to a third party, who then formally manumitted him. However, instead of becoming free (as a manumitted slave would), he reverted into his father's *potestas*.[9] The process of sale and manumission was repeated a second time. The father then sold him for a third time, at which point *potestas* was terminated. At this stage, the son was still *in mancipio* to the notional buyer. He was then remancipated to his father, who carried out a third manumission;[10] the purpose of this manœuvre was to give the father rights to inherit from the son, analogous to those that an owner manumitting had to inherit from his freedmen (see below).

Why were three sales necessary? Gaius derives this rule from a law of the Twelve Tables:[11] 'Si pater filium ter venum duit, a patre filius liber esto' (If a father thrice sell a son, from the father the son is to be free). It is not known for certain whether this law itself was intended merely to institute a procedure for release of a son from *potestas*. If this were the case, it is surprising that no provision was made until later to secure the father's rights of intestate inheritance from the son. Alternatively, it was originally meant to punish fathers who abused their power, and humiliated their sons, by repeated sale into bondage; however, as it created a means of ending *potestas*, it came to

---

[8] Livy 7. 16. 9; *Cod. Iust.* 8. 48. 6. A procedure by rescript was already made available in AD 502 by Anastasius in cases where the person to be emancipated was unavoidably absent, subject to subsequent declaration of consent (*Cod. Iust.* 8. 48. 5).

[9] Gaius 1. 132ff. Watson (1975) 118–19 plausibly explains this way of doing things by the derivation of the procedure from that used for giving into *nexum*, temporary bondage to work off debt, which was not intended to be a permanent transfer of *potestas*; sale of sons into bondage was obsolete by the classical period. For a summary and discussion of other modern views of the purpose of the law, which associate it with a more general paternal 'right of sale' (instituted, according to Dion. Hal. 2. 27, by Romulus), see Rabello (1979) 93–104.

[10] Gaius 1. 134, *Epit.* 1. 6. 3; Ulp. *Reg.* 10. 1.

[11] Twelve Tables 4. 2. Numeration and translations of texts from the Twelve Tables follow the recent edition in Crawford (1996) 555–721.

be used to permit this to be done. Daughters, and male descendants other than sons (i.e. grandchildren), were apparently not mentioned in the Twelve Tables; therefore it was decided that they needed to be sold only once, thus simplifying matters.[12]

Unlike marriage, emancipation was not a purely private act. It used the procedure of *mancipatio*, which was the appropriate method used in early Rome for conveyancing ownership of the main types of property that were commonly known in classical law as *res mancipi*—working animals, slaves, land in Italy and the buildings on it, and rights over rural land; the same procedure was used for making wills, i.e. for the conveyance of the *familia* (in the sense of property) to an heir. *Filiifamilias* were not slaves, but like slaves they were *in potestate*; in their case, the 'sale' was notional. All of these acts diminished in some way the *familia*, which was the basic structural unit of Roman society—the *paterfamilias* was at the interface between public and private. The procedure therefore had to be conducted in the presence of a magistrate and of five other adult male Romans (i.e. five *patresfamiliarum*) as witnesses.

The legal consequences were clear-cut. There were certain gains. The person emancipated became legally independent, *sui iuris*, and, if adult (minors had their affairs administered by tutors), both capable of and responsible for taking legal action on his own behalf. From now on, whatever he acquired was his, not his father's.

On the other hand, he ceased to be a member of the *familia*. He had to provide for himself. Children already born to him remained in his father's *potestas* but would not come under his own *potestas* when his father died; he therefore lost all legal control over them. He also lost his automatic right to a share of the inheritance should his father die intestate.

These were potentially serious disadvantages, which followed logically from the legal nature of the *familia*. The existence of such legal rules, however, does not necessarily mean that there were drastic effects in practice on the daily lives of emancipated children, still less that it was the intention of the emancipators that this should be so, or that friendly contacts abruptly terminated. Emancipation, it should

---

[12] Jolowicz (1965) 87, suggests over-ingeniously that the omission of daughters and grandchildren in the original law was deliberate: 'It was intended that the head of the family should be able to sell the less important members of the family as often as they were manumitted by a buyer.' If, however, the purpose was *nexum*, it is questionable whether these would be equally acceptable or effective in working off the debt.

be remembered, also created possibilities for mutual benefaction between the old *familia* and the new. *Emancipati* could, for example, receive gifts from their former *patres*, since they were no longer *in potestate*, and, being still related as cognates, relatives by blood, they were exempt from the restrictions on gifts imposed by the *lex Cincia* of 204 BC, which allowed valuable gifts only between cognates up to the sixth degree.[13] Though not heirs in civil law if their fathers died intestate, they could still be instituted heirs in wills, or left some part of the property as legacies; the possibility of disposition by will is already recognized in the Twelve Tables[14] (and therefore may predate the institution of emancipation itself—see below). Although outside the *familia*, the *emancipatus*, like the person given in adoption into another *familia*, was not necessarily socially and emotionally regarded as an outsider; he or she was still 'family'.

An example of this is the generosity shown by someone no longer in the *familia* of his birth, Scipio Aemilianus, son of L. Aemilius Paulus, towards his natural brother and sisters. Scipio had been given in adoption to the son of Scipio Africanus Major, who had married Aemilia, Paulus' sister. By the adoption, his paternal aunt thus became his paternal grandmother. Another brother had been given in adoption to Q. Fabius Maximus (praetor 181). Two daughters remained in Aemilius' family, and two sons, but since these two sons died before him he made his heirs the two whom he had given in adoption, even though they were now no longer part of his *familia*. Scipio Aemilianus, his brother Fabius and their sisters the Aemiliae were now in three different *familiae*. Polybius, drawing a distinction between the strictly legal position, and Scipio's devotion to his natural family, gave an admiring account of Scipio's generosity.[15]

Since Scipio knew that his brother Fabius was less well-off than himself, he did not take up his part of the inheritance from their father Aemilius but let Fabius have it all. Not only that, but when Fabius wanted to put on a gladiatorial display for their father's funeral, Scipio voluntarily supplied half the cost—Polybius estimated the total amount required for such a show was about thirty talents. Scipio had also received the inheritance, when she died in 162 BC, of his aunt-cum-grandmother Aemilia. Out of this he was asked to pay

[13] Watson (1971*b*) 73–4; Crawford (1996) 741–4; see 3.2 below.
[14] Twelve Tables 5. 3; Crawford (1996) 635–40.
[15] Polyb. 31. 26–8. For the adoption by Fabius, see 2.4 below, at n. 46.

the outstanding portion of the dowries of her two daughters, his adoptive aunts, and astonished their husbands by paying the whole amount at once, instead of spreading it out, as was customary, over three years. Aemilia's personal possessions—the rich clothes and jewellery, the gold and silver vessels, with which she was accustomed to appear in ceremonial processions at women's festivals, as well as her personal retinue of slaves—he handed over to his own natural mother, Papiria, whose means were much more modest, so that she did not any longer have to stay at home on ceremonial occasions, but could participate in a manner befitting her rank. When she died, Scipio (apparently inheriting also from her, by her will) passed these on to his natural sisters, even although, Polybius remarks, they had no legal title to it. That is, it was not part of the patrimony of this branch of the Aemilii—and, in any case, if the Aemiliae had been married with *manus* (as Polybius' calling their father 'legally childless' also perhaps implies), they would belong to the *familiae* of their husbands. Even if they had not married with *manus*, we do not know whether their mother had. If not, she would have been in a different *familia*, and daughters at that stage did not have any claim to inherit on intestacy from their mothers, if not in the same *familia*.

Polybius gets a good deal of moralizing mileage out of this account. His main theme is the stock one of 'virtuous poverty', or at least superiority to the materialistic attractions of wealth and luxury, exemplified by one of the heroes of Rome's glorious past (Papiria's allegedly modest means underline the theme); he also emphasizes, however, the nobility of character shown in Scipio's devotion to the members of his natural family.

The whole story goes to show that people who had departed from a *familia*—whether as here by adoption, or by emancipation—were still socially and emotionally regarded as part of the 'family'. One of the strongest indications that this is true of those emancipated is the eventual modification of the rules of intestate succession, greatly to the benefit of *emancipati*, in the praetor's edict. These changes, it is suggested below, are consequent upon a number of developments in the late Republic that intensify the importance of family, rather than *familia*, connections in resisting the dispersal of properties. Since examples of actual emancipations are lacking, these legal changes provide valuable indirect evidence of the way that Romans felt emancipated children ought to be treated. That the changes began so late after the institution of emancipation cannot, however, be taken as evidence of earlier coldness toward emancipated children, still less does it prove that emancipation (as suggested in Girard (1911) 190) was little used and lacking in social importance until the final stages of the Republic. Roman legal writing is one of our most important sources of evidence for social developments and attitudes among the Romans, scrappy and lacunose though it is, especially for the Republican period. It must be borne in mind, however, that legal writers in general mention only what is relevant to the legal point under discussion. Just as much of Roman law is equally relevant to males and females, and so it is unnecessary to specify sex,[16] so *emancipati*, for most practical purposes, are in Roman law like any other independent heads of household, and equally under the protection of the law. What lawyers are concerned to settle and clarify are the consequences of legal changes; they do not spend much time talking about the social and emotional reasons for them.

1.3 *Emancipati* and Inheritance in Roman Civil Law

If a *paterfamilias* died without leaving a will, or if his will failed for some reason (see below, nn. 175–6), certain rules of succession upon intestacy came into play. So far as property expectations were concerned, the rules of intestate inheritance in civil law, as laid down in the Twelve Tables,[17] strongly favoured the *familia* and have no place—or only a very low-level one—for emancipated children. In contrast, the rules which were applied in practice in classical Roman law, those of the praetorian edict, placed emancipated children on virtually the same footing as the *familia* remaining under *patria potestas*.

Intestate inheritance in civil law arranged claimants in three classes, with descending priority.

1. *Sui heredes*—those free people who were until his death in the *potestas* of the deceased, or *in manu*, that is his legitimate natural sons and daughters, his adoptive sons and daughters, descendants of sons no longer *in potestate* and his wife *in manu*—in other words, the *familia*. These inherited automatically.
2. The agnates (after the *sui*, who were themselves also agnates).

---

[16] D. 31. 45 pr.; 32. 62; 50. 16. 1, 152, 195.
[17] Twelve Tables 5. 4, 5. 5; Gaius 3. 1–17.

The patron, i.e. the former owner, of a freedman was also included, as the nearest thing, in law, to a relative that a freedman had. Freedmen had no agnates, since slaves had no legally recognized kindred. 'Agnates' were for practical purposes the deceased's brothers and sisters and the brothers' children; however inheritance was offered only to the *proximus agnatus,*[18] i.e. the agnate nearest in degree (or agnates, if there were several of equal degree). If he/they all refused or died before acceptance, the inheritance passed straight to the third category. The original purpose of this restriction may have been to control dispersal of property in this category; agnates of more distant degree could still claim in the third category.

3. The members of the *gens*—'Si agnatus nec escit, gentiles familiam ?pecuniamque? habento' (If there be no agnate, the *gentiles* are to have the *familia* ?and goods?). The law concerning them had fallen into disuse by the second century AD.[19]

There is no obvious place for emancipated children to succeed in any of the above categories, unless, possibly, as members of the *gens*, which would give them only a remote chance of succession. *Emancipati* were not counted as agnates, since emancipation broke the agnatic tie; nor were they *sui heredes*, since the *sui heredes* essentially constituted the *familia*, of which the *emancipatus* was no longer a member. They would be excluded from the inheritance by their own brothers and sisters, or children born to sons before their emancipation, and remaining in their grandfather's power, and also by their father's agnates; and they would have no more right to inherit at civil law than other members of the *gens*. *Gentiles* appear to have been admitted indiscriminately, not by nearness of degree.[20]

Under civil law, therefore, they were starkly excluded; their omission, however, may not have been deliberate. It seems likely, for two

---

[18] Freedman's patron: Twelve Tables 5. 8; Gaius 3. 40; other references and commentary in Crawford (1996) 646–8. *Proximus agnatus*: Twelve Tables 5. 4; cf. *D.* 26. 4. 9 (Gaius) and Gaius 1. 164, on *tutela* (of *impuberes* only, agnate *tutela* over women having been abolished by Claudius: Gaius 1. 171).

[19] Twelve Tables 5. 5; Gaius 1. 163; 3. 17.

[20] For the case for their continuing membership of the *gens* after emancipation see Watson (1967) 100–1; *contra,* Kaser (1971) 69. The *gens* was in theory a patrilineal descent group descended from a supposed common ancestor and with the same clan name, or *nomen gentilicium*. By classical times, this descent was notional and in practice unprovable, and *gens*-affiliation rested solely on the name; see Brunt (1988) 451–2, 525–6; for *gentes* in early Roman history, Cornell (1995) 84–5, with bibliography in notes.

reasons, that emancipation of a *filius* from paternal power was not yet practised at the time of the Twelve Tables.

The first is an argument—admittedly not conclusive—based on Twelve Tables 4. 2.[21] As mentioned above, a procedural possibility at least of emancipation was created under the provision 'si pater ter filium venum duit, a patre filius liber esto' (If a father thrice sell a son [i.e. bind him over to another in *nexum*, short-term bondage to work off a debt], from the father the son is to be free). However, it is not certain that the initial purpose of this provision in the Twelve Tables was to enable emancipation generally. It has also been suggested that it was meant as a means of punishing fathers who so abused their powers by repeatedly selling their sons' labour in this way. It has been argued that it was only by subsequent interpretation that this came to be used collusively as a means of releasing a *filiusfamilias* from *potestas*, i.e. of emancipating him.

Second, and a rather stronger argument, later legal sources are definite that certain rights, those of intestate succession and of *tutela* (guardianship), were awarded first to patrons, the former in the Twelve Tables, but that emancipating fathers were accorded them only later, under the praetor's edict.[22]

There was apparently no mention at all of emancipated children in the section of the Twelve Tables relating to inheritance on intestacy. According to Gaius, there was provision in the law of the Twelve Tables for the former owner of a freedman to succeed on intestacy, after the *sui heredes* (that is, after the freedman's freeborn legitimate children, if he had had any since his release). However, it is evident that there was initially no such provision for a father who had emancipated his child. This had to await the development of the praetor's edict, which, according to Ulpian, allowed the father to claim the inheritance of an emancipated child *exemplo patroni*, i.e. on the analogy of the right previously allowed patrons over the estates of freedmen. So, if a grown-up emancipated son died without having had any children of his own in his own *potestas*, and without leaving a valid will, his father, as the nearest thing to an agnate, could succeed to his property.

At the time of the formulation of the civil law of the Twelve Tables,

---

[21] Crawford (1996) 631–2, and bibliography there; cf. also Watson (1975) 188–9; (1977) 24, nn. 3–5.
[22] Gaius 1. 165–6. 3. 40; *D.* 37. 12. 1. pr.; Crawford (1996) 642–3, 646–8.

then, it is possible that account was not taken in succession law of the consequences of terminating a child or grandchild's membership of the *familia* by release from *potestas*, because this was not yet practised. Moreover, by later legal interpretation of the law of the Twelve Tables (i.e. resolving a matter not specifically mentioned in them), since patrons were the heirs on intestacy of their manumitted slaves in the category of agnates, the guardianship (*tutela*) of female freed slaves and of those of either sex who had not yet reached puberty was assigned to them; and, again according to Gaius, it was later still, and on the analogy of *tutela* of patrons, that guardianship was similarly assigned to emancipating parents of women and children.

This guardianship meant, incidentally, that fathers could, at least until the passing of the *senatusconsultum Orphitianum* in AD 178,[23] effectively prevent their emancipated daughters from leaving their property elsewhere, by refusing to authorise their making wills, since the veto of a manumitting parent, as *tutor legitimus*, could not be overriden on appeal to the praetor (Gaius I. 192). Children emancipated while very young, and dying while still *impuberes*, not yet adult, though legally capable of owning property, were unable to make wills and so necessarily died intestate.

Freedmen, of course, had no agnates, because as slaves they had had, in the eyes of the law, no recognized family relationships—the manumitting owner was the only person who, legally, had had any connection at all with the slave prior to his leaving *potestas*. By the same logic, the father (*parens manumissor*) of an emancipated child could succeed in this category, and, indeed, was bound to come first in this category, since the emancipation had broken the agnatic ties with any brothers and sisters remaining in his power, who in any case could not succeed in their own right while *in potestate*. However, no provision was made, it seems, in the law of the Twelve Tables for fathers of *emancipati*, and so in strict civil law they had no more right over the estates of children they had emancipated than the latter had over those of their fathers (unless, that is, both were regarded as among the *gentiles*). This was later remedied, by interpretation of the civil law

---

[23] The *senatusconsultum Orphitianum* gave children first claim to succeed to their mothers under the praetorian rules of succession, in the category of *legitimi*. It appears likely, from the wording of a clause of the *senatusconsultum* cited by Ulpian (*D*. 38. 17. 1. 9) that the deceased's children were given priority over others in this category, i.e. not only over agnates, but, in the case of an emancipated daughter, over her emancipating father. See Meinhart (1967) 198–200 and 3.3 below.

which gave manumitting fathers rights to inherit from their emancipated children, on the analogy of those granted in civil law to manumitting owners. The children emancipated, however, had to wait until the first century BC, when praetorian modification of the civil law rules (see 1.4 below) allowed them some right of inheritance from their fathers, although initially at a low level of priority, as blood relatives, *cognati*; later, by the end of the century, they could inherit almost on the same terms as their brothers and sisters who had remained *in potestate*.

There is little or no evidence for individual emancipations under the Republic. C. Licinius Stolo is said to have emancipated his son as a device to evade his own land law of 367 BC (see below, 1.13),[24] though this story may be unhistorical and the product of a later hostile tradition. Emancipations are likely, however, to have become more common with growing prosperity and expansion of economic opportunities in the second century BC. A certain frequency of emancipation by the first century BC is suggested by the improvement in inheritance prospects created for *emancipati* by changes to the praetorian edict.[25] This improvement, which had more than one stage, spread over some time, and was accompanied by other developments in the law of succession; some of these changes may have been in part a response to the harsher circumstances of the late Republic.

How early manumitting parents were admitted to succession by the praetor is not known, but it very probably occurred before the end of the second century BC. We may compare the further extension, under the praetorian edict, of patrons' rights over the estates of freedmen, even against a will, which is generally seen as occurring shortly after, and perhaps as a reaction against, the protection afforded freedmen in their lifetimes against the exactions of patrons by the edict of Rutilius (*c.*118 BC).[26]

The motive for the edictal change allowing fathers to inherit from *emancipati*, according to Ulpian, was economic, showing a concern not for *pietas* or blood ties, but, rather, for property:

[24] Livy 7. 16. 9; Val. Max. 8. 6. 3; Crook (1967a) 120; Cornell (1995) 334, 339. See 1.13 below.

[25] So Crook (1967a) 120; Crook, however, appears to associate this only with the development of the praetorian category *unde liberi*, and does not take into account what I argue below was an earlier stage, the introduction of the category *unde cognati*.

[26] Gaius 3. 40–1; D. 38. 2. 1; Watson (1967) 231–4; Waldstein (1986) 149ff.; Gardner (1993) 25ff.

This outcome appeared most equitable to the praetor, since [the emancipated son] received from his parent the benefit of being able to acquire property, whereas if he were a son in power, whatever he acquired for himself he would be acquiring to the profit of his father. Therefore the step was taken to admit a father to possession contrary to the terms of a will on the analogy of a patron.[27]

Under the praetorian edict, a patron passed over in his freedman's will could claim half the estate against his will, and could claim on intestacy if the only *sui heredes* were adopted children or wives *in manu*. Initially, fathers would be admitted under the edict to possession only if there was no valid will, and presumably not then if the deceased were an emancipated son and had died leaving *sui heredes*, i.e. legitimate children, born since his emancipation. It is not until the first century AD at earliest that there is mention of a father being admitted to possession contrary to the terms of a will, and then not against *sui heredes*.[28]

1.4 INHERITANCE UNDER PRAETORIAN RULES

In sharp contrast to the civil law are the praetorian rules of intestate succession. In the Republic and early Empire, the urban praetor at Rome was the magistrate (holding office for one year) chiefly responsible for the administration of the private law between citizens; it was his function to apply the basic rules of civil law in practice, and each successive praetor issued an edict at the start of his office in which he detailed those legal remedies and interpretations he proposed to offer in order to make this possible. The edict therefore became a source of

[27] *D.* 37. 12. 1 pr.: 'Quod aequissimum praetori visum est, quia a parente beneficium habuit bonorum quaerendorum: quippe si filius familias esset, quodcumque sibi adquireret, eius emolumentum patri quaereret. et ideo itum est in hoc, ut parens exemplo patroni ad contra tabulas bonorum possessionem admittatur.'
[28] *D.* 37. 12. 3. Paul, in the eighth book of his commentary on Plautius (for whom see Schulz (1946) 215 and 228) says: 'Paconius says that if a son, emancipated and manumitted by his father, had appointed as his heirs disgraceful persons (*turpes personas*), such as a prostitute, possession of the entire property contrary to the terms of a will is given to the parent; or possession of the appointed share, if the heir instituted is not *turpis.*' The 'appointed share' is presumably half, as for patrons. That this does not apply against heirs who are *sui heredes* is suggested by *D.* 5. 2. 14. By the late 2nd or early 3rd cent. AD, a father passed over in a child's will can bring a *querela inofficiosi testamenti*, complaint of unduteous will (on grounds of *pietas*—*D.* 5. 2. 15 pr., Papinian, *Questions* bk 14; this is our earliest evidence), but claims by the deceased's own children take precedence (*D.* 5. 2. 14, Papinian, *Questions* bk 5).

law, and was transmitted mainly intact from year to year, the principal period of innovative activity apparently falling between *c.*125 BC and AD 17. Under Hadrian, it was finally consolidated and applied without further change. In effect, the praetor's function was to 'aid, to supplement, and to correct the civil law in the public interest' (*D.* 1. 1. 7. 1 (Papinian) adiuvandi vel supplendi vel corrigendi iuris civilis gratia propter utilitatem publicam); the edict therefore responded more directly than the civil law to personal and private concerns.

This is particularly evident in the praetorian rules for succession on intestacy. Here, the emancipated children are found ranked alongside *sui heredes* in the first order of priority. Although no longer members of the *familia*, they have (almost) the same rights of inheritance as those who still were *in potestate* at the time of the death of the *pater*.

The edict as we have it is not pre-Hadrianic; it was codified by Julian under the instruction of the emperor Hadrian. At least one important change (discussed further below) is known to have been introduced by Julian himself (*D.* 37. 8. 3), and the likelihood is that the praetorian rules underwent numerous earlier changes and developments. Most modern commentators confine themselves to discussing the Hadrianic edict and subsequent legislation.[29] It is important, however, to try to reconstruct some of these earlier stages, for the light that they may throw upon changing Roman attitudes towards 'family', in the common sense, that is the group of closely related blood kin, as opposed to *familia*, the legally constructed 'family'.

The principal grades of succession in the edict as revised under the emperor Hadrian by Julian were:

1. *Unde liberi* (*D.* 38. 6). First in the order of precedence were the *liberi. Liberi* in this context were 'children' in a special technical sense, i.e. the *sui heredes*, and also those who would have been *sui* but for having been emancipated (but not those in another's *potestas*, i.e. adopted into other *familiae*: *D.* 37. 4. 6. 4). So, children emancipated (but not those in adoptive families) could claim in this category; so could those given into adoption, and subsequently emancipated by their adoptive fathers, as well as the children of deceased *emancipati*. The category *unde liberi*, therefore, comprised not only the children and grandchildren of the *familia*, but many of those of the deceased father's natural family outside the *familia*.

---

[29] See Watson (1971a), ch. 6, for attempts to date some of the developments in the later Republic.

2. *Unde legitimi* (*D.* 38. 7). 'Heirs at law', *heredes legitimi*, covered agnates, as in the civil law; patrons of freedmen and freedwomen were admitted in this category, but now sharing equally with certain *sui heredes*, i.e. adoptive children or a wife *in manu* (Gaius 3. 41); so were patrons' children (subject to certain limitations under the Augustan *lex Papia*: Gaius 3. 45–6). Also included in this category, as we have seen, on the analogy of patrons, was the *parens manumissor*, i.e. a *pater*, usually father or grandfather, who had emancipated the deceased person.

3. *Unde cognati* (*D.* 38. 8). The third category in order of succession under the praetor's edict were cognates, all blood relations within six degrees—i.e. the *gens* is supplanted by the extended family.

After these, with remoter rights of succession, and not really of concern to our discussion, are patron's family, and husband or wife of the deceased.

Certain points are worth remarking. A notable feature of these principles of succession is the importance accorded, in the absence of *potestas*, to the blood tie between children and their biological fathers. Adopted children, so long as they remain in adoption, have the same inheritance rights as natural children *in potestate* within the *familia* into which they have been adopted, and none to the inheritance of their natural fathers. This is why, for instance, as Polybius pointed out (31. 28), L. Aemilius Paulus was, legally speaking, childless. Of his four surviving children, the sons, Scipio and Fabius, had been given in adoption and were still in their adoptive *familiae*, and his daughters—whom he was less likely to regard as his principal heirs—had probably passed into other *familiae* by having married with *manus*. Scipio and Fabius were not therefore heirs on intestacy; their father had to name them as heirs in his will.

However, if an adoptive child is emancipated, this terminates the adoptive relationship, which was purely legal and dependent on no blood tie, and the original blood tie between him and his natural father takes effect again. His or her situation is as if merely emancipated from the original *familia*, without ever having passed into another.[30] That is, the rights of inheritance of *emancipati* and of manumitting parents, in the categories respectively of *liberi* and of *legitimi*, were interpreted as existing only between natural fathers and children. Later legal interpretation also decided the questions of how praetorian rules

[30] Gaius 2. 137; *D.* 1. 7. 13; 37. 4. 6. 4.

were to be applied to certain claims to inheritance from emancipated children on the part of their brothers and sisters who had remained *in potestate*, and likewise of sons' children already born before emancipation, who had remained in the grandfather's *potestas*.

With regard to the former, Ulpian, in the forty-fifth book of his commentary on the edict, remarks (*D*. 37. 12. 1. 5) 'liberos autem manumissoris non venire ad contra tabulas bonorum possessionem filii constat, quamvis patroni veniant' (It is established that the children of a manumitter are not admitted to possession against the will of an [emancipated] son, although the children of a patron are admitted). The grounds for the distinction are not explicitly stated, but may be deduced. Emancipation broke agnatic ties, and therefore destroyed the possibility of claims which otherwise might have existed (though presumably his siblings could still make a claim as cognates). However, the situation of the freedman and the patron was not parallel. There had never been any agnatic ties between them to be broken, nor, indeed, could a freedman have any agnates; the Twelve Tables *created* a right for the patron, on the basis of the property-power (*potestas*) he had held over this person in his *familia*, and this right was inherited by his civil law heirs.

Children left in their grandfather's *potestas*, and becoming *sui iuris* at the latter's death, would probably under the original edict have had no claim against the estates of their emancipated fathers except as cognates, relatives by blood; however, they were later allowed a claim in the category *unde liberi*. This may have happened some time before the final formation of the Hadrianic edict (the evidence is from Pomponius' commentaries on a jurist of the earlier part of the first century AD, Masurius Sabinus), although whether by interpretation or incorporation in the edict is unclear.[31]

The introduction of the category *unde liberi* had given emancipated sons a claim to their father's estates which, if they chose to exercise it, excluded the claim of their own children left in their grandfather's

---

[31] *D*. 38. 6. 5. 1: 'Quin etiam hi quoque, qui in potestate numquam fuerunt nec sui heredis locum optinuerunt, vocantur ad bonorum possessionem parentium. nam si filius emancipatus reliquerit in potestate avi nepotem, dabitur ei, qui in potestate relictus sit, patris emancipati bonorum possessio' (Indeed, even those also who have never been in the power [of the deceased] nor held the position of *sui heredes* are called to possession of the property of parents. For if an emancipated son has left a grandson in the power of his grandfather, possession of his emancipated father's property will be granted to him who was left in [his grandfather's] power). See also *D*. 37. 4. 21 pr. (Modestinus).

potestas—a change later introduced by Julian in the Hadrianic edict obliged them to share (*D.* 37. 8. 3: see below, 1.6). Giving these children a claim on their emancipated father's estates may have been intended to redress the effects of the clause *unde liberi* (although so far as the evidence goes this provision did not apply only to those who had actually been excluded from their grandfather's estates in this way).

Further, the institution of the category *unde cognati* created new possibilities of inheritance between members of the same family (but not *familia*). In Gaius' analysis of the degrees of cognation in the eighth book of his work on the provincial edict, the first degree of cognate relationship is defined as existing between parents and children. Mothers, therefore (if not *in manu*), and their children, who previously had no inheritance rights from each other under civil law, being not only not members of the same *familia*, but usually not of the same *gens* either, could now inherit from each other under the edict as cognates.[32]

1.5 CHRONOLOGICAL DEVELOPMENT OF THE PRAETORIAN RULES

There is an almost total lack of evidence for the details of the development of the praetorian rules between the civil law of the Twelve Tables and the Julianic edict, but at least a sketchy, if somewhat speculative, reconstruction may be attempted. In the Julianic edict, *emancipati* could claim in the first category, as *liberi*, that is, they enjoyed a right to share, should they choose to exercise it, with those who had remained *in potestate*.

Whether this was granted in the earliest form of the praetorian rules is uncertain and perhaps unlikely. It is more probable that they initially acquired a claim in the third category, as cognates, since this blood relationship was not destroyed by emancipation;[33] besides, as mentioned above, in civil law, if still members of the *gens*,[34] they would already have had a claim under that category, although no stronger a claim

---

[32] *D.* 38. 8. 1. 7, 8; 38. 10. 1. 1. Mothers were likely to belong to a different *gens*, since the evidence for endogamy—either among parallel kin or cross-kin—is limited: Y. Thomas (1980) 345–82; Saller and Shaw (1984*b*), 432–44. Parallel kin are the children of two brothers (agnatic cousins) or two sisters, cross-kin those of a brother and a sister, but only in the first of the three cases (agnatic cousins) is there an agnatic link.

[33] Children given in adoption into other *familiae* also retained a cognate relationship with their natural families: *D.* 38. 10. 4. 10.   [34] See n. 20 above.

than that of any other *gentiles*. Their claim as cognates, however, still ranked after the claims not only of children still in power but also, failing those, of agnates.

It is possible that this was the original—and sole—change that differentiated the succession rights of emancipated children under praetorian rules from the civil law, namely that the rights of the *gens* as a whole were displaced by those of blood relatives, *cognati*. Among the cognates the most nearly related were the deceased's own children, including those formerly members of the *familia* but now emancipated and outside it; those given in adoption, however, while subject to the *potestas* of someone else were ineligible. If the clause *unde liberi*, which extended the first category beyond *sui heredes* and significantly improved the inheritance prospects of *emancipati*, could be shown to have come later, we could then begin to discern the outlines of a development involving decreasing emphasis upon the legal rules of the *familia*, and more concern with the family relationships between persons related by blood, even if they were no longer technically part of the *familia*. *Emancipati*, originally excluded by civil law from the right to share in intestate inheritance to the property of the *familia*, are admitted again, and, despite their remoteness in law, increasing priority is given to them on the basis of their close blood relationship with the *pater*.

Unfortunately, dates for these changes are singularly hard to determine. There is a small amount of relevant literary evidence, some of which is discussed by Watson (1971*a*) 180–5, although he appears more concerned to trace evidence for the persistence of claims by *gentiles* to inheritance or *tutela*, than to date more closely the introduction of the clauses *unde cognati* and *unde liberi*, or to analyse the implications of these changes.

1.5.1 *Praetorian Succession* unde cognati

The earliest jurist cited in the *Digest* on cognates is Trebatius (*c*.84 BC–AD 4). He is twice referred to (*D*. 38. 10. 10. 15 and 18) for the terminology used in referring to relatives in the fourth and and seventh degrees of cognation. This obviously means that the clause *unde cognati* had been introduced to the praetor's edict before AD 4, but this could have happened much earlier. Trebatius' interest in the details of cognate succession could have arisen much earlier, and not necessarily immediately it was introduced.

Though claims to succession by members of the *gens* are referred to several times in texts from 60 BC onwards, this does not in itself imply that cognate inheritance had not yet been introduced under praetorian rules. The introduction of the praetorian categories of succession, though it resulted eventually in the effective disuse of the old civil law rules, did not abolish them. It is not known, either, how long the claim to guardianship (*tutela*) by the gens survived. Later references to these older institutions, therefore, do not prove that the praetorian changes had not yet taken place; situations could arise in which there were no eligible claimants under praetorian rules, in which case presumably civil law would take effect, and the *gentiles* could claim. In two of the three texts cited by Watson which mention such a claim the people affected seem to be almost entirely lacking in relatives eligible to succeed in any closer categories; this is why claims from members of the *gens* might have been possible.[35]

The well-known eulogistic inscription on a dead wife, the *Laudatio Turiae*, relates a fraudulent attempt, probably during the 40s BC, to void the father's will and claim gentile *tutela* over 'Turia', whose sole close relative appears to be a married sister. Apart from Turia herself, there is mention only of certain female relatives, *propinquae* (which suggests a fairly distant relationship, and we are not told whether it was through the father or the mother), who were apparently reared in the marital homes of Turia and her sister, and helped with dowries at marriage, Turia's husband and brother-in-law also contributing. Turia herself and her husband had no children, and Turia's sister was in the *manus* of her husband and therefore in another *familia*.[36]

When Turia's father died, she and her husband were named heirs in his will. Certain persons then tried to get Turia to have the will declared invalid, on the grounds that after it was made her mother had been taken into her father's *manus* (by a procedure known as *coemptio*).[37]

This would have added another *suus heres*, who had not specifically been instituted as heir in the will, and so the will would automatically have been invalidated (it made no difference that her mother had died at the same time as her father). Turia's sister was *in manu*, and therefore

---

[35] Watson (1971*a*) 180–1. *CIL* VI 1527=*ILS* 8393 (the *Laudatio Turiae*) 1. 13–26; Catullus 68. 119ff. The third, Cicero, *Pro Flacco* 84, delivered 59 BC, may obliquely refer to a succession claim (to a woman's estate) based on *gens* membership, though this is uncertain. [36] *Laudatio Turiae* 1. 42–9, 2. 41ff.
[37] For *coemptio* for purposes of entering *manus*, see Gaius 1. 114 and 136.

ineligible to inherit on intestacy, so the entire estate would have gone to Turia. At the same time, however, any provision for a tutor for her which her father had made in the will would also have become invalid. Since she had no agnates, these alleged members of the *gens*, as Turia's nearest heirs if she in turn died intestate, were hoping to claim guardianship over her. This, besides giving them some control over how she used her property in her lifetime, would enable them to prevent her from making a will, so that, if she continued childless, they would in due course inherit the estate.

Their manœuvre failed, since Turia denied that such a *coemptio* had taken place (and the *gentiles* were apparently unable to prove it), and in any case the claimants did not appear to be from the same *gens* at all (how this was demonstrated is not explained in the inscription). This text, obviously, cannot tell either for or against the existence by that date of the praetorian category *unde cognati*, since the question of any claim from that quarter does not arise.

Catullus 68. 119ff. (possibly written shortly after 60 BC) also depicts an extreme family situation; other than a daughter, the old man appears to be envisaged as having no surviving relatives or descendants who could claim on intestacy, either under civil law or under praetorian rules, in which case there might be a claim from a member of the *gens*. The situation is saved by the birth of a child to the daughter (see further below).[38]

The survival so long of succession by the *gens* was probably encouraged by the narrow meaning given to 'nearest agnate', *agnatus proximus*, which in practice eliminated many *agnati* from succession in the higher category, as agnates. 'Nearest agnate' meant the agnate (or agnates, if there were more than one of equal degree) nearest in degree at the moment when it was established that there was an intestacy; the inheritance was offered only to him/them, and if the nearest abstained from taking up the inheritance, or died before having done so, the next nearest were not invited under this category. Inheritance was *per capita*, by individual, and not (in contrast to *sui heredes*) *per stirpes*, by lines of descent through deceased males. This limited the numbers of agnates who could be eligible as being of the same degree.[39] The category was still further restricted, possibly as early as

---

[38] Cf. Gardner (1986*a*) 192.

[39] Gaius 3. 11–12; Watson (1971*a*) 181. Schulz (1951) 222–3 has a helpful diagram explaining the principle and its effects. For example, grandsons by a deceased son were not in the same degree as their late father's brother.

the middle of the second century BC, by accepting only those female agnates who were sisters of the deceased.[40]

The intention of limiting agnate succession in these ways appears to have been to limit dispersal of the patrimony outside the direct line of descent of the *familia*; the effect in practice, given social and demographic conditions in the later Republic,[41] was perhaps to increase the prospects of the property going to the *gens*, an effect likely to be exacerbated by the demographic effects of the civil and other wars of the last century BC upon the availability of *sui heredes* and agnates as claimants in the male line of succession. The Roman senatorial aristocracy, which was already having difficulty in perpetuating itself by natural reproduction (see 3.2), was still further depleted by these upheavals, to the extent that some noble families were actually dying out.

Several passages in Cicero, to be discussed presently, suggest that the clause *unde cognati* was introduced somewhere between 74 and 66 BC. That it cannot be dated as early as 74 BC, however, is suggested by a story in Valerius Maximus. Gaius, commenting on the provincial edict, remarks that *bonorum possessio* was promised on grounds of natural equity 'to those who by reason of the blood-tie are called to the inheritance, though they fail at civil law'. This principle of equity was, according to Valerius Maximus, the basis of a praetorian decision in 71 BC,[42] to give possession of an estate to the father of a son given in adoption, one of eight reared by him. The son had disinherited his father, who brought a complaint (*querela*);[43] the father could not claim as manumitting parent, because the son had not simply been emancipated but given in adoption, and had never been emancipated from his adoptive family.

Valerius Maximus gives details of the reasons which moved the

---

[40] Gaius 3. 14; according to Paul, *Sent.* 4. 8. 20 the change was *Voconiana ratione*, although it is uncertain whether he means that it was instituted by the law itself (for which see n. 50 below) or by later interpretation—for references to modern discussion, see Kaser (1971) 696 n. 12; for its intention and possible effects see Gardner (1986a) 191.

[41] Brunt (1971) chs. 8–9; Hopkins (1983) ch. 2 (with Graham Burton), esp. 69–99. See also 3.2 below. The fundamental study of demographic patterns in Roman families is Saller (1994) chs. 2 and 3.

[42] D. 38. 8. 2 (Gaius); Val. Max. 7. 7. 5; for the date, see Broughton, iii (1986) 46; the *praetor urbanus* in question is C. Calpurnius Piso.

[43] This is not a case of 'querela inofficiosi testamenti' (complaint of unduteous will), since it comes before the praetor, not the *centumviri* (see below, n. 56) though, as Watson (1971a) 70 n. 4 observes, 'it concerns a situation where the *querela* might have been appropriate'. On the implications of Valerius' account see Watson (1971a) 80–1.

praetor to decide in favour of the father. He mentions various grounds of equity, which indicates that he believes this to have been an *ad hoc* decision, not one given under the edict on the grounds of the cognate relationship, a relationship of blood, which still existed between father and son. The praetor was influenced, Valerius says, by the *maiestas* of fatherhood, the gift of life the father had bestowed, the benefit of upbringing which the son had received, and, to some extent, the number of siblings who had, against *pietas* (proper family feeling), been disinherited along with their parent.

This suggests that the clause *unde cognati* had not yet made its appearance in the edict. However, we cannot be entirely confident in this argument, since Valerius' main interest appears to be in the rhetorical ascription of moralistic motives to the praetor, rather than the legal niceties. Besides, Valerius is occasionally anachronistic on the details of Roman law (cf. 8. 2. 2, where a praetor in 66 BC is made to threaten someone with prosecution under the Augustan criminal law on adultery).

Valerius' story therefore suggests, but does not prove, that the clause *unde cognati* did not make its appearance until after 71 BC. A passage in Cicero's *Verrines*, however, referring to an incident dated 74 BC, shows that up to that date at least the praetor's edict still followed the civil law in giving inheritance to the *gens*. A certain Minucius had died intestate shortly before Verres became praetor. Cicero says (115): 'By law (i.e. the civil law) the inheritance was due to come to the Minucian *gens*. If Verres had had the edict that was followed by all his predecessors and successors, possession would have been granted to the Minucian *gens*.'[44] This possession, though, he goes on, was open to challenge by anyone claiming to be a testamentary heir. Verres, however, had altered the wording of the edict in favour of the (or rather, a) possessor, whom he carefully left unnamed; the intention, Cicero alleges, was to favour a particular individual who was in *de facto* possession, whereas Verres should rather have been enquiring into his right to possession. The preceding paragraph (114) quotes verbally from the edict: 'Since the introduction of praetorian rules,

---

[44] Cic. *Verr.* 2. 1. 114: Posteaquam ius praetorium constitutum est, semper hoc iure usi sumus: si tabulae testamenti non proferrentur, tum, uti quemque potissimum heredem esse oporteret, si is intestatus mortuus esset, ita secundum eum possessio daretur ... hoc vetus edictum translaticiumque esse. 115: ... Lege hereditas ad gentem Minuciam veniebat. si habuisset iste edictum, quod ante istum et postea omnes habuerunt, possessio Minuciae genti esset data.

this is the rule we have always used: "If no will is produced, then possession is to be given in the order of precedence for inheritance on intestacy." ... This is an old edict, taken over from year to year.'

This seems to show fairly clearly that at the date of the speech the praetor's edict had made no alteration to the civil law rules of intestate succession.[45]

Cicero's famous speech *Pro Cluentio*, made in 66 BC in defence of Aulus Cluentius Habitus, accused of poisoning, contains several relevant passages, some more helpful than others. The significance of Cicero's twice-repeated claim that in 74 BC, since Cluentius had not yet made a will, his mother Sassia would inherit if he died is not easy to determine.[46] It has been suggested that this may mean that the clause *unde cognati*, if not (on the evidence of the passage from the *Verrines*), already in place before 74 BC, may nevertheless have been introduced at about that time. Referring to events no later than that year, when Cluentius was contesting a case on behalf of his fellow townspeople of Larinum against his stepfather Oppianicus, Sassia's third husband, Cicero claims that Oppianicus and others were aware that on Cluentius' dying intestate his property would go to his mother Sassia.

However, this (if true) could have been by agnatic succession, not

---

[45] However, Watson's further argument in support of this (1971a: 183) does not convince: 'This part of the edict corresponded to the clause *Unde legitimi* in Hadrian's edict.' Since, he continues, in Cicero it is quoted immediately after the clause on succession according to will, whereas under Hadrian's edict the clause was immediately preceded by the clause *Unde liberi*, 'The conclusion must be drawn that *Unde liberi* did not exist in the seventies BC. It then becomes extremely likely that *Unde cognati* also did not exist.' The basis of this argument is that similar words occur in a passage cited by Julian at the start of the *Digest* title *Unde legitimi. D.* 38. 7. 1: 'Haec verba edicti "tum quem ei heredem esse oporteret, si intestatus mortuus esset" ' (The following words of the edict, 'Then the person who ought to be heir to him if he had died intestate'). These words require, however, to be read in context. They are not part of the clause *Unde legitimi*, but rather of a general introductory statement that an order of precedence is to be followed in granting claims to the estate. They are to be understood, says Julian, with reference not to the time of death but to the time at which a claim for possession of the estate is made; if someone is claiming in a particular category, they must at the time of the claim belong to that category. The words are cited under the title *Unde legitimi*, not because they are part of that clause in the edict, but because they are relevant to a point which Julian is making concerning claims under that clause, namely that if *capitis deminutio* (which breaks the agnate connection) has occurred, it excludes a person claiming as *heres legitimus*—unlike *liberi*, among whom *emancipati* were included.

[46] Cic. *Pro Cluentio* 45, 52. The possibilities are briefly discussed by Moreau (1983) 102ff.; (1986) 178ff. For Sassia and her family complications see also 3.3 below.

by praetorian rules. If Sassia had gone into *manus* when marrying his father, she would be agnatically related, and the unmarried Cluentius' nearest heir; but it then has to be supposed also that she did *not* go into *manus* in either of her subsequent marriages, to Aurius Melinus (her own daughter's former husband) and to Oppianicus, and it also has to be supposed that her daughter Cluentia, sister of Cluentius, *did* go into *manus* when she married Melinus and was therefore, if still alive, not eligible to inherit from Cluentius. If Sassia had not been *in manu* when married to Cluentius senior, then she could be Cluentius' nearest heir only if his sister was ineligible and if cognate succession had already been introduced. These are a great many suppositions, with no other evidence to establish them—in short, there is no evidence either way.

The only trace of anything which might conceivably be regarded as evidence is a single phrase. Cicero in both these passages says that all Cluentius' *bona* (property) would come to Sassia, suggesting perhaps a reference to praetorian rules (which admit claims to 'possession of property', *bonorum possessio*) rather than to civil law.[47] However, *bona* is a term of such general use that this is hardly conclusive enough evidence to justify the assumption that Cicero means inheritance under the edict, rather than by agnatic succession, and therefore to take these texts as evidence for the existence as early as 74 BC of the clause *unde cognati*.

There is, however, additional evidence which allows us to push back the date of introduction of the clause at least to 66 BC or even perhaps a few years before. In the speech made in that year on behalf of Aulus Cluentius Habitus, Cicero, briefly dismissing some of the additional subsidiary charges of poisoning brought against his client, remarks (165) *à propos* of one of these charges that the deceased, C. Vibius Capax, died a natural death in the home of so eminent a personage as the senator L. Plaetorius. Not only that, but, he continues, 'Intestatum dico esse possessionemque eius bonorum, ex edicto praetoris, huic, illius sororis filio, adulescenti pudentissimo et in primis honesto, equiti Romano datam, Numerio Cluentio, quem videtis' (I say that he died intestate and that possession of his property was given, in accordance with the praetor's edict, to this man, his (i.e.

---

[47] So, as Moreau notes, W. Y. Fausset in his edition of the text. This would also, if correct, rule out the assumption that Numerius Cluentius (see below) was Aulus' emancipated son.

Vibius') sister's son, a most well-behaved young man of outstanding respectability, a Roman knight, Numerius Cluentius, whom you see here).

Watson dismisses this, remarking curiously (although Cicero's words seem clear enough):'We know nothing of the relationship of these two and the text cannot be taken as evidence for the existence of *unde cognati.*'

Certainly, we do not know exactly how Numerius, son apparently of a Vibia and a Cluentius, fitted into the ramifications of the family tree which also bore Cicero's client on one of its branches. However, he obviously cannot have succeeded as one of Vibius' *gentiles*, and Cicero clearly describes him as in fact a cognate—sister's son. [48]

Other evidence suggests a connection between the two families. Two Vibii, suffect consuls in AD 5 and 8, are epigraphically attested as having links with Larinum, and the name of the earlier of these is A. Vibius Habitus. Numerius' father was a Cluentius, otherwise unknown, as is the nature of his connection, if any, with Aulus Cluentius. The possible alternative meaning of the text, that Numerius was Aulus Cluentius' son (supposing that the latter had married a Vibia) is difficult, though not quite impossible, to accommodate chronologically, since the most recent census at which he could have been registered as an *eques* (for which he would have had to be at least 17 years old) was 70 BC. Aulus Cluentius (born 106 BC) would have had to have been married and a father by 87 BC at latest; Numerius would also have to have been emancipated, in order to be *sui iuris* and able to succeed to Vibius in his own right. These, again, are rather too many suppositions. [49]

On the other hand, Cicero's description of the relationship between Numerius Cluentius and Vibius is clear and specific, as is his statement that possession was given under the praetor's edict. We may accept the passage, therefore, as establishing the existence of the clause *unde cognati* by 66 BC.

By 60 BC, the clause was firmly in place, and Catullus 68. 119ff. written soon after shows the difference made by its introduction. The

[48] Moreau (1983) 101–8; (1986), 169–89, esp. 180–1 and 188, stemma (1). Moreau (1983) notes that Cic. *Pro Cluentio* 165 is our earliest evidence for succession being given under the edict to *cognati*.

[49] Cic. *Pro Cluentio* 165; Moreau (1983) 101ff.; Watson (1971a) 185 n. 4. The Loeb editor oddly translates, 'my client's (i.e. Aulus Cluentius') sister's son'—without considering how in that case Cluentius came by his *nomen*.

possibility of a claim to succession by a member of the *gens* is mentioned:

> nam nec tam carum confectum aetate parenti
> una caput seri nata nepotis alit,
> qui cum divitiis vix tandem inventus avitis
> nomen testatas intulit in tabulas,
> impia derisi gentilis gaudia tollens,
> suscitat a cano volturium capiti.

For not so dear to a father worn out by age is the late born grandson nursed by his only daughter. He puts his name into his will, and so the child, found at long last as successor to his grandfather's fortunes, drives the vulture away from his hoary head, making mock of the *gentilis* and putting paid to his improper delight.

Watson remarks:'The birth removed the hopes of the *gens* to the *hereditas,*' and takes this passage as evidence that succession by the *gens* was still common *c.*60 BC. However, it provides even stronger evidence for the existence by that time of the praetorian clause *unde cognati*. Under civil law, whether the daughter had children or not, then either, if she were not *in manu*, she would succeed on intestacy, but the *gentilis* could claim the *tutela*, and so perhaps succeed in preventing her from willing the property away, or, if she were *in manu*, in the absence of other blood relatives through the *familia* the *gentilis* could claim the estate under civil law.[50]

How does the birth of a grandchild change the situation? If he were merely made extraneous testamentary heir, the will might still be broken for some reason, and any *gentilis* could then benefit; but if the edictal clause *unde cognati* is already in existence, the old man now has a cognate in the second degree, who can (assuming that his mother is *in manu* and therefore ineligible) claim to succeed under praetorian rules even if the will fails (*D.* 38. 10. 1. 4, 10. 13), so excluding the *gentilis.*

Catullus is not concerned to explore all the legal possibilities. It would, of course, have been possible for the old man to adopt one or more extraneous male heirs (preferably adult); then, even if the will failed, these adoptive sons would succeed as *sui heredes*, so totally ex-

---

[50] Catullus does not mention the option that (if she were not *in manu*) her father might make a will, in which he nominated a tutor for her; if he did make a will, however, then if he were a member of the élite class for whom this poem was written, the *lex Voconia* would prevent him from making her his heir; he could do no more than appoint an extraneous heir and leave her a legacy of no more than half the estate. For the *lex Voconia*, see Gardner (1986*a*) 170ff., with bibliography at p. 201 n. 14.

cluding the *gentilis* from all interest in and influence upon the patrimony (since these adoptive sons would also, as agnates, be the appropriate *tutores* (guardians) for their sister). However, Catullus is not nearly so much interested in the availability of heirs in law, as in family feelings, in the emotional value set upon having an heir of one's own blood, even if not of the name; one may compare the sentiments implicit in Pliny's letter to his wife's grandfather after her miscarriage (8. 10): 'quo magis cupis ex nobis pronepotes videre, hoc tristior audies neptem tuam abortum fecisse . . . necesse est graviter accipias senectutem tuam quasi paratis posteris destitutam' (Your desire to see great-grandchilden born from us will make you all the more sorry to hear that your granddaughter has miscarried . . . you must inevitably take it hard that your old age is robbed of a posterity which was, as it were, already to hand).

Pliny goes on to anticipate future offspring, whose career paths will be smoothed by association with distinguished names and illustrious ancestry (*imagines*) on *both* sides of their antecedents.

It appears probable, then, that the introduction of the category *unde cognati* to the praetor's edict can be narrowed down to the period between the later 70s and 66 BC.

1.5.2 *Praetorian Succession* unde liberi

As for the praetorian right of succession in the first category, *unde liberi*, there is reason to believe that it was in existence within the time of Augustus' ascendancy at latest. The change vastly improved the prospects of emancipated children, should intestacy occur. Instead of being ousted by their brothers and sisters (or brothers' children), who had remained *in potestate*, or even by their paternal aunts and uncles, they could now succeed among claimants of the first rank. A report of an opinion given by the jurist Labeo (died AD 10/11)[51] takes us part of

---

[51] *D.* 29. 2. 60, not cited by Watson, presumably since he was confining himself to strictly Republican developments. In support of the idea that the clause *unde liberi* is 'not later' than *unde cognati*, Watson produces a curious double-negatived argument (1971a: 184–5 n. 3): '*Laudatio Turiae* 1. 13–26 cannot be taken as evidence that *Unde liberi* was not in existence when "Turia's" father died between 49 and 43 BC', because, as he goes on to argue, if the will was broken, the sister of 'Turia' (on the assumption that she was still *in manu*) would have been ineligible for a share on intestacy whether or not the clause then existed; in other words, this is evidence neither way. On the evidence of Cic. *Verr.* 2. 1. 114–15 (see above) no change at all had been made to the civil law rules by 74 BC, but this does not enable us to assign a *terminus post quem* specifically to the introduction of the clause *unde liberi*.

the way towards establishing the date of its introduction, though not in itself providing enough relevant information to be conclusive. (Lawyers, as already remarked, have a habit, frustrating for historians, of omitting details of a situation save those essential to the particular legal point under discussion.)

A father instituted his emancipated son sole heir and, if he did not become heir, had ordered that a slave be free and heir. The son applied for possession of the property on intestacy, on the grounds that his father had been insane, and so took possession of the inheritance. Labeo says, if it were proved that the father made the will while of sound mind, the son was his father's heir by the will. I think this incorrect; for when the emancipated son did not want the inheritance given to him by will to belong to him, it passed at once to the substitute heir, and someone who, in order to avoid an inheritance, claims possession of property under another section of the edict, cannot be said to have acted as heir.[52]

We are not told, because it is not relevant to the point of law being discussed, what the son might have hoped to gain by this device of refusing the inheritance and claiming on intestacy (and this may be an invented example), but if the will failed, so did certain liabilities under the will, namely, manumissions, legacies save those to near relatives (who are not mentioned because they are not relevant in this scenario; at least, there are probably no *sui heredes*), and *fideicommissa* (trusts), i.e. requests to the heir to perform certain actions, or to dispose of parts of the property in specified ways.[53] The essential point, for our discussion, is that, although he is an emancipated son, he nevertheless is able to apply for possession of the estate on intestacy. Unfortunately, we are not told what we really want to know, that is, whether he could do so as *liber*, or merely as a cognate (possible in this instance, since the scenario seems to presuppose no alternative heir other than the slave).

---

[52] *D.* 29. 2. 60 (Iavolenus, *From the Posthumous Works of Labeo*, bk. 1): 'Filium emancipatum pater solum heredem instituit et, si is heres non esset, servum liberum et heredem esse iusserat; filius, tamquam pater demens fuisset, bonorum possessionem ab intestato petit et ita hereditatem possedit. Labeo ait, si probaretur sana mente pater testamentum fecisse, filium ex testamento patri heredem esse. hoc falsum puto: nam filius emancipatus cum hereditatem testamento datam ad se pertinere noluit, continuo ea ad substitutum heredem transit nec potest videri pro herede gessisse, qui, ut hereditatem omitteret, ex alia parte edicti possessionem bonorum petat.'

[53] Legacies were actionable under the edict (*D.* 29. 4. 1. pr.), probably as early as this, given the amount of known republican legislation on legacies, but *fideicommissa* were not yet actionable.

Taken alone, then, this text is not conclusive evidence for the existence of the clause *unde liberi* by Labeo's day. However, Labeo also knew of a praetorian provision that even sons given in adoption could in certain circumstances (see n. 55 below) make a claim to *bonorum possessio* of their natural father's property, but only if proceedings were initiated by 'alius praeteritus ex liberis qui solent committere edictum' (another of the *liberi* who usually initiate edictal procedure, who has been passed over). This ruling was evidently republican, since Labeo comments upon it as already established praetorian practice; it follows that the clause *unde liberi* itself was already well established.

These texts of course, do not provide us with a *terminus post quem* for the introduction of the clause *unde liberi* and enable us to date it more closely in relation to the clause *unde cognati*, nor, therefore, to trace the development of the inheritance rights of emancipated children. There is, however, one piece of literary evidence which, if the historical details are correctly reported by the author, lends some support to the idea that the category *unde liberi* was introduced later than *unde cognati*, which, as we have seen, is in place at latest by 66 BC.
Valerius Maximus 7. 7. 2:

Likewise the son of a distinguished Roman knight, M. Anneius Carseolanus, who had been adopted by his uncle Sufenas, had his natural father's will, in which he had been passed over, voided by the centumviral court, although Tullianus, a dependent of Pompeius Magnus, had been instituted heir in the will and Pompey himself had affixed his seal as witness. So in his suit the claimant had to contend more with the influence of a very prominent man than with the ashes of his deceased parent. But even though both these factors operated against him, nevertheless he gained possession of the property; for L. Sextilius and P. Popilius, blood relatives of M. Anneius, whom he had made heirs to equal shares with Tullianus, did not venture to enter into litigation with the young man, even though the very great power which Pompey had at that time might have induced them to defend the will, and it was of some assistance to the heirs that M. Anneius had transferred into the *familia* and the *sacra* of Sufenas. But the tie of paternity, the closest tie that exists between humans, overcame both the father's wish and the personal influence of the foremost Roman.[54]

---

[54] 'Item M. Annei Carseolani spendidissimi equitis Romani filius, a Sufenate avunculo suo adoptatus testamentum naturalis patris, quo praeteritus erat, apud centumviros rescidit, cum in eo Tullianus Pompei Magni familiaris ipso quidem Pompeio signatore heres scriptus esset. Itaque illi in iudicio plus cum excellentissimi viri gratia quam cum parentis cineribus negotii fuit. Ceterum quamvis utraque haec adversa

In order to bring suit at all, Anneius' son must have become *sui iuris* before his natural father's death; this means, either that Sufenas had died, or that he had emancipated him during his father's lifetime— perhaps in order to enable him to make this claim when the need arose, although that does not appear to have been necessary for a plea of this type, as it was to be for claims by *liberi* under the praetorian edict. Under the fully developed praetorian rules of succession, as finally established in the Hadrianic edict, emancipated children, as well as *sui heredes*, could claim, as *liberi*, 'bonorum possessio contra tabulas' (possession of property against a will), if they had been passed over, i.e. neither been instituted heirs nor expressly disinherited; this applied even to children given in adoption, if they had subsequently been emancipated during their natural father's lifetime, or even, in certain circumstances, those still in an adoptive family.[55] However, the son's claim is not of this type; the case is heard not by the praetor but by the centumviral court.[56]

This mean that the son is bringing a 'querela inofficiosi testamenti' (complaint of unduteous will),[57] a praetorian remedy instituted to help those unjustly disinherited or not properly provided for in a will, where the testator had some moral duty to do so; cases were heard before the centumviral court. This is one of three texts[58] which together provide some evidence for the existence of the remedy by the middle of the first century BC. In the other two the actual or poten-

---

nitebantur, tamen paterna bona optinuit: nam L. quidem Sextilius et P. Popilius, quos M. Anneius sanguine sibi coniunctos eadem ex parte qua Tullianum heredes fecerat, sacramento cum adulescentulo contendere ausi non sunt, tametsi praecipuis eo tempore Magni viribus ad defendendas tabulas invitari poterant, et aliquantum adiuvabat heredes quod M. Anneius in Sufenatis *familiam* ac sacra transierat. Sed artissimum inter homines procreationis vinculum patris simul voluntatem et principis auctoritatem superavit.'

[55] By the time of Labeo, at least, even children given in adoption into another family, and still in that family after the death of the adoptive father, could claim *bonorum possessio* against a will. However, this was possible only if they were instituted heirs in their natural father's will, and if the latter had left other children, one of whom claimed; they could not themselves initiate the procedure: *D.* 37. 4. 8. 11. Obviously they would claim only if this gave them more than the will itself.

[56] For centumviral jurisdiction in the Republic, see Kelly (1976) ch. 1.

[57] *D.* 5. 2; *Cod. Iust.* 3. 28. 21 (2173 Honoré). There is an extensive literature on the *querela*. See especially Renier (1942); Voci (1963) 670–726; Kaser (1971) 709–13 and references there.

[58] The others are Val. Max. 7. 8. 4 (where a complaint is not actually brought, but it is implied that it could justifiably have been) and Quint. *Inst. Orat.* 9. 2. 9, together with 9. 2. 34–5; see Watson (1971*a*) 61–70.

tial claimants are a man's brother (i.e. an agnate) and a man's mother (i.e. a cognate); in neither example are we told who the testamentary heirs were.

This story, therefore, suggests that the praetorian category *unde liberi* had not as yet come into existence as late as the 50s BC, since, as observed by Watson (1971*a*) 83, had this clause in the edict existed at the time, it is difficult to explain why the son did not simply apply, on the grounds of having been passed over, for 'bonorum possessio contra tabulas' (possession of property despite the will).[59]

Unfortunately, it is not quite conclusive evidence, since we do not know whether Sufenas died or had emancipated his adoptive son before his natural father's death; only in the latter case would he have been able to bring a claim under the edict, *unde liberi*. It tells neither for nor against the existence by this time of the clause *unde cognati*, since that clause admitted only to a claim on intestacy; however, we have already seen some reason to suppose that it was in existence by 66 BC.

Valerius Maximus attributes Anneius' success to the weight attached by the court to the blood tie between parent and child—in the absence, that is, of a counter-claim by two other blood relatives, when the remaining heir, though he had a powerful aristocratic patron, was extraneous. However, had Sextilius and Popilius chosen to assert their claims, then it is uncertain whether Anneius would have had as much chance of success against his father's expressed wishes, even although, all three being cognates of the deceased, the young man stood in a nearer degree of relationship to his late father than the two heirs. Valerius' phrase 'artissimum inter hominis procreationis vinculum' (the closest tie that exists between humans), expresses the sentiment of a period when the clause *unde liberi* was already in operation. However, it perhaps sheds some retrospective light on the thinking of the period leading up to the institution of that clause, which may—this is a tentative suggestion—have been influenced by experience of the use of this *querela inofficiosi testamenti*. The operation of the *querela* would perhaps tend to encourage the drawing of distinctions between moral claims, and attaching to them varying degrees

---

[59] See also *D.* 5. 2. 23 (Paul), the implication of which is that an emancipated son, if passed over, could claim *bonorum possessio contra tabulas*, but could not bring a complaint of undutiful will unless expressly disinherited. This text dates to a period *after* the introduction of the edictal clause *unde liberi*; before that, only *sui heredes* needed to be expressly instituted or disinherited.

of strength, particularly according to the nearness of the blood relationship.[60] Among those connected by blood, parents and children
were closest. Besides the bond of blood, the tie between father and
child had an additional element, the original legal tie of *potestas* which
had existed between them—that is, it combined considerations both
of family and of *familia*. Lacking that special legal bond, claims of
mothers and children to each other's inheritance took much longer to
progress beyond the cognate level.

I suggest, therefore, that the order of modifications made by various
praetors in their edicts to the civil law rules of succession on intestacy
was as follows. First, and quite early, came the inclusion of the emancipating *pater* under the category of *legitimi*. Next, some time between
71 and 66 BC, the third category of claimants, members of the *gens*,
were replaced by cognates, that is, actual blood relatives. Lastly, some
time in the latter half of the first century BC, but possibly not before
Augustus came to power, the edict extended *sui heredes*, which
covered only descendants still *in potestate*, to form the category of
liberi, which included emancipated children.

All these changes deal with situations where agnatic links have been
broken, or do not exist. The first allows the father to be a quasi-
agnate, to inherit if his son has no children; the second replaces the
gens with an 'extended family' of those with an actual, not merely notional, blood connection; and the third reasserts the closeness of the
blood tie between those who previously had also been the most
closely related agnatically, that is, father and child. All three modify

---

[60] For a later comment, see *D.* 5. 2. 1 (Ulpian, *xiv ad edictum*) 'Sciendum est fre-
quentes esse inofficiosi querellas: omnibus enim tam parentibus quam liberis de inofficioso licet disputare. cognati enim proprii qui sunt ultra fratrem melius facerent, si se
sumptibus inanibus non vexarent, cum optinere spem non haberent' (One should be
aware that complaints of unduteousness are common; for it is open to everyone,
parents as well as children, to argue want of duty. For one's cognates beyond the
degree of brother would do better if they did not trouble themselves with pointless
expense, since they have no hope of succeeding). By the end of the 3rd cent., it
appears to have been decided that this particular form of family squabbling by
remoter relatives was wasting too much judicial time, and it was simply barred: *Cod.
Iust.* 3. 28. 21 (2173 Honoré: Diocletian, 8 Feb., AD 294): 'Fratris vel sororis filii,
patrui vel avunculi, amitae etiam et materterae testamentum inofficiosum frustra
dicunt, cum nemo eorum qui ex transversa linea veniunt exceptis fratre et sorore ad inofficiosi querellam admittatur' (People are wasting their time alleging undutifulness
of a will of a brother's son or sister's son, of a paternal or maternal uncle, of an aunt
even, on the father's or mother's side, since nobody in the collateral line is admitted to
bring a complaint of undutifulness). On the *querela*, see further in 3.3 below.

the idea of family as male-oriented *familia* towards 'family' as biological kin.

The interests of emancipated children are unlikely to have been the only, or even the main, factor influencing the introduction of the praetorian category *unde cognati*, and the effective replacement of the civil law claim of *gentiles*. Probably a more immediately influential reason, and one already glanced at, was the threatened dissipation of estates due to the shortage among the élite both of direct heirs in the male line and of agnates, who could be named as testamentary heirs, but who also were eligible to succeed on intestacy (women could succeed on intestacy, but were excluded as testamentary heirs to the wealthiest Romans by the *lex Voconia* of 169 BC: see n. 50).

The decline of *manus* for wives[61] may also have been influential in prompting the development of the category *unde cognati*. When the mother was *in manu*, she was in the same *familia* as her children and she and they were related as agnates. If she outlived her husband and became legally independent at his death, her *tutor* (unless her husband had provided otherwise in his will) would be the nearest agnate, i.e. her own son. If for some reason she was intestate, her agnates, i.e. her own children, would have first claim to inherit any property she left (which would include not only anything inherited from her husband but anything subsequently acquired).

However, the financial interests of a Roman man as husband conflicted with those as father. The original motive for avoidance of *manus* (which was a possibility even before the Twelve Tables) was probably to prevent property passing away from the woman's *familia* of origin; a *pater* by not allowing his daughter to pass into *manus* was retaining control of the means of providing for the financial benefit of the other branches of the family descended from him (especially in the male line), although this was to the disadvantage of that daughter's own children.

To the Roman as husband also, however, especially among the élite, 'free' marriage for himself was an attractive option, though for not quite the same reasons, and increasingly attractive as Rome's wealth and empire grew—but it also had disadvantages. Competition for office and its rewards, already growing in the wake of Roman imperial expansion from the early second century BC onwards, was intensified by the enfranchisement of Italy after the

---

[61] Treggiari (1991) 30–4.

Social War, which greatly increased the numbers of those eligible for Roman magistracies and membership of the Roman senate. To have a wife not *in manu* was potentially advantageous, since she was among those with first priority in inheriting on intestacy from her father, should his will fail, and moreover since in the natural order of things her *pater* was likely to die before her husband, she would be able all the sooner to acquire property in her own right from external sources (including her claim, as a *suus heres*, to inherit something from her father's estate, if he did not otherwise provide for her in his will) and to have so much the more to leave, which in due course it was to be hoped that she would bequeath mainly to benefit her children, or the husband himself. In the meantime, the burden of maintaining an élite lifestyle could benefit from her day to day contribution to the running of the household.[62]

On the other hand, there was a severe drawback. If the will of a wife who had not been *in manu* should fail, under civil law rules her children stood to inherit nothing at all of her property. They had no defined place under the civil law rules, since they were neither agnates nor, usually, *gentiles* (and a woman had no *sui heredes*). In a period of wars, civil and external, women might be left with no surviving agnates, and yet their own children would be unable, in civil law, to benefit from their inheritance. It is such a context that perhaps provided one reason prompting the introduction of the praetorian category *unde cognati*. These and other developments in the Roman law of inheritance will be discussed further in 3.2–3 below.

As mentioned above, Gaius, commenting on the provincial edict, remarked that *bonorum possessio* was promised on grounds of natural equity 'to those who by reason of the blood-tie are called to the inheritance, though they fail at civil law.'[63] If mother and child, who had never been in the same *familia*, could claim inheritance from each other, at least as cognates, solely on the ground of the blood-tie, so

---

[62] Despite the long-standing ban on substantial gifts between husband and wife, it is evident from legal discussion that in daily life the resources of both might be drawn upon indiscriminately for household use: see esp. *D.* 24. 1. 18, 28, 29. 1–31. 1, 31.9 and 3.4 below.

[63] *D.* 38. 8. 2. By Gaius' time, illegitimate children also could apply for possession of their mother's estates on intestacy. He was commenting before the passing of the *senatusconsultum Orphitianum* of AD 178 (Gardner (1986a) 198–200), which placed children (probably including the illegitimate) in the category of *legitimi*—women, of course, had no *liberi*, because they did not have *potestas* over their children. See also 3.6 below, and Dixon (1988) ch. 3.

much the more acceptable would it be for former members of the *familia*, emancipated children, to inherit from their father at least at this level.

Next, at least by the time of the ascendance of Augustus at Rome, and possibly even before the death of Cicero (see n. 67 below) emancipated children were promoted from the level of cognates to a claim comparable with that of children still in power. This was on the basis of their blood relationship with their natural fathers, a relationship which, as observed by Valerius Maximus, was closer than any other. The reason for this change can only be guessed at. Actual behaviour of Roman fathers at a later period, as reflected in legal sources from the second and third centuries AD, shows fathers in their wills sometimes giving preference to emancipated chldren over those still *in potestate*, sometimes the other way round (see 1.12 below). In the context of the late first century BC, however, in the aftermath of a period of foreign and civil wars and of proscriptions, with a depleted ruling élite and a perceived shortage of natural born legitimate heirs, which Augustan legislation on marriage attempted to remedy, the extension of the first category of intestate heirs to include also those closely related by blood, even if formally outside the *familia*, may have been seen as desirable in the interests of resisting dispersal of patrimonies and the financial as well as numerical deterioration of the élite.[64] Hence the promotion of emancipated children to the same category as children still in power, with equal inheritance rights, should they choose to exercise them.

1.6 Other Related Changes

Another modification to the praetor's edict must have been either shortly subsequent to or, more probably, contemporaneous with this. In civil law, a will was invalidated if the testator did not either institute as heirs his *sui heredes* (i.e. those in his *potestas* up to the time of his death), or expressly disinherit them; since *emancipati* were no longer *sui*, they could presumably be passed over with impunity. The praetor's edict extended this protection (at least partially) from *sui* to *liberi* in general. A father's will was not invalid *ab initio* if he omitted his

---

[64] Cf. the argument of Wallace-Hadrill (1981), 58–80, that Augustus' aim was 'to stabilise the transmission of property, and consequently of status, from generation to generation'.

emancipated sons (as it would be in civil law if he neither instituted nor specifically disinherited his *sui*), but they could challenge it on these grounds and claim possession against the terms of a will.[65] In the case of intestacy, the estate was divided equally among the *sui heredes* and those *liberi* who were not *sui heredes* who claimed; if the claim was made against a will (*bonorum possessio contra tabulas*), certain legacies and express disinheritances were observed.[66]

Sui heredes, in turn, appear to have benefited from the introduction of the category *unde liberi*. Under civil law rules, *sui heredes* were 'necessary heirs', i.e. they inherited automatically, whether as instituted heirs under a will, or on intestacy (whereas all other heirs were free to refuse); the consequences for *sui heredes* could be unfortunate if it were a debt-ridden *damnosa hereditas*. However, the praetor's edict allowed them to abstain from the inheritance. The date of this innovation is not stated, but it seems unlikely that it pre-dates those changes in the rules of succession which were apparently intended to retain the possibility of resisting dispersal of property outside the blood relatives. A more probable context would be after *liberi* were admitted to succession on the same level as *sui heredes*, but with the option of refusal.[67] It might then begin to seem unfair that, while *sui* had to share wealthy estates with their emancipated siblings, they had to cope with ruinous debts all by themselves. The right of refusal was therefore extended to them too.

So, by the end of the Republic, or very soon after, certain members of the family outside the *familia* (namely emancipated children) had been given significant claims upon the estates of their fathers. Possible abuse was discouraged, and the interests of those heirs who had

---

[65] Gaius 2. 123–4; *D.* 5. 2. 23; Buckland (1963) 322.

[66] *D.* 37. 5 *passim*; this applied to legacies to children, parents, wives and to daughters-in-law; according to Ulpian (*D.* 37. 5. 1. pr.) 'children' and 'parents' was interpreted as covering all ascendants and descendants linked by cognate relationship.

[67] Gaius 2. 157–8. Girard (1911) 893 places the change before 70 BC, on the basis of Cic. *Phil.* 2. 42, the literal meaning of which appears to be that Mark Antony *chose* not to claim his paternal inheritance; cf. however, ibid. 2. 44—Antony, Cicero suggests, will say that his bankruptcy in youth was his father's fault. Bearing in mind the nature and purpose of this speech and Cicero's skill at putting his own preferred gloss upon matters, it seems more likely that Antony did not have the chance to refuse, Creticus, his father, aware of the parlous state of his own financial affairs, having instead disinherited his son and installed a slave as *heres necessarius* (Gaius 2. 153–4). If by 44 BC it was already possible for *sui heredes* to refuse an inheritance, Cicero's audience may not have noticed the discrepancy—though in the absence of other evidence, this argument should not be made to bear too much weight.

remained *in potestate* safeguarded, by the introduction, either simulta-neously with the promotion of *emancipati* to the category of *liberi* or soon after, of the requirement that the *emancipatus* making a claim must make a contribution from his own property to any of the *sui heredes* whose share was impaired by his intervention; this was known as *collatio bonorum* ('hotchpot' in the Watson translation of the *Digest*). Ulpian remarks that this was

> manifestly equitable (*manifestam habet aequitatem*); for when the praetor admits emancipated children to *bonorum possessio* against a will and makes them sharers in their father's property, along with those who are in power, he be-lieves it to be appropriate (*consequens*) that those who lay claim to their father's property should bring in their own property also to the whole.

> If there were more than one emancipated son claiming, they should not make, nor expect to receive, contributions from each other, but should each contribute separately to those who had remained in power.[68]

Later a further modification was introduced, by Julian himself, to protect the inheritance rights of grandchildren, and also of other *sui*, in the situation where adult sons had been emancipated, but their chil-dren remained in their grandfather's *potestas*. These grandchildren took their father's place as heirs on intestacy. In civil law, intestate suc-cession within the *familia* went not by individuals but by 'stocks' (*stirpes*)—that is by separate lines of descent from each male—and the nearer member excluded the more remote. What this meant was that each son and daughter of a *pater* counted as one share, but sons in power excluded their children also in power, and the children of each dead or emancipated son counted together as one share, that is, they 'represented' him.

The introduction of the praetorian clause *unde liberi* introduced a complication. Sons no longer in the *familia*, i.e. the *emancipati*, could now claim. Had they still been in power, they would have excluded their own children left in power. The latter, however, were now *sui*, and it was decided that they should not be excluded if their emanci-pated fathers chose to exercise a claim; instead, they split their intestate

---

[68] D. 37. 6. 1. pr., 5, 24; Lenel (1927) 345-6, §144. Schulz (1951) 229-31 gives some examples of how *collatio* would operate.

share with them. This clause is Julian's only definitely known addition to the edict.[69]

It is perhaps surprising that it took so long for the adjustment to be made, but this does not necessarily mean that emancipation was not common. It may reflect rather other situations, e.g. that many wills were successful, and inheritance under the terms of a will more common—and possibly, therefore, also that *emancipati* were usually sufficiently generously provided for in their fathers' wills[70]—or that, if not so provided for, many nevertheless were doing well enough on their own account to have nothing to gain, and perhaps even something to lose, by making claims on the estate.

The effect of the intervention was that the emancipated person took half of the share of his *stirps*, and his children still in their grandfather's power shared between them the other half (grandchildren already emancipated did not participate). As far as the remaining *sui* were concerned, the coming in of an emancipated son who had left children in his father's *potestas* had no effect upon their shares of the estate, since he merely took a part of the share that fell due in any case to his own children still in power. It was not necessary for him, therefore, to make *collatio* with the remaining *sui*. However, he did injure his own children's share, and so the rule was that he should make *collatio* only with them.[71]

Obviously, it would be in the interests of an emancipated person to make a claim and upset the will only if he or she stood to gain by intervention; this meant that it was inevitable that, should emancipated children choose to assert a claim, some or all of the *sui* would lose to some extent, though no more (at least, that was the intention) than they would have done had the others not been emancipated; and what the emancipated children stood to gain or lose by claiming would partly depend on how well they had done for themselves. The

---

[69] *D.* 37. 8. 'De coniungendis cum emancipato liberis eius' (On the joining of his children with an emancipated son). *Stirpes*: Gaius 3. 7–8. Julian's innovation: *D.* 37. 8. 3.

[70] Unfortunately, this is not an aspect discussed in Champlin (1991). The characteristics of some wills—actual or imagined—discussed in legal texts will be examined below.

[71] *D.* 37. 8. 1. pr. Ulpian (ibid. 1) remarks that this was 'most equitable', since in this way neither did the emancipated son by coming into the estate exclude the grandsons, nor did the latter hinder their father's claim.

anonymous praetor or praetors, then, who introduced the clause *unde liberi*, and instituted the requirement of *collatio*, may be seen as forestalling possible personal risks for *emancipati*, parental anxieties about the risks of emancipation (bearing in mind the possibility of failure of wills in which they had tried to provide for *emancipati*) and resentments on the part of those still in the *familia*.

The intention of these various modifications to the civil law was to allow all children, emancipated and otherwise, the chance of benefiting from the estates of their fathers. In the event, emancipations, sometimes combined with adoptions within the *familia* itself, together with the safeguards now built into the edict, came to be exploited by *patres* in support of their desire for 'playing favourites' within the family. They made use of it as a device to ensure the fulfilment of their wishes to favour some of their descendants against others in inheritance of their property, in the event of failure of the will. I have touched briefly upon some aspects of this topic elsewhere,[72] and also discuss in more detail below (1.12) the legal implications of some of the situations outlined in the *Digest*.

These changes to the praetor's edict are significant for our understanding of the intentions of those who emancipated their children. They indicate that the perception of emancipation, removal from the *familia*, in Roman society at the time was not primarily as punitive, or vindictive—i.e. as an exclusion or expulsion from the family group—but rather as a device intended to help the particular economic situation of the individual family and its members. However, it was one which could, given the civil law, entail unfortunate and unintended economic consequences. Changing the civil law itself was neither necessary nor, indeed, desirable, given the structural importance of the *familia* in Roman society;[73] it is evident, however, that it was not considered appropriate that the legal technicalities of the *familia* should take priority over family sentiment, but rather the other way round. The effect of the changes in the edict was to allow these family feelings some additional protection and support, which could be invoked if needed.

---

[72] Gardner (forthcoming –*a*).
[73] Gardner (1993) 78–9, 82–3.

1.7 AUGUSTAN LEGISLATION ON MARRIAGE AND INHERITANCE

It is likely that the praetorian clause *unde liberi* was already in place by the time of the passing of the Augustan legislation on marriage and inheritance, the *lex Julia de maritandis ordinibus* (18 BC) and *lex Papia Poppaea* (AD 9), and probably (though it is no longer possible to distinguish all the contributions of the later law) by the time of the former. This is suggested by what the—unfortunately late, terse and incomplete—sources say about the rules laid down by the legislation.

Did emancipated children count towards either achieving the benefits or avoiding the penalties of these laws? This is a question not considered in modern discussions.[74]

Potestas, obviously, was irrelevant as far as women were concerned. It is said to have been required in the original law for certain of the privileges or exemptions obtainable by men. According to Gellius, *NA* 2. 15. 4, chapter 7 of the *lex Julia* gave priority in taking the fasces to the consul with more children than his colleague, that is, children either in his *potestas* or having been killed in warfare.

On that ground, interpretation wished to allow children killed in warfare to count also for exemption from the duties of tutor. They already counted for exemption from service as judges in criminal and civil courts by chapters 26 and 27 respectively of the two *leges Juliae* on judicial procedure.[75] These concessions concern public offices or duties or, in the case of *tutela*, a quasi-public responsibility, since it affected the affairs of another *familia*: for most private benefits, as we shall see later, having children *in potestate* was not a requisite.

Much later, in the latter part of the second century AD, the emperor Marcus Aurelius and his brother may have extended this exemption so that emancipated children also counted for exemption from being tutor; at any rate, by the early third century legal interpretation appears to assume this. In a rescript preserved in part of an Ulpianic

---

[74] See e.g. Mette-Dittmann (1991), who provides extensive bibliography of earlier discussions, and Treggiari (1991) 60–80.

[75] *Frag. Vat.* 197 (Ulpian). The source of *Frag. Vat.* 198 (Ulpian?) thought that grandchildren by sons ought to count as well, although the wording of the two clauses was different, 27 merely mentioning *liberi*, which could (though of course it need not) cover grandsons *in potestate*, (*D.* 50. 16. 220. pr.), whereas clause 26 specified *se natos*—variously emended, but apparently taken by the writer as meaning 'born of him' and applying to sons only.

commentary (*Frag. Vat.* 168) the emperors tell an enquirer that the praetor would grant him exemption from undertaking *tutela* if he produced proof that he has *iustos tres liberos*, three legitimate children (who must still be living—this is implied by the tense of the verb, *habere* (have), rather than *habuisse* (have had)).[76] The text continues: 'But the mention of *iusti* is to be understood thus, *uti secundum ius civile quaesiti sint*, that they were begotten in accordance with civil law (i.e. in marriage).' This is punctuated by most modern editors as part of the rescript, but is perhaps better taken as belonging to the commentary. The comment is not unnecessary. Although *iusti liberi* is frequently used to mean, like *iuste quaesiti liberi*, children who are legitimate because born of lawful marriage, the two terms are not synonymous, since *iusti liberi* strictly refers to the legal, not the biological, relationship, meaning, as we learn from D. 1. 7. 2. *pr.* (Gaius), children who are in their father's *potestas*, whether by birth or by adoption. The emperors' rescript mentions only legitimate birth as a ground for exemption. The intention may have been merely to exclude adopted children, but it could be taken to imply that retention *in potestate* was not regarded as relevant.

This, at any rate, seems to have been the interpretation of the commentator, who continues (*Frag. Vat.* 169) 'Children given in adoption also are of benefit for this purpose.' Elsewhere we learn that not only did children given in adoption still serve to qualify a man for exemption from being a tutor, but those taken in adoption did not, 'quoniam soli naturales tribuunt excusationem' (since only natural children provide exemption).[77]

Was it always the case that adoptive children did not exempt a father from the law? For preference in election to office, the *lex Julia*, according to Gellius, specified only that the children be in the candidate's *po-*

---

[76] *Frag. Vat.* 168. Cf. Gaius 1. 55: 'Also in our *potestas* are our children whom we have begotten in lawful marriage (*iustis nuptiis*).' The formulation (*secundum ius civile*) of the reply of the *divi fratres* excludes the children of Roman women and *peregrini*, since although those by that time counted as *iusti liberi* it was not by civil law but in virtue of a *senatusconsultum* introduced by Hadrian (Gaius 1. 77). Treggiari (1991) 63 oddly cites *Frag. Vat.* 168 as evidence that a distinction was drawn between marriages which were valid in civil law and marriages valid according to the Augustan law; this is because she sides with modern commentators who believe (but see Gardner, *CR* 42 (1992) 387—review of Treggiari (1991) *et al.*) that marriages which contravened the (Augustan) law were not null.

[77] *Frag. Vat.* 168–9 (Ulpian, *lib. sing. de excusationibus*—edd.); cf. *Frag. Vat.* 196 (Ulpian, *de officio praetoris tutelaris*—edd.)

testas. For exemption from judicial duty, according to Ulpian, chapter 26 of the law on criminal courts mentioned *liberi*, while chapter 27 of the law on civil courts specified *ex* (supplied by edd.) *se natos*, children born to him. Ulpian's interest here is in a different question, whether or not grandchildren counted, but, if this citation of the law is accurate, then only natural children should have counted from the start.

There is, however, a strange story told in Tacitus *Annales* 15. 19 which suggests that, for some purposes at least, adoptive children had been allowed to count, for half a century or more after the Augustan legislation. In AD 62 action was taken against a piece of malpractice which had grown frequent around that time (*percrebuerat ea tempestate pravus mos*). Candidates for office or appointment to governorships acquired sons *fictis adoptionibus* (by pretended adoptions), and then immediately emancipated the adoptive children once they had gained their object. A senatorial decree was passed that for the future pretended adoption (*simulata adoptio*) was to be of no benefit either for qualifying for any public office or for obtaining inheritances.

The adoptions themselves were genuine in the sense of being legally valid. We are told that the successful candidates then went through the procedure of emancipation—which was public, observable, and involved the co-operation of a number of other parties—in order to undo them. Tacitus' words *fictis* and *simulata* do not mean that the adoptions were legally invalid, but refer rather to the deceitful intent behind them, shown by the fact that they were so promptly reversed.

Are we to take the wording of the senatorial decree as represented by Tacitus to be accurate? Taken literally, it ought to mean that *genuine* adoptions (i.e. those not immediately cancelled once the objective was attained) continued to count, for these purposes at least (and therefore that they had hitherto counted). However, there is a discrepancy with the later evidence from Ulpian, unless we wish to defy Occam's razor by positing an otherwise unattested later measure disallowing adoptive children. Alternatively, if the word *simulata* is disregarded, the implication of the *senatusconsultum* is that hitherto adoptive children had in practice given exemption, and were no longer to do so.[78] *Simulata* then becomes subjective (something like 'insincere') rather than legally descriptive. This seems to be borne out

---

[78] It is so understood by Buckland (1963) 320 (on inheritance): 'Adoptive children sufficed until Nero'; Kaser (1971) 321 does not discuss the implications of the passage.

by the account of Tacitus, who provides the indignant senators with suitably resentful remarks, in indirect speech.

They drew up the balance sheet—natural law, and the effort of rearing children, set against deceit and wiles and short-term adoption. It was a good bargain for the childless: completely carefree, with no burdens, they had favour, honours, everything ready to hand and presented to them. They themselves, on the other hand, found the long-awaited benefits, promised to them by the laws, turned to a mockery, when anyone could become a parent without anxiety, be childless without suffering, and in a moment attain the ambitions of fathers.[79]

The basis of their complaints is not that the device is unlawful because adoptive children do not, as the law stands, qualify a man for exemption, but only that these people have taken an easy way to make themselves successfully competitive while avoiding all the toil and effort that went into actually having and rearing children in order to qualify.

This, of course, is Tacitus' version. Even if he were using the reports of senatorial proceedings as a source, it is an open question whether and to what extent these *acta senatus* preserved a record of things said in the meetings.[80] The story is not conclusive evidence that either the *lex Julia* or the *lex Papia Poppaea* gave exemption to fathers of adoptive children; indeed, it is highly unlikely that laws aimed so clearly at encouraging procreation should from the start have allowed adoption as an effectual alternative.

The most perhaps that we can derive from Tacitus' story is that the original wording of the laws was vague enough in the relevant sections, perhaps saying merely *iusti liberii*, to allow deliberate misinterpretation, and perhaps also that the implementation of the laws, despite the institution by Augustus of the album for registration of legitimate births, was, either collusively or otherwise, sufficiently lax in checking the status of claimed offspring to allow abuse to develop. All the same, it is a strange story, since there must have been collusion among a number of people for each adoption not only to take place but to achieve its aim. Perhaps what we are seeing here is the remaining trace of a movement of resistance among part of the senatorial

---

[79] Tac. *Ann.* 15. 19: Ius naturae, labores educandi adversus fraudem et artes et brevitatem adoptionis enumerant. satis pretii esse orbis quod multa securitate, nullis oneribus gratiam honores cuncta prompta et obvia haberent. sibi promissa legum diu expectata in ludibrium verti, quando quis sine sollicitudine parens, sine luctu orbus patrum vota repente adaequaret. [80] Talbert (1984) 315–22.

class, aiming to have the marriage laws either subjected to further amendment, or reduced to a dead letter, a movement which arouses counter-resistance when it has become sufficiently widespread for realization to develop of the threat it poses to the future interests of those families in which the fathers have sired and reared their own natural children.[81]

It is likely, then, that the original law specified *iusti liberi*, perhaps with the intention of excluding illegitimate children. The drafting, however, was insufficiently precise. A move in the middle of the first century AD to establish an interpretation which included adoptive children was abortive.

There is little evidence as to how soon and to what extent emancipated children also came to be accepted as qualifying for exemption under various headings. The statement of Gellius is evidence only that *potestas* was mentioned in the original law; it does not necessarily imply that it was still made a requirement for preference in the middle of the second century AD that candidates for major public office have children *in potestate*. For Marcus Aurelius, we have a ruling, made in response to a specific query, about those children who counted for exemption from *tutela*, which may be interpreted as including *emancipati*.

Whether or not emancipated children were recognized at that time, or earlier, as qualifying their fathers to benefit also from other exemptions from the law (and specifically, to have priority in election to office) is not known, but seems not unlikely. The difficulty is rather to explain why *emancipati* were excluded in the first instance when the law was passed—after all they were legitimate natural children. Perhaps the feelings ascribed by Tacitus to the aggrieved senators in AD 62 provide a clue. Either the original drafters of the law (if Gellius is accurate), or a substantial portion of the senatorial order, may have intended to suggest an additional rationale for specifying not merely children born from them, but *liberi in potestate*. Their idea was that only those parents who were still shouldering the responsibilities of having children, by keeping them *in potestate*, deserved exemption from various duties, or preference in election. (This in itself would keep down the electoral competition in another way, since, obviously,

---

[81] Note that the interpretation put forward here differs somewhat from that originally put forward in Gardner (1989) 249 n. 29, on which the author has now had further thoughts.

only children still living could count). Although, from well before the end of the first century BC, emancipated children, as *liberi*, counted alongside children still *in potestate* for intestate inheritance from their fathers, they had ceased, like children given in adoption, to be part of the *familia* of their parents, and should not be allowed to count for exemption.

The supposed burdens of fatherhood did not, admittedly, provide a very satisfactory reason either for electoral preference or for exemption from the chore of undertaking *tutela*.[82] *Potestas* did not necessarily involve heavy responsibilities, nor its absence the opposite. Tacitus' rhetoric also conveniently overlooks the facts that in practice the adult *filiusfamilias* needed little or no looking after, while emancipating juveniles still left their fathers with the administrative responsibilities of *tutela impuberum*.

When emancipated children first gave their fathers exemption from the burden of exercising *tutela* is uncertain. Under Claudius, some relief was given from the obligations of being tutor, to agnates who willy-nilly became tutors on the intestacy of a relative, by the *lex Claudia* abolishing agnatic *tutela* over women. *Tutela* over children was considered less burdensome, according to Gaius, than that over women, since it terminated at puberty (whereas that over women was temporally open-ended), and it was therefore permitted to gain exemption from, or to resign to others, testamentary or *legitima tutela* over women (though not *tutela dativa*, that is, on appointment by a magistrate), but not *tutela*, of any sort, over children.[83] There may have been several intervening stages, extending the possible exemptions; these are not attested in our sources. At all events, by the latter part of the second century AD, legitimate[84] natural children, whether still *in potestate* or not, provided exemption from *tutela*, without

---

[82] In later legal discussion of exemption from *tutela* (D. 27. 1 *de excusationibus*, 'On Excuses', *passim*) exercise of a number of tutelages is a valid excuse for exemption from undertaking another; it does not appear, however, that *tutela legitima* of one's own emancipated under-age child counts; the *tutelae* considered are external—see esp. D. 27. 1. 32. However, if the interpretation suggested above of *Frag. Vat.* 168 is correct, emancipated children, whether still in *tutela* or already adult, already gave exemption. For the importance of *tutela* in Roman society, see Saller (1994) ch. 8.

[83] Gaius 1. 155, 157, 168, 171.

[84] In *Frag. Vat.* 194, Papinian is cited for the view that illegitimate children also qualify for exemption from *tutela*, as they do for exemption from judging; it is not clear, however, whether his comment is meant to apply only to Junian Latins, since they are mentioned in the preceding fragment.

mention of any qualification restricting this to relief from particular types of *tutela*.

Still earlier, in regard to eligibility at least for certain humbler public offices, emphasis appears to have been placed on procreation, rather than *potestas*. The Flavian municipal law, attested from Irni and elsewhere in Spain, apparently taking as model the political privileges awarded in the Julian law, laid down that opinions of *decuriones* were to be taken, first in hierarchical order by *ordo*, and then within each *ordo*, 'ut quisque in suo ordine plurimos liberos iustis nuptis (*sic*) quaesitos habebit' (in the sequence determined by the number of children each has, *begotten in legal marriage* [my italics]).[85]

In section 56 of the *lex municipalis Malacitana* (AD 82–4), choice between candidates for local office polling equal numbers of votes was determined *inter alia* by the number of children born to them, including those who had died since, even those young (therefore not, obviously, in war); two dying after their naming days were equivalent to one dying after puberty.[86] Procreation, rather than *potestas*, was held to represent the spirit of the law.

Potestas, of course, had no relevance to determining women's right to the *ius liberorum*, or their exemption from the restrictions on inheritance. What counted was being married and having given birth to the requisite number of legitimate children (later, illegitimate children also counted).[87] Both men and women were unable to accept legacies or inheritances from persons other than close relatives, if unmarried; if married but childless, they could take a portion.[88]

The fullest surviving evidence (such as it is) on inheritance is that for inheritance between husbands and wives.[89] They could take up to one-tenth for each joint child which had survived the naming day; surviving children from a previous marriage (of either husband or wife)

---

[85] *Lex Irnitana* Tab. V A, 15–18; Gonzalez (1986) p. 158, translation by M. Crawford p. 185. 'Begotten in legal marriage', i.e. not adopted—bachelors also could adopt.

[86] Cf. inheritance between husband and wife (below). The significance of the naming day (ninth after birth for boys, eighth for girls: Festus *Epit.* s.v. *lustrici*, Suet. *Nero* 6, Macrob. *Sat.* 1. 16) was that the child had been acknowledged and would be reared, not exposed.

[87] *D.* 38. 17. 2. 1; 38. 8. 2, 4; Gardner (1986a) 20–1, 194–8, esp. p. 198, on various relaxations of the rule; see also 3.6 below.

[88] The text of Gaius 2. 111 is defective at the crucial point. For the purpose of these restrictions, see Wallace-Hadrill (1981) 58–80.

[89] Ulp. *Reg.* 14. 1, 15. 1–3, 16. 1a. See Treggiari (1991) 69–71.

also entitled each spouse to a further tenth per child; they also had a right to a usufruct of one-third of the spouse's property, which would be converted into ownership if they had children by a subsequent marriage. As far as their own marriage was concerned, what was held to matter, to qualify them for their reward, was that they had shown good intent by the production of children, even if these had not survived very long; remarriage (already encouraged by the revival of penalties on those who stayed widowed and unmarried too long) and further procreation were encouraged by the provision about conversion of usufruct to ownership.[90]

However, children from previous marriages had to be still surviving. For what reason is this requirement introduced? We might amuse ourselves by envisaging a melodramatic scenario, on the basis of the allegations made by Cicero in his speech for Aulus Cluentius Habitus of Larinum, of a much-married couple proceeding, via encompassing the deaths not only of other kinsfolk but of offspring by previous marriages, to narrow down the inheritance lines to benefit their own joint descendants.[91] These allegations were, of course, tendentious and made on behalf of an interested party.[92] However, there was a much less dramatic, though equally regrettable reason for the proviso. Given the high level of spontaneous juvenile mortality in the ancient world, there was a consequent probability that many children would predecease their parents. People whose children in previous marriages had already succumbed must not rest on their oars, feeling that their social duty had adequately been fulfilled by their fecundity in a previous marriage. Both for the sake of keeping up the population and of providing themselves with *liberi* to be heirs, they ought to try to have more children. The purpose of this proviso, then, is likewise to encourage procreation, as well as to concentrate the transmission of property.

The above relates to the amount husbands and wives could inherit from each other (Ulp. *Reg.* 15). Limits were set also to the amount which they could validly bequeath to each other. There was a sliding scale, depending upon the number of surviving *joint* children and also

---

[90] As Treggiari notes (1991: 70), this appears also to have been a popular provision in the wills of husbands, who expected their widows to remarry.

[91] Cic. *Pro Cluentio,* esp. 11–28; Moreau 1983 and 1986. See further in 3.2 below.

[92] One may compare the slanderous accusations of domestic murder made for political purposes against Catiline (Cic. 1. *Cat.* 14; Sallust, *Cat.* 15), but neither pursued nor intended to be.

the ages to which they had survived (Ulp. *Reg.* 16. 1a). This indicates that what counted was not only the fact of procreation, but the durability of the marriage.

We are not told whether *potestas* affected the parents' inheritance rights, but since women did not have *potestas*, and were in a different *familia* anyway, it presumably made no difference to the inheritance rights of the wife whether or not the children of the present or any previous marriage were still in their father's *potestas* or had been emancipated (or even adopted), and it is difficult to see why it should have been held to make any difference to those of the husband either, since even deceased children of the present marriage counted.

Save, then, initially at least, for the relatively small number of élite citizens with aspirations to public office, and for those men who wished to avoid the chore of undertaking *tutela*, it seems that the Augustan legislation on marriage and inheritance did little to deter or discourage most freeborn people from emancipating their children. Even for these two groups of citizens, the rules were soon relaxed; and in general, in application of the law, emphasis was placed not on retention of the children in the *familia*, that is *in potestate*, but on their parents having earned a reward for having produced them in the first place.

1.8 EMANCIPATION IN FREEDMAN FAMILIES

Freedmen, however, are in some respects a special case. The extent of emancipation by freedman fathers under the Empire cannot be calculated.[93] Although, as will be seen presently, some incentive may have been provided by the wish to find ways of evading some of the consequences of Augustan legislation on marriage and inheritance, liability to *operae*, contractual service to the former owner, could perhaps make emancipation of children a less desirable option. Even under the Republic, there may have been less tendency to emancipation than among freeborn families (though this is something for which direct evidence is lacking). Some reasons among freeborn Romans for emancipation, attested in literary sources—such as fulfilment of conditions of inheritance from mothers or mothers' relatives—were less

---

[93] There are only two references in the *Digest* to the emancipated sons of freedmen (*D.* 38. 2. 20.4 and 5), in both of which the legal point at issue is affected by the son's emancipated status (see further below).

likely to arise; also libertine families perhaps tended to be smaller, on the whole, than those of the freeborn, because of the late start imposed by the necessity of waiting for manumission. This tendency was, if anything, increased by the *lex Aelia Sentia* of AD 4, which delayed manumission, save in exceptional cases, to an age (30) at which female freed slaves especially had, given average life expectations, a relatively short reproductive period to look forward to. What value, if any, exslaves placed upon having achieved not only citizenship but the status of *paterfamilias*, lawful marriage and *potestas* over legitimate children (i.e. not merely a family but a legally recognized *familia*) the evidence does not enable us to assess, since the biological relationships mentioned epigraphically need not also be legal relationships,[94] and Latin literature has little to say about freedman families.

The Augustan laws on marriage and inheritance introduced various measures to protect the interests of patrons, in ways that could make it sometimes undesirable for freedmen to emancipate their children, sometimes the reverse.

Only children *in potestate* counted to release freedmen from certain obligations to their former owners.

A freedman who shall have two or more male or female children fathered by him in his power (except for one who has been an actor or hired out his services to fight wild beasts)—no such freedman is to give, do, or perform for his patron, patroness or their children any services by way of gift, service, or anything else which he has sworn, promised, or committed himself to do in return for freedom.[95]

---

[94] *Lex Aelia Sentia*: Gaius 1. 17–21. That some ex-slave couples attached importance also to preserving the memory of their personal history and social ascent is suggested by such inscriptions as *CIL* 6. 15598, in which an imperial freedman commemorates his wife, with whom he lived 46 years, describing himself as her *contubernalis* and patron: 'Dis manibus. Claudiae Stepteni vix(it) annis LXXII fecit T. Claudius Aug. l. Nymphodotus patronus et contubernalis coiugi suae karissimae bene meritae de se cum qua vix(it) ann(is) XLVI' (To the infernal shades. For Claudia Stepte, who lived 72 years, Tiberius Claudius Nymphodotus, freedman of Augustus, her patron and cohabitant, made this, for his dearly beloved wife, well-deserving of him, with whom he lived 46 years). *Contubernalis* indicates that the relationship began in slavery; after manumission, Nymphodotus, who either had Stepte in his *peculium* or bacquired ownership of her otherwise, manumitted her also. See S. Treggiari (1981*b*) 42–69.

[95] *D.* 38. 1. 37 (Paul, *Lex Julia et Papia*, bk. 2): Qui libertinus duos pluresve a se genitos natasve in sua potestate habebit praeter eum, qui artem ludicram fecerit quive operas suas ut cum bestiis pugnaret locaverit: ne quis eorum operas doni muneris aliudve quicquam libertatis causa patrono patronae liberisve eorum, de quibus iuraverit vel promiserit obligatusve erit, dare facere praestare debeto.

Paul is apparently quoting directly from the law—at least, this is assumed by editors, who put the passage in quotation marks. The intention is apparently to exclude adopted children—though, strictly speaking, since the text does not speak of *iusti liberi* (i.e. legitimate freeborn children of a lawful marriage) but 'a se genitos natasve in sua potestate' (those fathered by him and in his power), this could be held to cover natural children born in slavery and manumitted, and/or illegitimate freeborn children, both subsequently adopted by their natural father. It is highly unlikely, however, that the law would have been interpreted in a way that made it easier for a freed slave to acquire sufficient children in his power, and so get out of fulfilling the *operae* contracted for.

In the first place, this would go against the spirit of the law. In a number of respects, the marriage and inheritance laws, like the *lex Junia*, offer inducements to freed slaves to marry and beget legitimate freeborn children.[96] Secondly, care is usually taken to protect patrons' interests; even before the passing of the *lex Papia*, the praetor's edict had admitted only natural children, not those adopted, to exclude patronal claims to a freedman's estate (Gaius 3.41, discussed above). Only natural children in power, therefore, were effectual in securing release of a freedman[97] from *operae*.

Inheritance was a different matter. Even before the legislation the praetor's edict, as we have seen, allowed natural (freeborn and legitimate) children to exclude the patron's claim to the freedman's inheritance, and this was extended to emancipated children (probably when the clause *unde liberi* was introduced to the edict) and even to those given in adoption, provided that their father had instituted them as heirs in his will. If they were passed over, they had the same right as other *liberi* to apply for *bonorum possessio* against the will. However, they could not bring a complaint of unduteous will if disinherited; the patron's right prevailed.

This requirement of the edict, known to us from Gaius 3. 41, that, in order to exclude the patron's claim, the emancipated son of a freedman must either be instituted heir or apply for possession, is relevant to two situations discussed by Julian at *D*. 38. 2. 20. 4 and 5, the only

---

[96] Gardner (1986*a*) 194–6, 226–8, (1993) 40.

[97] Freedwomen obtained release on marriage, even without children, or on reaching 50, the upper age limit set by the marriage laws: *D*. 38. 1. 13. 4–5, 14, 28, 35, 48 pr.

two *Digest* passages which mention the emancipated children of freedmen.

The first passage (*D.* 38. 2. 20. 4) starts from the situation in which an emancipated son has conditionally been instituted heir by his freedman father, with a substitute heir, to cover the possibility of the condition not being fulfilled (this was not an uncommon practice).

If a freedman has appointed his emancipated son as heir subject to a condition, and on the failure of the condition a substitute heir has accepted the inheritance, I ask whether the praetor ought to assist the patron against the substitute heir, in respect of the portion due to him [sc. the patron], or to assist the emancipated son in respect of the whole estate. I have replied that when a father has conditionally instituted his son heir in the first degree, if the condition under which he was instituted has failed and the estate passed to the heir of the second grade, or if the son has died while the condition was as yet unfulfilled, then the patron has a right to possession of the portion due to him, against the substitute heir. The same applies if the son either did not claim the inheritance or lost his claim through lapse of time.

The question is about the patron's claim. Is he entitled only to half, or to nothing? Julian's answer (which is rather condensed and does not cover all possible eventualities) is concerned, first, with the question of the patron's claim in the event of the condition not being fulfilled, and the substitute accepting the estate, or the condition being fulfilled, but the heir failing to enter upon possession within the due time, so that the substitute takes the estate; his answer applies the law as stated in Gaius 3. 41, that is, the patron can claim half against the substitute heir, but nothing against the son.[98] Since the estate can be held to have devolved under the terms of the will upon an external heir, the patron can claim half against that heir. The son's emancipated

---

[98] *D.* 38. 2. 20. 4: Si libertinus filius emancipatum sub condicione heredem instituerit et deficiente condicione substitutus adierit, quaero, utrum patrono adversus substitutum in partem debitam praetor an emancipato filio in totam hereditatem succurrere debeat. respondi, cum pater filium sub condicione primo gradu heredem instituerit, si deficiente condicione, sub qua filius heres institutus est, ad secundum gradum hereditas pertinet vel adhuc pendente condicione filius decesserit, patrono partis debitae bonorum possessionem adversus substitutum competere. idemque est et si filius vel non petierit bonorum possessionem tempore exclusus vel repudiaverit. Secondly, Julian goes on to consider the son's claim against the substitute heir should the condition have failed, but be one that was not in his power to fulfil, and therefore improper, so that the estate can be held not to have devolved. If he were a *suus heres*, he would inherit automatically on intestacy; since, being emancipated, he is a *liber*, he must actively claim *bonorum possessio*. The son's emancipated status is relevant to both parts of the discussion; the father's freedman status, however, affects only the first.

status is relevant to the question only in that, if things had turned out differently, he could have excluded the patron as instituted heir (had the condition been fulfilled), if he made a claim for possession; if he had been a *suus heres*, however, he would automatically have excluded the patron, whether he claimed the inheritance or not.

This is straightforward stuff. In the second passage, however (*D.* 38. 2. 20. 5), which is possibly hypothetical, but delineates a situation, in which seems to lurk an ingenious plot, in considerable circumstantial detail, Julian produces an interpretation which favours a patron. We may detect traces of awareness of suspect manoeuvres on the part of freedmen and their heirs, who are attempting to avoid sharing with patrons. The passage runs:

If a freedman has instituted his emancipated son as heir and has given him a testamentary instruction (*fideicommissum*) to hand over the entire estate to Sempronius, and the son, when [or 'although'] he was alleging that the inheritance was 'suspect' to him,[99] has entered upon it on the praetor's orders and has handed it over to Sempronius, it will not be unfair for the patron to be given possession of the portion due to him, just as if the freedman's heir was not the son but the person to whom the estate was handed over.[100]

The intention was obviously that the estate should go to an external person, Sempronius (who might or might not be related to the freedman's family), but that the patron should nevertheless be excluded entirely. The heir had to accept the estate, in order that the *fideicommissum* should be fulfilled, and the patron had no claim against him as instituted heir. But what was the point of the heir's declaration about the 'suspect' estate? *Diceret*, in the imperfect tense, suggests that he had not intended to maintain his protests to the point of failing to take up the estate entirely. In any case, it was not open to him to do this; one of the provisions of the *senatusconsultum Pegasianum* (early 70s AD)[101] was that 'if the instituted heir refuses to enter on the inheritance, alleging that he doubts its solvency (*eam sibi suspectam esse quasi damnosam*), then if the person to whom he was given a trust to transfer the

---

[99] Presumably 'unsafe' in the sense of being burdened with liabilities; the translation of the Watson edition has 'onerous'.

[100] *D.* 38. 2. 20. 5: Si libertus filium emancipatum heredem instituerit eiusque fidei commiserit, ut totam hereditatem Sempronio restitueret, et filius, cum suspectam sibi hereditatem diceret, iussu praetoris adierit eam et Sempronio restituerit: non inique patrono bonorum possessio partis debitae dabitur, perinde ac si non filius, sed is cui hereditas restituta est liberto heres exstitisset.   [101] Gaius 2. 254, 258.

estate wishes, he is to enter on the estate on the orders of the praetor, and hand it over'.

The heir had nothing to lose by accepting the estate since, because he was emancipated, the estate would have gone on intestacy to the patron anyway. Why, then, did he not accept it voluntarily? The reason is presumably that the patron, though he could not claim against the heir, could challenge (probably using the *actio Fabiana*—see below) on the grounds that Sempronius was the 'real' heir, and therefore the will was devised to defraud him of his patron's right. However, if the heir and Sempronius could get the praetor to *order* compulsory acceptance and transfer of the estate, the patron had no chance to intervene.

This is probably an imaginary example. How often the dodge had been tried successfully is unknown. Evidently, however, the loophole had eventually been spotted and blocked. It is clear from Julian's comment that by his time patrons in such circumstances were allowed to bring an action. The patron, he says, will not unjustly be granted a half share, since Sempronius, not the son, is the 'real' heir. In other words, an attempted fraud has been sniffed out and circumvented. (A similar view, he goes on, *D.* 38. 2. 20. 6, should be taken where a freedman's son, made co-heir with an *extraneus*, has not claimed his half of the estate.)

These passages from the *Digest* are of interest for their informativeness about the actual effects, for freedmen and their families, of patrons' inheritance rights. The first illustrates merely that things could go wrong and the testator's intentions (apparently innocent) not be fulfilled. In the second, it looks much more as if a deliberate attempt had been made to evade the patron's claim, in order that the entire estate, not merely a half, should be available for distribution to the persons to whom Sempronius was doubtless instructed to distribute legacies. The device, however, was too patently fraudulent.

The praetorian edict was the law that pertained even after the Augustan legislation, except for those freedmen who had done well for themselves, to the extent of amassing an estate of 100,000 sesterces or more. By a neat device, the *lex Papia Poppaea* gave them an incentive to have more legitimate children, while simultaneously depressing their prospects of further social mobility (since their due shares of the inheritance would be smaller). Natural children did not exclude the patron entirely, as with the less well-off freedmen. The patron took half, whether there was a will or not, if there was one child, one third if there were two; three or more would exclude him entirely.

The catch was that, with three children to share, each would get less. A further catch, for a freedman aware of the law, was the uncertainty of whether or not at his death the estate was going to exceed the critical figure of 100,000 sesterces, and also whether there were going to be as many as three eligible surviving children. It might be a gamble whether or not to emancipate any of the children—i.e. with the intention of helping to keep the father's own estate below the danger level, since property acquired by an emancipated child was acquired for himself, not for his father. If, in the end, the estate amounted to less than 100,000, even if there were fewer than three children surviving in total, the freedman could exclude the patron by instituting any surviving children, emancipated or otherwise, as heirs in his will. However, if the will failed, the emancipated children, if they wished to intervene in the estate, would have to bring their property into the total reckoning by making *collatio*. If this brought the total estate above the 100,000, and there were fewer than three children surviving in all, then they would have to share with the patron; alternatively, emancipated children would have to rest content with what they had and abstain from the estate. There were so many variables, that the decision on how best to plan ahead to provide for the next generation cannot have been easy.

In freedman families, therefore, calculation of the advantages and disadvantages of emancipation was not a simple matter. If a freedman had only one child *in potestate* and outstanding *operae* to fulfil, emancipation of that child would seem inadvisable, unless, that is, there was reasonable hope of further additions to the family. Once there were more than two children *in potestate*, or once the *operae* were fulfilled (whichever came first)—and depending on his estimate of his likely financial circumstances by the time of his death—then it was time to think of emancipation.

Clearly, the safest combination would be to have only one or two children *in potestate* and to keep the father's property down below the 100,000 sesterces level. A neat way of doing this, while at the same time making some provision for emancipated children (who, as seen above, might not safely be able to take up the inheritance without personal loss) would be to find ways of disposing of substantial amounts of the property in his lifetime, to the benefit of emancipated children.

That this had occurred to some freedmen and been put into practice is suggested by discussion in the *Digest* of measures instituted against fraud upon a patron. The context is claims made for possession of a freedman's estate, and the praetor had to take cognizance of complaints that fraudulent attempts had been made to deprive 'any one of those persons entitled to claim possession against a will' (eorum ... qui contra tabulas possessionem accipere possunt)—the rest of the discussion shows that the aggrieved parties are assumed to be patrons or their children.[102]

Only once or twice is the recipient of the freedman's generosity explicitly identified as one of his children (whether emancipated or otherwise is not stated). The possibility is not elsewhere excluded, however, that the persons concerned are his own children, either legitimate and emancipated (or their children, i.e. his grandchildren—loans to sons in power are mentioned: *D.* 38. 5. 6–8), or illegitimate, and not able to benefit on intestacy or to exclude the patron. Illegitimacy, for a variety of reasons, will not have been uncommon in freedman families.

There were two actions, one, the *actio Fabiana*, applicable where the freedman had made a will, the other, the *actio Calvisiana*, where he had died intestate. The dates of their institution are unknown, but fall somewhere in the first century AD. The earliest attested discussion of the *Fabiana* is by Javolenus (died *c.*107 AD).[103]

Expressions of simple family affection, and indeed duty (*pietas patris*) were not held to be fraud, as when a freedman gave his daughter a dowry.[104] A gift made in anticipation of death was treated in the same way as a legacy, but it was not recoverable on grounds of fraud if made to a son or daughter, 'for', Ulpian remarks, 'where a man was free to leave his *filius* as a legacy as much as he liked, he does not appear to have defrauded his patron by making a gift'. *Pietas* appears to be given recognition here also. Ulpian has discussed gifts *mortis causa* and legacies in general immediately before; separate mention of

---

[102] *D.* 38. 5; see especially 1. pr. and 3. 3. This is also discussed, more briefly, in Gardner (1997).

[103] Paul, *ad Plautium lib. viii* frag. 2 (=*Frag. de formula Fabiana*), 2–3; *D.* 38. 5. 12; Buckland (1963) 597.

[104] *D.* 38. 5. 1. 10; the phrase used is *pietas patris*. However, there was also legal discussion about the position of a dowry given to 'a woman' (*mulier*), not said to be a daughter, Javolenus and Octavenus both agreeing that the husband could be sued during the marriage (*Frag. de formula Fabiana* 3).

legacies to a *filius* may mean that this was separately mentioned in the edict. 'As much as he liked' would mean in practice only up to the amount that the law allowed.[105]

Only actual pecuniary loss to the patron was taken into consideration. Ulpian roundly declares that patrons' complaints against the alienation of property, based on amenity or sentiment ('in quam habet patronus affectionem vel opportunitatis vel vicinitatis vel caeli vel quod illuc educatus sit aut parentes sepulti' (which the patron fancies because of its convenience or neighbourhood or climate or because he was reared there or his parents were buried there)), were not to be entertained; he may have some real suits in mind. Again, since only actual pecuniary loss to the patron counted, both Julian and Ulpian held that it was not fraud if a freedman deliberately refrained from availing himself of the chance to acquire property, i.e. an inheritance, legacy, or gift. The tactic seems, at first sight, somewhat self-defeating, but much depends upon who the person was, in the circumstances, to whom the property in question reverted. This could be a fairly foolproof way, for instance, of benefiting an emancipated child.[106]

Another ingenious device was to make a loan to a *filiusfamilias*, who might, as suggested above, be the child of an emancipated son or daughter. Under a Vespasianic enactment, the *senatusconsultum Macedonianum*, loans to a son in power were irrecoverable, but the *senatusconsultum* did not apply if the son were acting with his father's consent; of course, the colluding *paterfamilias* would deny that he had consented, and the loan could not then be recovered at law. This loophole was blocked; according to Julian it was to be understood in such a case that the freedman had made, not a loan, but a gift with intent to defraud the patron.[107]

A battery of other devices is briefly outlined in D. 38. 5. 12–13,[108] all

---

[105] *D.* 38. 5. 1. 2. The amount would therefore be limited by the *lex Falcidia* of 40 BC, which specified that at least a quarter of an estate must be reserved for the heir or heirs, and by the regulations about patron's rights in the Augustan marriage laws. In addition, a *senatusconsultum* dating somewhere between Vespasian and Hadrian (Talbert (1984) no. 148; *D.* 39. 6. 35) brought such gifts under the same conditions of acceptance as applied to legacies in the Augustan legislation; if *filius* may be taken here also to mean an illegitimate son the latter, as an *extraneus*, might take only if qualified by marriage and children.

[106] *D.* 38. 5. 1. 6, 15.   [107] *D.* 14. 6. 1, 11; 38. 5. 6–8.

[108] With a number of ingenious variants, in which the money or the property is passed on to a third party, or money lent or borrowed and similarly passed on: *D.* 38. 5. 14–19.

of which involve placing a false valuation on property which was alienated, purchased, let out, or exchanged; these were in due course brought within the application of the actions. If the freedman sold, let out, or exchanged property at a ridiculously low valuation, the sale, lease, or exchange was not directly cancelled, but the person benefiting was given the option of either renegotiating the deal at a fair price, or else giving up the property and getting his money back. Again, the freedman might buy at an exaggeratedly high valuation; the seller who benefited was then given the option of dropping the price or cancelling the sale. The person benefiting from these sales or purchases is identified only as the buyer or seller or vendor, but it is a fair presumption that in many cases he or she will have been someone personally connected with the freedman, i.e. his wife, or one of his children, who was not subject to his *potestas*, either because illegitimate, or legitimate and deliberately emancipated.

Another possible reason for freedman fathers to emancipate children was the possibility of their inheriting directly from their mother. If, however, as was quite likely, the mother was herself a freedwoman, this was not easy to achieve; the situation could arise also for freeborn men married to freedwomen. A freedwoman had no agnates and, at the date of the edict, children inherited from a mother only as cognates; this did not change until AD 178 (the *senatusconsultum Orphitianum*—see 3.3 below). If she died without making a will (and, until the *lex Papia*, this was something that every patron, as *tutor legitimus*, could effectively prevent), the entire inheritance would go to the patron (Gaius 3. 44).

A *tutor legitimus* could not be compelled by the praetor to give his authorization for a woman to make a will, nor indeed for her to alienate certain types of property, *res mancipi* (slaves, working animals, land, and buildings in Italy), nor to incur obligations. Gaius explains: 'All this is provided in the interest of the tutors themselves, in order that, since they are entitled to inheritance of the women on intestacy, they may not be excluded from the inheritance by a will, nor receive it with its worth reduced because the more valuable items have been alienated, or debts incurred.'[109]

---

[109] Gaius 1. 192: Eaque omnia ipsorum causa constituta sunt, ut, quia ad eos intestatarum mortuarum hereditates pertinent, neque per testamentum excludantur ab hereditate neque alienatis pretiosioribus rebus susceptoque aere alieno minus locuples ad eos hereditas perveniat.

It would not be easy for freedwomen to evade patrons' control over their property. Most freedwomen were perhaps unlikely to have much in the way of *res mancipi*, the alienation of which was directly under the tutor's control; those women epigraphically attested as having skills or businesses are in the main retail traders or providers of personal services.[110] Any other kinds of property they could dispose of without tutor's authorization, although the Fabian and Calvisian actions would be available, as with the property of freedmen, against possible attempts to dispose of it to the benefit of their children and the detriment of the patron. Gifts, of course, would be possible at all only to emancipated children, since not only were gifts between husband and wife legally invalid, but this applied also to gifts to anyone in the husband's *potestas*.[111]

Gifts disguised as debts, or as loans written off (by fictitious release, *acceptilatio*) would need the collusion of witnesses, but would be much easier for freedmen to pass off than freedwomen, since the latter needed the authorization of tutors both for the incurring of the obligation and for issuing of formal release from it.[112] The active involvement of tutors in both types of transaction may be observed in the waxed tablets, dating to the middle of the first century AD, from Pompeii and Herculaneum, documenting women's business activities in both places, and also in Puteoli. From Pompeii, the archive of L. Caecilius Iucundus (*CIL* 4. 3340) includes sixteen private receipts for payment to women creditors or their slaves. Two tablets from Herculaneum, and several of those from Pompeii concerning business conducted in Puteoli (the archive of the Sulpicii),[113] document loans to (and sometimes also by) women; those concerning Puteoli mostly are not the texts recording the women's liability but that of the men (either certainly or probably their tutors), who have also stood guarantor for the debt. It has been observed that, unlike similar documents relating to debts incurred or payments received by men, none of these is a *chirographum*, written personally by the woman principal; the probable reason is not, however, as has hitherto been suggested, feminine

---

[110] Julia Sp(urii) f(ilia) Felix of Pompeii may have been a freedwoman's daughter; she had acquired real estate, of which baths, shops and various other properties are advertised for rent (*CIL* 4. 1136=*ILS* 5723).

[111] D. 24. 1. 3. 4; see also 3.4 below.

[112] Gaius 1. 192, 3. 171; Ulp. *Reg.* 11. 27.

[113] Herculaneum: *Tab. Herc.* 70 and 71. Puteoli: re-edited recently in Camodeca (1992); see *TP Sulp.* 60–2 (borrower and tutor both Greek), 63 (possibly), 64, 82.

illiteracy, but rather the legal requirements of tutorial authoriz-ation.[114] Tutorial control could therefore be very effective in circum-venting any attempted deceptions of this kind by freedwomen.

For most freedwomen, it was also very difficult to leave their estate as they wished, even to their children, and to avoid patrons' claims. Before the *lex Papia* a patron, as *tutor legitimus*, could prevent a freed-woman from making a will, by refusing his authorization. Therefore he had no one but himself to blame if he gave his consent for the making of a will, and he was not made heir.[115] If he had not given his consent, then the woman died intestate and the patron was her heir. The *lex Papia*, however, altered the rules of the game. Women were encouraged to become mothers by awarding freeborn women who had borne three children, and freedwomen who had borne four, freedom from the requirement to have tutorial authorization. It was perhaps not very likely that many freedwomen would, by the time they achieved manumission, manage to go on to have as many as four freeborn children (especially as, initially at least, these had also to be legitimate—illegitimate children did not count), but in regard to any woman who did the patron's control over her estate disappeared.

The *lex* therefore changed the rules in that respect also. Henceforth, patrons were entitled to a share, will or no will, of the estates of freed-women (apparently all freedwomen, not merely those with property over a specified amount), calculated, even if there were extraneous heirs, on the hypothetical basis of equal shares between the patron and the surviving children. What it would take to exclude the patron entirely (or whether this was provided for at all) is not clear from the account in Gaius 3. 44. The text is defective, but enough survives to make it clear that Gaius said that, if four children survived, one-fifth was due to the patron, and very probable that he continued that in the event of none surviving the estate went to the patron (i.e. will or

---

[114] So Gardner (forthcoming–*b*). Illiteracy: suggested for tablets from Pompeii (with women as creditors) by Mommsen (1877) 104f., followed in *CIL* 4. 3340 by Zangemeister; so also Harris (1983) 107ff., with some rather daring statistical extrapola-tions from a small amount of evidence; he expresses himself more cautiously in (1989) 200 n. 126, as does Camodeca (1992) 32 n. 34; at 230 n. 66, Camodeca suggests that women 'could not' draw up *chirographa*, without going on to discuss what he means by this.

[115] Gaius 3. 43. No rules are specified for the content of the will, unlike those of freedmen under the praetor's edict (Gaius 3. 41). This is because in the latter case the question of invalidity arose only *ex post facto*, and on account of the terms of the will; no consent was needed for the actual making of the will.

no will). There is no indication (unlike the provision in the *lex Papia* for freedmen with over 100,000 sesterces) whether the patron's share would decrease in the event of there being more than four children, or whether, by any given greater number of surviving children, the patron could be excluded entirely.[116] These are not likely to have been events of frequent occurrence.

Emancipation by the fathers, therefore, might, depending on circumstances, be of some use in enabling the more prosperous freedwomen mothers to benefit their children in their lifetime. However, neither children in power nor emancipated children stood much chance of benefiting from their wills, so long as the patron was alive or had children surviving him.

1.9 EMANCIPATION IN PRACTICE: HOMES AND INCOMES

How much did emancipation change someone's daily life? To speak of 'casting out' or 'throwing onto the streets' is probably to misrepresent the physical situation of many or most emancipated offspring. Much depends, of course, on the circumstances, including the age and single or married state of the person concerned, and also the economic situation; but there is no obvious reason why a change in the son's legal status *vis-à-vis* his father (or, indeed, in the daughter's) should necessarily involve a change of residence.

Where the *emancipatus* was still an underage child, he would naturally continue to live at his father's house, especially since the latter was also his *tutor legitimus* and responsible for ensuring that his care, maintenance, and education were provided for.[117] This is clearly what happened with the son of the egregious Regulus, emancipated by his father in order that he might inherit his mother's estate (she apparently, as was not uncommon, having made such a condition in her will).[118] Pliny alleges that the notorious legacy-hunter (*captator*)

---

[116] Cf. Gardner (1986a) 194–5.

[117] *D.* 27. 2: 'Ubi pupillus educari vel morari debeat et de alimentis ei praestandis.' In the case of fatherless wards, the financial responsibility was the tutors', but the children were likely to stay with their mothers or other close relatives: Fayer (1994) 466–472.

[118] Not infrequently there is also express animosity on the part of the testator towards the child's parent. Besides such well-known literary examples as Pliny, *Ep.* 4. 2 (Regulus' son) and 8. 18 and Suet. *Vit.* 6, there are numerous references to such testamentary conditions in legal sources: *D.* 5. 3. 58; 26. 5. 21. 1; 28. 5. 47; 28. 7. 18. 1; 29.

Regulus, then began to spoil the boy: 'mancipatum (ita volgo ex moribus hominis loquebantur) foeda et insolita parentibus indulgentiae simulatione captabat' (having mancipated [i.e. 'sold'] him—as people, making an inference from the man's usual behaviour, generally spoke of it—he began to ingratiate himself with him by a show of indulgence, disgusting and unwonted in parents).

This 'indulgence' (although the only specific indication mentioned is the quantity of exotic and costly pets the boy had—ponies, dogs, and birds) is unlikely to have included such behaviour as sending the child away from his father's house and presence to live elsewhere. Besides, this would have been something which, given his extreme dislike of Regulus, who had frequently opposed him in court, Pliny could scarcely fail to have mentioned, as an additional ground for disapproval.[119]

Many adult sons still *in potestate*, specially if married, but also some bachelors, will have lived elsewhere than in their fathers' houses; so would married daughters, emancipated or otherwise. This, at any rate, seems to have been taken for granted by the time of the late Republic. Two *filiifamilias* whom Cicero defended on criminal charges were living, we learn from his speeches on the cases, apart from their fathers. Roscius of Ameria, at the age of 40, lived apart from his father, in the countryside, managing some farms of which he had the usufruct. This probably served as his *peculium*, i.e. property assigned to his use by his father for the purpose of generating a personal income (Cic. *Pro Rosc.* 39 and 42). Given his age, Roscius was probably already married and perhaps also a parent. Young bachelors, especially those heading for a career in public life, were perhaps as likely to have their own establishments, if this could be afforded, as to continue living at home. Cicero's young friend and legal client Caelius left home in his early twenties and lived in a flat on the Palatine which he rented from Publius Clodius (Cicero, *Pro Caelio* 17-18).

Naturally, the prosecution tries to make something of this separa-

---

4. 27. 1; 29. 7. 6 pr.; 30. 114. 8; 32. 50; 35. 1. 70, 77. pr.,92; 36. 1. 23. pr.; 37. 4. 16; 45. 1. 107; *Cod. Iust.* 2. 20 (21). 5; 3. 28. 25; 5. 16. 16; 6. 25. 3; 6. 42. 15; 8. 54. 5 (respectively 1903, 2714, 829, 434, 1325, 2562 Honoré).

[119] Regulus' legacy-hunting: Pliny, *Ep.* 2. 20; his son's emancipation and death: 4. 2; the extravagance of his mourning: 4. 7; his performance in court: 1. 5; 1. 20. 14–15; 2. 11. 22; 6. 2.

tion from the father in both instances. Cicero rejects their criticism of Caelius, on the grounds that it was appropriate for his time of life; he did so with his father's permission, and indeed encouragement, and for the purpose of furthering his social and political advancement. [120] Cicero also makes short work of the prosecution's rather desperate ploy of describing Roscius' life in the country as a banishment, revealing his father's dislike; he gives us to understand that, on the contrary it shows parental esteem and trust, and indeed is nothing out of the ordinary, but something that *patres*, specially rural gentry like Roscius senior, commonly do (Cicero, *Pro Rosc. Am.* 42–4).

That Cicero finds it necessary to answer criticisms of this sort is not sufficient evidence that living away from the paternal home was exceptional or ill-regarded; the prosecution are merely doing their job, and trying to impose an unfavourable interpretation upon all details of the accused's way of life. For an adult son, in particular, to continue living with parents was regarded, in the late Republic and early Empire, as fairly unusual; this is evident, not only from the way in which Seneca and the younger Pliny speak of sons who choose to continue living with parents, but also from other references in Cicero and in Plutarch to extended households in the earlier Republic; [121] that they are commented upon suggests that they are by this time regarded as exceptional.

Seneca (*Ad Marc.* 24) cites as an instance of Metilius' strong affection for his mother that, although a young man with a house of his own, he preferred to live with her 'cum vix paternum [contubernium] liberi ferant' (when children can scarcely endure living with their fathers). Pliny (if 'cum . . . vivebat' (lived with) is to be taken literally as referring to domicile) remarks approvingly on the *pietas* shown by Pompeius Quintianus in living with a father very unlike him in disposition.

Cicero's description (*Cato* 37) of the tight control exercised by Appius Claudius the Blind (the famous censor of the late fourth century BC) over his four sons and five daughters implies that these

---

[120] Cic. *Pro Cael.* 18: 'et, cum domus patris a foro longe abesset, quo facilius et nostras domus obire et ipse a suis coli posset, conduxit in Palatio non magno domum' (and, since his father's house was a long way from the Forum, in order that he could get to our houses more easily and be visited more easily by his own [sc. friends and clients], he rented a house on the Palatine, quite cheaply).

[121] These examples are mostly drawn from Fayer (1994) 70–2, who, however, discusses them in rather less detail.

formed a single household, though the characterization of the sons as *robustos* (sturdy) perhaps suggests that they were adult and therefore some at least of them likely to be married. Among Cicero's own contemporaries, Marcus Crassus, Plutarch tells us (*Crass.* 1. 1), was brought up with his two brothers in a small house. The brothers married during his parents' lifetime, and the whole family had their meals together. Plutarch continues that this may have been one of the main reasons for the temperance and moderation of Crassus' personal way of life. It is not clear whether he is referring only to the regular family meals just mentioned or to the whole set-up. Nor is it clear whether he believes that all seven adults continued to live together in the same modest house (the date will not have been much after the end of the second century BC—Crassus senior was away serving in Lusitania 97–93 BC), or merely that they continued, unusually, to meet daily for meals, the married sons having moved out.

Appius Claudius is cited as an archetypal *paterfamilias* of the 'good old days'. The sixteen Aelii Tuberones, that is, Q. Aelius, (probably tribune of the plebs 177 BC, legate of Aemilius Paulus in 168, and married to one of his daughters) and his relatives, who all shared one little house and one small farm, although of interest to modern scholars of Roman law as a possible example of *ercto non cito* or *consortium* (undivided inheritance), rare in classical law,[122] typified for the ancients the virtuous poverty of early Rome; Valerius Maximus places them, under the heading *De paupertate*, between other such exemplary figures as the humble farmers Atilius Regulus and Cincinnatus, and the opponents of Perseus and Hasdrubal respectively, Aemilius Paulus and Cn. Scipio, whose womenfolk's dowries presented financial problems. Regulus had only seven *iugera* for the maintenance of his wife and children, and this land was run in his absence apparently only by a bailiff and one hired help; Cincinnatus, who became dictator, had only four *iugera*, having pledged three to cover a friend's debt to the treasury; Aemilius Paulus, conqueror of Perseus, died in such poverty that the estate did not cover the return of his wife's dowry and his (allegedly) sole piece of landed property had to be sold; Cn. Scipio had asked to be relieved of his Spanish command during the second Punic war in order to return home and raise the

---

[122] Tuberones: Plut. *Aem. Paul.* 5. 7, 28. 12; Val. Max. 4. 4. 8; Broughton, i (1951) 398, 431. *Ercto non cito*: Gaius 3. 154a, with Zulueta's commentary ad loc.; Kaser (1971) 93 n. 12; Crawford (1996) 649–51 (on Twelve Tables 5. 10).

wherewithal to pay his daughter's dowry, and was made a grant from the treasury (whether merely as a loan is not stated—that would spoil the effect of the story). [123]

Plutarch, again, informs us (*Cato Mai.* 24) that the elder Cato's son by his first marriage (married after Cato's wife died) and the latter's wife[124] lived with him. Mistrusting Greek doctors, Cato prescribed remedies for himself and his household; healthy and still sexually vigorous until late in life, as a widower he regularly took a slave-girl to bed, and as it was a small household, this could not be kept secret, and scandalized his son and daughter-in-law. This story incorporates several of the old-fashioned virtues attributed to this famous figure: his frugality, his sturdy health, and his anti-Hellenism.

Stories of this sort probably contain a core of truth, in that they derive plausibility from the relative poverty of earlier Rome; as told by writers of the late Republic and early Empire, however, they have a moralizing purpose. Virtuousness is associated with all aspects of the *mores* of a less prosperous (and therefore, it is assumed, more idealistic and less materialistic) period while those of the wealthier present are *ipso facto* venal and corrupt. It would be unwise, however, to take them at face value as factual evidence that in the earlier Republic cohabitation of the generations was the norm.

Some of the same distinguished *pauperes* of early Rome appear also as illustrations of virtue, in the proper use of wealth. Aemilius, despite his deathbed 'poverty' in ready cash, was earlier able to dower one daughter (the one who married Tubero) with five pounds' weight of silver from the spoils of his Macedonian campaign. There are different accounts of the dowering of Scipio Africanus' daughters: according to Valerius Maximus the senate bestowed on one daughter, in his lifetime, the relatively modest sum of 40,000 sesterces, whereas, according to Polybius, Scipio had made arrangements (presumably by *fideicommissum*) for two daughters, apparently still unmarried at his demise, to receive via their mother a total of 100 talents between them. Scipio's namesake, the younger Africanus, as we have seen, showed that he knew the proper use of wealth by generously sharing out his inheritances from his father and his aunt among members of the family.

---

[123] Val. Max. 4. 4. 6–7, 9–10.

[124] This wife was one of the two daughters of L. Aemilius Paulus; coincidentally, the other daughter was married to one of the domestically crowded Aelii Tuberones (Val. Max. 4. 4. 9).

Tubero's son, however, got it wrong. When he was invited to fit out the dining-room for a ceremonial banquet in honour of his late uncle Scipio Africanus, his décor, intended to honour the moral principles of his uncle, was ostentatiously austere—pottery instead of silver, and deerskins on plain couches—and this lost him a praetorian election. 'The Roman people,' said Cicero, 'hates private extravagance, but it adores public ostentatiousness.'[125]

So if, among the special features characterizing Rome's virtuous ancients in these exemplary stories meant for the moral edification and instruction of the decadent present, is mentioned the cohabitation of parents and adult children, the inference that may be drawn is not so much one about domiciliary habits in the earlier Republic, as that in classical Rome at least parents and adult children were more likely to live apart than together, whether these children were still in power or not.[126] Married sons who themselves had young children would naturally have these children living with them. Emancipation of the father did not include emancipation of the children, who remained in their grandfather's *potestas*, and were therefore officially still under his legal control; however, they always had been in his *potestas*, and there is little reason, therefore, to suppose that he would now want to have them physically with him, any more than he had before. Much, of course, would depend upon personal relations between fathers and their adult sons; the interfering grandparent, with or without *potestas*, critical of his children's methods of bringing up *their* children, is a feature of many ages and societies. Such evidence as we have, however, about individual grandparents does not provide examples of a grandfather *paterfamilias* insisting upon his legal power and carrying off the youngster to his own establishment.[127]

---

[125] Cic. *Pro Murena* 75: 'odit populus Romanus privatam luxuriam, publicam magnificentiam diligit'; Val. Max. 4. 4. 9 and 10. 7. 5. 1; Polyb. 31. 27.

[126] On factors influencing the composition of Roman households, see e.g. Dixon (1988), esp. chs. 1, 7, and 8; Bradley (1991*a*) chs. 6 and 7 and (1991*b*).

[127] See e.g. the various instances mentioned in Wiedemann (1989), s.v. 'grandparents' in index. In most of these it appears (particularly where letters from the grandparent are mentioned) that they are in separate residences. Augustus took his grandsons Gaius and Lucius (to whom he was not originally *pater*) to live with him, but only after adopting them directly as his sons. They, however, were being groomed for potential succession to political power; nor does it follow that, when (as appears from Ulpian *D*. 37. 4. 3. 4 and 8 occasionally to have happened) a grandfather adopted children born to an emancipated son *after* his emancipation, this change of legal status necessarily entailed a change of residence; on such adoptions, see 2.9 below.

As far as the practical conduct of daily business for the maintenance of an income was concerned, the change of status will have made little difference, since sons in power, like slaves, were able to carry out most types of transaction, including buying by mancipation.[128] The main differences were that, should litigation be required, *emancipati* would now be able, and indeed obliged, to undertake it themselves, or appoint their own representatives, instead of leaving that to the parent; and any gains or losses would be theirs, not the parent's (though that difference would be less obvious, in the short run, if the son in power had been operating with a *peculium*).

Daughters might or might not have a *peculium*, and could operate in much the same way as sons, except that, unlike sons, they were unable, while still in power, to incur contractual obligations for which they were personally liable after becoming *sui iuris*;[129] that at least would alter on emancipation, but tutorial authorization—i.e. the *auctoritas* of their fathers—would be required.

Daughters still *in potestate* and not yet married would still be resident with parents; those 'between marriages', and possibly with children in their care, might or might not be. Again, it is unlikely that change of status would involve a change of residence. If married, they would be resident with their husbands and in part supported by them. If they were married before emancipation, a dowry would normally have been provided, which, while the marriage lasted, would be legally, and not merely *de facto*, the husband's property. The position regarding the recovery of dowry could be complicated, and will be discussed in a later section (2.11 below).

Sons and daughters who were already adult when emancipated will often have been in possession of a *peculium*—especially sons, who if already married will themselves often have had children to support. As these grandchildren remained in the grandfather's *potestas*, he had a moral, if not legal,[130] obligation to provide for them. There was additional incentive, therefore, for him to continue to help out with the upkeep of his son's household, that is, by making appropriate provision, if he did not allow the emancipated son to retain the *peculium*. The children of married daughters, of course, would be the responsi-

---

[128] Gardner (1993) 55–63, 72–78.   [129] Ibid. (1993) 84; see below at n. 148.
[130] The right of *liberi* to *alimenta* (maintenance) is not attested until late classical law: *D.* 25. 3; *Cod. Iust.* 5. 25. 4 (Honoré 35), and see also below 1.10.

bility of their husbands, whether or not they themselves were emancipated.

1.10 PROVISION FOR THE PRESENT: MAINTENANCE

As far as the patrimony was concerned, it does appear true that, in early Rome at least, an emancipated son might well find himself 'cast out', dependent on the goodwill of his father for what the latter might choose to leave him in his will, but with little or no claim on the intestate estate. This state of affairs, however, had, as we saw, largely been remedied by the end of the Republic, or soon after, by which time the prospects of an emancipated son of inheriting on intestacy were as good or bad as those of *filiifamilias*. How well or badly in practice, on the other hand, fathers' wills treated their emancipated offspring compared with those still in power may perhaps emerge from examination of discussions of real or imaginary wills in legal texts (see below). Meanwhile, what indications are there of paternal provision for emancipated sons during the father's lifetime?

Again, comparison may be made with relations between patrons and freedmen. Strictly speaking, a patron, after freeing his slave, had no longer any legal responsibility for his welfare—not that he had had much while he was a slave. Measures to protect slaves from neglect and ill-treatment were late in appearing, limited in scope, and of doubtful efficacy; however, owners had strong practical incentives to keep slaves 'adequately fuelled'.[131] The earliest known requirement that a patron provide maintenance for his freedman is attributed by Modestinus to the *lex Aelia Sentia* of AD 4:

If a patron has not maintained his freedman, the *lex Aelia Sentia* takes away anything imposed as a condition of his freedom, both from the patron and from an interested party;[132] likewise the inheritance is taken away from the patron and his children, unless he has been instituted heir, and possession of property, except according to the terms of a will.[133]

---

[131] Bradley (1994) ch. 5; Watson (1987) ch. 8.

[132] i.e. the patron's heirs, including his children if instituted heirs, since they were entitled to claim certain *operae* unfulfilled at the patron's death: D. 38. 1. 6, 7, 15.

[133] D. 38. 2. 33: 'Si patronus non aluerit libertum, lex Aelia Sentia adimit eius libertatis causa imposita tam ei, quam ipsi ad quem ea res pertinet, item hereditatem ipsi et liberis eius, nisi heres institutus sit, et bonorum possessionem praeterquam secundum tabulas.'

The patron or his heirs stood to lose not only any *operae*, services stipulated for as a condition of manumission (and presumably also any money alternative), but also their entitlement to a share in the freedman's intestate inheritance. This must refer only to maintenance of freedmen in actual want; legal interpretation of the section of the praetor's edict relating to *operae*, for instance, was that freedmen were normally expected to provide for themselves while performing *operae*, being allowed time to do so if necessary, while the patron was required to provide food only if the freedman himself found this impossible.[134] The patron was not expected to volunteer assistance; this penalty applied only if the freedman actually asked for support and was refused (*D.* 25. 3. 6. pr.).

Freedmen could likewise be required to provide maintenance to patrons and their families, but only if the latter were in need, and made application to a magistrate to oblige them to do so. This rule was stated in 'several imperial constitutions' (*D.* 25. 3. 9); the only mention of a penalty for non-compliance is a *constitutio* of the emperor Commodus prescribing forced service to the patron and, for persistent offenders, sale and re-enslavement to a different owner. This penalty upon the freedman was prescribed not only for failure to support a needy patron but also for insulting behaviour (*contumelia*) and physical abuse.[135]

Both requirements may originate with the *lex Aelia Sentia*, which instituted a praetorian *actio liberti ingrati*, a legal remedy for patrons against 'ingratitude' on the part of ex-slaves whom they had done the favour of manumitting. How 'ingratitude' was described and defined in the original law and what penalties were prescribed does not emerge from our legal texts, which all date from considerably later. However, it is quite probable that both the reciprocal requirement of patrons and freedmen to provide support in case of need, as well as the restrictions, grounded in *pietas*, on the ability of patrons and freedmen to bring suit against each other,[136] come from the same section of the *lex Aelia Sentia* as the provisions on 'ingratitude', and Modestinus may well be right in assigning also to this law the specific

---

[134] *D.* 38. 1. 18, 19; cf. Duff (1958) 48–9.   [135] *D.* 25. 3. 5. 18–26, 6. 1, 9.
[136] Gaius 4. 46; *D.* 22. 5. 4; 37. 15. 2, 5, 6, 7; 38. 2. 14; *maiestas* ('treason') was an exception: 48. 4. 7. 2.

penalty mentioned for non-provision of maintenance for a needy freedman.[137]

As far as emancipated children are concerned, however, evidence for any comparable obligation to provide maintenance is late and scanty and, again, apparently confined to cases of need. Ulpian discusses maintenance between parents and children (or, more generally, ascendants and descendants, including emancipated children and cognates not connected by *potestas*), in the second book of his *Duties of a Consul*. However, even in his time, there still seems to be uncertainty as to how far the duty should extend among those related by blood. Ulpian initially expresses a personal opinion:

But it must be considered whether a man is compelled to maintain only those children who are in his power, or also those who have been emancipated or have become legally independent in some other way. And my opinion is that, even if children are not in power, the preferable view is that they must be supported by their parents and, reciprocally, they ought to support their parents.[138]

This applies also to a son who was emancipated before puberty: 'For everyone would quite properly say that it would be most unfair (*iniquissimum*) for a father to be in want, while his son had resources' (*D.* 25. 3. 5. 13). This is a curious remark, since a son emancipated before puberty would have his father as tutor, with powers of administration over his property. Perhaps Ulpian is indicating that a parent who, in such circumstances, appropriated the child's funds to supply his own necessities could plead stress of need if subsequently accused by a third party[139] of maladministration and embezzlement. Does a real case perhaps lie behind this?

Although it is accepted that illegitimate children and mothers should support each other, it does not seem as yet to be firmly established whether the duty of maintenance applies only between relatives on the paternal side, or also to those on the maternal side: 'And the pre-

---

[137] See also Gardner (1993) 20–50.

[138] *D.* 25. 3. 5. 1: 'Sed utrum eos tantum liberos qui sunt in potestate cogatur quis exhibere, an vero etiam emancipatos vel ex alia causa sui iuris constitutos, videndum est. et magis puto, etiamsi non sunt liberi in potestate, alendos a parentibus et vice mutua alere parentes debere.'

[139] The accusation, since conviction brought *infamia*, could not be brought by the *emancipatus* himself, or through someone acting as *procurator* on his behalf even after he came of age (*D.* 2. 4. 4; 3. 2. 1; 37. 15. 2, 5)—nor indeed by his mother, so long as the parents remained married, though she presumably could do so after divorce: *D.* 25. 2. 2, 3. pr.

ferable view is that the judge should intervene equally in each case, to relieve the necessities of some and the infirmity of others: and since this derives from equity, and affection between blood relations, the judge ought to weigh the requirements of each individual.'[140]

Ulpian supports the general principles enunciated by mentioning several imperial rescripts and constitutions of Marcus Aurelius and Antoninus Pius, some evidently issued in response to individual enquiries.[141] No fixed rule is laid down; each case is to be determined according to the individual circumstances. In general it appears to have been accepted, on grounds of equity and natural affection (*pietas*) that parents and children could, if necessary, be forced to support each other. In their case, however, unlike that of freedmen and patrons, no further penalty is mentioned for failure to do so. The legally recognized rights lost by a patron (sc. to inheritance even against certain *sui heredes*, and to *operae*) had never been considered appropriate for a manumitting parent to have, and there was no question in classical law of forcing a freeborn *emancipatus* to render slave service.[142]

In several respects, the parent–*emancipatus* relationship differs from that between patrons and freedmen. Claims could be made by patrons against the estates of freedmen under the Fabian and Calvisian actions (*D.* 38. 5), where it was alleged that freedmen had deliberately tried to deprive patrons of some of their share by disposing of property fraudulently in various ways during their lifetime; such claims could not be brought by a parent against the estate of an emancipated child, 'because it is unfair (*iniquum*) that freeborn men should not have freedom to alienate their own property' (*D.* 37. 12. 2). The praetor's edict gave emancipating fathers no power to require *operae* or monetary payments from their sons (*D.* 37. 12. 2, 4; 37. 15. 10). Emancipated children also, as we have seen, acquired by or soon after the end of the Republic inheritance rights from their fathers equal to those of children who had remained in power, unlike freedmen, who had no claim at all to their patron's intestate estate.

However, both between patrons and freedmen, and parents and

---

[140] *D.* 26. 3. 5. 2–4. 'Et magis est, ut utrubique se iudex interponat, quorundam necessitatibus facilius succursurus, quorundam aegritudini: et cum ex aequitate haec res descendat caritateque sanguinis, singulorum desideria iudex perpendere oportet.'

[141] *D.* 25. 3. 5. 5–14; cf. *Cod. Iust.* 5. 25. 1 (Pius), 2–3 (Marcus and Verus).

[142] By AD 330, children who had seriously injured their parents could have their emancipation cancelled: *Frag. Vat.* 248; this is reiterated in an imperial rescript of AD 367: *Cod. Iust.* 8. 49.

emancipati, the fact of having been part of the same *familia* was considered to lay upon the parties concerned—whether as former holders of *potestas,* or those subjected to it—certain obligations of respect or considerateness, *pietas,* which extended also to other members of the household such as the patron's wife, and, in the case of freeborn members, to other relatives by blood though not necessarily members of the same *familia.* Significantly, the title of *D.* 37. 15 is 'On the obedience to be offered to parents and patrons'. By the third century AD at least, children, including *emancipati* and the illegitimate children of ex-slave mothers, could be disciplined by the urban prefect for verbal or physical assault on parents (*D.* 37. 15. 1. 2). Children and parents, and other close relatives, like patrons and freedmen, were expected to refrain from bringing 'defaming' actions against each other, that is lawsuits defeat in which could incur for the defendant the socially and to some extent practically awkward penalty of *infamia.*[143]

That is, requirements of *pietas*—provision of maintenance, abstention from bringing defaming actions, refraining from abuse or physical violence—apply to freedmen and *emancipati* alike, but they differ in respect of property rights. A freedman became a *paterfamilias* only by grace of his manumitter; a son's independence was merely anticipated, and the development of the praetor's edict restored to him those property rights which he—but not the freedman—had had as a member of the *familia,* but, in the early stages of Roman law and society, had lost as a consequence of being released from *potestas* by legal device, rather than in the natural course of events, on the death of the *pater.*

Were manumitting parents inclined to make provision voluntarily for their children after emancipation? This depended on the individual, though there is evidence that some did, if their means allowed. Sons and daughters who were already adult when emancipated will often have been in possession of a *peculium*—especially sons, who if already married will themselves often have had children to support. As already suggested, since these grandchildren remained in the grandfather's *potestas,* there was additional incentive for him to continue to help out financially or in some other way.

---

[143] Physical assault: *D.* 37. 15. 1. 2; defaming actions—d'Ors (1986), 2575–90; see also *lex Irnitana* ch. 84 with the commentary of Gonzalez (1986) 228; Gardner (1993) 66–8, 111–26 (the effects of *infamia*); 152–3; Dixon (1992) 58.

Nevertheless, it is evident that practice was not uniform. Parents were under no legal obligation to allow their sons and daughters to retain a *peculium* on emancipation, any more than slaves on manumission. The nearest the Romans seem to have come to compulsion, in the latter instance, is the general rule that a slave manumitted in his owner's lifetime was tacitly allowed to keep his *peculium*, unless it was expressly withheld; conversely, on the master's death the *peculium* was absorbed into the estate unless a specific legacy was made, either to the slave, manumitted in the will, or to the inheritor of the slave.[144]

The same general rule seems to have been applied to the *peculium* of sons on emancipation. It could frequently arise that lawsuits arose after emancipation in respect of transactions which had been carried out by a *filiusfamilias*, working with a *peculium*, while still in power. The praetor's edict allowed actions, to the extent of the *peculium*, directly against the *pater* or his heir for one full year from the date of the end of *potestas* (by emancipation of the son, and also on the death of the *paterfamilias*, or, in the case of a slave, by alienation or manumission). The emancipated son (though not the daughter—this follows from Gaius 3. 104, on which see below) could be sued for whatever he was able to pay. The son was liable 'whether the *peculium* has been taken away or not'.

Some opinion held that a father, as well as an emancipated son, could sue for formal discharge from debt (when this had been left as a legacy by a creditor) even where the father had allowed (*concessisset*) the *peculium* to the son after emancipation, since he was regarded as having an interest in maintaining his son's right intact. On what may be a real instance, Papinian reports that a father who had given his daughter, while she was in his *potestas*, some slaves for her personal use, and who did not take away her *peculium* when he emancipated her, was regarded as having in effect made her a gift of them.[145] It is clear, from the form of expression, particularly in the last example, that some positive action by the *pater* was required if he did not wish to let the *peculium* go with the son or daughter on manumission. However, it is equally clear that it was by no means a foregone conclusion that he would normally concede it.

---

[144] D. 15. 1. 53 (Paul); *Cod. Iust.* 7. 23. 1 (2392 Honoré: Diocletian); *Frag. Vat.* 261 (Papinian); legacy of a slave with his *peculium*: D. 10. 2. 39. 4 (Scaevola).
[145] D. 15. 2. 1; 26. 7. 37. 2; 34. 3. 6. 1; 39. 5. 31. 2.

As this example shows, assistance, whether as *peculium* to a *filiusfamilias* or gift after emancipation, need not necessarily be cash but could be in kind. It is reminiscent of the younger Pliny's delicately phrased presentation of a cash gift[146] to his friend Quintilianus, to help with the costs of fitting out his daughter in a style befitting her future married state: 'She ought to be equipped with clothes and attendants in keeping with her husband's status . . . I know that you, though rich in intellect, have modest means, therefore I am taking upon myself part of your burden, and, like a second father, am contributing to our girl 50,000 sesterces.' Pliny cannot make a direct gift to the girl, who is still in power. He is, however, making a gift to her father, and so helping him to increase the amount in her *peculium*. Pliny then has no further control of the money; it would be for Quintilianus to decide what dispositions to make in the event of his death, or if he emancipated her.

An emancipated married daughter, if her father had allowed her to keep her *peculium* and/or if she had subsequently acquired property from other sources, was in a good position to make an independent economic contribution to the marital household.[147] It is an interesting speculation, but one which cannot be illustrated with specific evidence, to what extent the role of the father of an emancipated wife, as *tutor legitimus*, enabled him to exercise some control over how she managed the resources on which she drew for the benefit of the

---

[146] Pliny, *Ep.* 6. 32: 'Debet secundum conditionem mariti augeri veste, comitatu . . . te porro animo beatissimum, modicum facultatibus scio. itaque partem oneris tui mihi vindico et tamquam parens alter puellae nostrae confero quinquaginta milia nummum.' This was not, *pace* Gardner (1986a) 31, a direct contribution to the dowry. It would have been tactless of Pliny to phrase it in a way that suggested that her husband would not voluntarily keep her in a suitable style; besides, there was no way of obliging a husband, who owned the dowry so long as the marriage lasted, to apply the money to any such particular purpose.

[147] Although in law the property of husband and wife was and remained separate, this became active and important in practice only at the end of the marriage, by divorce or the death of one spouse, when a general sorting-out and settling-up had to be made. *D.* 24. 1. 29. 1, 31. pr.–1, from the *Digest* chapter on gifts between husband and wife, is the *locus classicus* for demonstrating that in practice, during the marriage, items belonging to both were put to use to serve the needs of the household; the text concerns the making of clothes for the wife, the husband, and (perhaps) males and females in the household, using wool and slaves belonging to one or other spouse; cf. *D.* 24. 1. 18 and 28. Similarly, in the two *Digest* titles on legacies of stores of provisions, *penus*, and of furniture and furnishings, *supellex* (*D.* 33. 9 and 10), although in the few instances where the legatee is mentioned it is usually a wife or mother, nothing excludes the possibility that both spouses might own and bequeath such items, which during their lifetimes were used in the joint household.

marital household. There was no appeal to the praetor against the refusal of *auctoritas* of a *tutor legitimus*, as there was against that of other tutors (Gaius 1. 192). Such interference, of course, was unlikely to be on a daily basis, but a father could certainly interfere to prevent any rash entry into large debt, or liquidation of valuable assets which happened to be *res mancipi*. In emancipating a daughter, and allowing her to keep her *peculium*, he was in fact taking less risks than when emancipating a son. On the other hand, the son bore the future of the *nomen*, and, in a sense, of the *familia*; the grandchildren through a daughter bore the *nomen* and descended from the *familia* of someone else.

From the daughter's point of view emancipation in these circumstances could perhaps be a mixed blessing. While she remained *in potestate*, it would be most convenient both for herself and for her *pater* if, as a remark by the jurist Paul (*D.* 15. 1. 46) indicates was common practice, he gave her a blanket authorization for administration of the *peculium*, which could cover all obligations arising from contractual undertakings by guaranteeing the liability of the *pater* under the 'actio quod iussu' (action for authorized undertakings: *D.* 15. 4). However, according to Gaius (3. 104) neither daughters in power nor slaves could incur obligations to other persons.[148] This did not mean that they could not engage in contractual undertakings; slaves routinely did so, in the conduct of their owners' affairs. What it did mean was that, should the daughter be emancipated, an aggrieved third party could bring suit only against the *pater* himself within the one year allowed for bringing an action, but not against the daughter.[149] Whether, if at all, this made fathers in practice less willing to grant daughters *in potestate* general freedom to manage their *peculia* is not determinable.

It would still have been more convenient for fathers to give a general grant of power of administration, than to have to authorize each individual transaction. The tutor, however, of a woman *sui iuris* had no such powers to give a blanket authorization.[150] The property in question was hers, not his, and any legal liability for transactions was hers, not his. As *tutor mulieris* he had no administrative authority

---

[148] Gardner (1993) 58–9 and 84.

[149] Though slaves, like sons, were liable during the one year allowed: *D.* 15. 2. 1.

[150] And so women normally had to apply to the praetor for a replacement tutor, should their own tutor be absent, in order to carry through individual transactions. Freedwomen and emancipated daughters—i.e. women who had a *tutor legitimus*—were permitted to do so only in special circumstances; Gaius 1. 173–80.

(unlike the *tutor impuberum*); his responsibility was confined to the power to interpose a veto on any transaction he considered likely to endanger the woman's resources. All of this presumably meant that daughters of even the most compliant fathers would nevertheless have to observe the irksome formality of obtaining consent repeatedly, as the occasion arose, for individual transactions; worse still, these would not be confined only, as formerly, to anything affecting whatever might have been put at the woman's disposal by the *pater* himself, but would apply to *all* her property, including also any acquired from other sources since her emancipation. Father, in other words, was capable of being much more interfering, if it suited him, after he emancipated her.

What provision, if any, emancipating fathers made for their sons and daughters would depend, as with assignment of *peculium* to a child in power, on a number of factors—their own particular circumstances and those of the person being emancipated, not to mention social pressures from customary behaviour in one's peer group. Cicero showed himself aware of such pressures in determining on a desirable amount for the personal allowance to be paid to his son-in-power Marcus, aged 19, when the latter was about to go to pursue his studies in Greece (unfortunately we have no detail on what provision, if any, he made for his daughter Tullia during her marriages).[151]

Young Marcus Cicero has a parallel in an example—perhaps theoretical, but credibly realistic—of provision for an adult, but unmarried, emancipated son discussed by Ulpian:

> If a father provided financial aid for his emancipated son while he was living abroad in pursuit of his studies, and if it is proved that the father did not send this with the intention that it was to be a loan, but under the influence of natural affection (*pietas*), then fairness does not allow that it be taken into account when reckoning what share of the deceased's property has passed to the son.[152]

Pietas, fatherly affection, is assumed as a natural and credible motive. There is nevertheless the implication that it would be as well if fathers took the trouble to make it quite clear (and somehow put on record)

---

[151] Cic. *Ad Att.* 12. 7. 1, 14. 16. 4.
[152] D. 10. 2. 50: 'Quae pater filio emancipato studiorum causa peregre agenti subministravit, si non credendi animo pater misisse fuerit comprobatus, sed pietate debita ductus: in rationem portionis, quae ex defuncti bonis ad eundem filium pertinuit, computari aequitas non patitur.'

at the time how far their generosity was intended to extend and what the legal status of the generous act was.[153] Future uncertainties must be provided for, and in particular, in the event of the father's death, it must be made clear what was to be included as among the total assets of his estate, including debts owed to it. It is assumed that the emancipated son will have some share in the father's estate (whether by will or on intestacy). There is perhaps a hint, as well, of squabbles and jealousy among other members of the family whose shares were affected by father's generosity.[154]

Ulpian's example, even if perhaps theoretical, has parallels in life, which show that generosity could go too far. In AD 265 Valerian and Gallienus replied to a certain Aetia (*Cod. Iust.* 3. 29. 2: 1324 Honoré). Her complaint was that her father before his death had, on an impulse of boundless generosity (*impetu quodam immensae liberalitatis*), exhausted the patrimony by flooding his son (presumably Aetia's brother) with gifts. The imperial reply is that, if her brother was not emancipated, she can make a complaint of unduteous will (*querela inofficiosi testamenti*), which will be satisfied by giving her a quarter of her share on intestacy (i.e. the amount due under the *lex Falcidia* (see n. 105). If he was emancipated, then the gift is legally valid and must stand, but, in accordance with constitutions (*iuxta constitutiones*)[155] she may obtain assistance from the provincial magistrate on grounds of equity, on the analogy of the *querela inofficiosi*.

Diocletian gives a similar response both to a daughter complaining about her father's lavish gifts to her—presumably emancipated—brother, and to two sons complaining about their mothers' favourit-

---

[153] Unfortunately, Antoninus Pius had abolished the requirement that gifts must be conveyed in due legal form, either *mancipatio* or *traditio* as appropriate: *Cod. Theod.* 8. 12. 4 (Constantine, AD 319). Later, though perhaps not long before Constantine, it was recognized that, to avoid fraud, some means of proof of the gift must be provided for (ibid. 4, 5). The legal record on the subject is confused: Buckland (1963) 256. Although gifts made *mortis causa*, i.e. to take effect only at the donor's death, were relatively safe from interference, they were made liable to the *lex Falcidia* by Septimius Severus (*Cod. Iust.* 6. 50. 5; 610 Honoré); however, legal interpretation (Papinian) allowed recipients to fend off family members' claims on that score if the gift was made only on the father's deathbed (*D.* 39. 6. 42. 1). The *lex Falcidia* of 40 BC limited legacies to three-quarters of the estate; the heir or heirs must receive at least a quarter, and this amount was held to satisfy claims under the complaint of unduteous will.

[154] On *pietas*, see Saller (1991b) 146–51 and (1994) ch. 5, and on strategies of succession in Roman families, Saller (1991a) and (1994) ch. 7.

[155] Cf. *Cod. Iust.* 3. 29. 9 (Constantius AD 361), from which it appears that a separate action for 'unduteous gift' was introduced by law, on the analogy of the complaint of unduteous will.

ism towards their brothers (by this time, of course, the *senatusconsultum Orphitianum* was in operation, and children had the same priority in intestate inheritance from mothers as from fathers). In one of these instances, the mother is said to have made these lavish gifts in her lifetime with the specific intention of forestalling the *querela*. All these enquirers are told firmly that they may appeal on the analogy of unduteous will.[156] How much justification these jealous siblings had for their complaints is unknown; some exaggeration might not be unnatural. In the most striking example, however, Diocletian is actually appealed to by the father himself, who is still alive. The reply is (*Cod. Iust.* 3. 29. 5: 1471 Honoré):

If you have totally exhausted your resources by the gifts you have made to your emancipated sons, that portion which must, to avoid complaint of unduteous will, be left to children not disinherited for ingratitude will be subtracted from the gifts already made and returned to your patrimony, so that sons or grandsons who have subsequently been born (*nati sunt*) from whatsoever legitimate marriage may receive the due provision from your property.[157]

The petitioner Cottabeus had apparently, from unstated motives, emancipated his entire family (at least two sons); then after handing over his entire property in gifts (which were legally valid) to them, he began belatedly to think of the future (and may possibly, given the tense and mood of *nati sunt*, have already started a second family), and panicked. Diocletian's admirably restrained response rescues him from the guilt consequent on his folly and forestalls future family rows and difficulties for the second family (though not, perhaps, hostility and resentment from the first).

---

[156] *Cod. Iust.* 3. 29. 6, 7, 8 (1485, 1491, 2366 Honoré). The response of Philip the Arab to a similar enquiry from a brother and sister (*Cod. Iust.* 3. 29. 1=1251 Honoré: AD 245), though less clearly expressed, is to the same effect. Severus Alexander ordered the urban prefect that a grandmother's gifts to her grandson, made with similar intent to forestall the *querela*, were to be reduced by half: *D.* 31. 87. 3. See also 3.4 below. In *Cod. Iust.* 3.29.4 (1467 Honoré) a woman complaining that her son has exhausted his patrimony in making immoderately large gifts to unspecified recipients, is told to apply to the provincial magistrate to have the gifts revoked, not on grounds of unduteousness, but of equity. This appears, however, to be an instance of action against a *prodigus*, a spendthrift (see Buckland (1963) 168–9).

[157] 'Si totas facultates tuas per donationes vacuefecisti, quas in emancipatos filios contulisti, id, quod ad submovendas inofficiosi testamenti querellas non ingratis liberis relinqui necesse est, ex factis donationibus detractum, ut filii vel nepotes, qui postea ex quocumque legitimo matrimonio nati sunt, debitum bonorum subsidium consequantur, ad patrimonium tuum revertetur.'

It seems, then, that far from casting out their offspring by emancipating them and leaving them to their own resources, some fathers during their lifetimes actually favoured them at the expense of their families still in power, to the extent that eventually legal controls had to be introduced on paternal generosity. What testamentary provision they may have made for them will be considered below.

1.11 DAUGHTERS, DOWRY, AND EMANCIPATION

Dowries to daughters are a special case, subject to particular rules; they were not absolute gifts, being recoverable by the wife, or the father, depending on circumstances, at the end of the marriage. Though not legally compulsory, it was expected, and probably would have been difficult to arrange a marriage otherwise, that fathers would provide a dowry when giving their *filiaefamilias* in marriage. A father who had already emancipated his daughter might also wish out of natural affection (*pietas*) to provide a dowry. This, while the marriage lasted, was the property of the husband. Whether the daughter had been emancipated before or during the marriage, or not at all, if the marriage outlived the father, neither he nor his heirs could expect to have anything more to do with the dowry (except in the special case posited in D. 24. 3. 44—see below, n. 168).

Where the daughter had been married while *in potestate*, the dowry provided by her father was known as *dos profecticia*.[158] If the couple divorced or the husband died after the death of the wife's father, the wife could recover the dowry in her own right; if she died, the husband retained the dowry. If her father was still alive, and she had not been emancipated, when the marriage ended either in divorce or the death of either spouse, then he could recover the dowry from her husband or the husband's estate, but only with his daughter's consent.[159] This Cicero began to do after he arranged the divorce between his daughter Tullia and her third husband P. Cornelius

---

[158] The following account of the legal rules on the return of dowry where daughters had not been emancipated is a little simplified in the interests of clarity and brevity; for a more detailed discussion, see Gardner (1986a) 105ff. which does not, however, consider in detail what happened where daughters had been emancipated either before or after marriage.

[159] If recovery was on divorce, the daughter had to consent to her father's bringing an action for its recovery: Ulp. *Reg.* 6. 6; *Frag. Vat.* 116; *Cod. Iust.* 5. 18. 7 (2183 Honoré).

Dolabella towards the end of 46 BC. In two letters, *Ad Att.* 12. 8 (late October 46) and *Ad Fam.* 6. 18 (January 45), he mentions arrangements for the recovery of the first instalment of the dowry. Cicero, so far as we know, had initiated the divorce, and Tullia was pregnant, but the letters do not indicate whether there was any agreement that Dolabella should retain a portion for the child.[160] Despite Dolabella's unsatisfactory behaviour, it was politically inexpedient for Cicero to attempt to insist upon immediate total repayment on grounds of Dolabella's misconduct. Repayment was due to be made in three instalments over as many years. However, Tullia was dead by the end of January 45, and her child only a few months after, Dolabella in June 43 and Cicero himself by the end of the same year, and the letters tell us no more about the fate of the dowry.

How did emancipation affect the right of recovery of dowry? A dowry payment made by someone other than the bride's *pater* was known as *dos adventicia*. The wife herself, if legally independent, *sui iuris*, by the end of the marriage, could recover it on divorce or her husband's death, but the original donor could not (presumably since as far as the law was concerned he had made to the husband a valid gift, which was not recoverable).[161]

Strictly speaking, this ought to mean that a dowry given by a father for a daughter who was already emancipated before marriage[162] was *adventicia* (since he was no longer her *pater*), and was no more recover-

---

[160] In two letters written from Astura towards the end of March, 45 BC (*Ad Att.* 12. 28. 3, 30. 1), Cicero asks Atticus to visit little Lentulus and to assign (*attribuas*) some slaves to him. Although Dixon (1986) 108 relates this to the second instalment of the divorce repayments, nothing in the texts supports this, and Cicero's language indicates rather that the slaves are *not* any in the dowry (and therefore already in Dolabella's ownership), but some, mentioned in the first letter, just acquired by Atticus on Cicero's behalf from a certain Castricius. Cicero may merely have wished to make them available for use, as a kind of loan, so that his little motherless grandson was properly looked after.

[161] D. 23. 3. 5; Ulp. *Reg.* 6. 3–4; *Frag. Vat.* 116. By custom, and probably from an early date in the Republic, gifts between husband and wife (or the *pater* of either, if they were *in potestate*) were not valid (D. 24. 1. 1; Stein 1985); that may be the rationale for allowing an action to the wife and her father for recovery of dowry. If, however, the external donor had made a stipulation for the return of the dowry at the end of the marriage, it was recoverable, and was termed *dos recepticia* (Ulp. *Reg.* 6. 5); for a stipulation of this sort, see D. 24. 3. 45, where the donor is the bride's maternal grandfather.

[162] Borkowski (1994) 203 curiously remarks: 'A daughter would often be emancipated on her marriage and be given a dowry'; however, legal sources on emancipated daughters do not justify such a generalization.

able than that given by any other external donor. However, legal interpretation, possibly as early as the first century AD,[163] was that in these circumstances also the dowry could be considered *profecticia*, and therefore recoverable by the father.

This is stated in *D.* 23. 3. 5. 11, which clearly refers to a daughter emancipated before marriage:[164] 'If a father gives a dowry on behalf of an emancipated daughter, there is no doubt that nevertheless [i.e. despite the fact that she is emancipated] the dowry is proficicious, since it is not the right of parental power, but the name of parent, that makes a dowry proficicious.'[165] Although Ulpian seems to appeal to sentiment (*pietas*) as a reason for the interpretation, the main concern behind this interpretation appears to be the preservation of the integrity of the paternal patrimony for a *pater* who is, after all, still alive. Ulpian does not mention whether or not the daughter is also still alive. However, as we shall see presently, it appears that there had been discussion among jurists, from the first century AD onwards, about the status of dowry where a wife had been emancipated, and by the third century AD the generally accepted view was that if the

---

[163] *D.* 23. 3. 5. 11: the source is Ulpian's commentary on the *Libri tres iuris civilis* of Masurius Sabinus, and it is apparently known also to Julian—see on *D.* 24. 3. 59 below.

[164] In *D.* 23. 1. 10 and 23. 3. 44 and 51, which also refer to dowry in connection with a daughter emancipated before marriage, special conditions apply. In 23. 3. 1. 10, the question is asked whether a father can cancel the betrothal of a daughter who has been emancipated (apparently after he had given his consent to the marriage), and whether he can sue for return of the dowry. The answer is that, though he cannot prevent the marriage, he can sue for return of dowry, if it can be argued that his original gift was conditional on his not withdrawing his consent. In 23. 3. 44, the argument is that a promise of dowry made by a father is contractually binding (cf. Gaius 3. 95*a*), even if he has subsequently emancipated his daughter before the wedding; in 23. 3. 51, the property used by an emancipated daughter as dowry was previously given to her as a gift by her father, and therefore is held to come from her, not from him.

[165] *D.* 23. 3. 5. 11: Ulpian, *xxxi ad Sabinum.* Si pater pro filia emancipata dotem dederit, profecticiam nihilo minus dotem esse nemini dubium est, quia non ius potestatis, sed parentis nomen dotem profecticiam facit. The principle is observed in a reply given in AD 225 by Alexander, possibly to the woman's bereaved husband (*Cod. Iust.* 5. 18. 4=735 Honoré). (The same did not apply, however, to dowries given by mothers, which were adventicious, like those of any other external donor.) A fragmentary tablet from Herculaneum (*Tab. Herc.* 87) records a process for recovery of dowry. The wife was no longer *in potestate* and the dowry was constituted by a woman, probably but not certainly her mother; nevertheless, the terminology of the *actio rei uxoriae* (normally granted only to the wife's *pater* or the wife herself) is used, although in the only specific item recoverable the retentions for children are to be one-fifth each (as on the wife's death) rather than the one-sixth allowed on divorce. The most likely explanation is that the donor had made a contractual agreement specifying these terms for return of the dowry.

marriage ended while both father and daughter were still alive, she was the one who had the right to recover it, whereas if the marriage was ended by her death her father, if he was still alive, could recover it. Certain questions remain. Does it make a difference whether the emancipation takes place before or during the marriage? Again, Ulpian does not say whether this interpretation is to be held applicable in all circumstances, i.e. when the marriage ends in divorce, when it ends in the husband's death, and when it ends in the wife's death. In the last-mentioned case, if the wife died while still in power, a dowry, if adventicious, would normally remain with the husband; if profecticious, it could be claimed by the wife's *pater* (Ulp. *Reg. 6.* 4–5).[166]

At first sight Ulpian's statement, if taken to apply only to a daughter emancipated before marriage, does not seem entirely logical, since, whether emancipated before marriage or during it, in both cases the daughter became independent only through the father's act and intention. Besides, in two texts (*D.* 24. 3. 22. 5; 44 pr.), both concerned with daughters emancipated after marriage, the opposite view is held, with regard to recovery of dowry after divorce or after the husband's death. Once the daughter, married while *in potestate*, becomes independent, she no longer has a *pater*. Since her father and she are no longer in the same *familia*, he is *extraneus*, the dowry is no longer *profecticia*, but *adventicia*, and it is she, not he, who has the right to bring an action for recovery of dowry.

Now the daughter ought to give her consent to the father [bringing the action for return of dowry] at the time when the issue is joined. It follows from this that if a daughter says that she gives consent to her father and changes her mind, or also if she is emancipated, before the issue is joined the father's action will be ineffective.[167]

---

[166] Pomponius remarks elsewhere (*D.* 23. 3. 6. pr.): 'Iure succursum est patri, ut filia amissa solacii loco cederet, si redderetur ei dos ab ipso profecta, ne et filiae amissae et pecuniae damnum sentiret' (The law comes to the aid of the father [i.e. the praetor grants him an action], in order to give him some solace for the loss of his daughter, by restoring to him the dowry which originated from him, so that he should not feel both the loss of his daughter and that of his money). *Profecta* suggests *profecticia*, but it is not clear that Pomponius had in mind merely the case in which the daughter had died while still in power; this text pre-dates Ulpian's comment.

[167] *D.* 24. 3. 22. 5: Ulpian, *xxxiii ad edictum*. 'Eo autem tempore consentire filiam patri oportet, quo lis contestatur. secundum haec si filia dicat se patri consentire et ante litis contestationem mutaverit voluntatem vel etiam emancipata sit, frustra pater aget.'

The situation is that there has been a divorce. If the daughter is still *in potestate*, her consent is necessary in order for the *pater* to bring an action, but only he can bring it. If, however, she has become *sui iuris*, she has no need of his consent; not only that, but only she can bring the *actio rei uxoriae*.

The same applied where the marriage was ended by the husband's death, as shown by an example from the *Questions* of Paul:

> If a father-in-law instituted as heir by his son-in-law accepts the inheritance, when the father dies the daughter will bring an action against his heir for the dowry. This was the response of Nerva and Cato, as reported by Sextus Pomponius in the fifth book of his *Digest of Aristo*; there he agrees with Aristo. I would therefore say also that if the father had emancipated the daughter, a suit could be brought against him as well.[168]

The marriage has ended with the death of the husband. The daughter, being still *in potestate*, is unable to bring an action for recovery of dowry. Her father does not need to do so, since the dowry has been willed to him by his son-in-law along with the rest of his son-in-law's estate, and he is entitled to it anyway. His heir, however, has no such entitlement, and legal opinion[169] is that an action can be brought against him by the daughter, once she is out of *potestas* by the death of her father. The situation is different when the daughter has already been emancipated before the death of her husband. Then, the dowry has become *adventicia* and she can bring an action for it against the husband's heir—even, Paul thinks, if this happens to be her father.

So, where the marriage is ended by divorce or by the death of the husband, a daughter who has been emancipated during marriage is, it seems, the person who has the right to bring an action for return of the dowry. There are, however, two more texts which perhaps shed some light upon the extent of application of *D. 23. 3. 5. 11.*

(i) The husband of my daughter, who was emancipated and ill, sent her

---

[168] *D.* 24. 3. 44 pr. 'Si socer a genero heres institutus adierit hereditatem, quandoque mortuo patre cum herede eius filiam de dote acturam Nerva et Cato responderunt, ut est relatum apud Sextum Pomponium digestorum ab Aristone libro quinto; ibidem Aristo consensit. ergo dicerem et si emancipasset pater filiam, ipsum quoque conveniri posse.'

[169] Since earlier discussion was reported by Aristo (a member of Trajan's advisory council, *consilium*), who cites Nerva (presumably Cocceius Nerva, cos. suff. AD 24), this view goes back at least to the early part of the 1st cent. AD, or even the mid-2nd cent. BC, if 'Cato' refers to the well-known jurisprudent, son of the Censor and author of a work on civil law.

notice of divorce in order that when she died he should restore the dowry rather to her heirs than to me. Sabinus said that an *actio utilis* for the recovery of the dowry should be granted to me. Gaius said the same.

(ii) If a daughter who had been emancipated divorced in order that she could give her husband the benefit of the dowry and defraud her father, who could sue for the dowry as *profecticia* if she had died while the marriage still existed, the father ought on that account to be assisted, to prevent his losing the dowry. Therefore he is to be allowed the right to claim the dowry, just as if his daughter had died during marriage.[170]

In neither instance is it stated whether the emancipation occurred before or during the marriage (perhaps because this is irrelevant). In both, a divorce takes place after the emancipation, with the express intention of defrauding the father of his claim to return of the dowry. The dowry is *adventicia*, because of the emancipation, and the daughter is the person with the right to claim its return. In *D.* 24. 3. 59 the divorce is apparently carried out in the knowledge that her death is imminent, with the express intention of ensuring that the dowry, now part of her property (or rather, a debt owed by the husband to her estate), will be passed on to her heirs (most likely her husband or children).

D. 24. 2. 5 probably in fact refers to the same (real or hypothetical?) case as *D.* 24. 3. 59. We are not told that the wife's death is anticipated, but this is implied. The text makes it clear that the purpose of the divorce is to block the father's claim to the dowry—a claim which he would not have were she alive when the marriage ended. If she died still married, however, the dowry would be regarded as *profecticia* (even though, strictly speaking, it was now *adventicia*; that is why the father would have to be accorded a special action, *actio utilis*, since the regular *actio rei uxoriae* was not available).

It appears, then, that emancipation made a dowry *adventicia* and reclaimable by the daughter (but not by her father) if the marriage ended during her lifetime; if it ended by her death, it was to be re-

---

[170] (i) *D.* 24. 3. 59. 'Iulianus ii ad Urseium Ferocem. Filiae meae emancipatae et aegrae vir in hoc repudium misit, ut mortua ea dotem potius heredibus eius quam mihi redderet. Sabinus dicebat utile mihi eius dotis reciperandae iudicium dandum esse: Gaius idem.' (ii) *D.* 24. 2. 5: Ulpian, *xxxiv ad edictum.* 'Si filia emancipata idcirco diverterat, ut maritum lucro dotis adficiat, patrem fraudet, qui profecticiam dotem potuit petere, si constante matrimonio decessisset, ideo patri succurrendum est, ne dotem perdat; non enim minus patri quam marito succurrere praetorem oportet. danda igitur est ei dotis exactio, atque si constante matrimonio decessisset filia.'

garded as *profecticia*, and a special action given to the father for its recovery. It was probably irrelevant from the first whether the emancipation took place before or during the marriage, since the principle was the same; Ulpian's reference to a daughter emancipated before marriage may merely be intended in clarification of something left unclear in Sabinus. Once the daughter was emancipated, the father was, legally, an *extraneus*, and the rules of *dos adventicia* applied—except, it came to be felt, where the daughter was dead and the fate of the dowry no longer in her control.

We have already seen two references to emancipated daughters who deliberately divorce, apparently in order to try to ensure that the dowry remains with their husbands and does not revert to their fathers. Twice also a father is found denying that his daughter had ever been emancipated.[171] In the first instance this is after the daughter's death; in the other she is very much alive and has appealed to the emperor Gordian.

After the death of a daughter who had been living as a *materfamilias*[172] as if lawfully emancipated, and who had made a will and appointed heirs before she died, her father is barred from starting litigation that denies his own deed, on the claim that he did not carry out a lawful emancipation or did not do it with witnesses present. No one can adopt or adrogate in his absence, nor carry through any solemn act of that kind through an agent.[173]

The father is patently attempting fraud. If his daughter made a will, it can only have been with his consent, as *tutor legitimus*; but he has become greedy, and now wants to overturn the will and hang on to all the property she had in her possession (and probably to the dowry as well). Moreover, as Papinian points out, there was no room for

---

[171] *D.* 1. 7. 25; *Cod. Iust.* 2. 26. 2: 987 Honoré. Compare *Cod. Iust.* 8. 46 (47). 1 (Antoninus and Verus), in which a father is claiming to have his son still in his *potestas* despite having long since allowed tutors, nominated in the will of his mother (evidently mistrustful of her husband), to have the management of the child's property: Rabello (1979) 250–3.

[172] This text should be included with a small group in which the term *materfamilias* is used merely to refer to a woman who is *sui iuris*, legally independent, as distinct from one still a *filiafamilias*: cf. *D.* 1. 6. 4; 24. 3. 30. 1; 24. 3. 34. *Paterfamilias* is frequently used in the same way.

[173] *D.* 1. 7. 25 (Ulpian, *Opinions* bk. 5): 'Post mortem filiae suae, quae ut mater familias quasi iure emancipata vixerat et testamento scriptis heredibus decessit, adversus factum suum, quasi non iure eam nec praesentibus testibus emancipasset, pater movere controversiam prohibetur. Neque adoptare neque adrogare quis absens nec per alium eiusmodi sollemnitatem peragere potest.'

mistake or misconception, because the *pater* himself must have been personally involved in the emancipation.

In the other instance, from the year AD 238, litigation has been allowed to progress further. When Serena's father claimed that she was in his *potestas* and, though admitting that he had gone through an emancipation, denied that it was valid, the proconsul who heard the case found in favour of the father. Serena thereupon appealed directly to the emperor Gordian, who now refers her to the provincial governor, saying that he 'in impertienda cognitione suas partes secundum leges exhibebit' (in bestowing a hearing will perform his part according to the laws).

We are not told what the father's motive was. Greed suggests itself; any property acquired by Serena since her emancipation was hers during her lifetime, not his (and by now the *senatusconsultum Orphitianum* has taken effect, so that even if, as tutor, he prevented her from making her will, should she die first he could not hope to inherit on intestacy, if she had children). It is not clear whether the provincial magistrate to whom the appeal is referred is the same as the one who initially found against Serena, but the emperor's phrase about conformity with the laws may contain a hint that he suspects corruption, and a veiled warning against any repetition.

Some fathers, apparently, regretted the financial consequences of emancipation, not only that what their emancipated daughters acquired they acquired for themselves and not for their *pater*, but also that part of the father's own property might become irrecoverable. It was one thing to bestow on her husband, for the daughter's welfare, part of the patrimony that she would ultimately be able to recover (i.e. the dowry); it was another to allow it, while the original donor, the *parens manumissor*, was still alive, to be absorbed after her death in the property of an *extraneus*, her husband, with no guarantee that it would go to her children, if any, since there were as yet no restraints upon how the husband chose to dispose of what was legally his own property. Measures restricting the capacity of a father to dispose of maternal property and obliging him to preserve it intact for offspring of the marriage begin to appear only in late law.[174]

As far as dowry property is concerned, legal opinion sides with fathers. Pomponius (n. 166) and Ulpian, telling us that the dowry is to be regarded as *profecticia*, may draw attention to the regard paid to

---

[174] Fayer (1994) 264–7; Evans Grubbs (1995) 115–18; Arjava (1996) 98–105.

fatherly emotion, but concern for the patrimony is even more to the fore. Nevertheless, care is taken to provide for the emancipated daughter in her lifetime. The provision her father made for her in marriage was still there for her to fall back on if the marriage failed.

1.12 FAMILY FAVOURITES: PROVISION IN WILLS

In civil law, the first category of heirs were the *sui heredes*, i.e. sons and daughters and sons' descendants, who inherited automatically upon intestacy. When a man made a will, these *sui heredes* must either be instituted as heirs or, if not, expressly disinherited; if this was not done, the will was void. By the end of the Republic, as we saw, the praetor's edict admitted emancipated children also to intestate inheritance on the same level as *sui heredes*, and the same rule was applied to wills in regard to them. Unless they were either instituted heirs or expressly disinherited (the sons individually by name, while for the others a general reference, sufficient to identify the persons meant, sufficed), the will was void.[175]

There were numerous ways, of which this was only one, in which wills might fail. Acquiring an additional *suus heres* was one of the principal ways. Adopting a son would have this effect; so did having a child, or bringing a wife into *manus* after the will was made, and also undergoing a 'capitis deminutio' (change of status) either voluntarily, e.g. by allowing oneself to be adrogated, or involuntarily, by being sentenced to slavery or exile for crimes committed.[176] Wills could also fail if none of the named heirs was willing, or survived, to take up the inheritance. Moreover, even if the formalities of disinheritance had been properly observed, it was still possible both for *sui heredes* and for *liberi* to complain that they had been unjustly disinherited (the 'complaint of unduteous will') and to claim the share due to them on intestacy; they could also claim under this heading if they had been left too small an amount.[177]

---

[175] Gaius 2. 123–35. [176] Gaius 1. 160–3; 2. 130–1, 138–40.

[177] In practice, under the Empire, complaints of unduteous will were regarded as satisfied if the *liberi* received their share of one-quarter of the estate. The *lex Falcidia* of 40 BC had required that one-quarter of an estate be left among the instituted heirs. If a complaint of unduteous will succeeded, the will was not rendered completely void, the instituted heirs still being entitled to up to three-quarters of the total estate, and legacies and manumissions still being due.

Not surprisingly, Roman legal texts have little or nothing to say about wills which succeeded in meeting all the legal requirements, not because they were rare (we are not justified in assuming that) but because correct wills offered little of legal interest for discussion. 'Good news is no news', or, from a legal point of view, thousands of boringly correct wills are less worth commenting upon than the occasional flawed one. We cannot, therefore, assume that the fairly numerous references in the *Digest* to emancipated sons being passed over in wills, or disinherited, are representative of Roman social practice, and can be used as evidence that it was *common* for Roman fathers to make no provision in their wills for their emancipated offspring; we have no way of calculating what proportion of all wills these instances represent. The motives for these disinheritances or omissions are not usually stated, either; this is because the jurists commenting upon them are interested only in the legal points involved.

The examples given in the legal sources, however, do provide some evidence that not all Roman fathers with emancipated children provided equally generously for descendants still *in potestate* and those emancipated—though not that one group is consistently favoured over the other. They also illustrate the variety of ways, either actual or deemed probable, in which property might be distributed among them. Emancipated children are not always less generously treated than those in power, and an important factor, recurring frequently in the texts, is the bequests made to the children of the emancipated sons, who have remained in their grandfather's power.

Were emancipated children generally treated better or worse in their father's wills than children kept in power? As far as disinheritance is concerned, there is little evidence to go upon. Of the thirty or so references in the *Digest* to emancipated children in connection with disinheritance, many have nothing to do with the content of actual wills. A few are merely procedural, indicating how the law is to be applied, and whether or not emancipation or disinheritance makes a difference, for instance: on liability for obligations contracted while a son was *in potestate*, after being emancipated or disinherited (*D.* 4. 4. 3. 4, 14. 5. 2 and 5, 12. 6. 38. 2); on the right to burial in a family or hereditary tomb (*D.* 11. 7. 6); on marriage between a tutor's son and his ward (*D.* 23. 2. 67); on claims to fulfilment of a *fideicommissum*, i.e. a testamentary instruction (*D.* 30. 114. 16);[178] and rules on dowry, and

---

[178] On failure of a son to observe a *fideicommissum* of his father's forbidding alienation of property away from his descendants; the text reports Marcellus' view that the

on legacies (*D.* 37. 7. 4). Several others, also procedural, have to do
with the praetorian rules of succession[179] or inheritance problems
which may be created or solved by emancipation.[180]

Two texts (*D.* 28. 2. 23; 37. 4. 8. 7) concern particular legal problems
raised when emancipation is combined with subsequent adrogation
by the original *pater*, and there has been a previous disinheritance;
these will be considered later in the context of adoption (2.9). These
manœuvres may seem bizarre to us, but Paul, in a longish text (*D.* 45.
1. 132. pr.), discussing how a verbal undertaking is to be understood,
by which someone promises to pay a penalty if someone put in his
charge is treated 'aliter quam ut filium' (otherwise than as a son), asks:
'primum in eum, qui legitime adoptavit, an possit committi, si eum
exheredaverit vel emancipaverit' (Can the stipulation apply to
someone who adopted [the person in question] in legal form, then disinherited or emancipated him?).

He answers his own question positively: 'haec enim pater circa
filium solet facere: igitur non aliter eum quam ut filium observavit'
([Yes,] for fathers customarily treat their sons like this, therefore [the
adopter] did not treat him otherwise than as a son).

However, if the son was merely put in the man's charge, but not
legally adopted, then Paul does not see what meaning can be attached
to the words 'treats him otherwise than as a son'. Disinheritance and
emancipation are inappropriate (*ineptas*), where no legal tie has been
established, therefore the promise is 'vacuous', i.e. no particular performance can be required. Nevertheless, he continues oddly, 'it will
be able to be said that the stipulation takes effect'.

These last words perhaps suggest that in Paul's view, where there
was no adoption, and therefore no legal relationship, 'treating like a
son' can bear only the meaning of showing some, albeit unspecifiable,

grandsons can claim fulfilment of the *fideicommissum*, whether instituted heirs, disinherited or emancipated. On such trusts, see Johnston (1985) 220–90.

[179] *D.* 28. 2. 32 (a theoretical example)—emancipated son disinherited, son in
power passed over in will (contrast 37. 4. 20. pr. emancipated son passed over, son in
power disinherited); 36. 1. 28. 6; 38. 2. 13; 38. 2. 20. 4; 38. 6. 5 pr.

[180] Problems about child heirs dying still *impuberes*, about grandchildren with
lunatic or spendthrift fathers, about entitlement to the estates of freedmen: *D.* 28. 6. 2
pr.; 27. 10. 16. 2; 38. 2. 11; 38. 2. 38 pr. Disinherited sons had no claim upon the
estates of their father's freedmen (cf. *D.* 38. 2. 13); however, they could re-establish a
claim for the next generation of the family, if they emancipated their children.

kindness beyond what would normally be shown to persons unconnected either by blood or by *familia* membership.

It is apparent, however, from his discussion of the topic, not only that legal manœuvres such as disinheritance and emancipation were not regarded as unusual, but that we cannot expect to find legal discussion treating them as, in themselves, being evidence of ill-feeling of father towards son. Legal discussion is concerned primarily with the legal effects of these actions, not their motivations. As we shall see presently, when we come to examine various dispositions of property by fathers, passing over and disinheritance appear to be applied without distinction both to emancipated children and to those still in power.

Occasionally, however, the curtain is drawn aside a little and it is possible, besides the purely legal considerations discussed, to discern something of the motivations—usually hostile or discreditable—involved. Not all families are happy ones. In *D*. 37. 7. 6 a disgruntled daughter, who had been disinherited whereas her emancipated brother was instituted heir, successfully brought a complaint of unduteous will, and took away half the estate. Not content with that, she seems to have tried to get an order for her brother to make *collatio* of his property; Papinian replied, however, that he was not to be compelled to do so: 'for it was decided also that manumissions were valid.' In other words, the will as a whole had not been voided (as it would have been had this been a successful suit for possession *contra tabulas*), and the brother retained his share not as if on intestacy, but as instituted heir.

A family fight (perhaps, the language suggests, only a hypothetical one, though the grandfather's resentment and huffiness is realistic enough) appears to lie behind the discussion in *D*. 37. 4. 3. 5 (from Ulpian's commentary on the Edict, book 39) about what should be decided when a grandson, whose father was already dead, applied for possession of the estate of his grandfather. The clause *unde liberi* of the edict allowed not only emancipated sons, but the children of deceased *emancipati*, to succeed on intestacy. This case, however, is presented as involving certain special circumstances.

The son, who was emancipated, had been disinherited by his father for marrying a woman father did not approve of. His son applied for possession against his grandfather's will, on the grounds that the will was invalid, since he himself had been left out of the will, when the law required that, as one of the *liberi* (being the surviving son of an *emancipatus*)[181] he should either be made heir, or specifically disinherited.

If an emancipated son marries a wife not in accordance with his father's wishes and obtains a son by her, and then after his father's death the grandson wishes to come into possession of his grandfather's property, he is to be admitted; for someone who is a legitimate son will not, by cancellation, cease to be a son, since cancellation is employed to increase the number of those admitted, not to diminish it. For even if the son married so base a wife that it disgraced him as much as his father for him to have such a wife, we will say that the son born to her is admitted to possession of the property of his grandfather, since the grandfather could have exercised his right and disinherited him: for the judge hearing a complaint of undutiful will in the case of this grandson will weigh up the offences of the father no less than the deserts of the grandson; [or, more plausibly, with the reading of F², *merita nepotis quam*, 'will weigh up the deserts of the grandson no less than the offences of the father'].[182]

The marriage of the emancipated son evidently caused his father bitter offence, which continued to rankle. The son is already dead, but grandfather has vented his continuing resentment by ignoring his grandson in his will. If his grandfather had disinherited him, he could have brought a complaint of unduteous will (cf. *Cod. Iust.* 3. 28. 7: 395 Honoré). The judge's decision, Ulpian points out, ought then to turn on the question of whether the grandson, not his father, had done anything to deserve disinheritance; the mother's alleged unworthiness is irrelevant.

We may assume that the men involved are not of the senatorial class, since the marriage to a 'base' wife would otherwise be invalid as a result of the *lex Julia de maritandis ordinibus* (emancipation did not result in loss of status: *D.* 1. 9. 7. pr.). If the son had still been in power, his father could have refused consent to the marriage, and his child would be illegitimate; as it was, being emancipated, he did not

---

[181] D. 37. 6. 2 pr.; 38. 6. 5. 1 fin.

[182] 'Si emancipatus filius uxore non ex voluntate patris ducta filium fuerit sortitus, dein nepos patre iam mortuo ad bonorum possessionem avi velit venire, admittendus est ad eam: non enim per rescissionem is, qui filius iustus est, efficietur non filius, cum rescissio, quo magis admittantur, non quo minus, adhibeatur. nam etsi tam ignominiosam duxerit uxorem filius, ut dedecori sit tam ipsi quam patri mulierem talem habere, dicemus ex ea natum ad bonorum possessionem avi admitti, cum possit avus iure suo uti eumque exheredare: nec enim minus in hoc nepote is, qui de officio cogniturus est, quam merita nepotis [So Mommsen-Krueger text; F¹ omits *quam*; F², however, reads more plausibly *merita nepotis quam*] patris eius delicta perpendet.'

require his father's consent to marry. The grandson therefore was legitimate, and so is now eligible to make a claim for *bonorum possessio.* Ulpian's view is that in such a case the grandson should be admitted to possession of the estate.

At first sight, it is unclear why there should be any doubt on the matter; however, the word *rescissio,* 'cancellation' provides a clue. At *D.* 37. 1. 6. 1 Paul (in book 41 of *his* work on the Edict) offers a rationale for the introduction to the edict of the clause *unde liberi,* admitting *emancipati* on the same level as children in power: 'Even though children who have ceased to be automatic heirs because of a change of status fall short in civil law, the praetor *rescindit* (literally 'cancels') their change of status on the grounds of equity.'[183]

This is a theoretical explanation, unrelated to the actual historical context of the introduction two centuries before of the clause, the original reasons for which are no longer remembered. (This kind of pseudo-explanation occurs elsewhere in Roman legal writings—the alleged reason for women being in *tutela* is a notorious example.) If the edict treats an emancipated son on the same basis as the *sui heredes,* this must be by a legal fiction. It is pretended that he has never been emancipated; therefore he or, if he is already dead, children born after the emancipation and in his *potestas* are eligible to inherit; this is the point of Ulpian's comment about increasing, rather than diminishing the number of those eligible.

How is this relevant to the situation described in the passage? Ulpian perceives that, in the situation described, this way of accounting for the praetorian rule could create a problem.

If the emancipation were regarded as *literally* 'cancelled', then it could be argued that, if it is assumed never to have occurred, then the situation becomes one in which someone to be regarded not as *emancipatus* but as a *filiusfamilias* has married without his father's consent, and therefore has a son who is illegitimate. Ulpian, however, sensibly takes the view that such a literal interpretation of the meaning of the praetorian rule is inappropriate.[184] 'Someone who is a legitimate son

---

[183] 'Quamvis enim iure civili deficiant liberi, qui propter capitis deminutionem desierunt sui heredes esse, propter aequitatem tamen rescindit eorum capitis deminutionem praetor.'

[184] *Rescissio* and the corresponding verb are found elsewhere in the *Digest* mainly with reference to cancellation of contracts or of wills or parts of wills. In only two other places is there a reference to change of status, at *D.* 38. 6. 1. 7, 'cancellation' of the adoption back into *potestas* as a grandson of a son, previously emancipated, by his re-emancipation; and *D.* 37. 1. 6. 1, quoted in text above, where the praetor is said to

(i.e. the grandson) will not, by cancellation (i.e. the legal fiction that his father had not been emancipated), cease to be a son.'

Underlying the discussion, however, we may perhaps detect traces of a current theoretical debate among jurists of the early third century. To what extent does an emancipating father continue to have any right to control the actions of his son? Expectations founded on *pietas* are, as we saw above, accorded some recognition, as having the force of moral obligations, though, unlike freedmen, no sanction is as yet suggested for emancipated sons who do not fulfil them, and to some extent the obligations are reciprocal. The emancipating parent has also been placed under an obligation by the edict either to institute his emancipated child as heir in his will, or disinherit him, in the same way as children in power. This does not, however, give him any right in his lifetime to try to exert authority over him. As far as concerns the autonomy of the emancipated son, in his new role as a fully-fledged *paterfamilias*, Ulpian and others are clear that his parent has no legal right to interfere.[185] The emancipated son in the present instance, therefore, did not need his father's consent to marry and, whether grandfather approved of his choice or not, the grandson was legitimate.

Wills in which someone with a claim *unde liberi* was passed over (i.e. neither instituted heir nor specifically disinherited) were invalid, and there is a good deal of discussion in the *Digest* (especially, of course,

'cancel' (i.e. to ignore) emancipated sons' change of status on grounds of equity, and to admit them to *bonorum possessio* in the same way as *sui heredes*. *Rescissio*, in the present text is not be taken literally as meaning 'cancellation' of the son's emancipation, i.e. his return into *potestas*, by adrogation (for which see D. 28. 2. 23; 37. 4. 8. 7–8). This could be done only by the son's consent, and scarcely fits with the scenario presented. Enforced cancellation of emancipation as a punishment for failure in *obsequium*, obedience, by a son is first attested in a constitution of Constantine from AD 330 against children who 'raise themselves up arrogantly and cruelly' (*superbe crudeliterque se tollere*) (*Frag. Vat.* 248) against their fathers, then again later, in AD 367, in a rescript in the names of Valentinian, Valens and Gratian (*Cod. Iust.* 8. 49), where it is as punishment for those who 'parentes vel acerbitate convicii vel cuiuscumque atroci iniuriae dolore pulsassent' (have stricken their parents with harsh reviling or with the pain of outrageous insult). Although it is perhaps not impossible that recall to *potestas* was employed in individual cases, it seems unlikely that it could have been in use for such a relatively slight offence as early as Ulpian, especially in a matter (the choice of wife) where the parent no longer had any legal right; according to Ulpian, in cases of verbal abuse or physical assault, the prefect of Rome administered punishment appropriate to the degree of the offence (D. 37. 15. 1. 2). Re-enslavement for freedmen found guilty of offences against their patron dates only from Constantine (*Cod. Iust.* 6. 7. 2).

[185] See 1.10 above and D. 37. 12.

though not only, in Title 37. 4, *De bonorum possessione contra tabulas*, 'On possession against the terms of a will') of the appropriate division of inheritances in such cases, in relation to families in which one or more of the eligible parties is emancipated. However, it is not possible on the basis of these texts, any more than of those concerning disinheritance, to assert either a tendency to favour children in power against those emancipated, or vice versa. A wide range of permutations is discussed—emancipated children or grandchildren are *praeteriti* (passed over) while those in power are instituted heirs, or vice versa, or a mixture of one and the other. Motivation is not usually discussed (as irrelevant to the legal point), and cannot be assumed to have been economically rational—the institution of the *querela inofficiosi testamenti* probably owed as much to parents' tendency to have favourites as to sibling jealousies. Sometimes children really were getting less than their fair share, sometimes they only thought they were.[186]

In addition, although the situations envisaged are possible and could occur in actuality, a good many of the examples are clearly hypothetical. Passing over and disinheritance are often discussed together, since both afforded opportunity for claims against the will, in the former case as invalid, in the latter as undutiful; Paul, for example, in his single book on undutiful wills summarized the options open, depending upon circumstances, to an emancipated son not provided for:

Suppose that an emancipated son has been passed over and a grandson by him has been kept in power and instituted heir: the son will be able to claim possession of the estate against his son, the testator's grandson, but he will not be able to bring a claim of unduteous will. But if the emancipated son has been disinherited, he will be able to bring a complaint, and thus he will be conjoined with his son (the change instituted by Julian: cf. above on *D.* 37. 8. 3) and acquire the estate along with him.[187]

Paul is providing a helpfully brief rule of thumb which can be applied in giving appropriate legal advice in individual instances. The

[186] Cf. Papinian's remark, *D.* 31. 77. 20, concerning a *fideicommissum* in a father's will to his sons, requesting them to hand over to his brothers, their uncles, the property he inherited from his mother: 'cum discordiis propinquorum sedandorum prospexerit, quas materia communionis solet excitare' (Since he wished to allay discord among relatives, which tends to be stirred up by what may be considered joint property).

[187] *D.* 5. 2. 3 pr.: 'Si ponas filium emancipatum praeteritum et ex eo nepotem in potestate retentum heredem institutum esse: filius potest contra filium suum, testatoris nepotem petere bonorum possessionem, queri autem de inofficioso testamento non poterit. quod si exheredatus sit filius emancipatus, poterit queri et ita iungetur filio suo et simul cum eo hereditatem optinebit.'

will can be contested as invalid if the emancipated son is passed over; it can be contested as undutiful if he has been disinherited.

The position is the same when it is a son in power, rather than an emancipated son, who is passed over. For instance, Marcian remarks:'If, when an emancipated son has been disinherited, a son in power has been passed over, the emancipated son will not have effective action if he claims possession against the will; however, both the emancipated son and the *suus heres* will have a claim on intestacy.'[188]

His point could equally well have been expressed by supposing the situation to be the other way round. If the *filius familias* had been disinherited and the *emancipatus* passed over, the former could not bring an effective claim for possession against the will, but both could claim on intestacy. In other words, the particular dispositions are irrelevant: the legal point is that leaving out one of the *liberi* (whether in power or not) invalidates the will.

Similarly, and at rather greater length, Paul discusses (*D*. 37. 5. 15. pr-2) the complex problems that can arise regarding individual liability to pay legacies, in various permutations of situations involving sons in power and *emancipati*, whether *praeteriti* or instituted heirs, whether making claims or not for *bonorum possessio*, and whether an instituted heir has accepted the estate.

Virtually all the discussion in the *Digest* of the consequences of the passing over of *liberi* is of this theoretical sort, whether expressed as general rules or by analysis of hypothetical (and usually problematical) cases. The rescripts in the *Codex Iustinianus* are likewise of little help in assessing tendencies in the treatment of emancipated children in comparison with those in power. Between AD 193 and 305, seven rescripts refer to persons *praeteriti*, omitted in wills. Of these, three are *postumi*, children not yet born when the will was made, two concern the wills of a mother and a sister (against which only a complaint of unduteous will can be brought), and in the remaining two an alleged son of the deceased has to prove his claim to be such.[189] Nothing of any relevance

---

[188] *D*. 28. 1. 32: 'Si filio emancipato exheredato is qui in potestate est praeteritus sit, ipse quidem emancipatus si contra tabulas petat, nihil agit, ab intestato autem et suus et emancipatus venient.'

[189] *Postumi*; *Cod. Iust*. 6. 21. 10, 6. 20. 11, 6. 29. 2 (1268, 2102, 2209 Honoré); mother's will: 3. 28. 15 (1247 Honoré); sister's will 3. 28. 17 (1435 Honoré); alleged *filius*: 8. 2. 1, 6. 33. 2 (55, 612 Honoré).

is to be found in the nine rescripts[190] directly mentioning disinheritance, none of which relate to emancipated children.

Although a number of rescripts[191] mention claims to *bonorum possessio*, and *collatio* by *emancipati*, in the absence of further details it is mostly impossible to say what provision was or was not made for the emancipated person, in what circumstances the will failed or was challenged, or whether indeed there was a will. Exceptionally we learn in one instance that the will failed because of the omission of a posthumous child; in another that *emancipati* have apparently been instituted heirs. One father appears to have made a dotal pact at the time of his emancipated daughter's marriage barring her from making any claim to her father's inheritance; the enquirer is told that this has no legal validity against her rights to a share of his intestate estate. However, her emancipated condition appears to be less relevant to the father's decision than the pre-emption of part of his property by the constitution of a dowry.[192]

Of more significance, perhaps, is the attention paid in the *Digest* to situations in which sons have been emancipated, but children already born to them have been kept in the *potestas* of their grandfather. This, as already noted, was apparently sufficiently commonplace for it to be thought advisable at the time of Julian's revision to introduce a modification to the edict concerning the respective claims of these grandchildren and their emancipated parent to the estate (*D.* 37. 8. 3).

In the ordinary run of events, if their fathers had not been emancipated, these grandchildren would in due course, on the grandfather's death, have come under the *potestas* of their fathers. Once the latter had been emancipated, however, this could be achieved only if they were first emancipated by their grandfathers and then adopted by their natural fathers. This does not, however, seem to have been a course of action that was particularly favoured. Why not? The reason may have been that more importance was attached to safeguarding

---

[190] In chronological order: *Cod. Iust.* 6. 28. 1, 6. 12. 2, 6. 25. 4, 6. 28. 2, 6. 21. 9, 6. 21. 10, 3. 28. 18, 3. 28. 22, 6. 23. 14 (104, 656, 666, 720, 965, 1268, 1469, 2198, 2531 Honoré).

[191] *Cod. Iust.* 2. 20. 6; 1. 18. 3; 6. 9. 4; 4. 5. 5; 6. 20. 9; 6. 20. 12; 6. 20. 15; 6. 19. 1=2. 6. 4 (1217, 1219, 1811, 1812, 1829, 2150, 2565, 2615 Honoré); *Cod. Iust.* 6. 20. 4 (1008 Honoré): *collatio* of dowry.

[192] *Postumus*: *Cod. Iust.* 6. 20. 11 (2102 Honoré). In *Cod. Iust.* 6. 20. 1 (693 Honoré), an applicant is told that emancipated children who have been instituted as heirs are not required to make *collatio* with their brother of gifts from their father; the situation appears to be that a sibling—whether also emancipated or not is not specified—is challenging the will. Dotal pact: *Cod. Iust.* 6. 20. 3 (844 Honoré).

the continued economic well-being of a particular branch of the family (so far as this depended upon intestate inheritance) than to perpetuating legal control from one generation to another within it. Financial provision could always be made in wills, which were specially useful for favouring individuals, but wills could fail. It was better, therefore, to keep grandchildren born before the emancipation in grandfather's *familia*; they could then, under praetorian rules, be sure of at least an equal share, along with any other heirs on intestacy, of both inheritances.

Before the development of the rules of succession under the praetor's edict, already discussed, grandchildren kept *in potestate* retained the right to succeed to the share of their grandfather's estate which their fathers would have had; they had, however, no claims on their emancipated fathers' estates. This they could have had only if they had been emancipated and then adopted by their natural fathers; this, however, would have meant that *both* generations forfeited a share in grandfather's intestate estate (since in civil law emancipated sons did not inherit).

Later, they could succeed to each other, under praetorian rules, but only *unde cognati*.[193] The grandchildren kept in power, however, had priority over their emancipated fathers in succession to their grandfathers' estates, since they were his *sui heredes*, while their fathers inherited only as cognates.

The introduction of the clause *unde liberi*, while improving the position, if necessary, for emancipated sons, worsened that of grandchildren retained in their grandfather's power; since the latter were held to 'represent' their father's line, he could, if he chose, intervene and exclude them from their grandfather's estate. They might find themselves, therefore, in difficult present circumstances; they would have to wait until their emancipated father died before they could (if necessary) bring a claim on his estate, which they also could now do as *liberi*.[194] Julian's modification to the edict improved matters by allowing both generations a share of the grandfather's estate; and in due course, when the emancipated son died, the grandsons were able to inherit from him.

In practice families adopted a wide range of strategies for the transmission of property, some of which are reflected in the legal

---

[193] This appears to follow from Ulp. *Reg.* 28. 9; *D.* 38. 10. 4. 10.
[194] *D.* 37. 6. 5; 38. 6. 6.

discussions cited above; but they appear not to have been content to leave matters to the ordinary operation of the rules of intestate succession, if their wills should fail. Instead, *patres* sometimes employed means of 'engineering' the structure of the *familia* in the interests of particular individuals, by means of emancipations, alone or in combination with strategic adoptions within the family (to be discussed later, in 2.9), especially with a view to favouring the claims of those individuals in the event of failure of a will. The resulting complications in calculating inheritance claims and the considerations of equity raised were matters on which lawyers had to be prepared to give advice.

1.13 MOTIVES FOR EMANCIPATION

A lot of emancipation appears to have been going on—but for what reasons? Very few individual emancipations are attested in literary sources. Legal sources are on the whole unhelpful for enquiry into the motives of emancipators, since for the most part discussion ignores motives, and concerns legal problems consequential upon emancipation; it may sometimes be possible, however, to infer motives from consideration of the effects. To some extent, consideration of the question will have to be speculative.

In three of the four (if one includes Clodius: Cic. *Dom.* 37)[195] well-known references to emancipation in literary sources (the exception is that by C. Licinius Stolo, on which see further below), and in the score or so of examples in legal sources where a motive is indicated, the initiative comes not from the potential emancipator but from a third party (and emancipation does not always take place). The common factor is that a *paterfamilias* is offered an inducement to emancipate, in order that either he himself or the *filiusfamilias* may benefit under the will of this interested third party. Most often, the instigator is mother of the child in power, occasionally grandmother[196]

---

[195] The others are Regulus' son, and Domitia Lucilla, mentioned in the text above. The text of Pliny, *Ep.* 10. 4 implies that Voconius Romanus was emancipated (since his mother was apparently able to make a legal gift to him in his father's lifetime: 'matris liberalitatem et statim patris hereditatem' (his mother's generosity, followed shortly by his father's inheritance)), but no motive is stated; he was subsequently adopted by his stepfather: cf. *Ep.* 2. 13. 4.

[196] *D.* 28. 7. 18. 1; 35. 1. 77 pr.; paternal in 35. 1. 93.

(whether maternal or paternal is not specified) or other relative. Notoriously, the maternal grandfather of Domitia Lucilla (future grandmother of Marcus Aurelius) so disliked his son-in-law that he made her his heir on condition that she be released from her father's control; his intention was thwarted, however, since she was promptly adopted by her father's brother, and it was a close-knit family.[197] Once the initiative comes from a paternal uncle, once from an emancipated son, apparently anticipating early death, who wishes his son left in his grandfather's power to benefit directly from his estate without it passing into grandfather's ownership, once from a natural father wishing to benefit his son given in adoption to another man and still in the latter's *potestas*.[198] This last is noteworthy. As we have seen, emancipation of an adopted child left him without any of the inheritance rights from his adoptive father retained by natural children; unless he was emancipated, however, the bequest would simply be merged into the property of his new *paterfamilias*. Giving in adoption was a gamble; it could matter who died first.

In two instances (*D.* 28. 5. 47 and *Cod. Iust.* 6. 42. 15: 1325 Honoré), the testator is not stated to be a relative, and may be an *extraneus*. The latter is an answer to a specific enquiry by two brothers, confirming that the wording of the will constituted a *fideicommissum* requiring their emancipation; the testator is identified only as *aliquis*, 'someone'.

---

[197] Pliny, *Ep.* 8. 18. There is a little legal puzzle here, since Pliny seems to say that she was first emancipated, then adopted: 'emiserat pater, adoptaverat patruus, atque ita circumscripto testamento consors frater in fratris potestatem emancipatam filiam adoptionis fraude revocaverat' (Her father had emancipated her, her uncle had adopted her. Circumventing [Mancia's] will in this way, one partner-brother [*consors* is usually taken to mean that the brothers had maintained the old-fashioned practice of retaining their joint inheritance undivided: see Gaius 3.154a] after emancipating his daughter, had recalled her into the *potestas* of his brother by the fraud of adoption). Adrogation (the method of adoption for persons *sui iuris*), was not originally available for females, since it was carried out in earlier Roman practice before a meeting of the *comitia*. This may (though Pliny does not say so) be an early instance of individual dispensation by imperial rescript. *Contra*, Russo Ruggeri (1990a) 105–12, who compares Cic. *De fin.* 1. 7. 24 'quem in adoptionem D. Silano emancipaverat' (whom he had given in adoption to D. Silanus) and Tert. *Apol.* 9. 17 'filios exponitis . . . vel adoptandos melioribus parentibus emancipatis' (You expose children or free them for adoption by better parents), and argues that Pliny's phrase 'in fratris potestatem emancipatam filiam etc.' means only that he gave her in adoption to her brother. This, however, does not explain 'revocaverat in potestatem adoptionis fraude' (called her *back* into *potestas* by the fraud of adoption), nor does it sufficiently account for the tense of *emancipatam*, which in classical Latin usage ought to refer to an action preceding and distinct from that in *adoptionis fraude revocaverat*, not to a constituent part of the adoption procedure.

[198] *D.* 29. 4. 27. 1; 37. 4. 16; 45. 1. 107.

D. 28. 5. 47 (from Africanus *Questions,* bk. 2) is rather curious; the *filiusfamilias* who is intended to benefit asks his would-be benefactor for a condition of emancipation *not* to be included, to avoid offending his *pater,* and so a friend of his is instituted heir instead; however, there was no explicit *fideicommissum* in the will. This has the air of an invented example, though perhaps shedding some light on the ambivalent status of *patria potestas* in the second century AD. On the one hand, the particular situation underlines the son's practical dependence on paternal goodwill; while on the other, the apparent normality of a condition of emancipation, in that an outsider could consider asking for it, indicates a generally relaxed attitude to retention of *patria potestas.*[199] There was agreement, however, as we shall see below, that there could be no question of forcing fathers to renounce what was peculiarly their prerogative.

Nor was a condition of emancipation introduced only in order to enable someone to receive all, or a major part, of an inheritance. Several of our examples involve only *fideicommissa,* or legacies; the person for whom emancipation is requested is not always heir.[200]

For the most part, however, the wills that figure in the sources are those of mothers,[201] divorced or otherwise, and sometimes with express indications of hostility or distrust towards the *paterfamilias.* Severus ruled that if sons had been emancipated to fulfil a condition of inheritance in their mother's will, their father was not subsequently to be appointed curator to his sons, since this would circumvent her intention. Such bad feeling towards a present or past marital partner may have been the most common motive prompting such a proviso. In one case decided by Marcus Aurelius it was held that a *fideicommissum* from a divorced wife, to be paid when her sons' father died, fell due upon their previous emancipation, on the grounds that her

---

[199] Cf. *D.* 35. 1. 42, where a bequest on the opposite condition, that the son remain in paternal power, is remarked by Africanus to be tantamount to leaving the father the legacy: Rabello (1979) 162–3. Africanus in *D.* 28. 5. 47 is interested in the technical question whether, in the event of the friend not fulfilling his part, an action is available, and if so, what kind of action (on *fideicommissum* or mandate), and to whom (*pater* or son).

[200] *D.* 32. 50; 35. 1. 92; 36. 1. 23. pr. (two examples, of which the second is Claudius Brasidas' ex-wife); 37. 4. 16.

[201] Suet. *Vit.* 6; Pliny, *Ep.* 4. 2 (Regulus' son); *D.* 5. 3. 58; 26. 5. 21. 1; 29. 7. 6 pr.; 32. 50; 35. 1. 70; 36. 1. 23 pr.; *Cod. Iust.* 2. 20. 5; 3. 28. 25; 6. 25. 3; 8. 54. 5 (1903, 2714, 434, 2562 Honoré). The beneficiaries in both *Cod. Iust.* 2. 20. 5 and 5. 16. 16 (1903, 1674 Honoré) may already have been emancipated.

reason for imposing such a condition had been that she had not believed that their father would emancipate them.[202]

There is one curious passage of Ulpian which suggests the possibility that a testator, with or without the collusion of the *filiusfamilias*, might induce a *pater* to emancipate by, in effect, bribing him: 'If a parent has accepted money to emancipate, or the son later, while living, has given him enough to stop him from upsetting what he has thought fit to do (sc. in making his will), then he (i.e. the father) will be warded off by a counterplea of fraud.'[203]

The context is discussion of a manumitting parent's right—on the analogy of patronal rights over freedmen's property—to bring a claim of *bonorum possessio* against a freed child's will. Two distinct situations are envisaged. The money offered might have come from a third party, either directly (perhaps in the form of a conditional legacy) or by agreement with the son (rather as in the collusive arrangement for manumission of a slave, *suis nummis emptus*),[204] as an inducement to emancipate; or the son himself might have paid it, for another purpose, some time after the emancipation. In the latter instance, the son, already emancipated (and apparently childless), is for some reason expected to die before his parent, but does not wish to make him heir. 'Enough', in that case, would presumably be an amount equal to the 'Falcidian fourth' (n. 153 above) of the son's estate; if the parent accepted that, then any further attempt at a claim upon the son's property would be dismissed. In the former, the parent has agreed to emancipate, in return for money. Slave-owners who accepted money for manumission did not damage their inheritance rights, but they could not also exact *operae*. *Operae* could not be exacted at all from freeborn children as the price of emancipation (*D*. 37. 12. 4), but parents who did it for money forfeited their right to inherit.

In all the above situations, the initiative for emancipation is not from the parent. Fathers, however, were not necessarily reluctant in such circumstances to emancipate, depending upon the age and sex of the child in question and the date at which the occasion arose. If the

---

[202] *D*. 36. 1. 23 pr. For possible legal considerations involved, see Gardner (1987) 52–4.

[203] *D*. 37. 12. 3: Ulpian, *Edict* 45. 'Si parens vel accepit pecuniam, ut emanciparet, vel postea vivus in eum filius quantum satis est contulit, ne iudicia eius inquietet, exceptione doli repelletur.'   [204] 2.6 p. 171 below.

children were still *impuberes*, not yet adult, their father as *tutor legitimus* had powers of administration over the property, and would inherit should they die, like Regulus' son, before reaching adulthood and the capacity to make a will. Adult daughters could effectively be prevented from making a will until the last quarter of the second century AD, and again the manumitting parent would inherit on intestacy. The passing of the *senatusconsultum Orphitianum* in AD 178 changed the situation in respect of both. There was no longer anything to be gained from preventing an emancipated daughter with children of her own from making a will, since her children now inherited on intestacy. On the other hand, if sons and daughters in power had been instituted heirs in their mother's will, it was safe for the father to ignore the condition of emancipation, and break the will, since on intestacy the children would automatically inherit—which meant that the property became his, as their *pater*. Wise or well-advised mothers, of whom perhaps Brasidas' ex-wife (see nn. 200, 202, and Gardner 1987) was one, would therefore frame their wills in such a way, by the use of other heirs, charged with *fideicommissa* or legacies, and/or substitution of heirs, that the father's failure to fulfil the condition did not bring about automatic intestacy.

Deferment of bequests until the child came of age was another tactic used by testators. Ulpian, in an interesting discussion of the interpretation of phrases such as 'cum in sua tutela pervenerit' (when he comes under his own tutelage),[205] remarks that, though a legacy left in those terms to a *filiusfamilias* is held to fall due when he reaches the appropriate age, when a divorced woman 'quae suspectam habuit mariti ... vitam' (who entertained suspicions of her husband's mode of life) left such a legacy it was held to fall due when the child should both have reached adult age *and* become legally independent.

In all the above instances, the intended beneficiaries are the children, and it is assumed that the decision whether or not to emancipate rests with the *pater*. In two cases, points of principle are raised in relation to situations in which a *pater* is asked to emancipate children as a condition of himself becoming a beneficiary under someone's will.

In *D.* 30. 114. 8, a man has been appointed heir and asked to emancipate his children. Marcian's view is that fulfilment of this *fideicommissum* is not to be required. 'Non cogitur hoc facere: potestas enim

---

[205] *D.* 32. 50 pr. For other uses of this and similar phrases, cf. *D.* 28. 5. 55; 28. 8. 11; 30. 1. 32; 32. 51; 37. 11. 8; 42. 4. 5; Gaius 2. 179.

patris inaestimabilis est' (He is not compelled to do this; for a price cannot be set on paternal power).

The issue is presented in more detail by Ulpian,[206] who has evidently had cases of this type to consider in the past. Like Marcian, and also Papinian, whom he cites, he agrees that a man is not to be obliged to emancipate his children. The praetor in charge of trusts will not support their request (unlike demands for fulfilment of *fideicommissa* for the emancipation of slaves). However, bad faith must be checked; Ulpian thinks that someone accepting a bequest on the understanding that he will emancipate his children should be obliged, outside the ordinary course of procedure (*extra ordinem*), to do so. He draws a comparison with a legacy left subject to a condition of emancipation, or for the purpose of emancipation; this is a helpful procedural analogy.

As precedent he cites a rescript of Severus (in which the situation is in fact rather more complicated):

A certain woman instituted her grandsons heirs with her son, their father, as co-heir, and made them substitute heirs to each other. She asked the son (i.e., gave him a *fideicommissum*) to emancipate them, but did *not* ask him to hand over the inheritance to them. Severus compelled him to do both, with the additional proviso of a penalty (payment of interest) if he delayed.

This was a singularly badly framed will, especially in the omission of a trust to hand over the inheritance to the children, and the substitution of father and children to each other, which conflicted with the grandmother's obvious intention that the children and their father

---

[206] *D.* 35. 1. 92 pr. (paraphrased in the text above). 'Si cui legatum fuerit relictum isque rogatus sit liberos suos emancipare, an cogi debeat manumittere? et retineo me dixisse defici eos a petitione fideicommissi; neque enim praetor fideicommissarius eos ad libertatem tuetur ut servos. Papinianum quoque libro nono responsorum scribere referebam non esse cogendum emancipare filios suos. arbitror tamen extra ordinem debere constitui eum qui adgnovit id, quod sibi relictum est hac contemplatione, ut liberos suos emanciparet. cogendum emancipare: neque enim debet circumveniri testantium voluntas: sic deinde accipiendum, quemadmodum si sub condicione liberorum emancipandorum ei fuisset legatum vel ita relictum, ut eos emanciparet. cui rei consequens est, quod divus Severus rescripsit. nam cum quaedam mulier nepotes suos heredes instituisset et ipsum filium coheredem filiis suis dedisset eosque invicem substituisset rogassetque filium, ut filios emanciparet, non autem rogasset, ut hereditatem eis restitueret: ex auctoritate divi Severi emancipare eos compulsus est hisque restituere hereditatem. et adiectum est, ut, si tardius id faceret, quasi ex more usuras praestaturum: videri enim eum, qui moram faceret emancipationi, moram restitutioni eam facere.' On this text, see also Honoré (1982) 246–7. There is an echo of this view at Paul, *Sent.* 4. 13. 1.

should share the estate. As they had been made substitute heirs to each other, if he did not, on the children's behalf, accept their part of the inheritance, he as substitute heir could take the lot.[207] Legally, he was not in the wrong, especially as there had been no *fideicommissum* to hand over the estate, but Severus decided that he was obviously acting in bad faith, and treated the matter as one of a valid *fideicommissum*, on which interest was due if there was delay in fulfilment (cf. Gaius 2. 280).

Severus was doing what Ulpian recommends as generally desirable in similar situations, that is, acting *extra ordinem*. For Ulpian, the difficulty was procedural. If it was generally agreed that it was morally improper to make such *fideicommissa* enforceable, how was acting in bad faith to be prevented? The solution he suggests is that they be treated not as *fideicommissa* but as conditions. A father cannot be forced to emancipate his children; but he cannot accept the inheritance unless he does.

Fideicommissa, first enforced by Augustus only on an *ad hoc* basis, had been regularly enforceable at law only since the institution of a special jurisdiction by the middle of the first century AD, followed by a string of *senatusconsulta* providing against contumacy or evasion on the part of the heir or legatee charged with carrying them out; exceptional provision was made to allow slaves to sue for liberty.[208] Before that, fulfilment of *fideicommissa* depended entirely upon the good faith of the heir or legatee in fulfilling the testator's intentions, and there could be no question of attempting to force a *paterfamilias* to emancipate children in his power. It is clear from the discussions reported above that there was agreement as to the moral impropriety of making such *fideicommissa* enforceable as a general rule. Slaves, who might either have come with the inheritance or already belong to the beneficiary, were under his *potestas* merely as part of his property; it was quite another thing, however, to interfere with the autonomous authority of the *paterfamilias* over family members. Such inroads on *patria potestas* were acceptable only when it was blatantly being abused.

This attitude is illustrated by the one instance cited in the *Digest* of forced emancipation. Trajan exceptionally compelled a father who

---

[207] A tactic comparable with that mentioned above of the freedman's son, made co-heir with an *extraneus*, who deliberately does not take his half of the estate (*D.* 38. 2. 20. 6).

[208] Gaius 2. 246–89: Johnston (1988); trusts on manumission: Impallomeni (1963) ch. 3.

was ill-treating his son to emancipate him. The father was later refused a claim to *bonorum possessio*, when he had the gall to try to take over his son's property after his death. The emperor, advised by Neratius Priscus and Aristo, was of the opinion that he must pay for neglecting the *pietas*, proper paternal feeling, expected towards a child.[209]

These cases, however, were exceptional, *extra ordinem*. The generally accepted view appears to have been that a *pater* could not be compelled by anyone, either a child in power or anyone else, to emancipate.[210]

Unfortunately, the historical record is singularly lacking in mention of individual emancipations, with or without mention of a paternal motive. A rare example in the Republic (the collusive emancipation of Clodius by his adoptive father—Cic. *Dom.* 37—can hardly be said to count) is that of C. Licinius Stolo, found in slightly, but significantly, different versions in Livy and Valerius Maximus. Licinius had had a law passed limiting individual ownership of public (i.e. conquered) land to 500 *iugera*.[211] According to Livy, Licinius was fined for violation of his own law, 'quod mille iugera agri cum filio possideret emancipandoque filium fraudem legi fecisset' (because he was occupying 1,000 *iugera* together with his son, and had defrauded the law by emancipating his son). Valerius Maximus says, on the other hand, 'ipse mille [iugera] comparavit dissimulandique crimina gratia dimidiam partem filio emancipavit' (he himself obtained 1,000 *iugera*, and to conceal his offence he emancipated his son).

In Valerius' version, Licinius had clearly broken the law, since the emancipation was subsequent to the acquisition of the land. However, he may merely be trying to tidy up an apparent anomaly in Livy, who seems to suggest that the emancipation came first, and Licinius and his son then were able to own 1,000 between them. If that were so, then there would have been no crime, but he was fined nevertheless for fraudulent intent. The authenticity of the story is doubtful; however, it is interesting that tradition accepts emancipation

---

[209] *D.* 37. 12. 5. Rabello (1979) 237-9. Compare Marcianus' comment (*D.* 48. 9. 5) on Hadrian's sentence of deportation on a father who had, it was felt, exceeded his paternal right in killing his son, who had committed adultery with his stepmother: 'nam patria potestas in pietate debet, non atrocitate, consistere' (For paternal power ought to be manifested in affection, not cruelty). On *pietas* in the Roman family, see especially Saller (1994) ch. 5.

[210] Gaius 1. 137a; *D.* 1. 7. 31 (Marcianus again); *Cod. Iust.* 8. 48. 4 (2691 Honoré); still asserted by Justinian, *Inst.* 1. 12. 10. An exception was made in the case of someone previously adrogated as an *impubes*: Gaius 1. 102; *Inst.* 1. 11. 3.

[211] Livy 7. 16. 9; Val. Max. 8. 6. 3. Licinius' land law: Cornell (1995) 328-9.

as apparently already an established practice in the first half of the fourth century BC.

The real historical interest of the story rests in the clue that it gives to reasons for an early spread of emancipation among the Romans. As the resources available, publicly or privately, to the Romans increased in the wake of Italian conquest and, later, imperial expansion, it was both practically possible, and desirable, to make separate provision for one or more sons, emancipating them, so reducing the numbers directly to be provided for from the patrimony.

In other words, emancipation was intended to enhance the economic well-being of the family as a whole, not to blight the prospects of those emancipated. They were not 'cast out'; on the contrary, the development of family law in such areas as succession rights and maintenance, examined above, indicates that in general the feeling, to which law was responding, was that the interests of the emancipated child had to be protected and some kind of 'safety net' provided, in case he or she did not prosper.[212]

At what level of society was emancipation most likely to be practised? Among the less prosperous, emancipation could be used to ease the financial strains upon the resources of the *familia*. Among freedmen, as we saw, it could be a way of avoiding at least some of the patronal depredations on the inheritance.

Among the better off, it could be a way of favouring one line of descent, by emancipating, with some provision, a son, but retaining his children in power. (More effective favouritism could be shown by the use of wills, but this was a fall-back in case the grandfather's will should fail). Sometimes the initiative came from outside, from testators wishing particular individuals to benefit. Among the élite, however, emancipation may have been less popular in general as a strategy. Both in the Republic and the early Empire, there were more social and economic, and in the Republic, it has been suggested,

---

[212] There is little to be said for the idea put forward by Aubert (1994) 91–5, that the number of emancipations increased in consequence of (i) the social and economic rise of Roman freedmen, (ii) the Vespasianic *senatusconsultum Macedonianum* which, according to him, barred sons-in-power from taking out loans, and (iii) the consideration that it 'must' have been desirable for all parties involved, i.e. principals and third contracting parties, to enlarge the pool of potential agents while retaining the same conditions of credit. Contrary to what Aubert seems to believe, freedmen and emancipated sons were less convenient as agents than slaves and sons-in-power. For the actual legal position, see Kirschenbaum (1987), esp. chs. 2–3, and Gardner (1993) 57–9.

perhaps also more political, benefits to be obtained from giving children in adoption to others.

However, among Romans of any means, by the early second century at latest, there are signs that emancipation had also come commonly to be used as a necessary preliminary to readoption of someone already a member of the *familia*, simply as part of strategic manœuvres within a *familia*, to forestall possible upsets to the testamentary provisions of a *paterfamilias* by adjusting in advance the relative entitlements on intestacy of different branches of the family. In other words, it was a way of enabling grandfather to play favourites. This will be discussed in more detail in 2.9.

2

Into the *Familia*: The Practice
of Adoption

2.1 INTRODUCTION

Modern legal systems vary widely in the regulations they lay down as to who may adopt or be adopted. Some bear a closer resemblance to those of ancient Rome than do others, among those most at variance being the law of England and Wales, which reflects a different conception of the nature and purpose of adoption from that of the Romans.[1]

In English law, only children, i.e. persons under 18 years of age,[1] which is the legal age of majority, may be adopted, and a court or adoption agency has the duty to give prime consideration to the welfare of the child, but also to consider the child's wishes. There is a minimum age for the adopter, lower for a relative (21 years) than for an unrelated person (25), and waived if the intending adopter is the child's natural parent; although no maximum age is set, agencies in practice frequently refuse applications from intending adopters over the age of about 35. Only sole unmarried persons (of either sex) may adopt, or natural parents acting together, or married couples with the agreement of both spouses. Once completed, the adoption cannot normally be revoked. Adoption is usually associated with the desire to nurture and protect the child as if one's own, and orphans or illegitimate children are the most frequent candidates for adoption.[2]

---

[1] In a case originally reported in the British press in the winter of 1995 (*Sunday Times*, 31 December), a British millionaire was refused permission to adopt the son of the Nepalese policeman who once saved his life and whom, at the latter's request, he had brought to Britain at the age of 14 when his father died. Permission was refused on the grounds that the boy had now passed the age of 18.

[2] The priorities, as stated by the representative of the social services department of an English county authority on BBC Radio 4, 21 April 1996, are: 'Our first concern is to find homes for children in need, not to help those unable to have children of their own to find children. The welfare of the child is paramount.' (The context was discussion of a suggestion that smokers should not be allowed to adopt.)

This has little in common with adoption among the Romans. There, concern for the welfare of the person being adopted is mentioned mainly with regard to adrogation (adoption of someone who is already *sui iuris*), and then concern is shown for the property as well as—or even more than—for the physical and moral welfare of the person being adrogated. Those given in adoption are mostly adults; special attention is paid, at least in later law, to those adrogated while still under age. Persons, of whatever age, in the *potestas* of a living father are commonly given in adoption, and no enquiry is made, since Roman law respects the autonomy of the *paterfamilias* in the disposal of his *familia*. It is not certain even—and on balance seems unlikely—that an adult *in potestate* had to consent to being given in adoption (see 2.7 below). Women cannot adopt at all, and while adopters have to be male, they do not have to be married (*D.* 1. 7. 30); a married man adopts alone, without reference to his wife, who has no legal authority in the matter and acquires no adoptive relationship to the person being adopted.

Very few adoptions are directly attested. Roman legal writings are one of our best sources of evidence for the actual practice of adoption among the Romans; inscriptions are insufficiently specific for certainty in detecting adoptions, and the adoptions mentioned in literary sources are numbered in tens rather than hundreds. There is even less direct evidence about the reasons for adoptions. Of the adoptions that are mentioned in literary sources, those in successive imperial families are not entirely typical of Roman society at large, since they generally have a specifically dynastic and political purpose. As in private families, however, a definite preference is shown for adopting persons related by blood, or at least by marriage, where any are available. This is the case between Trajan and Hadrian, among the Antonines and the Severi, and is most evident among the Julio-Claudians. The transmission of a claim to political power is to some extent held to be additionally validated by strengthening a 'family' relationship into one of *familia*.[3] Others, however, including those attested among the senatorial aristocracy of the Republic discussed in 2.4 below,[4] cannot simply be assumed to be 'political' in intent; the wish to provide oneself with a secure and unchallengeable heir to property is an important motive, and appropriate in many of the

---

[3] Prévost (1949), ch. 2; Russo Ruggeri (1990) 143–202; Fayer (1994) 336–51.
[4] Prévost (1949) 17–34; Russo Ruggeri (1990a) 12–36.

attested cases. More instances of adoption are attested or can be inferred for the Republic than for the Empire. This is partly the consequence of the nature of our literary sources, which reflect the altered nature of Roman politics, and the relatively lesser importance of individual senators under the Empire. Nomenclature also becomes a less reliable guide to adoption in the later period (see 2.4 below), as it begins to be used as a means of drawing attention to maternal pedigree. Like the changes in inheritance law (discussed in 1.5–6 above and 3.3 below), it indicates the attachment of increasing importance to maternal family ties. The transmission of property remained important, that of *nomen* became less so; adoption may not therefore have been in all cases the preferred alternative. That is the most that can be said. Too few actual (or possible) adoptions are attested for any period to allow any kind of statistical guess.

Certainly adoption continues, and the laws controlling it undergo change and alteration, as will be seen in detail below. There is a great deal of legal discussion, reflecting not the incidence of adoption but the legal complexity of its consequences. In themselves, legal texts are concerned only with working out the legal consequences of specific adoptions or adoption-related actions; they do not generally comment on the purposes or motives of the persons acting. The consequences of membership of a *familia* (including change of *familia* by adoption) with which the law concerns itself are almost entirely material, to do with property and succession rights. Essentially, Roman adoption is about property entitlement.

There could be many personal reasons, however, for favouring recourse to adoption, varying in individual cases not only from the point of view of the three persons involved—the person giving in adoption, the person being adopted and the adopter—but also according to the particular circumstances of each. Some of these will be explored in more detail below, as will some of the disadvantages. For instance, a number of attested adoptions, particularly those known among members of the republican senatorial aristocracy, are by close relatives, especially on the maternal side. This suggests that concern for keeping property, if not within the agnatic line of descent, at least within the family, played a major part in the choice of an heir. Lower down the social scale, it is possible that the desire to integrate a family legally as a *familia* was a motive prompting some ex-slaves to resort to adoption, or rather adrogation, of blood relatives (in particular, of illegitimate children, freeborn or otherwise); but such desire could be countermanded by consideration of the damaging effect that adoption into the ex-slave's *familia* could have on the material prospects of the children, because of the claims of patrons. Another type of 'family' concern we shall observe in operation (2.9) is in the curious phenomenon of adoptions inside the *familia* itself, with the effect of restructuring the inheritance prospects of its members (father playing favourites again).

What does not seem to have caused anyone concern—except, technically, under the Republic, the pontiffs, where adrogation was proposed, since that involved extinction of the cults of a *familia*—was that adoption involved interference with the composition of *familiae*. One *familia* had a part broken away, or was extinguished entirely, and another had a 'foreign body' inserted. The *familia* was not treated as an end in itself, but a means to various ends, both on the part of the adopter and of the person giving (or giving himself) in adoption.

2.2 THE LEGAL EFFECTS OF ADOPTION

Adoption was a device for taking a person out of one *familia* and placing him or her into another, under the *potestas* of its *paterfamilias*. If the person being adopted was already a *paterfamilias*, his existing children came into *potestas* along with him. The legal relationship between a *pater* and his adoptive sons was the same as that between him and children born to him in lawful marriage. This meant, incidentally, that the adopting *pater*, since he had acquired another *suus heres*, had to make a new will; until at least the time of Gaius this applied even if he adopted someone whom he had already instituted heir.[5]

All agnatic connections with the *familia* of origin were extinguished (though cognatic ones survived), and the person adopted acquired the same agnatic inheritance rights as a natural child in the new *familia*, and ceased, so long as he or she remained in the adopter's *potestas*, to have them in the old one.[6] The adoptive child did not acquire any additional cognatic inheritance rights to his adoptive father's wife and her kin, since he acquired cognate relationships only

---

[5] Gaius 1. 107, 2. 136, 138–40; *D*. 28. 3. 8 and 18; *Inst*. 1. 11. 8, 2. 13. 4.

[6] With the exception (see Ch. 1 n. 55) that, by the time of Labeo at least, they could claim *bonorum possessio* against a natural father's will, so long as they had been instituted heirs in that will, and a procedure had been initiated by remaining *sui heredes* or *liberi*: *D*. 37. 4. 8. 11.

to those to whom he also became an agnate. However, as he still had a blood relationship with all members of his original family, he could still inherit—though only as a cognate—from kinsfolk on both his natural mother's and father's sides.[7] For an economically hard-pressed *paterfamilias*, therefore, it could be more advantageous to give a child in adoption, should the opportunity arise, than to emancipate. Both involved truncation of one's *familia*, and sacrifice of legal control over one of its members, but whereas emancipation reduced immediate pressure on the resources of the family, without necessarily adding to them in the long run, adoption potentially increased them, by opening access to those of another *familia*.

There were also, however, economic risks. The son given in adoption was economically dependent on the new *paterfamilias*, but could not, any more than could a natural-born *filiusfamilias*, force the *paterfamilias* to emancipate him. Moreover, the consequences could be serious should his new *pater* choose spontaneously to emancipate him—an event which he was equally unable to prevent. This emancipation cancelled all the rights he had acquired by the adoption. If his natural father was still alive when he was emancipated by his adoptive father, then his status was as if he had been emancipated by the natural father, with concomitant rights of succession on intestacy in his original *familia*; but if his natural father were already dead, then he had the worst of both worlds, since he had no inheritance rights from his former adoptive father and had lost the chance to inherit from his natural father. Worse still, the same applied even to grandchildren who were born while their father was in what was to him an adoptive *familia*, and then were emancipated by their *paterfamilias*.[8] Clearly, there must be a certain trust between a father giving his son in adoption and the person adopting; it was not a step to be taken lightly.

Someone already legally independent took an even greater gamble by giving himself for adoption (or rather, in his case, adrogation), since it meant allowing the entire property which he already possessed to be absorbed in that of his adoptive father, without any certainty that he or his children would profit in the long run. Moreover, any children he already had in his *potestas* went into *potestas* with him (whereas existing children of a *filiusfamilias* remained in the power of

[7] *D.* 2. 4. 7; 38. 10. 1. 4.
[8] Gaius 2. 136–7; *D.* 1. 7. 13 and 14, 31, 37. 4. 6. 4; 38. 6. 1. 6, 4; *Cod. Iust.* 8. 47 (48). 10. pr. (AD 530).

their natural grandfather and had inheritance rights from him); in other words, the *familia* which he headed was extinguished. For that reason, among others, adrogations were subject to particularly careful preliminary scrutiny by the appropriate public authorities, namely (since extinction of family cult, *sacra*, was involved) the pontiffs.[9]

Since the adoptive child and the natural child have legally the same status within the *familia*, the consequences of adoption, for both parent and child, extended far beyond the acquisition of inheritance rights. For marriage, the same prohibited degrees applied for adoptive as for natural relationships, although for most of them only while the adoption lasted. Even after an adoption was dissolved, former adoptive ascendants and descendants were still excluded as possible spouses, as were their former marriage partners.[10]

Natural brothers and sisters, whether with one or both parents in common, could not marry. A couple related as brother and sister by adoption could not marry either, but the emancipation of either made marriage possible, and this manoeuvre appears occasionally to have been employed by fathers of daughters, seeking a male heir to the name (i.e. the daughter was emancipated and the son-in-law adopted). There is a possible example in a couple epigraphically attested in Pompeii:

M. Alleio Luccio Libellae patri, aedili IIvir. praefecto quinq. et M. Alleio Libellae f., decurioni, vixit annis XVII, locus monumenti publice datus est. Alleia M.f. Decimilla, sacerdos publica Cereris, faciundum curavit viro et filio.

(To M. Alleius Luccius Libella senior, aedile, IIvir., prefect, quinquennial magistrate, and M.Alleius Libella his son, who lived 17 years, decurion, a site for a monument has been publicly given. Alleia Decimilla, daughter of Marcus, public priestess of Ceres, saw to its construction for her husband and her son.)

Alleius' additional *nomen*, Luccius, could possibly derive from his

---

[9] At least in theory this was so; not surprisingly, Cicero, *De domo* 34–6 protests at permission having been given by the *pontifices* for the politically-motivated adrogation of Clodius by Fonteius, despite the fact that it failed to conform to customarily accepted criteria.

[10] Gaius 1. 59–63; D. 23. 2. 14. 4, 17. 2. Volterra (1966) 140–3; Russo Ruggeri (1990) 398–416. Volterra's explanation, that the continued ban on marriage between those formerly related by adoption as ascendant and descendant rested on the legal identification of the adoptive child with a biological descendant, is preferable to Ruggeri's suggestion that it arose from moral and religious scruples.

maternal family, but, given the coincidence of name with that of his wife, the probability is that he was adopted by her father (she having been emancipated). The family is evidently one of some social eminence and, probably, wealth—hence the early co-option of the son to the decurionate. Alleius Luccius himself was evidently freeborn, otherwise he would not have been eligible to be a magistrate, but his previous history and descent cannot now be traced with any certainty.[11]

The consequences of Augustan legislation on marriage and adultery applied to adoptive as well as to natural children (although, as already discussed in 1.7 above, adoptive children did not earn benefits for the adopters). Except for freedmen (who, at least in classical law, despite the legal fiction of agnatic descent from the adopter, still did not count as freeborn after adoption), adoption could enhance status, but it did not diminish it. This applied not only to members of the senatorial and equestrian orders, but also to the city élites under the Empire, the *decuriones*, although after the political and economic upheavals of the third century the last-mentioned order had lost much of its former prestige, and indeed might be disrespectfully treated by provincial governors. In AD 285, a provincial decurion (of unknown provenance) complained to Diocletian that his adoptive son had been subjected by the provincial governor to corporal punishment, normally reserved for the lower classes, the *humiliores*. In his reply, the emperor, referring to this treatment as 'atrocibus iniuriis' (atrocious outrages) and 'illicitis corporibus cruciatibus' (unlawful bodily torments) assures him that the offending governor will be suitably punished.[12]

Not surprisingly, when discussing these status differentials, legal interpretation concerns itself particularly with the composition of the senatorial order. Someone adopted by a senator ranked as a senator's son; a senator's natural son given in adoption to someone of lower rank was still *senatorius*. Senators and their descendants could not lawfully marry either the adoptive children, or the natural children, of freedmen or actors.[13]

---

[11] Gaius 1. 61; *D.* 23. 2. 17. pr.–1; *CIL* 10. 1036=*ILS* 6365; Minieri (1982) 278–84; Castrén (1975) 67, 71, 104, 133. For criticisim of Castrén's analysis of the Pompeian governing class, see Mouritsen (1988) 115–22.

[12] *Cod. Iust.* 10. 32. 4 (1456 Honoré). The incident is reminiscent of the maltreatment by Roman magistrates of Italian quaestors of Teanum Sidicinum and Ferentinum, related by Tiberius Gracchus in 123 BC (Gellius 10. 3), or (a closer parallel) Verres' public flogging of a Roman citizen in Messana in 70 BC (Cic. *Verr.* 2. 5. 161–3).

[13] Senatorial rank: *D.* 1. 9. 5, 6 and 10; marriage restrictions: *D.* 23. 2. 44. There

2.2 The Legal Effects of Adoption

These interpretations,[14] all of which, save *D. 1. 9. 10* (Ulpian *xxxiv ad edictum*) are from commentaries on the *lex Julia et Papia*, sit well with the hierarchical assumptions of Augustan legislation. So long as base connections were avoided, it was apparently felt that weight was to be accorded to the judgement of the senatorial *paterfamilias* on the choice of suitable persons for the purpose of enlarging his social class for posterity, either by taking or giving sons in adoption (naturally status is not transmitted through women: *D. 1. 9. 8, 12*).

A *paterfamilias*—including one by adoption—had, in certain circumstances, the 'power of life and death' over those in his *potestas*. Jurists' explanations of the power given by the Augustan adultery law to a *paterfamilias* to kill his daughter (and her lover)—that is, if they were actually taken in the act of adultery—may seem strange to modern ideas, but conform to Roman conceptions of the social role of the *familia*. Papinian remarks that the *lex Julia de adulteriis* did not distinguish between a natural and an adoptive father—each had the right to kill a *filiafamilias*, i.e. a daughter or granddaughter, caught in adultery, so long as she was in his *potestas*.[15]

That she may be an adoptive, not a natural, daughter is not a

---

seems to have been some legal debate, however, about the extent to which the natural father's status counted, even after the adoption. Pomponius opined that it should not, if he had already died. Paul agrees. Octavenus presumably would not have agreed, since he had held that the parent's condition counted also for illegitimate children.

[14] Which appears to be what they are, rather than direct citations of the law; indeed, Paul's verbatim quotation (*D. 23. 2. 44*) from the clause concerning unlawful marriages contains no mention of adoptive children.

[15] Opinions differed on the father's right to priority in bringing an accusation of adultery. It did not depend entirely on *potestas*, according to Papinian (*Coll. 4. 7. 1*), since he could exercise it even against an emancipated daughter (in this, he differed from Scaevola: *D. 48. 5. 15 (14). 2*). However, although Papinian would extend the *ius occidendi*, the right to kill, to a father whose daughter had with his consent left his *potestas* by entering into a *coemptio in manum* (Gaius 1. 114), by this time merely fiduciary (Rabello 218 attributes the mention to compilers), it would be going too far to see this, with Russo Ruggeri (1990a) 436–8, as a manifestation of continuing recognition of the moral power-cum-duty of blood relatives to curb their women's immorality, illustrated in historical and quasi-historical anecdote from the early Republic onwards; still less is it evidence of any recognized authority over offspring no longer in power. With regard to the latter, the story cited by Russo Ruggeri, of Manlius Torquatus and his son Silanus (Cic. *De fin. 1. 7. 24*; Val. Max. 5. 8. 3), is irrelevant; Manlius' 'punishment' of his son, already given in adoption, extended only to a symbolic disowning of him, and he had to ask the Senate for permission to preside over the enquiry. Papinian, it should be noted, speaks only of the right to prosecute, *iure patris*, regarding children no longer in *anyone's* power; he does not claim it for those who had given their children into the *potestas* of another.

problem for Papinian, since he stresses the legal authority of the *paterfamilias*, as well as his wider social responsibility for the moral welfare of his house, rather than any personal feelings. If the father is himself a *filiusfamilias* he does not have the right to kill his daughter—a restriction based on his lack of legal authority over his daughter. Paul remarks that this prohibition, though not quite directly stated in the law, is implicit, and disagrees with it, holding that he ought to be permitted to kill her. This perhaps indicates that Paul is prepared to give some weight to emotional factors. Ulpian, on the other hand, approves the reservation of the right to kill to a father with *potestas*, but offers only the curiously vacuous justification that someone who is not legally independent (*suae potestatis*) cannot have *potestas* over others. Like Papinian, he stresses the legal authority of the *paterfamilias*, but like Paul he omits discussion of some of the further implications of the law. According to Papinian, the *lex Julia* specified that only a father with *potestas* over the adulterous woman had the right to kill her: 'itaque nemo alius ex patribus idem iure faciet' (no other father will have the right to do this). This would exclude not only a father who was himself *in potestate*, but a *paterfamilias* who was the natural father, but had emancipated his daughter or given her in adoption.[16] In other words, the right was inherent in the legal, not the biological, relationship.

Again, a contrast is drawn between the right accorded a *pater* and that of a husband. The husband's feelings are regarded as purely private; the father's authority lays upon him a public duty. A husband may kill an adulterer taken with his wife, though only if he belongs to certain categories of 'base persons' (pimp, actor, someone condemned of a criminal offence) or is a freedman of his or her family—but he may not kill his wife, because, says Papinian, his naturally inflamed feelings should be restrained, whereas 'pietas paterni nominis consilium pro liberis capit' (the sense of duty inherent in the title of father takes counsel for his descendants (plural)). It is ambiguous whether Papinian thinks this *pietas* would be better exercised in clemency than in setting examples.[17]

---

[16] *D.* 48. 5. 21 (20) (Papinian); 22 (21) (Ulpian); 23 (22). pr. (Papinian); Paul, *Sent.* 2. 26. 2=*Coll.* 4. 12. 2: 'verbis quidem legis prope est, ut non possit occidere; permitti tamen etiam ei debet, ut occidat.'

[17] *D.* 48. 5. 23 (22). 4; 25 (24) pr. 39 (38) 8. For the husband's presumed distress, see also *D.* 48. 5. 38 (37).

2.2 The Legal Effects of Adoption

All three jurists accept the primacy of *familia* over personal affections. Adultery is a public, not a private, matter. It affects the stability of society at large and private feelings must not be allowed to interfere with its repression and punishment.

The husband's social duty is to preserve the integrity of his own *familia*, and to that end his priority should be to separate himself and it without delay from the outsider, his errant wife, by divorcing her; he is liable to prosecution himself for 'pandering' (*lenocinium*) if he does not. He also has first priority in putting society's disapproval into practice in a socially approved manner by prosecuting her. To do this is his duty, rather than to indulge in the venting of his own personal feelings. The *paterfamilias'* first responsibility also is the soundness of his own *familia*, and his duty, in the interests of society at large, is to exercise discipline within it over all those who are legally its members, whether by birth or by adoption, and subject to his authority.

That, at any rate, was the legal view. In practice, in the nature of things it might be relatively rare, if a couple were reasonably careful, actually to be taken in the act. Also, enforcement of this part of the law was perhaps not easy, given the relative difficulty, for outsiders, of finding evidence, and although fear of a prosecution for *lenocinium* may have deterred some husbands and fathers from turning a blind eye, it would not be surprising if many preferred not to safeguard society at large, at the expense of their wives and daughters—whatever exponents of the law might have to say about social duty.

The disciplinary authority of the *paterfamilias* is grounded solely in a legal relationship; on the other hand, the expectation of proper respect and affection (*pietas*) between parent and child not only survived the dissolution of a legal relationship based on blood, but also arose from the artificial creation of a relationship by adoption, lasting, however, in the latter case only as long as the adoptive relationship did. A son in power was expected to display *pietas* both toward his natural father and his adoptive father; as just observed, Papinian takes this for granted. *Pietas*, as a legal obligation, was recognized by jurists in regard to certain types of behaviour between *patres* and former members of the *familia*, such as their freedmen and emancipated children, as also between these last and their mothers. As an expression of the affection and respect regarded as appropriate and morally desirable between family members, both inside and outside of the *familia* (including children in power, wives, mothers and other close relatives), it was also invoked to provide a reason on grounds of equity for modifying strict legal rules (as with the 'complaint of unduteous will').[18]

However, because of the artificial origin of their relationship, the restraints affecting adoptive children were not co-extensive with those for natural children. Because of the obligation to *pietas*, a natural son—whether emancipated, in an adoptive family, or *sui iuris* in the ordinary course of nature—was not permitted under the praetor's edict to bring a lawsuit against parents (*parentes*), defined by Ulpian (*D. 2. 4. 8 pr.*) as referring to ascendants through both the male and female line; but an adoptive son could summon the *parentes* of his adoptive father because they were not his relatives, 'cum his tantum cognatus fiat quibus et adgnatus' (because he becomes a cognate only to those to whom he is also an agnate). Presumably this meant, for instance, that, unlike the natural son, he could sue the father of his adoptive father (assuming the latter had been emancipated), and also the mother and the wife. If after being adopted he was emancipated, he could also sue the adoptive father himself, since emancipation cancelled the agnatic as well as the cognatic relationship.[19]

It was also assumed that he would show *pietas* towards his natural father when making a will; the latter could bring a complaint of unduteous will. There was less agreement that the duty was reciprocal. In the 50s BC, according to Valerius Maximus, a son given in adoption (M. Anneius, already mentioned) was apparently successful in bringing the *querela* when his natural father had omitted him from his will. However, according to a Justinianic rescript to the praetorian prefect, there was no agreement among jurists under the Empire as to whether sons given in adoption could claim in this way. Papinian said that a son given in adoption could not bring the *querela*, Paul *sine effectu derelinquit* (an obscure expression—perhaps 'set it aside as futile'?), but Marcian was prepared to allow the action if the son was likely to lose out on both inheritances, having been let down by his natural father, and if his adoptive father happened to be hard up.[20]

---

[18] Examples in Saller (1994) 110–12; see also Gardner (1993) s.v. *pietas* in the index, and 1.10 above.   [19] *D. 1. 7. 13; 2. 4. 4; 6; 7 pr.; 8 pr.*

[20] Val. Max. 7. 7. 2; *D. 5. 2. 30; Cod. Iust. 8. 47 (48).* 10 pr. (AD 530). Russo Ruggeri (1990a) 452–5. Paul's reasoning may be that the cognatic tie, being now merely natural and not civil (*D. 38. 10. 4. 2*), was insufficient basis for a plea, which was unlikely to succeed; cf. *Inst. 2. 18. 1*: 'Ultra fratres et sorores cognati nullo modo aut agere possunt aut agentes vincere' (Relatives more distant than brothers or sisters cannot sue, or if they do they cannot win). Constantine excluded uterine brothers and

What was the cause of this apparent change of attitude between the late Republic and the third century AD? When Anneius won, it was because, Russo Ruggeri suggests, it was repugnant to the Romans' moral and social sense that an outsider should be preferred to a natural son (though Anneius, as much as the other cognates, was *extraneus* in the eyes of the law). Valerius Maximus, it will be remembered, stressed the 'tie of procreation' between father and son. No such rationale is offered by the imperial jurists. The reactions of Papinian and Paul appear to be a stronger and weaker version of the same point of view; Paul's, in particular, is reminiscent of Ulpian's remark on the pointlessness of appeals by cognates beyond the degree of brother.[21]

A son given in adoption is a cognate, but only by 'natural law', not by civil law—that is, he is essentially in the same relationship to his natural father as to his mother. It is evident from Valerius' story that there were no other close blood relatives of the deceased, and this will perhaps have helped Anneius. Other things being equal, where there were several cognates (all technically 'extraneous' from a legal point of view) wishing to claim the inheritance, the praetor's decision may have turned upon the relative closeness of their blood relationship to the deceased.

Moreover, at the time of Anneius' appeal the clause *unde liberi* may not yet have been added to the praetor's edict, and there was therefore as yet no difference in priority between a son given in adoption and still in the adoptive *familia*, and one already emancipated by his adoptive father (and therefore cut off from his hopes of inheritance from him); both had a claim *unde cognati* on the estate of their natural father, but only if there was no will. By the time of the Empire, however, the emancipated son was among those acknowledged as having first priority to inheritance from his natural father, and had to be specifically instituted heir or disinherited, while the son given in adoption but not afterwards emancipated still ranked merely as a cognate. The imperial jurists are discussing the situation of someone still in the adoptive family; their hard line may be accounted for by the consideration that he had either already received, or still had first claim upon, another inheritance, that of his adoptive father.

Marcianus, however, sees a difficulty, if the adoptive father should

---

sisters, and allowed the others to apply only if the instituted heirs were persons of ill repute or undeserving freedmen (*Cod. Iust.* 3. 28. 27: AD 319).

[21] *D.* 5. 2. 1; cf. *Cod. Iust.* 3. 28. 21 (2173 Honoré: AD 294). See above 1.5.2 at n. 60.

become poverty-stricken. Then the natural father's (presumed) intention to provide for his son by giving him in adoption had *not* been effectual, and a case could be made for allowing the *querela.* The adoptive father's future financial failure was one of the possible risks of giving one's son in adoption; Justinian draws attention to another, the helplessness of the son should the adoptive father emancipate him after his natural father has died. It was against such hazards, Justinian says, that he had decided to change the whole system.[22]

2.3 THE PROCEDURES OF ADOPTION

Adoption could be effected by two procedures,[23] and was possible only between Roman citizens, not between citizens and *peregrini* (aliens).[24] The procedures are distinguished by Gaius 1. 98ff. as that 'by the authority of the people' (*populi auctoritate* or *per populum*), and that by order of a magistrate; we may distinguish these as respectively 'public' (since it required a legislative act) and 'private'. Private adoption was used when the person being adopted was still *in potestate*; he (or she, though there is much less evidence for adoption of females) was given in adoption by the *paterfamilias.* The procedure, conducted before a magistrate, was essentially the same as that for emancipation (1.2 above), except that the final remancipation was omitted, and the adoptee remained in the *potestas* of the adopter.

Public adoption, also known as *adrogatio*, was necessary when the person being adopted was already legally independent, *sui iuris*, i.e. head of a *familia.*[25] Originally it proceeded in two stages. First there

---

[22] *Cod. Iust.* 8. 47 (48). 10 (AD 530); *Inst.* 1. 11. 2; Kurylowicz (1979) 163–82, (1984) 3305–35, and, for preceding developments in post-classical law, (1993) 187–201.

[23] Cic. *De domo* 34–8; Gell. *NA* 5. 19. 1–14; Gaius 1. 99–107; *D.* 1. 7.

[24] So, correctly, Volterra (1966) 134, who remarks that this limitation is a consequence of their structure (because, as he does not specify, one involves *mancipatio*, the other a *lex curiata*). Russo Ruggeri (1990a) 209–11 asserts the contrary, assuming that the procedure of *mancipatio* was available to Latins. This she deduces by misinterpretations of Livy 25. 3. 16 and 41. 8. 6–12, both of which are about manumission from *mancipium*, a form of short-term bondage. Neither implies the legal capacity of Latins to engage in *mancipatio* at the relevant dates; Ulpian's statement in the early 3rd cent. AD (*Reg.* 19. 4; cf. 20. 8) that Latins could mancipate represents a change from Gaius' earlier statement (1. 119) that the procedure of *mancipatio* was exclusive to Roman citizens. In any case Ulpian is quite clear that no *peregrinus* could have a Roman citizen *in potestate* and vice versa (*Reg.* 10. 3).

[25] For the possibility that in early Rome it was used for those *in potestate*, see Watson (1975) 41–2; *contra*, Kaser (1971) 66 n. 11.

had to be an enquiry by the college of pontiffs to determine the admissibility of the proposed adoption; this was required because *adrogatio* terminated the *familia* of the person being adopted, and with it the *sacra*. This was followed by a meeting, presided over by the *pontifex maximus*, of the curiate assembly (later represented by a token assembly of lictors), which passed an enabling law, a *lex curiata*. The proposal put to the people for enactment as a law (*populi rogatio*) makes it clear that the person so adopted is legally to be fully equated to a *filiusfamilias* born from lawful marriage. The formula of the *rogatio*, framed in archaizing language, is given by Gellius, *NA* 5. 19. 9 as:

May it be your will and command that L. Valerius may be to L. Titius in right and in law his son, just as if he were born from him as *pater* and from his *materfamilias*, and that he (Titius) may have in relation to him (Valerius) the power of life and death, as there is to a father in the case of a son.[26]

This meeting of the curiate assembly was eventually replaced by an imperial rescript (while the pontiffs' role became essentially consultative, to the emperor as Pontifex Maximus).[27] Details of this development, and the implications for the availability of adoption by this method, will be discussed further below.

Private adoption was possible as early as emancipation, i.e. as discussed in 1.2 above, when interpretation of a rule in the Twelve Tables provided an appropriate procedure. Theoretically at least, *adrogatio* could already have been available in the time of the kings of Rome, since the institution of the curiate assembly is traditionally attributed to Servius Tullius. The pontiffs, of course, were given origins of the remotest possible antiquity, being traditionally the creation of Romulus (Dion. Hal. 2. 21, citing Terentius Varro). There is no evidence, however, for any *adrogationes* in early Rome, and few are directly attested later. The procedure is unlikely ever to have been as widely used as adoption of *filiifamilias*, because of its drawbacks. It extinguished a *familia*, and involved surrender of legal independence and absorption of one's property into that of the adopting *pater*; and, since it could not be used for adrogating females, this meant that for a long time women already *sui iuris* could not be adopted. It was also difficult to arrange, since the necessity of a formal vote in the *comitia curiata* meant that the procedure could be completed only in Rome.

---

[26] 'Velitis, iubeatis, uti L.Valerius L.Titio tam iure legeque filius siet, quam si ex eo patre matreque familias eius natus esset, utique ei vitae necisque in eum potestas siet, uti patri endo [=in] filio est.'　　　　　　　[27] Millar (1977) 359–61.

Replacement of the comitial procedure by imperial rescript removed the geographical restriction, but still involved arranging a direct approach to the emperor himself.

Because of the implications for *familia* and property, the circumstances of a request for *adrogatio* required careful examination; 'adrogationes non temere nec inexplorate committuntur', says Gellius (5. 19. 5): (adrogations are not carried out lightly nor without investigation). Enquiry was made into the age of the would-be adopter, his potential for begetting children of his own, and the possibility that the whole thing was merely an underhand device to get hold of the property of the adoptee. Gellius adds that Q. Mucius the pontifex maximus had instituted the administration of an oath to the *adrogator*. Ulpian (*D.* 1. 7. 15. 2) supplies a few more details. No more than one person should be adrogated, except for just cause, the adrogator should be the older of the two (unlike Fonteius, the adrogator of Clodius), and someone else's freedman was not to be adrogated.[28] The relevant age for the expectation that the adrogator might sire his own children was 60 (i.e. the same as the top limit for liability under the *lex Julia et Papia* to the penalties for bachelordom or childlessness), though exceptions might be made on grounds of health. Under the age of 60, according to Ulpian, the would-be adrogator 'ought rather to be making an effort to beget children'.[29]

The requirements as to the age and state of health of the adrogator, and the limitation to one person, obviously derive from the view that extinction of one *familia* line was acceptable only if another was otherwise about to become extinct. In contrast, there was apparently no limit to the number of persons *in potestate* who might be adopted. On requirements of age, see further in 2.5.1 and 2.6 below.

Both procedures were conducted during the lifetime of the adopter. There is, however, a persistent belief among some modern scholars in the legal reality of so-called 'testamentary adoption', a form of posthumous *adrogatio*, which, it is alleged, had all the legal effects of adrogation by a living adopter, save, of course, for the creation of *patria potestas* (the adopting father being already dead). Evidence for this

---

[28] For exceptions to this rule, see Gardner (1989) 243–4; certain 'just cause' appears to have been recognized under the Empire (see further below in 2. 8).

[29] *D.* 1. 7. 15. 2: 'magis liberorum creationi studeat'; cf. 1. 7. 17. 2; 'an melius sit de liberis procreandis cogitare eum quam ex aliena familia quemquam redigere in potestatem suam' (whether it would be better for him to think of begetting children than to bring someone from another *familia* into his power).

view is not forthcoming; besides the total lack of mention of such a form of adoption in juristic sources, there is no legal discussion at all of its possible legal consequences (even where, as in Gaius 3. 58, such mention would have been pertinent, and not susceptible to Justinianic deletion).[30] Belief in its reality rests entirely on the action taken by C. Octavius on his return to Rome in September 44 BC, when, as consul, he had a *lex curiata* passed, ostensibly to ratify his testamentary adoption by Julius Caesar, but in reality to consolidate his claim to succeed to Caesar's political influence.[31]

So-called 'testamentary adoption' amounted to no more than the institution of an heir under a *condicio nominis ferendi*, a condition that the heir take the adopter's name.[32] Practice in adopting and using the name seems to have varied, even under the Republic, and by the time of the Julianic codification of the edict fulfilment of the condition seems to have been discretionary.[33] Although legally non-existent, the practice is nevertheless of importance for social history, and a considerable number of examples have been detected, especially from the epigraphic evidence of anomalous names among men of the senatorial élite in the early Empire.[34] Caution must be observed, however,

[30] As Gaius 3. 58 explains, patronal rights over a citizen freedman are inherited only by an owner's *liberi*, even if disinherited, whereas those over Latin (i.e. Junian Latin) freedmen belong to testamentary heirs, even if extraneous.

[31] Kunst (1996), 87–104, esp. 93ff.

[32] Saller (1994) 79 assumes that the adoption mentioned by Pliny (*Ep.* 8. 18) by Domitius Afer of the two sons, Lucanus and Tullus, of a man whose property he had had confiscated, was testamentary. Seventeen years had elapsed between the making of the will and Afer's death, with a change of heart towards their father in the interval. Pliny's words, however at 8. 18. 6, seem to separate the adoption from the will ('Domitius Afer, qui illos in nomen adsumpsit, reliquit testamentum' (Domitius Afer, who adopted them into his name, left a will)), specially since he remarks that Afer 'shared his children with [their father]' ([eum] socium etiam in liberis habuit); a testamentary 'adoption' would have come into effect only at his death.

[33] Octavius' *lex curiata*: Appian, *BC* 3. 94. Appian's explanation muddles this with ordinary *adrogatio inter vivos*. His suggestion that the purpose was purely financial, to allow Octavius patronal rights over Caesar's rich freedmen, makes the silence of Gaius 3. 58 all the more surprising. Testamentary 'adoption' by women: Cic. *Att.* 7. 8. 3; Suet. *Galba* 4. For various arguments by 'believers', and (for the curious) further bibliography, see Prévost (1949) 29–34; Schulz (1951) 145; Salomies (1992), 7–10; *contra*, Champlin (1991) 144–6. Testamentary 'adoption' by women is to be distinguished in its effects from the special grant made by Diocletian to Syra (see 2.5.3 below).

[34] Syme (1984) 1159–68 and (1988) 159–73; Fayer (1994) 352–61. At a lower social level, Castrén (1975) tentatively identified on the basis of nomenclature a number of magistrates and members of the local Senate of Pompeii as possibly adopted (2.4 below).

since similar results may appear from the aristocratic practice of (apparently) voluntary assumption, for its prestige value, of nomenclature from the maternal ascendance, or even from a wife's family (see 2.4 below for some examples).[35]

Significantly, the adopters in 'testamentary adoption' are occasionally women (who, of course, since they did not have *potestas* could not legally adopt). This sort of 'adoption' by women is not to be confused with the privilege, discussed in 2.5.3 below, given later by imperial grant to some women, of 'adopting' an heir 'as if born of you'; the latter had specific legal consequences.

Adoption of someone *in potestate* could take place both in Rome and in the provinces, or indeed, anywhere where there was access to a competent magistrate and the requisite number of citizen witnesses; it was therefore relatively easy and convenient. Adrogation was unlikely ever to have been as widely practised,[36] not only because of the drawbacks of its legal consequences, already discussed, but also because of the practical difficulties of transacting it. Under the Republic, because a *lex curiata* was required, the formal procedure could be carried out only at Rome. It has, indeed, been suggested that persons living in the provinces could obtain *adrogatio* by indicating their wishes to the pontiffs by letter 'or deputy'; however, the derivation by Gaius of the term *adrogatio* from the putting of questions (*rogare*) to the two parties and to the *comitia* suggests that he believed that they were personally present. By the time of Diocletian, the *lex curiata* passed at Rome was no longer in use; all adrogations were obtained by imperial rescript, which obviously removed the geographical limitation, although adrogation still involved more effort and delay than adoption.[37]

For some time, both procedures coexisted, although there is scanty evidence for the details of the rise of adrogation by imperial rescript, and its generalization. Adoption by emperors of their successors was

---

[35] Syme (1988) 164–6; Salway (1994) 131–3. An additional clue to distinguishing between 'testamentary' and real adoption may be provided by *praenomina*; in 'testamentary adoption' the patronymic may differ from the *praenomen* of the man commemorated, whereas in regular adoption that of the adoptive father is taken: Salomies (1992) 6.

[36] Few examples are known; apart from Clodius, one may cite P. Cornelius Dolabella (n. 72 below), Domitia Lucilla, and Voconius Romanus (Ch. 1 n. 195).

[37] Schulz (1951) 146: Gaius 1. 99–100. The traditional view, that adrogation *per populum* lasted effectively until the end of the fourth century and the disappearance of the college of pontiffs, has been effectively countered by J. A. C. Thomas (1967) 413–27, esp. 413–18.

something of a commonplace in the first two centuries AD, and literary accounts of the circumstances of three of these adoptions (those of Piso by Galba, Trajan by Nerva and Hadrian by Trajan) represent the emperors as replacing the normal procedure of adrogation by unilateral declaration, in various forms and various locations; in the latter two instances, the adopted son was absent. These, however, were arrangements of state, not normal adoptions, and the circumstances were exceptional; adoptions of imperial successors later in the second century are described in terms suggesting conformity with normal legal procedure.[38]

For adoptions among private citizens, it is possible, as already suggested, that special authorization from the emperor was obtained in the latter part of the first century AD for Domitia Lucilla's adoption, and this may not have been an isolated instance. By the late second or early third century the emperor was the port of resort in special cases, e.g. for remedying an improperly executed adoption, or seeking exemption from the rule against adopting the freedmen of others, in order to adopt one's natural child.[39] Adrogation of *impuberes*, those not yet legally adult, was for the first time made possible by Antoninus Pius; according to Gaius, he permitted it to be done *per populum*, i.e. in the *comitia curiata*, subject to a satisfactory preliminary enquiry and the provision of guarantees by the adopter. This development was unknown to Aulus Gellius when he was writing his *Noctes Atticae*; he declares 'adrogari non potest nisi iam vesticeps' (Only someone who has already attained puberty can be adrogated). However, here Gellius was apparently relying on an out-of-date source, Masurius Sabinus (named a few lines later and quoted, on the adoption of freedmen).[40]

It is possible that imperial rescript was in regular use still earlier to permit the adrogation of women (see 2.5.4 below). Adrogation 'by the people' was still in use, but already in his *Institutes* Gaius indicates that the original reason for the ban on adrogating women by this

---

[38] Galba—privately, before the consuls, praetorian prefect and urban prefect, then before the praetorians: Tac. *Hist.* 1. 15–16; Nerva—at the temple of Jupiter Optimus Maximus, before the assembled populace: Dio 68. 3. 3–4, Pliny, *Paneg.* 6–8; Trajan either by letter or deathbed declaration (allegedly faked). Russo Ruggeri (1990a) 163–79; Fayer (1994) 340–51.

[39] *D.* 1. 7. 38 (Marcellus); 1. 7. 46 (Ulpian); Gardner (1989) 244; see 2.8 below.

[40] Gaius 1. 102; Ulp. *Reg.* 8. 5; Gellius 5. 19. 8. For this and other instances where Gellius' information is behind the times, see Holford-Strevens (1988) 15, 222.

method was either forgotten or of little relevance; they could, he says, be adrogated by imperial rescript.[41]

Clearly, imperial rescript became an established alternative procedure used by those for whom adoption by a *lex curiata* was for technical reasons not permissible. Whether (and if so to what extent) it was also used as a special favour to assist those for whom *adrogatio per populum* was simply inconvenient, the evidence does not permit one to judge. At all events, the availability and (comparatively, at least) greater convenience of the method was likely to lead to the disuse of adrogation 'by the people'. Given the emperor's approval of a request, there was little point in retaining the requirement of performance of what had long been merely the token ritual of a comitial assembly; likewise, since the emperor himself was *pontifex maximus*, his approval effectively rendered unnecessary an examination by the college of pontiffs.

In AD 286, Diocletian assured an enquirer, Timotheus, that adrogation by imperial rescript was legally valid, just as if it had been transacted under the old rules (*iure antiquo*), by the people's authority. The phrase *iure antiquo* strongly suggests that the procedure of adrogation by *lex curiata* was already obsolete, rather than that Diocletian himself was the first to abolish it. That the old procedure had indeed disappeared is shown by a response of the same emperor almost seven years later: 'Adrogations of those legally independent can take place neither in the imperial city (i.e. Rome) nor in the provinces except by imperial rescript.'[42] Therefore, it seems that adrogation 'by the people' had been totally supplanted by imperial rescript well before the end of the third century.

---

[41] Gaius 1. 101: 'Item per populum feminae non adoptantur, nam id magis placuit' (Also, women cannot be adopted by authority of the people, for this opinion has prevailed); *D.* 1. 7. 21 (Gaius, *libro singulari regularum*): 'Et feminae ex rescripto principis adrogari possunt' (Women also can be adrogated by imperial rescript). The latter remark has been impugned as an invention of the Justinianic compilers; J. A. C. Thomas (1967) 423–7 reviews (and regrettably accepts) the alleged evidence against adrogation of women before Diocletian, all of which amounts essentially to no more than argument from silence.

[42] *Cod. Iust.* 8. 47(48). 2. 1 (1474 Honoré), 11 March, AD 286; *Cod. Iust.* 8. 47(48). 6 (1762 Honoré), 2 April, AD 293. Kurylowicz (1981) 43–4 takes these passages only as evidence for the practice of adrogation by rescript in the provinces, and maintains the view that *adrogatio per populum* persisted at Rome 'until the end of the classical period'.

2.4 ADOPTIONS IN ROMAN HISTORY

The adoptions (including testamentary 'adoptions') for which we have some kind of evidence do not offer much help in determining the prevalence of adoption in Roman society at large. Literary evidence occupies itself almost exclusively with the concerns of the ruling élite. Outside the imperial house, most of the persons adopted known from the Republic and the Empire are of senatorial rank; a few—such as Anneius' son,[43] already mentioned, Cicero's friend Atticus and the younger Pliny—are equestrian. There is a very little evidence for practice below this social level, and even within the élite the number of attested adoptions is very small—a few dozen at most, even counting those of imperial heirs—so that any generalizations drawn from such evidence cannot be relied upon to be representative of society as a whole.[44]

A further problem in identifying persons who have been the objects of adoption is in the nature of the evidence itself. Some adoptions, specially those of and by emperors, are explicitly identified in the literary sources, but for the most part deduction that an adoption has occurred is based upon nomenclature alone.[45] For some this is fairly secure. For instance, men when adopted usually took the *praenomen* (forename) and *nomen* (*gens*-name) of the adopting *pater*, and the adaptation of the original paternal *gentilicium* for use as a *cognomen* (or, more correctly, *agnomen*, where there is also a *cognomen*), with the suffix *-anus*, is a practice well attested for the Republic.[46] Another

[43] Val. Max. 7. 7. 2. The status of the father in Val. Max. 7. 7. 5 who gave his son in adoption is unknown, but his motive may be inferred from the fact that he had an unusually large family, no less than eight other children.

[44] For those from the Republic, see Prévost (1949) ch. 1, Russo Ruggeri (1990a) 72–4, n. 8, 82–4, nn. 23–4, Shackleton-Bailey (1976) 81ff.; for the imperial period, Prévost (1949) ch. 2; Russo Ruggeri (1990a) 141–91—mainly imperial adoptions, but with a selection of possible non-imperial adoptees from *PIR* I–IV at 141–2 n. 5 (some of the latter are identified by Syme (1988) as testamentary adoptions). Salomies (1992) ch. 3 lists fifty-eight examples, mainly from inscriptions; for most of these, however, no more than probability is claimed, and details of possible connections between them and their likely adopters are equally lacking.

[45] Salomies (1992) *passim*, with references to earlier literature.

[46] e.g. L. Manlius Acidinus Fulvianus (cos. 179 BC), son of Q. Fulvius Flaccus, and the two adopted sons of Q. Fabius Maximus (pr. 181), Q. Fabius Maximus Aemilianus (cos. 145 BC) and Q. Fabius Maximus Servilianus (cos. 142 BC), sons respectively of L. Aemilius Paulus and Cn. Servilius Caepio. The father of the empress Livia, originally a Claudius Pulcher, became by adoption in about 50 BC M. Livius Drusus Claudianus.

common practice was to take the adopter's name, but retain one's original *cognomen*. Some adoptees may therefore be identified by bearing *cognomina* which are traditionally associated with a different *gens*.[47]

Such names alone, however, without additional information cannot be relied upon as indicators of adoption. By the end of the Republic, both types of name were also used to provide children with *cognomina* which indicated their maternal pedigree. For instance, in the early first century, the cousins Sex. Nonius Quinctilianus, son of L. Nonius Asprenas, and Appuleia Varilla have *cognomina* derived from their mothers' family, the Quinctilii, and from their ill-fated maternal uncle P. Quinctilius Varus (cos. 13 BC). Another likely example, later in the century, is the florid-complexioned (*facies* ... *multo sanguine, multo rubore suffusa*) senator, aged thirty-something, from Brixia, whom Pliny recommends as a husband for the young niece of his friend Junius Mauricus. The senator, Minicius Acilianus, son of Minicius Macrinus, has a maternal uncle named Publius Acilius.[48]

The practice spread. In three inscriptions from central Spain sons appear to derive a *cognomen* from the mother's name.

Licinius Julianus Uxsamensis an(nis) xx h(ic) s(itus) e(st) Julia mater f(aciendum) c(uravit).

(Here lies Licinius Julianus of Uxama [modern Burgo de Osma], aged 20. His mother Julia had it set up.)

D(is) M(anibus) s(acrum) Co(rnelio?) Juliano ann. XV Jul[i]a He[l]pis mater fil(io) pientissimo p(onendum) c(uravit).

(Sacred to the infernal deities. For Cornelius Julianus, aged 15, his mother Julia Helpis had this set up, for a most dutiful son.)

C(aio) S(empronio) Valeriano an(norum) xxiii et C(aio) S(empronio) Semproniano p(atri) et Val(eriae) Paternae m(atri) S(empronius) Primitivus lib(ertus) p(atronis) op(timis) d(e) s(uo) f(aciendum) c(uravit).

---

[47] e.g. M. Terentius Varro Lucullus (cos. 73 BC), originally a Licinius. The father of Pompey's final wife, Cornelia, Q. Caecilius Metellus Pius Scipio Nasica, after a 'testamentary adoption', kept the two *cognomina* of his original name. See also Shackleton-Bailey (1976) 83–7.

[48] Varus' kindred: Syme (1986) 313–8; Salway (1994) 128–9. Minicius: Pliny, *Ep.* 1. 14.

(For C. Sempronius Valerianus, aged 23, and C. Sempronius Sempronianus his father and Valeria Paterna his mother. Sempronius Primitivus, freedman, had it constructed at his own expense.)

These are not examples of adoption. Enough information is provided about the family for it to be clear that the sons take their *nomen*, in the normal way, from their fathers, and have a *cognomen* derived from the mother's name, not from the *nomen* of an adoptive *pater*. However, matters are seldom so clear-cut. Even with relatively well-attested families, more than one interpretation of the surviving evidence is possible.

A striking example is the family of L. Aelius Seianus, Tiberius' praetorian prefect, and son of L. Seius Strabo. The explanation of Seianus' name has been long assumed to be that he was adopted by L. Aelius Gallus, prefect of Egypt, although Q. Aelius Tubero (consul 11 BC) has been suggested as an alternative. An Aelia, sister of an Aelius Tubero, has been suggested as another wife of Strabo, so linking L. Seius Tubero (suffect consul AD 18) as Strabo's son by that wife, with a cognomen from his maternal family; alternatively, it is suggested that Tubero was an adopted son, or even stepson, originally the son of Strabo's wife (and Seianus' presumed mother) Junia by a putative previous marriage to Q. Aelius Tubero. That Seianus' mother was a Junia itself rests on Tacitus' repeated reference to Q. Junius Blaesus, the suffect consul of AD 10, as his *avunculus*, maternal uncle. That is, starting from nomenclature, hypotheses proliferate, based on the suppositions of repeated marriages, either by Seius Strabo or by a wife, and/or the use of adoption.[49]

Under the Empire, examples also are found of persons with two *nomina*, both with and without an additional *cognomen* and patronymic, and this also may indicate either actual adoption, or maternal descent or inheritance.[50] Domitius Lucanus, the father of Domitia Lucilla (see below), whom we know to have been adopted (Pliny *Ep.* 8.18), had not just two sets of *nomina* and *cognomina* but three, the first deriving from his adoptive father, the third from his natural father, and that in the middle presumably from his maternal family. In his case, the adoption is also clearly indicated by his patronymic; although

---

[49] Knapp (1992) 393–5, nos. 127 (Complutum), 242 (Segovia), 300 (Segovia); other possible examples are nos. 230, 240, and 267, all from Segovia. For Seianus and possible members of his family see Syme (1986) 301–7; Salomies (1992) 23 n. 5.

[50] Syme (1988)—although note the cautionary remarks of Salomies (1992) 75 about Syme's interpretations; Saller (1994) 87–8; Salway (1994) 128–9, 131–3.

his adoptive father was Cn. Domitius Afer, Lucanus is named in an inscription as *Sex.f,* 'son of Sextus'.

Examples of both types of nomenclature, i.e. derived *cognomen* or double *nomen,* are epigraphically attested from Pompeii—nineteen *cognomina* ending in -*anus,* and as many examples of double *nomen*—and on the basis of these Castrén identifies adoption as a major element in the development of the Pompeian governing élite in the first century AD.

All but a handful of those bearing names of these types are either local magistrates or magisterial candidates, and Castrén remarks, 'Adoptions and political marriages became much more frequent in the Augustan and Julio-Claudian periods, and almost always the adopting family was either new to Pompeii, or in a socially inferior position.'[51]

He makes the suggestion—although on little or no positive evidence—that some wealthy freedmen gained entry to the *ordo* for the next generation of the family in this way, either by giving their own sons[52] in adoption, or by adopting the sons of others. That is, social developments at Pompeii might seem to resemble in some ways, at a lower level of society, those described by Wiseman among the Roman senatorial élite in the late Republic, although Wiseman emphasized exogamy, rather than adoption, as the means used to secure perpetuation of the family name, or financial aid for continuance of status. It is notable that Castrén, though his emphasis is rather on adoption, speaks also, and in the same breath, of marriages; indeed, the nomenclature patterns could be the consequence of either—though in themselves they do not suffice to prove either type of connection.[53]

His hints of adoption, moreover, are not developed—actual examples are not forthcoming. In his text he tends instead to suggest that individuals are 'related to' other families, without specifying the basis of the relationship; moreover, save for one uncertain example (see n. 53) of direct adoption by a freedman, he speaks of persons as merely of freedman descent. His hesitancy is understandable; apart from the

---

[51] Castrén (1975) 100; see also his Index of Families, pp. 129–244.

[52] Giving themselves in adoption would not have sufficed, since it would not allow them to count as freeborn: see 2.8 below.

[53] For example, the adoptive father of Cn. Alleius Nigidius Maius (*quinquennalis* AD 55/6) was probably, according to Castrén, and his wife certainly, freed. However the relevant (and unpublished) inscription is now lost: Castrén (1975) 109; see also index under 'freedmen' for other magistrates and decurions whom he thinks to be of possible freedman descent. Exogamy: Wiseman (1971) 53–64.

ambiguous evidence of names, proof of these supposed adoptions is lacking.[54]

Indeed, from the point of view of the Pompeian governing class, as a strategy for perpetuation of either name or status, marriage—and with the freeborn offspring of freedmen, rather than with freedmen themselves—might seem likely to have commended itself (if it did so at all) more than adoption of the offspring of wealthy freedmen. For those lucky enough to have sons, marrying them to the daughters of wealthy freedmen (an option taken, for instance, for his own first marriage by the debt-ridden Mark Antony) would be much more attractive than financing their careers by giving them in adoption to freedmen. Marriage had the advantage of keeping the freedman connection at slightly longer arm's length. It would be one thing for a grandchild to have a freedman grandparent;[55] it was quite another to hand over one's own son for adoption and have him henceforth acknowledge a freedman as father—and perhaps only marginally less unacceptable to have a new son in the family whose natural father was well known locally not to be freeborn. However, evidence for such marriages, as for the suggested adoptions, is again mere conjecture, based on nomenclature. Essentially, Castrén can do no more than suggest, on the basis of names, that some families intermarrying with the 'local aristocracy' may have originated, at some unspecified time in the past, from freed slaves.[56]

There is, however, other evidence which indicates that, both for aspirants to social acceptance in public life and those bestowing it, neither marriage nor adoption was the preferred route for ex-slaves and their families. On the contrary, successful freedmen used what they had, and what local authorities needed—their wealth. A freedman without a son of his own need not adopt a stranger to satisfy his

[54] See also the trenchant criticisms made by Mouritsen (1988) 115–22, of Castrén's whole theory of the historical development of the Pompeian governing élite from the foundation of the colony until the Flavian period, and especially (121–2) of Castrén's suggested identifications of 'new' families of freedman descent.

[55] Or, preferably, great-grandparent, although the requirement for membership of the councils of Italian and provincial towns and even the Senate at Rome seems to have been only that the candidate himself be freeborn, not the 'three-generation rule', apparently of ancient origin, governing eligibility for membership of the Areopagus at Athens: Gordon (1931) 65–77; Treggiari (1969) 52ff.; Oliver (1970) 20–1, 31–2, 44–65; Garnsey (1975) 167–80.

[56] For evidence of a tendency, within municipal élites, for those families derived from imperial freedmen to intermarry among themselves, see Gordon (1931) 72–3.

ambitions vicariously; he could by his munificence in public benefaction achieve directly for himself, not indeed public office, but the trappings of magisterial or decurional status. Between those with sons and their local councils there was an understanding. Public generosity by the father could secure adlection, sometimes even before puberty, of his freeborn son into public office; there was no need to give away his son into another man's *potestas* and name.[57]

Much of the other evidence for possible adoptions which is derived from names is equally indirect and problematic. If two men, said to be brothers, have a different *nomen*, this may mean that one has been adopted; equally, it may indicate that their mother married twice. Where a son has a different *nomen* from that of his natural father, that may mean that his parents were not married. Most troublesome of all are the polyonymous appellations (the longest has fourteen *nomina*) fashionable from the second century AD onwards as a demonstration of ancient pedigree among the older Roman senatorial aristocracy; these could be built up in a variety of ways.[58]

For the Republic, there are, including so-called testamentary adoptions, about three dozen fairly clear examples of adoption in the Roman senatorial élite, plus a few more among the equestrians (see above). Obviously, this number is too low to allow confident statistical assertions about adoption among the upper orders as a whole, let alone Roman society in general. Nevertheless, it is striking that even among this small population a substantial proportion—no fewer than eleven, of which three may be testamentary adoptions, the rest real— are known to be already related to their adopters, as are two equestrian examples, M. Anneius and Cicero's friend Atticus, both adopted, the latter probably by will, by their maternal uncles—as later, was the younger Pliny. C. Sallustius Crispus was adopted by his maternal great-uncle, the historian.[59]

Two of the certain Republican adoptions are by relatives in the

---

[57] Gordon (1931) 66–8. Castrén's readiness to detect servile descent among the decurions of Pompeii in the 1st cent. AD is perhaps premature; most of the positive evidence for freedmen in local public life belongs to the following century: Gordon (1931) 70–1; cf. Garnsey (1975) 170–1.

[58] Salomies (1992) 15–19, 83–7; Salway (1994) 132–3.

[59] Syme (1986) 159–60; Salomies (1992) 14, 24; in due course he himself adopted the son of L. Passienus Rufus (cos. AD 4); Crispus Passienus was consul twice (suff. 27, II ord. 44).

agnatic line, one by a paternal uncle,[60] the other by his father's cousin.[61] The rest are adopted by relatives through females. Four, or possibly five,[62] are adopted by maternal uncles, and two (possibly both as testamentary 'adoptions') by maternal grandfathers.[63] Of these, particularly interesting is L. Licinius Crassus Scipio, along with his brother, two sons of P. Cornelius Scipio Nasica (praetor 93 BC) who both changed their names. Licinius was 'adopted' in the will of his maternal grandfather, the orator L. Licinius Crassus (cos. 95 BC) and took his name, as requested; his brother was adopted (again possibly by will) by a remoter relative, Q. Caecilius Metellus Pius, whose grandfather had been the brother of Scipio's paternal grandmother. Most famous of all, perhaps, is Scipio Africanus Minor, son of L. Aemilius Paulus, adopted by the relatively undistinguished son of Scipio Africanus Maior; his adopter was the son of Scipio Maior and Aemilia, and adopted the son of his maternal uncle. Another son of Aemilius was given in adoption to Q. Fabius Maximus (see 2.1 above and n. 46). Maximus in fact adopted not just one, but two, sons.

One of the most striking and interesting instances is this double giving in adoption by L. Aemilius Paulus, and double taking in adoption by Q. Fabius Maximus, *praetor peregrinus* in 181 BC, involving four families in all. Both financial considerations and those of family ambition may be supposed to have played a part, both on the part of those giving, and those taking, in adoption. One donor, L. Aemilius Paulus, having four sons, would appear to be making provision both for the financial and for the political future of all of them by giving the two elder in adoption, so making it easier to advance the two younger from his own resources—an intent which was, however, forestalled by their early deaths. As remarked by Valerius Maximus (5. 10. 2) *ad donandos usque abundaverat.* he had had plenty of sons he

---

[60] The younger son of C. Claudius Pulcher, adopted by the latter's brother Appius Claudius Pulcher (cos. 54 BC).

[61] Q. Caecilius Metellus Celer (cos. 60 BC), son of Nepos (cos. 98), adopted by Celer (tr. pl. 90). Nepos and the elder Celer were the sons respectively of Balearicus and Diadematus, sons of Q. Metellus Macedonicus (cos. 143 BC).

[62] M. Marius Gratidianus (tr. pl. 87), son of C. Marius' sister and adopted by M. Marius, his brother; M. Satrius (later pr., 45 BC), adopted by L. Minucius Basilus; C. Rabirius Postumus (pr. ? 48 BC), son of C. Curtius, an equestrian tax-farmer; M. Junius Brutus, adopted by Q. Servilius Caepio; possibly one may add Mam. Lepidus Livianus (cos. 77 BC), son of M. Livius Drusus (cos. 112 BC) and a Cornelia: see stemma XIX in Syme (1986).

[63] L. Licinius Crassus Scipio and T. Annius Milo (pr. 55 BC).

could spare to give away. One was given in adoption into a prominent political family, that of the Cornelii Scipiones, to whom he was already related by marriage through his paternal aunt (his adopter was his cousin). The other was given in adoption to Fabius, a prominent politician whose line was otherwise likely to die out. The same appears likely of the other recipient, P. Scipio, the son of Africanus Maior; Cicero remarks (*De Off.* 1. 121) that because of his poor health he could not be as like his famous father as Africanus Minor was like his (sc. Aemilius). This suggests not only that Scipio's poor health barred him from a political career, but that he had been unable to have sons. Both of the sons given in adoption by Aemilius to Scipio and Fabius duly became consuls, in 147 (and again 134) and 145 respectively. Similarly, Fabius' other donor, Cn. Servilius Caepio, who had two other sons to provide for, gave his eldest in adoption, and all three reached the consulship in three successive years (142–140). Aemilius, though he failed to perpetuate his own *nomen*, assisted two other families (one already related to him) to continue their traditions, and also provided them with male heirs to their property. In due course, his two surviving natural sons inherited from him, as well as from their adoptive fathers.

Admittedly this is a small sample; nevertheless the proportion of instances in which there is a blood relationship—especially one through females, and not through the direct agnatic line—is striking. If we knew the names and family connections of more of the Roman nobility's wives and mothers (many of whom are not attested), then there is some likelihood that more adoptions would involve relatives, a probability which is enhanced by the Roman practice of serial marriage.[64]

Trying to establish the general characteristics of adoptions among the *nobilitas*, Prévost[65] describes them as essentially 'dynastic', drawing attention to the political importance of the noble families studied, in relation to the number of adoptions they performed. The argument is in some danger of circularity, since his research design explicitly confined investigation to consular, or at least senatorial, families of the last two centuries BC, and those families in whom he

---

[64] See the remarks of Syme (1986) 505–6 in the prolegomena to the Appendix of stemmata; in table I he hazards the suggestion that no fewer than three of Pompey's marriages connected him remotely, via other series of marriages, with the Caecilii Metelli.   [65] Prévost (1949) 25–9.

found most adoptions are, not surprisingly, among the best-attested in the sources, and the most extensively intermarried, of the political élite. His conclusions are based on 27/28 adoptions, over more than a century, of which 18/19 are from six prominent families (Cornelii, Licinii, Caecilii Metelli, Livii Drusi, Fabii, Terentii), with the Caecilii and Licinii accounting for nine between them, and the Fabii having two adoptions by one man in the early part of the period; among the rest, the Aemilii, Claudii and Servilii Caepiones show one each.[66]

These families, Prévost tells us (p. 27) constitute the most important part of the senatorial oligarchy, 'that restricted political caste which reserved to itself, by hereditary right, the government of the Republic'; more recent scholarship calls attention, on the contrary, to the discontinuity in consular families in the last two centuries of the Republic.[67] In calling these adoptions 'dynastic', moreover, Prévost is using a model of political life in the Roman Republic which few would accept today, or at least not without major qualifications. The untenability of the notion of 'factions', bound by ties of kinship, as a governing force in Roman politics or in the behaviour of Roman aristocrats has been cogently demonstrated.[68] Adoption created a prospective heir to property. What was additionally transmitted was not power, but status, to which wealth was inextricably linked because of the high cost of public life.[69]

The motives both of the adopter and the person giving in adoption are relevant. For members of senatorial families, fathers giving in adoption found a way of 'maintaining a son's status from someone else's funds',[70] adopters a way of perpetuating the family name and dignity. Family sentiment, if a kinsman were available, rather than the political factionalism of modern theory, provides a credible motive for the choice of person. Besides adoption, there was, of course, an alternative method for noble families to use to avoid

---

[66] He refrains from comment on the examples of an adoptive Annius, Atilius, Aufidius, Junius, Manlius, and Postumius, possibly because these six families lack the prominence in the magisterial record on which he bases his thesis.

[67] Hopkins (1983) ch. 2, who concludes (p. 117), 'The senatorial aristocracy ... never developed, either in law or in fact, into a hereditary Estate.' See also Wiseman (1971) 53–70. [68] Brunt (1988) ch. 9.

[69] Inheritance is explicitly attested in a number of instances and probable in several others. Exceptionally, M. Junius Brutus does not seem to have been his adoptive uncle's heir (Plut. *Cat. Min.* 11. 3), but details of his landed estates and financial transactions indicate considerable wealth of his own. On the significance of transmission of the nomen, see Saller (1994) 79–80. [70] Hopkins (1983) 49.

extinction, namely, exogamy; both could also provide an avenue for outsiders to gain entry to the élite.[71]

A few—a very few—adoptions can be shown to have an overtly political motive. This is clearly the case with the adoptions of the patricians Clodius and Dolabella into plebeian families, so enabling them to hold the tribunate, Clodius in 58 BC, Dolabella in 47.[72] It has also been suggested that the adoption of one son of the plebeian Q. Fulvius Flaccus into the patrician family of the Manlii Acidini was in order to allow both sons to be consuls together in one year (179 BC).[73] This however (besides perhaps misinterpreting the scope of the *lex Genucia* and, given the date, overestimating the strength of surviving feelings of 'class' distinction between patrician and plebeian) is to argue from fact to assumed motive, and is also belied by what we know of the careers of the two. Manlius' adoption preceded his consulship by a decade at least, since, as Manlius, he was praetor in Hither Spain in 188 BC. His brother's praetorship (also in Hither Spain) was six years later. Even overlooking the uncertainty of success for the candidacies, it stretches credibility that such long-term advance planning for Rome's most competitively sought office can even have been contemplated—especially as we have no information at all about the age of Manlius when adopted.

Manlius' adoption is, as it happens, the earliest securely attested adoption among the Roman nobility, though the adoption into a plebeian family of a patrician Aemilius, father of the consul of 147 BC, C. Livius M. Aemiliani f. Drusus,[74] may for all we know have preceded it. Another adoption of a patrician by a plebeian is that of the notorious D. Junius Silanus Manlianus, praetor in Macedonia in 141 BC. For the first century BC, a number of adoptions in both directions are attested;[75] by then, it is clear that patricians and plebeians were ef-

---

[71] Wiseman (1971) 53–64.; Mratschek-Halfmann (1993) 95–127.

[72] Clodius: Cic. *Att.* 8. 3. 3, *Dom.* 37. Dolabella: Dio 42. 29. 1, Ascon. 5C; Plut. *Cic.* 41. 1.

[73] Russo Ruggeri (1990a) 80. According to Velleius Paterculus 2. 8. 2 this fraternal consulship created a record unmatched up to his own day. A *lex Genucia* of 342 BC (for which see Cornell (1995) 337–8) apparently ruled that one consul in each year should be plebeian (which arguably meant that both could be). For almost two centuries each year had one plebeian, one patrician consul; but in 172 BC, both consuls were plebeian for the first time, and this was repeated on numerous subsequent occasions.

[74] Prévost (1949) 23.

[75] Prévost (1949) 26; Fayer (1994) 336 n. 185. To those listed by Prévost may be added two plebeians adopted by patricians, Cornelius Scipio Pomponianus (*RE* 4.

fectively integrated, as indeed they were also in marriage. The son of the patrician P. Cornelius Scipio Nasica, for instance, is 'adopted' by the will of his plebeian maternal grandfather L. Licinius Crassus. Adoptions in the imperial family, however, are overtly 'dynastic'. Starting with Augustus, the central concern was the transmission of power to successive leaders without opening it to ruinous internecine competitition such as bedevilled the late Republic. The hereditary principle was the most obvious alternative. In default of direct descendants through the male line, there was resort to personal selection of a successor, but reinforced preferably with blood kinship through women, or connection by marriage (and so, again, through women).[76]

From time to time, if these later possibilities also failed, personal designation alone was used. Although Pliny (*Paneg.* 7. 4) contrives to make the absence of connection by blood or marriage a virtue—the best man chosen by the best—it is clear that what confers acceptability on Trajan is the designation as 'son' of his predecessor. Septimius Severus, almost a century later, appears to model his behaviour in more than one respect on the early tactics of Augustus. After a brief flirtation with representation of himself as avenger of Pertinax, whom he had had deified, by AD 195 he had begun to issue coinage styling himself son of Marcus Aurelius.[77] In this way, the hereditary principle, with or without actual family connection, is used for the transmission of imperial power during the first three centuries of our era.[78]

Outside the imperial house, very few adoptions are directly attested in the sources for the imperial period. The best-known example is the younger Pliny, son of a L. Caecilius, and adopted by his maternal uncle C. Plinius Secundus (*Ep.* 5. 8. 5). His adoption by his uncle has

---

1505; Pliny, *NH* 35. 8) and D. Junius Brutus Albinus, adopted by a Postumius Albinus, perhaps the one who was the last consul of the line in 99 BC (*RE* Suppl. 5. 369–85; for Brutus' hybrid nomenclature, found also on coins, see e.g. Plut. *Caes.* 64. 1, App. *BC* 2. 464, 479; 3. 102; Dio 44. 14. 1), and a patrician adopted by a plebeian, M. Livius Drusus Claudianus, the father of the empress Livia (*RE* 13. 881–2; Suet. *Tib.* 3. 1; Tac. *Ann.* 6. 51).

[76] Corbier (1994), 243–91 and (1995) 178–93.

[77] Dio 74. 4. 1–5. 5; SHA *Pert.* 15. 1–5, *Sev.* 7. 8–9; *BMC* v. 136.

[78] Adoptions of successors to the imperial power are discussed in several modern works, and will not be examined in detail here. For a summary down to Diocletian and the tetrarchy, see Russo Ruggeri (1990*a*) 143–91.

commonly been assumed to be testamentary (i.e. not a legal 'adoption' at all), since Pliny mentions it only once, in this letter, and elsewhere refers to him as his uncle (*Epp.* 1. 19, 6. 16 and 20), and since Pliny's father in his will appointed not his uncle but L. Verginius Rufus to be his tutor (*Ep.* 2. 1). However, neither argument is cogent. Pliny mentions the legal relationship (father) only incidentally in that one letter, but there also the elder Pliny is primarily identified as his uncle. In *Ep.* 1. 19, Pliny is discussing his correspondent's father's personal friendship with Pliny's own maternal relatives (his mother and uncle) in their common home town of Comum; the other two letters are to Tacitus, who has approached him for information because he knew of the family relationship, and also that Pliny and his mother had at the time of the eruption been living with his uncle (*Ep.* 6. 16). In other words, it is not the legal relationship, but the personal one, that is of main interest. Though Verginius was appointed as Pliny's tutor in his father's will, this does not preclude a subsequent adrogation when he came of age; Pliny was in his eighteenth year when his uncle died (*Ep.* 6. 20. 5). As well as having two *nomina*, Pliny in his official titulature claims two fathers; he is 'C. Plinius L.f. Ouf. Caecilius Secundus' (Gaius Plinius Secundus, son of L. Caecilius of the Oufentina tribe (*CIL* 5. 262 (=*ILS* 2927) and 5623)). Separately attested are a L. Caecilius L.f. Cilo who had two sons, L. Caecilius Valens and L. Caecilius Secundus, the latter perhaps Pliny's father (*CIL* 5. 5279 (=*ILS* 6728)).

As for other adoptions of which something is known, we may add, besides Domitia Lucilla, adopted by her paternal uncle (1.3 above), also her father and that uncle, his brother. They were adopted by the orator Cn. Domitius Afer (Pliny, *Ep.* 8.18; see also n. 32 above, for reasons to believe that this was a real, and not a testamentary, adoption). Their natural father was Sex. Curvius Tullus, and this is preserved in the nomenclature. The full name of one of the brothers, Domitia's natural father, is epigraphically attested as Cn. Domitius Sex.f. Afer Titius Marcellus Curvius Lucanus (*ILS* 990). He has no fewer than three sets of *nomina* and *cognomina*, the middle one of which, Titius Marcellus, may provide information on the family of his mother, Curvius' wife. It is worth noting that Pliny's comment on their adoption by Domitius seems to take it for granted that when someone unrelated was adopted, a strong feeling of friendship may be presumed between the adopter and the donating father. He comments on Domitius Afer's subsequent change of heart, some time after he made his will in their favour, in that he had had their natural father's property confiscated (the reasons are not specified). Pliny's suggestion that Afer had also changed his mind about the will (*improbatum*) and about the beneficiaries (*divites fierent invitissimis*, 'they became rich against their—sc. Afer's and Curtilius Mancia's—wishes') is plainly rhetorical, to match up with the story about the hostility of Lucanus' father-in-law. Had Afer really turned against them, he could have disinherited them, something which they might have found difficulty in contesting because of their natural father's disgrace, or, easier still, emancipated them. As usual, we have tantalizingly little information about the circumstances of the adoption. It would be helpful to know why Domitius adopted both brothers, and why Curvius was willing, or able, to allow the adoption of two sons.

Few adoptions are attested so directly in the literary sources. For the rest, they are identified mainly on the basis of nomenclature. Extreme caution is necessary, however, since, as already observed, the same types of names are sometimes possibly adoptive, sometimes certainly not. At best, all that can be claimed on the basis of nomenclature alone is a possibility that there has been an adoption.

2.5 CAPACITY TO ADOPT: QUESTIONS OF AGE AND SEX

2.5.1 *Requirements of Age—the Generation Gap*

There was no minimum age limit for the adoption of someone *in potestate*. The adopter, obviously, had to be legally adult, but for much of Roman history there was no clear agreement about the relative ages of the two. Under Hadrian, Javolenus remarked, 'Adoption may take place between those persons between whom the natural relationship also can exist,'[79] which, coming from a commentary on Cassius, may represent also the view of his predecessor. The remark is ambiguous; it is not indicated whether he is referring to age alone, or to the procreative capacity of the aspirant adopter.

As to age-difference, a hard and fast rule of general application appears to be laid down, several centuries later, by Justinian, who not only states that the adopter, for both methods, must be older, but

[79] Gaius 1. 102 'apud praetorem ... cuiuscumque aetatis adoptare possumus' (we can adopt [persons] of any age before the praetor): *D.* 1. 7. 16 (Javolenus): 'Adoptio enim in his personis locum habet, in quibus etiam natura potest habere.'

specifies a minimum age difference, 'debet ... plena pubertate, id est decem et octo annis praecedere' (he must be the older by a time long enough for full achievement of puberty, i.e. eighteen years). We shall hear more presently of this figure of eighteen years, and Justinian's does not appear to be the first statement of the rule. Cicero's complaint about the fraudulent nature of Clodius' adrogation, evinced, *inter alia*, by the relative ages of Clodius and his adrogator, suggests that in general practice in his day adopters were usually significantly older than those adopted: 'You were made son of the man of whom, in terms of age, you could have been the father.' Nevertheless, it was still matter of debate in Gaius' time whether the adopter *need* be older, for either form of adoption. Ulpian states, apparently as a generally accepted rule, that an older person is not to be adrogated by a younger.[80]

Verisimilitude in age difference between 'parent' and 'child' may sometimes have been strained by such practices as the reshaping of family structures by emancipation and re-adoption within the *familia* (see below). Generations could become confused, as in the situation hypothetically presented, but without hint of criticism or surprise, by Ulpian: a man with two grandsons emancipated one and re-adopted him as father of the other grandson. The matter appears to be settled within a generation after Ulpian. Modestinus says: 'Not only when someone is adopting, but also when adrogating, he must be older than the person he is making his son by adoption or adrogation, and at any rate he must be the older by a time long enough for full achievement of puberty, i.e. eighteen years.'[81] Why eighteen years? The last phrase exactly corresponds to the words of Justinian's *Institutes*, but it does not follow that the text has been interpolated by a Justinianic compiler.[82] The age of 18 assumes importance in a number of other contexts, being accepted as a (not the) definition of adulthood.

As late as the mid-second century AD, on the evidence of Gaius, the long-running debate had not been settled between those who wished to define legal adulthood for males by physical development and those who defined it by the attainment of a fixed age, i.e. 14 years—

[80] Justinian: *Inst.* 1. 11. 4; Cic. *De dom.* 35; Gaius 1. 106: *quaestio est*; D. 1. 7. 15. 3 (Ulpian): *Item* non debet *adrogare maiorem minor*, cf. Russo Ruggeri (1990a) 290–1.

[81] D. 37. 4. 3. 1; D. 1. 7. 40. 1: 'Non tantum cum quis adoptat, sed et cum adrogat, maior esse debet eo, quem sibi per adrogationem vel adoptionem filium facit, et utique plenae pubertatis, id est decem et octo annis eum praecedere debet.'

[82] As supposed e.g. by Kurylowicz (1984) 3314.

and in practice, to judge from the examples of Cicero and his brother, Roman fathers might not get round to giving their sons the *toga virilis* until a year or two after they reached that age.[83] It does not appear from our evidence, however, that as a general rule 18 replaced 14 under the Empire as the conventional age for ceasing to be *impubes*; on the contrary, it is clear that 14 remained the conventional age of adulthood, but that the attainment of 18 was regarded as an appropriate criterion to be applied in certain special circumstances, where for some reason or other it was thought desirable to allow a comfortable margin.

Ulpian, for instance, discussing manumissions permitted for 'just cause' under the terms of the *lex Aelia Sentia*, where the manumitter is under the age of 20 and the slave under 30, says that someone may be manumitted in order to be a *procurator* (estate manager) for the owner, 'dummodo non minor annis decem et octo sit' (provided he is not less than 18 years old). *Procurator* was a responsible position, requiring some maturity; the slave to be manumitted must therefore be above the minimum age for adulthood. Elsewhere, he reports an instruction of Hadrian, reiterated by Septimius Severus, that legacies of *alimenta* to children were to be interpreted as due until the fourteenth year for girls, the eighteenth for boys; this, he observes, was not the general definition of puberty, but from considerations of *pietas*, in this one instance, it was public-spirited (*non incivile*) to make an exception. That is, a comfortable margin is allowed (as with the lower age limits for producing children in the Augustan *lex Papia*) before cutting off the benefit. Papinian, saying that the terms of conditions in wills are to be interpreted according to the testator's intention, gives as an example the case where persons nominated in a will as tutors (sc. *impuberis*, for a minor) have instead chosen to act as curators, on the grounds that the young person has already come of age (*adoleverat*). The will had asked them to exercise the *tutela* until the ward reached eighteen; their point was that the young man was no longer *impubes*. Here, the testator was anxious not to put an immature young heir in full control of his property too soon; the tutors, on the other hand, were in a hurry to discharge themselves of a burdensome responsibility, and wished to stand upon the letter of the law.[84]

---

[83] Gaius 1. 196; Cic. *Att.* 6. 1. 12, 9. 19. 1.

[84] D. 40. 2. 13; 34. 1. 14. 1 (Ulpian); D. 35. 1. 101. 2 (Papinian). To qualify for inheritances, women were expected by the *lex Papia* to have begun to produce children

Possible fraudulent exploitation of the unresolved ambiguity between the criteria of age and physical development appears to underlie a comment in Paul, *Sententiae*: 'Males can make wills after the completion of their fourteenth year, women their twelfth, with tutor's authorization if they do not have the *ius liberorum*. *Spadones* can do so from the age by which most people reach puberty, i.e. the eighteenth year.'[85]

The generally accepted rule was that age (14 for males) rather than physical development determined, among other aspects of legal adulthood, the capacity to make a will.[86] *Spado* is the general term for someone constitutionally impotent; obviously, there would be a problem in his case in applying physical development as the criterion for his attainment of adulthood. If a tutor (with, perhaps, a particular interest in postponing the requirement to render account of his administration) was refusing to resign his charge on the excuse that his ward, not having become physically mature, was not legally adult, this could be extended only until the ward reached 18, when he could represent himself as *spado*, and claim recognition as adult.

For adoption, then, eighteen years became accepted as a conventional generation gap—time enough for a person to have become legally adult, married and a parent. We have no evidence as to how such a rule was enforced in practice. Presumably for adrogation the pontiffs and, later, the emperor, would simply reject the application where the appropriate age gap did not exist, and the praetor or provincial magistrate for adoptions of *filiifamilias*.[87]

2.5.2 *Power to Adopt and Sexual Capacity*

In order to have the capacity to adopt, it was not necessary to be physically capable of fathering children, any more than to be mar-

by the age of 20, men by 25 (Ulp. *Reg.* 16. 1), that is, some years later than even late developers would normally reach puberty. For the distinction between tutors and curators, see Buckland (1963) 142–3, 169–73; curators normally acted for persons already adult.

[85] Paul, *Sent.* 3. 4a. 1–2: 'Testamentum facere possunt masculi post impletum quartum decimum annum, feminae post duodecimum, (sed non) habentes ius liberorum tutore auctore. Spadones eo tempore testamentum facere possunt, quo plerique pubescunt, i.e. anno decimo octavo.'

[86] Gaius 1. 40, 2. 113; *D.* 28. 1. 5; *Cod. Iust.* 6. 22. 4 (2462 Honoré: AD 294).

[87] Or the municipal magistrate, under the Empire, if he had *legis actio*: Paul, *Sent.* 2. 25. 4. For the competent magistrates for private adoption, see Russo Ruggeri (1990a) 327–34.

ried—even bachelors could adopt. All that was required was that the intending adopter was a Roman citizen *sui iuris*, who was classified as legally male, and therefore a *paterfamilias*. The title *paterfamilias* designated not a person, but a legal right (in current parlance, a 'gender role'); actual paternity was not required. The relevant qualification was the possession not of potency, but of *potestas*.[88]

In classical law, therefore, it was apparently possible for men incapable of fatherhood, whether from natural impotence or even because of castration, both to adopt and to adrogate. Gaius says as much: 'This is common to both kinds of adoption, that those also, such as *spadones*, who cannot procreate can adopt,'[89] and it would seem natural, especially for adrogation, since one of the conditions normally required was that the adrogator did not or could not have children of his own.

This, indeed, was probably the main purpose of Gaius' remark, simply to confirm the appropriateness of allowing *adrogatio* by *spadones*. His mention of both methods of adoption need not imply reservations about either. There could be no doubt about whether *spadones* should be allowed to adopt *filiifamilias*, since no external criteria had to be satisfied, provided that both the adopter and the *paterfamilias* giving his son in adoption were legally adult Roman citizens, while for adrogation the case for allowing the *spado* to adopt was more straightforward, indeed, than for other men. It was not that they, of all people, were shirking the civic duty of procreation (implied by Ulpian's 'they would do better to think of begetting children'), but rather that this option was not in practice available to them. *Spadones* are not 'difficult', and requiring some kind of special dispensation to allow them to adopt; rather, whereas careful enquiry was necessary into the motives of other would-be adrogators, it is accepted that *spadones*, once their physical condition is established, have a specially strong case.

However the power of adopting—apparently by either method, and so the paraphrase of Theophilus understands the text—was denied to *castrati* by Justinian, 'This is common to both methods of adoption, that those people also who are unable to beget children, such as *spadones*, can adopt, but *castrati* cannot.'

---

[88] *D.* 50. 16. 195. 2 (Ulpian). Marriage: *D.* 1. 7. 30; 24. 1. 32. 13; cf. 35. 1. 15; 50. 17. 30; see also Gardner (forthcoming–c). Adoption: *D.* 28. 2. 6 pr.

[89] Gaius 1. 103: 'Illud vero utriusque adoptionis commune est, quod et hi qui generare non possunt, quales sunt spadones, adoptare possunt.' Cf. *D.* 1. 7. 21.

The last three words are Justinian's addition to Gaius' text, and have the effect of making the generic term *spado* apply specifically only to men possessing genitals, albeit not in working order, in distinction to *castrati*, who no longer have theirs.[90] The latter are no longer to be allowed to adopt. The opposite view, that *castrati* were already excluded from adopting in classical law, has been held by some modern scholars,[91] mainly on the basis of *D.* 28. 2. 6 (Ulpian), which contains some choice examples of legal reasoning:

The question is raised, whether someone who cannot easily beget can institute a posthumous heir. Cassius and Javolenus write that he can; for he can also marry and adopt. Both Labeo and Cassius write that a *spado* also can institute a posthumous heir, since neither age nor sterility is an impediment to him. 1. But if he has been castrated, then Julian agrees with the opinion of Proculus that he cannot institute a posthumous heir, and that is the principle we follow. Clearly a hermaphrodite, if male characteristics are prevalent in him, will be able to institute a posthumous heir.'[92]

This text has provoked a great deal of—in the main misguided and irrelevant—discussion, mainly because of the mention of adoption in Cassius' and Javolenus' opinion concerning the case of those who cannot easily procreate; but there is no reason at all to consider adoption in relation to the rest of the text.

---

[90] *Inst.* 1. 11. 9: 'Sed et illud utriusque adoptionis commune est, quod et hi, qui generare non possunt, quales sunt spadones, adoptare possunt, castrati autem non possunt.' The point is observed by Kurylowicz (1981) 76; he therefore takes the view that *castrati* could adopt under classical law. For the use of *spado* as a generic term, covering not only impotent men but those with destroyed or damaged testicles (*thlibiae, thliasiae*) and even *castrati*, see *D.* 50. 16. 128 (Ulpian): 'quo nomine tam hi, qui natura spadones sunt, item thlibiae et thliasiae, si quod aliud genus spadonum est, continentur' (The term covers those eunuchs by nature, those made so, and any other kind of eunuchs), and esp. *D.* 23. 3. 39. 1 (Ulpian) 'Si spadoni mulier nubserit, distinguendum arbitror castratus fuerit necne' (If a woman marries a *spado*, a distinction ought to be made whether he has been castrated or not). In the latter case, it is held that property given him does not constitute a dowry; sexual capacity is relevant, since dowry in certain circumstances might remain at the end of the marriage in the husband's *familia*, and that of a *castratus* must end with himself.

[91] References, and a summary of the argument, in Fayer (1994) 368–71 and Russo Ruggeri (1990a) 293–305.

[92] 'Sed est quaesitum an is, qui generare facile non possit, postumum heredem facere possit. et scribit Cassius et Javolenus posse: nam et uxorem ducere et adoptare potest. spadonem quoque posse postumum heredem scribere et Labeo et Cassius scribunt: quoniam nec aetas nec sterilitas ei rei impedimento est. 1. Sed si castratus sit, Iulianus Proculi opinionem secutus non putat postumum heredem posse instituere, quo iure utimur. Hermaphroditum plane, si in eo virilia praevalebunt, postumum heredem instituere poterit.'

2.5 Capacity to Adopt: Questions of Age and Sex

In the first place, the text as a whole is not about adoption at all, but about a purely technical legal point, whether, if a *postumus* (a child not yet born at the time a will was made and who was or would be a *suus heres* when born) is instituted as heir in a will, attention has to be paid to that institution. Such institutions had the effect of invalidating a previous will. The final settlement of an estate had to be delayed, should a widow's pregnancy be alleged, until the anticipated child (whether it was in the will or not—if not, its birth invalidated the will) either finally appeared, or was manifestly not going to. Questions of paternity (in which reversionary heirs would have an obvious interest) could also arise over *postumi* already born when the testator died.[93]

The passage as a whole discusses four groups of people about whose capacity for procreation there is doubt; but, just as the reasons for doubt vary, so do the principles on which the treatment of each group is decided. The four are (i) those merely having difficulty in procreating; next, those incapable of procreating, who are further subdivided into (ii) *spadones*, the chronically impotent, but still possessing genitals, and (iii) *castrati*, who no longer have theirs. The first three groups are all classified as men. With group (iv), the hermaphrodites, there is no real problem at all. It is simply a matter of gender role assignment—those without appropriate genitals would not be classified as male at all (*D.* 1. 5. 10), and so, not being legally capable of having *sui heredes*, need not institute *postumi*.

On group (i) Cassius and Javolenus base their opinion upon the male gender role as *paterfamilias*, which is a social and legal construct, and not dependent on generative capacity. A Roman *paterfamilias*, unlike a woman, could have *sui heredes*. To provide in their wills for the possibility of *postumi* was a desirable precaution for Roman men to take, since their omission automatically invalidated a will; like any other *sui heredes* they had to be specifically instituted heirs or disinherited.

[93] *D.* 28. 2. 9 (Paul): 'Si quis postumos, quos per aetatem aut valetudinem habere forte non potest, heredes instituit, superius testamentum rumpitur, quod natura magis in homine generandi et consuetudo spectanda est, quam temporale vitium aut valetudo, propter quam abducatur homo a generandi facultate' (If someone who for reasons of age and health is perhaps incapable of having them institutes posthumous heirs, a previous will is broken, because regard must be had to the nature, and customary capacity of generating, in a man, rather than to a temporary defect or ill-health on account of which the man is deprived of the faculty of generating). On the arrangements in the praetor's edict for verifying the pregnancy and confinement of a widow, *D.* 25. 4. 1. 10. Paternity: *D.* 37. 10 on the *Edictum Carbonianum*; cf. *D.* 1. 6. 6.

The jurists back up their argument from a man's status as *paterfamilias* with reference to two other activities associated with the male gender role, namely taking a wife and adopting. Incapacity to consummate did not of itself invalidate a marriage (although the legal effects of lawful marriage, *matrimonium iustum*, might be declared not to be operative, where these involved a presumption of sexual activity and the production of children), and it was unnecessary to be married to be able to adopt.[94]

The second and third groups apparently cannot procreate at all. For the *spadones*, the reasoning of Labeo and Cassius may be explained by a view expressed by Paul:

If someone who for reasons of age and health is perhaps incapable of having them institutes posthumous heirs, a previous will is broken, because regard must be had to the nature, and customary capacity of generating, in a man, rather than to a temporary defect or ill-health on account of which the man is deprived of the faculty of generating.[95]

In other words, the men in question may be chronically impotent, but, since they *are* physically whole men, there is at least a possibility that this condition might not be permanent.

Group (iii), however, are different. Since they manifestly do not possess the necessary sexual organs, they are obviously never going to sire any children. Proculus' argument is based on this physical fact.

The reasons, then, for the juristic interpretations vary from group to group; adoption is mentioned only incidentally, and as a point of comparison, in relation to group (i). As far as the legal evidence goes, therefore, there is no reason to believe that a *castratus* in Roman classical law was any less capable of adoption than any other man.

It is also important to recognize that D. 28. 2. 6 as a whole is concerned with *postumi* only in the strict sense of a testator's own natural children, born after his will was made. It is not concerned at all with

---

[94] Cf. 23. 3. 39. 1 (n. 90 above) on dowry, and *D.* 40.2.14.1, where manumission *matrimonii causa* by a *castratus* may be presumed to be a fraudulent attempt to circumvent the restrictions of the *lex Aelia Sentia* (Gaius 1. 18); Gardner, (forthcoming–*c*) Bachelors could adopt (*D.* 1. 7. 30), although presumably, at least after the reign of Nero, this would not exempt them from the inheritance restrictions placed by the Julian marriage laws on the childless: see 1.7 above.

[95] *D.* 28. 2. 9: 'Si quis postumos, quos per aetatem aut valetudinem habere forte non potest, heredes instituit, superius testamentum rumpitur, quod natura magis in homine generandi et consuetudo spectanda est, quam temporale vitium aut valetudo, propter quam abducatur homo a generandi facultate.'

either of the two other ways in which *sui heredes* might come into existence after the making of a will, that is by adoption of children, or by the birth of grandsons to *filiifamilias* (whether natural or adoptive) who themselves pass out of *potestas* before their father dies (so-called *postumi nepotes*: *D*. 28. 2. 29 pr.). By the time of Ulpian, it was accepted that *sui heredes* emerging by both of these other routes could also be instituted in wills in advance as *sui*. This was applied to grandsons (whether born before or after their own father's death), by interpretation and by legislation, between the first century BC and the early second century AD. It was not applied to adoptive *sui heredes* until some time after Gaius, but at latest by the time of Papinian (and so in the period from late second to early third century AD); before that, even if previously instituted by name, their subsequent adoption invalidated a will.[96]

Each type of 'posthumous' heir must, of course, have been appropriately identified in the will in order to be instituted. So, the *postumus* properly so-called would be instituted in terms such as 'if any son shall be born of me' or 'to my wife', and the grandson by a *filius* no longer *in potestate* by some such words as, 'if my son dies during my lifetime, then any grandson born of him'; persons subsequently adopted would presumably simply have been instituted initially as heirs by name.

Therefore the opinion of Proculus, followed by Julian and later jurists, that a *castratus* cannot institute a *postumus*, that is, a posthumous heir actually born of the testator, certainly does not imply that in classical law they could not adopt children, and so acquire 'posthumous' *sui heredes* in that way. This latter possibility was removed by Justinian. *Castrati* could not beget *postumi*, but neither, after Justinian's change in the rules of adoption (discussed in 2.5.3) could they acquire *sui heredes* directly or indirectly (i.e. through adoptive sons) by adoption. The same rule was applied to other men (except for paternal or maternal ascendants) who adopted children who were still *in potestate*; the effect of these adoptions was to make the adoptive children, who did not come into *potestas*, *sui heredes*, in so far as their claim to the intestate estate could not be toppled by other claimants,

---

[96] Gaius 2. 138–40; *D*. 28. 2. 4; 10; 13 pr.; 28. 2. 23. 1 (Papinian). On grandchildren, see esp. *D*. 28. 2. 29. Grandchildren born after their father's death were admitted to institution as *postumi* by interpretation (Aelius Gallus) and then by the *lex Junia Vellaea* (? AD 26); Julian extended this to cover those born during their father's lifetime but after the making of the will.

but, as Justinian's rescript on the subject (see n. 97) makes clear (§ 1d), their omission did not invalidate a will. However, it was still open to other men, whether relatives of the adoptee or not (but not to *castrati*), to adopt by adrogation, which carried the same legal force for both parties that it had before.

There seems no reason, therefore, to believe that *castrati* were unable, in classical law, to adopt; certainly, they could not perpetuate their line by natural means. Justinian's reasons for excluding *castrati* not only from adrogating, but also from adopting children in power, are unclear. His own reform of the legal rules for adoption, enacted a few years earlier, meant that adoption of someone *in potestate* by anyone other than a male ascendant (which, obviously, excluded both congenitally impotent and castrated males) did not involve the acquisition of *potestas* by the adopter, nor did the person adopted lose agnatic inheritance rights in his family of origin. Only adrogation continued to have these legal effects.[97] One would have expected therefore that *castrati* of all people might safely be allowed, if not to adrogate, at least to adopt, in order to have direct heirs; after all, something with the same effect had in certain circumstances been allowed even to women at least since the time of Diocletian (see 2. 5. 3 below).

Dalla suggests tentatively that the basis of Justinian's distinction might be the idea that adoption should imitate nature; the impotent male might, at least theoretically, be held to have hope of generating, the *castratus* obviously could not.[98] Another possible explanation may be put forward. The ban may have been actuated by moral objections—even though castration in most instances was neither self-inflicted nor voluntary, the condition was often associated with homosexual activity and male prostitution, both fiercely denounced and menaced with ferocious penalties in late Roman law. It may have been held objectionable that men who had engaged in such activities should be allowed even titular parenthood, without *potestas*, over other Roman citizens. Since no freeborn Roman could legally have been castrated (castration being prohibited, on pain of severe penalties, within the bounds of the empire, and most *castrati* therefore having

[97] Justinian's adoption reforms: *Cod. Iust.* 8. 47 (48). 10 (AD 530); Kurylowicz (1979) and (1984).
[98] *Inst.* 1. 11. 4: 'adoptio enim naturam imitatur' (which, however, in context refers to the relative ages of the parties); cf. the general and unqualified remark of Modestinus in *D.* 1. 7. 16. Dalla (1978) 180ff.

entered Roman society from slavery), those affected will in the main have been freedmen. The objection underlying the Justinianic ban would rest not solely on their libertine status (freedmen were otherwise capable of adoption) but rather on the presumed purposes of the castration. This is in some contrast to the more tolerant attitudes of an earlier age. The emperor Severus in a rescript said that what a woman had done for money while she was a slave was not deleterious to her standing (*fama*) once free; moreover, while retirement from various disgraceful professions (prostitute, actor, gladiator, beast-fighter) did not in classical law remove *infamia* from those who had practised them when free, they were not disqualified from adopting—the legal effects of *infamia* were much more restricted than that.[99]

2.5.3 *Adoption by Women*

Women could not adopt; this is stated, with varying amounts of emphasis, a number of times in the sources. The reason given is straightforward and obvious; women, unlike men, cannot have *potestas* over any other free persons, not even over their own children. This applied whether the children were legitimate or illegitimate; a married woman had no legal authority over her husband's children, and, unless she was *in manu*, was not even a member of the same *familia*. Children were not adopted by married couples, but by the husband alone, and his adoptive children were not related to his wife even as cognates.[100]

This situation did not change. Women in Justinianic law are still without *potestas*, and still declared to be unable to adopt; the statement in Justinian's *Institutes* is virtually identical with that in Gaius' *Institutes*. In the early third century, however, we begin to hear of the apparent possibility that some women may adopt, by special permis-

[99] Legal penalties for catamites (whether professional or amateur): Gardner (forthcoming-*c*). For repeated prohibitions against castration, whether of slaves or free men, from the late Republic onwards, see Dalla (1978) 78–116; for the persistence of trade in imported *castrati*, e.g. *D*. 39. 4. 16. 7 (Marcianus); *Cod. Iust*. 4. 42. 2 (AD 457–65); Justinian's efforts to eradicate the practice: *Nov*. 142 (AD 558). *Infamia* and disgraceful professions: *D*. 3. 2. 24; *D*. 48. 5. 14 (13). 2; Gardner (1993) 111–26, 150–1 and 223 n. 80.

[100] Gaius 1. 104: 'Feminae vero nullo modo adoptare possunt, quia ne quidem naturales liberos in potestate habent' (Women cannot adopt by any method, since they do not have *potestas* even over their own natural children); cf. Ulp. *Reg*. 8. 8a; *D*. 5. 2. 29. 3; *Cod. Iust*. 8. 47 (48). 5 (1711 Honoré), 7. 33. 8 (2547 Honoré); *Inst*. 1. 11. 10. The rule was not always observed in practice, at least in the provinces; there is some evidence from late Roman Egypt: Arjava (1996) 85. Adoptive children of husband: *D*. 38. 8. 1. 4.

sion from the emperor. 'Since', says Ulpian, 'a woman cannot adopt a son without an order from the emperor, neither can someone who supposed—wrongly—that someone was his adoptive mother bring a complaint of undutifulness against her will.'[101] This remark, attributed to Ulpian's' *Opinions*,[102] may originate in a real case, and the context is inheritance. If genuinely Ulpianic, this means that by the early third century at latest it was possible in certain circumstances for fictitious parenthood to be established between a woman and an unrelated person (even illegitimate children could by that time bring the complaint of unduteous will), which had at least some of the legal effects of blood relationship. It is important to note that the concession, as described by our sources, applies only to persons not descended by blood from the woman. There is no trace at all anywhere in our sources of women being given powers at any time to take steps to alter the existing legal relationship between themselves and their own children, legitimate or illegitimate, on the basis of their blood connection. We learn a little more from the first, and only, attested instance of such a grant, made by Diocletian to a certain Syra:[103]

Indeed, it is certain that it is impossible to be adrogated by a woman, who does not have even her own sons *in potestate*. However, since as consolation for the loss of your sons you desire to have your stepson in the place of legitimate offspring, we assent to your request, on the terms we have noted, and we allow you to have him, just as if he were born from you, as an honorary natural and legitimate son.

The grant is made in exceptional circumstances—the woman's own

---

[101] *D.* 5. 2. 29. 3: 'Quoniam femina nullum adoptare filium sine iussu principis potest, nec de inofficioso testamento eius, quam quis sibi matrem adoptivam falso esse existimabat, agere potest.' Cf. 5. 2. 29. 1: 'de inofficioso testamento matris spurii quoque filii dicere possunt' (illegitimate sons also can bring an action for undutifulness against a mother's will).

[102] A work wrongly attributed to Ulpian, but possibly deriving from his lengthy commentary on the praetor's edict: Schulz (1946) 182. It is unnecessary to suppose that *sine iussu principis* is a later interpolation; however, there is no justification for the supposition of Russo Ruggeri (1990*a*) 261–5, (1990*b*) 75ff., that Suetonius, *Galba* 4 refers to anything other than a 'testamentary adoption', or that it is evidence for such a use of imperial dispensation in the 1st cent. AD.

[103] *Cod. Iust.* 8. 47 (48) 5 (AD 291: 1711 Honoré): 'A muliere quidem, quae nec suos filios habet in potestate, adrogari non posse certum est. verum quoniam in solacium amissorum tuorum filiorum privignum tuum cupis in vicem legitimae subolis obtinere, adnuimus votis tuis secundum ea, quae adnotavimus, et eum proinde atque ex te progenitum ad fidem naturalis legitimique filii habere permittimus.'

sons have died—and so, the mention of adrogation suggests, has her husband. Evidently Syra is the widow of his second marriage, and there is at least one surviving son from his first; the stepson and Syra are the two remaining members of the household. In the sixth century, Justinian reiterates the general ban, and cites, as the one instance in which permission might be obtained for such 'adoption', mothers who have lost their own children: 'ex indulgentia principis ad solacium liberorum amissorum adoptare possunt' (as a special concession by the emperor they are allowed to adopt as consolation for children lost).[104]

What does such 'adoption' amount to? There can be no question of *potestas*; that is made abundantly clear. Ulpian's reference to the complaint of unduteous will makes it clear that certain inheritance rights—including, apparently the right to the *querela*—were acquired, and Diocletian's response indicates that these were the same as those that the woman's own natural children would have had. It is unlikely that such concessions began to be made very long before the time of Ulpian's comment. Until the passing of the *senatusconsultum Orphitianum*[105] in AD 178, even legitimate children succeeded to their mothers on intestacy only as cognates; 'adoption' of others would give them no more protection, if there were no valid will, than legitimate children. Both could still be ousted from the succession by the woman's agnates (or by her patron, if she was a freedwoman). After the *senatusconsultum*, her own children were secure, even if the will failed, but other heirs still were not. Permission to 'adopt' meant in effect that a woman without surviving children could have an heir of her own choice, secure in the knowledge that, even should her will fail, he or she would still have priority over other possible claimants. There is no evidence whether freedwomen, to whom such a provision was likely to be of particular interest, were particularly active in asking the imperial indulgence; we do not know even the status of Diocletian's petitioner Syra.

Were the benefits of being 'adopted' confined solely to inheritance of the money and property? A woman's natural children, whether legitimate or not, inherited patronal rights over her freedmen, if she had any. It is possible that this was so even before the *senatusconsultum*

---

[104] *Inst.* 1. 11. 10; that permission was granted only to childless women is the implication also of *Cod. Iust.* 7. 33. 8 (AD 294=2547 Honoré), below.

[105] For the *senatusconsultum Orphitianum*, see 1.2 at n. 23 and 3.3 below.

Orphitianum, since it is referred to in Paul's commentary on the edict; illegitimate children were probably added by legal interpretation.[106] Presumably 'adopted' children also inherited these patronal rights.

It is much less likely that such 'adoption' carried with it other legal consequences of normal adoption, such as bans on 'incestuous' marriages, obligations of *pietas* towards various members of the adoptive family, and so on (of course, some of these already applied to Syra's stepson, because of their existing relationship). This view is supported by Justinian's explanation of what is or is not comprised in the new-style adoption (by men) without *potestas*, which he introduces in AD 530.

In future, he says, the full traditional legal consequences of adoption, including *potestas*, will apply only to persons adopted by paternal or maternal (an important addition) ascendants, and not to adoptions by outsiders. The former (and so by implication *not* those adopted by outsiders) are expected to show *reverentia* towards their adoptive ascendants (something which would be expected of them in any case because of the blood relationship), and their acquisitions belong to their adoptive *pater*. There is, however, one signal difference: an extraneous adoptive father is free to leave the adoptive son nothing at all in his will, and there is no recourse to the complaint of unduteous will. This, Justinian explains, is because, since the adoptee had remained in the *potestas* of his natural father, whatever the son had acquired had been absorbed into the property of his natural, not his adoptive, father, and the latter therefore *owed* him nothing.[107] Obviously, this particular distinction would not exist between a natural and an 'adopting' mother, and, just as the *querela* was already available to children of the former, so it was to those 'adopted'.

In sum, then, this type of 'adoption' allowed a childless woman to pick an heir of her choice, who would take priority, should her will fail, over her agnates and/or her patron. The person adopted inherited patronal rights over her freedmen. He also had a right to expect gener-

---

[106] D. 38. 2. 18. Normally, inheritance of patronal rights went only to *sui heredes*, not to extraneous heirs (Gaius 3. 58). The public advantage of allowing women's children to inherit, from the point of view of social control, was that this reduced the number of *orcini*, freedmen without living patrons, so it may originate, at least for legitimate children, at the time of Augustan legislation on manumission (by which time children inherited as *legitimi*, the nearest thing a woman had to *sui heredes*).

[107] *Cod. Iust.* 8. 47 (48). 10. 1a, 1d.

ous treatment in her will (in practice, at least a quarter of the estate), failing which the 'complaint of unduteous will' was available to him. Every concession finds a fraudulent exploiter—or someone puzzled by it. Three years after his reply to Syra, Diocletian was approached by a certain Celsus,[108] who was having trouble over his mother's inheritance. An unnamed person was disputing the ownership of some slaves with him, on the pretext that they were his because Celsus' mother had adopted him, or perhaps merely intended to do so (*destinatae adoptionis*). All this had apparently happened some time ago, since the time limit for making a claim had passed; that does not matter, Diocletian tells him, since the other party had only recently got hold of the slaves. In any case, his opponent cannot claim ownership on the basis of an adoption which was not only merely prospective, but was not lawful (i.e. since, Celsus himself being alive, the woman still had a natural son). We are not told what evidence, either in a will itself, or of some other kind, the other man offered in support of his claim. Celsus' adversary may simply have been trying it on—or may have been a favourite (perhaps an *alumnus*, fosterling) of Celsus' mother, and both of them genuinely confused about the legalities of 'adoption' by women.[109]

2.5.4 Adoption of Women

Women *in potestate* could be adopted—there was no difficulty about that—though there is a dearth of evidence for actual instances of adoptions of women.[110] They may in practice (especially if there was a choice) have been less commonly chosen for adoption than men, since some at least of the usual purposes of adoption would not be served by the adoption of women. Women, even if closely related by blood, would not serve to preserve the family name and the agnatic line. Those adopting in order to perpetuate the family name would not choose for preference a woman as heir; rather, in the absence of kin on the paternal side, males in the female line of descent would be chosen for adoption. Gaius, discussing forbidden degrees of kinship for marriage, mentions 'a woman who has come through adoption

---

[108] *Cod. Iust.* 7. 33. 8 (AD 294: 2547 Honoré).

[109] B. Rawson (1986) 170–200, esp. 173–97; Nielsen (1987) 141–88. Cf. also the instance of mistaken belief mentioned by Ulpian, *D.* 5. 2. 29. 3 (above).

[110] None during the Republic; in the 1st cent. AD, the daughter of Domitius Tullus; plus three, or possibly four, attested in inscriptions: Salomies (1992) 20 n. 1.

to be in the position of daughter or granddaughter to me',[111] i.e. not one directly adopted, but the daughter of an adopted son (cf. D. 1. 7. 1. pr.—also Gaius—the sole reference under that title to female descendants), or someone transferred, by adoption within the *familia*, who comes into the *potestas* of an adopted son.

Moreover, adoption of women by adrogation was not possible at all until the imperial period. Gellius explains this by women's inability, as women, to participate in meetings of any voting assembly: 'feminis nulla comitiorum communio est.' Since adrogation was effected through a vote at a meeting of the *comitia curiata*, adrogation of women could not take place. However, Gaius raises no such formal objection, saying merely 'id magis placuit' (this is the opinion that has prevailed), which says nothing about the reason for the bar, and represents it merely as the majority opinion (after some debate) among jurists.[112]

There would have been no reason for such debate had there existed 'an obstacle of formal nature'.[113] However, Gellius' explanation and Gaius' are not incompatible. Gellius provides 'an obstacle of formal nature' (though not its original *raison d'être*), but it is one which by the second century AD was not obviously self-justifying, given the loss of political function of the *comitia* in the previous century. One may compare Gaius' doubts about the necessity of women's being in *tutela*, and his and other jurists' lack of awareness of its original purpose; similarly, Paul is content to ascribe women's incapacity to perform certain public functions to 'custom' and 'received practice'.[114]

Schulz dismisses Gellius' explanation out of hand, believing that the personal presence of the parties—the adrogator and the one being adrogated—in the *comitia* was unnecessary for what was merely the passing of a legislative act: 'the motion of the presiding magistrate and the vote of the assembly were the only requirements.' The

---

[111] Gaius 1. 59: 'quae mihi per adoptionem filiae sue neptis loco esse coeperit.' Contrast D. 23. 2. 17 pr.: 'eam, quam pater meus adoptavit et emancipavit' (whom my father adopted and emancipated); this, however, is in the context of manœuvres to permit marriage, where the emancipation of the natural daughter and adoption of the son-in-law is the more expected procedure (see n. 10 above) although the converse, emancipation of son and adoption of daughter-in-law, is also mentioned, perhaps for reasons of symmetry (or perhaps because Gaius had in mind a specific instance, where special motives operated).   [112] Gellius, *NA* 5. 19. 10; Gaius 1. 101.

[113] Donatuti (1961) 138.

[114] Gaius 1. 144, 190; Paul: D. 5. 1. 12. 2, 16. 1. 1; cf. Ulpian D. 50. 17. 2; Gardner (1993) 87–91.

consent of the two individuals, he suggests, would be ascertained by the Pontifex Maximus beforehand. For the same reason, as already remarked, he believes that *adrogatio* was also available under the comitial procedure to persons living in the provinces. However, this argument also involves his dismissing as 'simply erroneous' the explanation of Gaius of the term *adrogatio*, which derives it from actual direct question and answer between persons physically present.[115]

This is rather too cavalier a way of treating evidence. Gaius' account accords well with what is known of other areas in which the Romans persist in requiring the performance *viva voce* and face to face of certain traditional legal procedures of long standing, despite their inconveniences (not all successfully overcome).[116] Certainly, in the rescript procedure consent will have been obtained indirectly from the parties in their absence, and this may have been permitted also in the later stages of the life of the comitial procedure, when the *comitia* consisted of merely a token gathering of lictors. Gaius' hesitancy about the *raison d'être*, however, even if it might be held to provide some slender support for the view that personal physical presence was no longer absolutely requisite in his day, serves, if anything, to strengthen reason to believe in the accuracy of Gellius' explanation of the origin of the ban. The exclusion of women originated in early Rome, when the curiate assembly was an active political assembly, serving a compact community, and it is neither surprising nor, as just remarked, unparalleled to find the practice retained when the original technical reason for it was outmoded.

There was, however, a practical reason for continuing to refuse adrogation of women—not, as Schulz suggests, that 'the republican pontiffs apparently did not wish to have families maintained by the adoption of women', but rather that families *could* not be maintained in that way, since women had no *sui heredes* and therefore the agnatic line of descent must fail again after a generation. There was small advantage, therefore, in allowing it in general,[117] and perhaps also some resistance, since inevitably the interests of a woman's own civil heirs (her agnates) suffered. Imperial rescripts, on the other hand, began as isolated individual grants (like, probably, that for the adoption of Domitia Lucilla), for the benefit initially of a few favoured persons, and these in due course created a precedent.

---

[115] Schulz (1951) 144–5; Gaius 1. 99.
[116] Gardner (1993) 75–6, and chs. 6 and 7.   [117] So Buckland (1963) 125.

It is not surprising that, once the purely technical procedural difficulty of the *comitia* was removed, it should have been found perfectly acceptable for women to be adrogated. Neither the purpose nor the consequences of adrogating a woman were the same as those of adrogating a man. In both instances, a *familia* was terminated—but that of the woman was due to end with herself anyway, and her cognatic relationships were unaffected. Besides, there was an ancient institution, going back before the time of the Twelve Tables, which had virtually the same legal effects as adrogation, and that was taking into *manus* (normally found in connection with marriage, and so not excluding it, as adoption by a husband or his *pater* would). It would be more appropriate to think of the adrogation of a woman not in terms of termination of a *familia*, or failure to continue the *familia* of the adopter, but rather, like entry into *manus* or ordinary adoption, as an absorption into another *familia*. If the emperor was satisfied that there were good grounds for it in a particular instance, there was no reason to refuse.

Unfortunately, examples are lacking of adrogations of persons of either sex. Suitable occasions may be imagined—when, for instance, it was desired to secure an inheritance more safely than by will, in favour of a particular person who happened to be already *sui iuris*. It also provided a means of legitimating illegitimate children, whether freeborn or freed—but only, if they happened to be girls, after the rescript procedure was introduced.

Also, the possibility should not be overlooked that, even when procedurally possible, adrogation of females was not a favoured tactic. The development of increased rights of inheritance through the female line (to be discussed further at 3.3), especially the *senatusconsultum Orphitianum* of AD 178, which gave women's children (*liberi*) priority in inheritance over agnatic heirs, on the one hand weakened a possible motive for opposition to the adrogation of women (since they were no longer a 'dead end'), but on the other hand reduced the importance of adoption of women in general as a tactic for ensuring the transmission of property within families—while in freedman families, other considerations might make such adrogations an undesirable option (see 2.8 below).

When did adrogation of women by imperial rescript first become possible? Antoninus Pius was the first to allow adrogation by the *comitia curiata* for the other previously excluded group, the *impuberes*, i.e. those not yet adult, but that does not mean that an alternative method had not previously been used for women; reasons were given above[118] for believing that it was used, for instance, to permit the transfer of Domitia Lucilla into the *potestas* of her uncle while honouring her maternal grandfather's wish that she be released from her father's *potestas*. There is no reason to suppose that Antoninus Pius' measure in relation to children under age 'removed the last remaining *legal* objection to the adrogation of women';[119] the objections to the adrogation of *impuberes* were different in kind from those to the adrogation of women, and were overcome by different means, principally by the introduction (by Pius) of safeguards to protect the interests of *impuberes* (see 2.6 below).

Nor is it necessary to suppose that, despite the opportunity allegedly first created by Pius, Diocletian was the first, a century and a half later, to allow adrogation of women by imperial rescript.[120] Gaius declares that women could be adrogated by imperial rescript. There is no incompatibility between his two statements, (i) 'Also, women cannot be adopted by authority of the people, for this opinion has prevailed'; and (ii) 'Women also can be adrogated by imperial rescript'.[121] The first says only that adrogation of women before the *comitia curiata* is not possible, the other only that their adrogation by imperial rescript is possible; nothing in these texts excludes the supposition that both methods coexisted for a time, though only one could be used for the adrogation of males. There is therefore no reason to reject as interpolated and in need of emendation this and other references in the *Digest*[122] which speak of the adrogation of women.

---

[118] I.13, n. 197.

[119] J. A. C. Thomas (1967) 423, who rather misguidedly tries to draw parallels between legal objections to the adrogation of *impuberes* and of women; he notes that neither could have *sui heredes*. The two are not, however, parallel. Male *impuberes* once they became adults could have *sui heredes*; females never could. The legal objection to adrogating women was procedural.

[120] So J. A. C. Thomas (1967) 423–7, siding 'on balance' with those who take this view; cf. Kurylowicz (1981) 79.

[121] (i) Gaius I. 101: 'Item per populum feminae non adoptantur, nam id magis placuit'; (ii) D. I. 7. 21 (Gaius, *libro singulari regularum*): 'Et feminae ex rescripto principis adrogari possunt.'

[122] D. 28. 3. 8 (Ulpian) 'adoptione vel adrogatione filii filiaeve testamentum rumpi' (a will is broken by the adoption or emancipation of a son or daughter). D. 38. 17. 7 (Paul) 'Si quis intestatus decesserit relicta matre et fratre consanguineo vel sorore quamvis per adrogationem quaesitis, eadem iura in personam matris servantur, quae et naturalibus extantibus liberis' (If a man has died without a will, survived by his mother and by a blood brother or sister, even if they have been acquired by adrogation, the same rights are preserved in the person of a mother as where natural children exist). In other words, the mother gets nothing, since under the order of succession in

The one remaining text from the intervening period which might be held relevant is Ulp. *Reg.* 8. 5: 'Both males and females, and minors and adults, can be adopted by the praetor or provincial governor. However not even now can women be adrogated by the people [i.e. by the *comitia curiata*]; but minors indeed could not be adrogated, and now can, upon due enquiry, as a result of a constitution of the deified Antoninus Pius'.[123]

In the second part of the passage, dealing with adrogations, Ulpian omits to mention the possibility of the adrogation of women by imperial rescript; but this does not mean that it did not yet exist. The two halves of his statement are not symmetrical in their expression. On women, he specifies the method by which they *still* cannot be adrogated (which does not preclude the possibility of another method by which they can). On *impuberes*, he says that they are now able to be adrogated—without specifying any method at all.

In AD 294, Diocletian issued a reply to a certain Ison. 'When a *pater* gives a freedwoman's daughter, who is in his *potestas*, for adoption, the mother's patron is not prevented from adopting her. For the adrogation of a legally independent woman never proceeds unless by our rescript.'[124]

The question appears to be whether it is proper for a girl to be adopted by her mother's former owner. The situation appears to be that the freedwoman is married either to the *pater* (who is probably Ison) or to his son. The reply is so concise as to be elliptic, but may be understood as follows: Ison appears to think that the mother's status in relation to the intending adopter excludes adoption by the ordinary method. The reply, while including a brief outline of the facts, says in effect that this is irrelevant. The daughter is given in adoption by

the *sc. Tertullianum* both *liberi* and consanguineous brothers and sisters preceded her, or, if there were sisters only, they shared with her (Ulp. *Reg.* 26. 8). *Consanguineus* in the terminology of Roman law means agnate, with the same adoptive or natural father, not cognate: cf. *D.* 1. 7. 44; 38. 8. 4.

[123] 'Per praetorem vel praesidem provinciae adoptari tam masculi quam feminae, et tam puberes quam impuberes possunt. per populum vero feminae ne nunc quidem arrogantur; pupilli autem quidem [*qui olim* item Huschke] non poterant arrogari, nunc c(ausa) c(ognita) possunt ex constitutione divi Antonini Pii.'

[124] *Cod. Iust.* 8. 47 (48). 8 (2182 Honoré): 'In adoptionem patre, in cuius est potestate, libertae filiam dante, matris patronus adoptare non prohibetur. nam sui iuris adrogatio feminae nisi ex rescripto nostro numquam procedit.' The drafter of the rescript is identified by Honoré (1994) 177, with the eponymous Hermogenianus of the *Codex* of that name.

her *paterfamilias*, so there are no contra-indications to adoption by the normal method, and no need for special permission. If, however, she were legally independent, imperial rescript would be necessary.

In other words, the writer is drawing a distinction, for the benefit of a rather muddled enquirer, between the applicability of *adoptio* and *adrogatio*. The text tells us merely that adrogation of women by imperial rescript was by now possible—*not* that it now became possible for the first time. There is no reason, then, to postpone the appearance of the possibility of adrogating women to the end of the third century AD, since nothing in the evidence precludes its existence at a much earlier date, as much as two centuries previously.

2.6 PROTECTION OF THE *IMPUBES*

Children still in their father's *potestas* could be given in adoption at any age, even as infants. Augustus' adoption from their father Agrippa of his grandsons by Julia, Gaius and Lucius, when the elder was about 3 years old and the other an infant, was therefore legally unexceptionable. On the other hand, Agrippa Postumus, the last son of Agrippa (died 12 BC) was not adrogated until AD 4, when old enough to have already taken the *toga virilis* and become legally adult.[125] At that period, adrogation of *impuberes*, those not yet adult, was not permitted in Roman law. The reason given by Gellius is different from the one he reports for the ban on adrogating women. Obviously, someone not yet an adult had no independent power of legal action, and therefore could not personally take part in the *comitia curiata*, but neither, says Gellius, could he be represented there by his tutor: 'It is not right (*fas*) that tutors should have so much authority and power in regard to their wards, as to subject to the control of another person a free person entrusted to their good faith.'[126]

That is (or so the use of words like *fas* and *fides* suggests), it would be a moral abuse of the tutor's authority to attempt to use it in this way. Gellius' language, however, obscures the basic legal reason. Though

---

[125] Gaius 1. 102 says that private adoption of persons of any age whatever (*cuiuscumque aetatis*) is possible; D. 1. 7. 42 (Modestinus): 'Etiam infantem in adoptionem dare possumus' (We can give in adoption even an infant); Suet. *Aug.* 64–5.

[126] Gell. 5. 19. 10: 'tutoribus in pupillos tantam esse auctoritatem potestatemque fas non est, ut caput liberum fidei suae commissum aliena dicioni subiciant.'

sometimes more loosely described,[127] the responsibility and authority of a *tutor impuberum* was not over the person but over the property of his ward, *pupillus*. He had powers of administration over the property, and must give his authorization for any necessary legal actions relating to it, but no authority over matters affecting the personal status, *caput*, of the young person. He therefore did not have the legal power to speak in the ward's behalf and give consent for a *capitis deminutio*, a change of status, such as would be involved in adrogation.[128]

Here again, Gellius' information is out of date.[129] Antoninus Pius, Gaius informs us, had already made it possible for *impuberes* to be adrogated before the *comitia curiata*: 'Adoption by the people's authority of a person under puberty has at one time been forbidden, at another allowed. At present, as the result of a letter written by the excellent emperor Antoninus to the pontiffs, if there shall appear just cause for the adoption, it is permitted, subject to certain conditions.'[130]

From the time of Antoninus' letter, therefore, it was possible for *impuberes* to be adrogated, at least at Rome, and, as indicated, after careful preliminary enquiry and with provision for certain safeguards. There is no direct evidence as to how early imperial rescripts were used to permit the adrogation of people living in the provinces; as we have already seen, by the time of Diocletian imperial rescript was the only method in use in the Roman world as a whole.

Gaius does not discuss how the procedure in the *comitia* was modified. Someone would presumably have to consent to the child's being given in adoption, but we are not told whether this was the tutor or, perhaps more likely, a representative of the pontiffs. We do, however, know a good deal more about the 'certain conditions' which had to be satisfied before adrogation of an *impubes* was per-

---

[127] e.g. Servius cited by Paul (*D.* 27. 1. 1 pr.), 'vis ac potestas in capite libero ad tuendum eum, qui propter aetatem sua sponte se defendere nequit, iure civile data ac permissa' (force and power granted and permitted by civil law in the case of [*not* 'over'] a free person, for protecting someone who on account of his age is unable to take the initiative in protecting himself). Too much should not be read into this; it is an exaggeration to call it, as does Buckland (1963) 143, a new conception, that of guardianship; as Buckland observes, the rules remain essentially confined to matters relating to the patrimony. [128] See the discussion in Donatuti (1961) 137–41.

[129] Holford-Strevens (1988) 15, 222.

[130] Gaius 1. 102: 'Item, impuberem apud populum adoptari aliquando prohibitum est, aliquando permissum est. nunc ex epistula optimi imperatoris Antonini, quam scripsit pontificibus, si iusta causa adoptionis esse videbitur, cum quibusdam condicionibus permissum est.'

mitted, and also about the protection afforded him after adrogation. To the emperor's credit, he did not simply permit the adrogation of *impuberes*, but followed up this innovation with measures to safeguard their interests.

We already know that the pontiffs were expected, in ordinary applications for *adrogatio*, to enquire into such matters as the age of the would-be adopter, his state of health, and possible motives for *adrogatio*;[131] where the person to be adopted was a young child, there was much more to be guarded against. Attention is paid to two factors in particular. One is the danger of immoral motives—unless themselves blood relatives, the adopters must satisfy the enquiry as to the purity and disinterestedness of their affection (*sanctissima affectione ducti*), especially if they are less well-off than their intended wards. Particular care is taken, however, to avert possible damage to the financial interests of the *impubes*. Adrogation may be disallowed if there are other existing children and they and the *impubes* are both likely to inherit significantly less in consequence. Adrogation by tutors, not merely of an *impubes*, but of persons under the age of 25, is not normally allowed, to forestall the possibility of fraud, an exception being made by Pius in the case of a stepfather. There are additional safeguards. If the adrogation turned out not to have been in the interests of the *impubes*, he could on reaching adult age have it cancelled, subject to satisfying a judicial enquiry; this, notably, is the only instance in which a *filiusfamilias* could compel his *paterfamilias* to emancipate him.[132]

Since the entire property of the *impubes* was absorbed into that of his new *pater*, it was necessary to protect him from being exploited by the adopter and then left high and dry and bereft of property when his *pater* died or summarily emancipated him; the nature of the protection provided by a constitution of Pius is summarized by Paul:

By a constitution of the deified Pius on the adoption of an *impubes*, it is provided that of the property which at the time of death belonged to the person who adopted him one quarter is to go to the person adopted; but it is ordered also that the property which he acquired for his *pater* is to be restored to him; if he shall have been emancipated after judicial enquiry, he loses the quarter. If, therefore, anything has been alienated to defraud him, it can be recovered as if by a Calvisian or Fabian action.[133]

---

[131] *D.* 1. 7. 15. 2–3.

[132] *D.* 1. 7. 17, 31, 32, 33—on 31–3, see further below, and also in 2.7.

[133] *D.* 38. 5. 13: 'Constitutione divi Pii cavetur de impubere adoptando, ut ex bonis,

First, the *impubes* should not be left destitute at the death of his adoptive father; he was entitled to at least one-quarter of the estate (the amount that a testamentary heir was entitled to under the *lex Falcidia*, or a natural child under the *querela* of unduteous will).[134] Second, any property gained by the adoptive father as a result of the adrogation was to be returned to him (this could cover not only his original property but that accruing afterwards, e.g. legacies from natural relatives).

To prevent an unscrupulous person adrogating the *impubes* in order to get his hands on his property, then abandoning him, it was further provided that the adrogator could emancipate his adoptive son only after satisfying a court of enquiry as to the honesty of his motives; a possible case that comes to mind is to allow the *impubes* to accept an inheritance to which a condition of emancipation was attached. If the emancipation was allowed, i.e. if it was accepted that it was to the overall benefit of the *impubes*, then in that case he was not entitled to claim one-quarter of the adopter's property (though presumably he got his own back).[135] Paul adds, apparently as an interpretation of Pius' constitution, that he had a right, analogous to that provided for in the Calvisian and Fabian actions, to make a claim in respect of property he believed his adopter to have alienated in order to defraud him of his entitlement.

In short, in return for giving up ownership and control of his own property, he acquired a right to be treated in some respects as well as a natural child in the disposal of the estate of his adoptive father, and with some measure of additional guaranteed protection. Adults who

quae mortis tempore illius qui adoptavit fuerunt, pars quarta ad eum pertineat qui adoptatus est: sed et bona ei, quae adquisiit patri, restitui iussit: si causa cognita emancipatus fuerit, quartam perdit. si quid itaque in fraudem eius alienatum fuerit, quasi per Calvisianam vel Fabianam actionem revocandum est.' For the Calvisian and Fabian actions, see 1.8 above.

[134] This was due to him automatically, under Pius' constitution; to recover his due, he should bring a praetorian action. He need not have been instituted heir nor applied for *bonorum possessio* of the estate, nor was it necessary for him to bring a *querela* of unduteous will; if he mistakenly did bring the *querela* and lost, Ulpian advised that this should not impair his entitlement: *D.* 5. 2. 8. 15, 10. 2. 2. 1. The complications referred to by Ulpian (*D.* 37. 6. 1. 21) in regard to the requirement of *collatio* by someone, adopted as an *impubes* by adrogation, who is making a claim for possession of his *natural* father's property, could arise only in a situation where the natural father had previously been emancipated by his *pater* (cf. *D.* 37. 6. 5 pr., where, however, grandfather is still alive and claiming on behalf of the grandson in his *potestas*).

[135] The rule as stated by Justinian (*Inst.* 1. 11. 3) was that the adrogator returned the property if he emancipated the *impubes* with court approval; if he did so without court approval, he must also leave him one quarter of his own property.

gave themselves for adrogation were not accorded this right, since they were presumed to have been fully aware of what they were doing when they gave up their property and independence. However, someone adrogated as an *impubes*, and realizing when reaching adulthood that it had not after all been for his good, could obtain a court hearing; if successful he would be emancipated and 'recover his original legal right' (*pristinum ius reciperare*), which presumably covered property.[136]

A rescript issued to a certain Timotheus in AD 286, in the names of Diocletian and Maximian, provides some additional detail as to the mechanisms used at that time to ensure the provision of these safeguards; the enquiry by the pontiffs seems substantially to have been replaced by a combination of enquiry by the praetor or provincial magistrate, and declaration to a public slave. Timotheus is told

You wish to adrogate a person under the age of puberty to the position of a natural son. If those persons related to him by blood confirm to the prefect of the province that it is in his interests, you will have him as son, subject to the proviso that either in your will, or if you should emancipate him, one quarter of your property shall be given him; and concerning his patrimony that suitable guarantors be given and an undertaking made to a public slave, so that you may not under pretext of adoption make inroads into his property, which is to be kept for him with diligent forethought.[137]

Support for the adrogation must be obtained from the child's own family. Then existing law is stated; the adrogated child is entitled to one quarter of the property of the adopter if the latter dies or emancipates him (presumably without court approval). The new element is the imposition on the adopter of a liability, backed by an undertaking made to a public slave,[138] to manage the patrimony of the *impubes*

---

[136] *D.* 1. 7. 32–3. This, originating as a proviso laid down by Pius when giving exceptional permission for a tutor to adrogate his stepson, was generalized. On *pristinum ius reciperare*, see Buckland (1963) 126.12, a view followed by Donatuti (1961) 135.

[137] *Cod. Iust.* 8. 47. 2 pr. (1474 Honoré) 'Impuberem, quem ad vicem naturalis subolis adrogare desideras, si hi, qui sanguinis necessitudine iunguntur, id ei expedire apud praesidem provinciae confirmaverint, filium habebis, ita ut bonorum tuorum quarta pars tam in postremo iudicio tuo, quam si a te emancipatus fuerit, ei praebeatur et super patrimonio eius idoneis fideiussoribus datis servo publico caveatur, ne sub copulandae adoptionis obtentu in facultates eius, quae ei diligenti provisione servandae sunt, inruas.'

[138] For the procedural technicalities and the practical convenience of this declaration to a public slave, see Buckland (1963) 126 and the detailed discussion by Donatuti (1961) 145–57.

with the care and attention of a good head of household, for eventual return to him.

Justinian went further (*Inst.* 3. 10. 2), and gave adrogators, irrespective of the age of the persons adrogated, only the usufruct of the property acquired through the adrogation, 'ad similitudinem naturalium parentum' (on the analogy of natural parents)—a development resembling that of children's rights to maternal property (see 3.3 below). The reason for all this care and concern is obvious. Save for exceptional cases, such as the *prodigus* (the spendthrift, judged incompetent to manage his own affairs) and the madman,[139] the adult *paterfamilias* is autonomous in running the affairs of his own *familia*; whether he gives his child into adoption, or himself and those in his *potestas*, it is his decision, and not to be questioned by anyone else. The child *sui iuris*, however, who is adrogated is as yet neither mentally nor legally competent to make independent decisions about his *familia* (which for the moment consists only of himself and his property); additional legal protection is therefore provided.

What is more surprising is to find the interests of certain other persons receiving protection also. According to Marcellus, even if the case for adrogation was found satisfactory in other respects, the adrogator still had to give an undertaking to a public slave that in the event of the child dying before puberty his property would be restored to 'those to whom it would have come, had he remained in his original status'. Even if not in Pius' original constitution, this requirement must have been introduced fairly soon after, since it is known to Marcellus.[140]

We learn from Ulpian that eligible claimants were interpreted as including the beneficiaries of secondary wills made by the child's father, by the practice known as 'pupillary substitution' (*substitutio pupillaris*). Since a child could not make a will, it was commonplace at least as early as the late Republic for a father instituting a child in his *potestas* as his heir to appoint an alternative heir to take the inheritance should the child, after inheriting, die before reaching puberty, i.e. before being legally capable of making a will—and so in effect to make a will on his child's behalf. Since adrogation, like emancipation,

---

[139] Twelve Tables 5. 7; Crawford (1996) 643–6.

[140] D. 1. 7. 18 'ad quos res perventura esset, si adrogatus permansisset in suo statu'; 20. Later Ulpian adds (*D.* 1. 7. 19. 1) that claimants were allowed an action even if the adrogator had failed to give an undertaking.

had the effect of cancelling the pupillary substitution, this secondary will failed.[141]

It is clear, however, that it was not primarily the testamentary intentions of a previous *paterfamilias* which were being respected. 'Those to whom the property would have come' meant in the first instance those who would have inherited, but for the adrogation, had there been no secondary will on the child's behalf at all, that is, the child's own legitimate heirs[142]—who had ceased to be *heredes legitimi*, because adrogation broke the agnatic links.

Who were these *heredes legitimi*? The range was potentially wide—agnates (that is, brothers and sisters and brothers' children), some mothers (since this post-dates the *senatusconsultum Tertullianum*, for which see 3.3), living natural fathers (if the *impubes* had been emancipated), and perhaps even patrons who (presumably showing just cause before a tribunal as required by the *lex Aelia Sentia*: Gaius 1. 18–19) had manumitted a child slave.[143] What was being protected? Not the child's economic well-being—he was already dead. If the child had not been adrogated, they would have been bound to inherit on intestacy, since he died too young to make a will. If the adrogated child had survived to puberty, they had no claim, since he could then free himself from *potestas* if that was in his interests, and could make a will; but if he died before puberty, they were regarded as having a better right than the adrogator to inherit whatever property he had taken with him into his new *familia*.

The grounds were perhaps equitable—they were linked by blood (the mother) or *potestas* and the gift of freedom (the patron) or both blood and *familia*, in the case of the manumitting parent and the siblings, and their claim was held to outweigh that of the new *paterfamilias*, who otherwise might make a profit from the dead child, without much expenditure of time, emotion, or responsibility. The situation and the handling of it bears a curious, if only partial, resemblance to that of the freed slave 'suis nummus emptus' (bought with his own money). In this latter arrangement of convenience, the person who collusively bought the slave from his owner, purely for

---

[141] Gaius 2. 179–84; *D.* 1. 7. 17. 1; 19 pr.; Watson (1971a) 53ff.

[142] So Papinian, *D.* 28. 6. 40. who treats the application to *substituti* as rising from interpretation.

[143] Though the general rule was that one was not to adrogate someone else's freedman, there were some exceptions: Gardner (1989) 242–8.

the purpose of manumitting him, had his purchase money refunded, but did not have *gratis* the full rights of a patron.[144] Similarly, the adrogator who had acquired a child complete with property was not to have the rights of an heir, if there were better claimants extant from the child's previous status.

Why was the possibility of adrogating *impuberes* introduced by Pius, and why just then? Fatherless young children were neither a rare nor a new phenomenon in Roman society. The alternative, however, to taking the children into *potestas* was that a tutor should undertake the responsibility, in the child's interest, of administering his property and arranging for his maintenance out of his resources. There was provision for this in the Twelve Tables; if the *paterfamilias* had not nominated a tutor in a will, the agnates automatically took on the *tutela*, as *tutores legitimi*.[145] Failing either of these, by legislation beginning from some time early in the second century BC tutors were appointed by those magistrates specifically authorized to do so by law, decree of the senate, or imperial appointment.[146]

Both women and young children required tutors. There are signs, however, that the tutorship was often a duty reluctantly undertaken, and one which many made efforts to avoid; correspondingly compulsion increased. The rules for exemption were developed and elaborated under successive emperors up to Marcus Aurelius, perhaps beginning with Claudius. Tutors appointed by magistrates could not refuse unless they had a very good excuse; testamentary tutors could, but risked losing their benefit under the will. Of *tutores legitimi*, who were in civil law heirs on intestacy, only those of women were free to refuse; tutors of young children could not obtain exemption.[147] Gaius' explanation of the difference is curious: 'Agnates, patrons and manumitters of free persons are allowed to make a legal cession of *tutela* over women to someone else; but *tutela* over male wards cannot be ceded, because it does not appear burdensome, since it terminates with puberty.'[148]

[144] W. W. Buckland (1908) 640; Gardner (1993) 36–7.

[145] Twelve Tables 5. 6; Crawford (1996) 642; Watson (1975) 71–5.

[146] Gaius I. 185; *D.* 26. 1. 6. 2 (Ulpian); so, Claudius assigned the duty to consuls: Suet. *Claud.* 23. 2; Buckland (1963) 147–8.

[147] Gaius I. 165–6, 168; *Vat. Frag.* 123–47; *D.* 27. 1; Buckland (1963) 149–50; Kaser, (1971) 356.

[148] Gaius I. 168: 'Agnatis et patronis et liberorum capitum manumissoribus permissum est feminarum tutelam alii in iure cedere; pupillorum autem tutelam non est permissum cedere, quia non videtur onerosa, cum tempore pubertatis finiatur.'

2.6 Protection of the Impubes

The implication is that *tutela* both of women and of young children was generally regarded as a burdensome chore, but that over women was accepted as being more irksome simply because it lasted longer. However, the responsibilities of women's tutors, though potentially longer-lasting, were in fact much less onerous than those of *tutores impuberum*. *Tutela* over women, unlike that over children, did not carry the burden of administrative responsibility or accountability, nor extend over all kinds of property (women, indeed, had a large degree of freedom in the management of their property), and it had lost much of its remaining importance with the introduction by Augustus of the *ius liberorum*. On the other hand, the tutor of a child had full responsibility until the child reached adulthood for proper care and management of the property, and he was accountable.

Gaius' statement is evidence for attitudes current in his day towards the chore of *tutela*, but not for the reason for the rule. Though the short duration of the responsibility of *tutela impuberum* is presented as a reason for refusal, that may be merely his attempt to account for a discriminatory rule which was in fact of long standing,[149] and based on the much more important factor of what was at stake. Young children could not make wills and necessarily, should they fail to reach puberty, died intestate. Women, however, being adults, could make wills, and, especially if they had children, there would be considerable moral pressure on tutors to allow them to do so.

It is likely, therefore, that the original reason for the discrimination was not the laboriousness or duration of the respective responsibilities borne (in common with other types of tutor) by the agnate tutors of women and children, but rather consideration of the future of the patrimony. As we have already observed in 1.6, from an early date there was a conflict of interest between agnates in a woman's *familia* of origin and her blood descendants, with increasing emphasis upon the claims of the latter. Dispersal of property outside the *familia* through women was therefore to some extent accepted as desirable, and there was less reason to insist upon available agnates, even though they were the civil law heirs on intestacy, fulfilling the role of tutor if

---

[149] As Gaius remarks elsewhere (1. 157, 171), automatic agnate *tutela* of women, where no other provision had been made, had been abolished by Claudius, and therefore the mention of agnates is no longer applicable; this implies that he is here quoting a long-established rule, an idea supported also by the secondary, analogous origin of other forms of *tutela legitima*, exercised by patrons and manumitting parents (1. 165–6).

the deceased had made no other provision. The property of the *impubes*, however, should the child die, had no destination other than his agnates; they, more than anyone else, had a responsibility to preserve the property which was part of the patrimony of the *familia* to which they also belonged.

Granted the correctness of this explanation, the question remains of why Gaius gave a different one. The answer, I suspect, is that the true reason was no longer obvious by his time, the rule being of early origin and originally applying only to agnates. Agnate *tutela* was by now probably rare, both because of the prevalence of the practice of naming tutors in wills, and also because of the demographic conditions of Roman society where, as already indicated, there seems to have been a chronic shortage of agnates. Most *tutores legitimi* will not have been agnate guardians of orphans, but rather patrons and manumitting parents, whose tutelary status was self-inflicted; reluctant though some might be to exercise it, exemption was scarcely to be expected. Only a minority, however, were *legitimi*; most tutors were responsible for orphans.

Gaius' suspiciously inapt explanation therefore perhaps indirectly indicates the reasons for which adrogation of *impuberes* began to seem acceptable in Rome of the second century AD. In a society in which an appreciable proportion of young Romans were fatherless before puberty,[150] in which agnate tutors were scarce and the reluctance of nominated tutors to perform necessitated magisterial coercion with increasingly formalized rules for exemption, and in which also other demographic factors perennially threatened the extinction of *familiae*, adrogation of the young fulfilled the double function of providing heirs for dying houses, and care for the economic affairs of orphan children (with an incentive for the adopter, not offered to tutors, in the use of the child's property). Above all, it was a way of ensuring the continuance of the Roman élite.

What event or events, if any, in particular stimulated the emperor initially to take action cannot be determined. There is only one reference in our texts to what was possibly an individual approach to the emperor; in a rescript Antoninus Pius gave permission for a tutor to adopt his stepson, to whom he was tutor. This, however, has the appearance of a special exception to an existing rule. According to

---

[150] Saller (1994) 189 estimates the proportion as one-third, basing this on computer simulations detailed in pp. 43–69.

Ulpian, adrogation of wards by their tutors was normally forbidden; the exception in favour of adopters who were blood relatives or otherwise of unimpeachably pure affections may have been generalized from an original rescript in response to an individual approach, or may have been introduced as a general regulation in an attempt to reduce the scale of what was beginning to be felt as a widespread social problem.[151] *Tutela* features quite prominently in the legal evidence for Pius' reign. Whereas for Hadrian there are a dozen mentions,[152] all but one concerned with reasons for being excused from the performance of *tutela*, for Pius there are almost twice as many,[153] on a variety of matters including tutorial liabilities and fraud, and almost all cited as rescripts. This—not so much the relative numbers, which cannot be taken as statistically significant, as the variety of problems—suggests that the emperor and his legal department had some inkling of the scale and legal complexity of the problem of fatherless children. Adrogation, given suitable safeguards, may have seemed a sensible way of reducing the legal workload while providing for those too young to manage their own affairs.

2.7 CONSENT TO ADOPTION

Referring to the adoption of a son in power, Buckland (1963) 124 remarks cautiously: 'The question whether the consent of the *adoptatus* was necessary for classical law is obscure'—an uncertainty shared by a few scholars, although most come down against the necessity of such consent.[154] Modern discussion is based essentially on two texts.

Justinian in AD 530 asserts that by an old rule of law a *filiusfamilias* can object (*contradicere*) to being given in adoption, and is not compelled to be transferred to another *familia* against his will; his own rules for

---

[151] D. 1. 7. 32. 1 (Papinian); 1. 7. 17 pr.–1 (Ulpian): the references to tutors suggest that *pupilli* in this text is not merely a synonym for *impuberes* but means specifically 'wards'.

[152] D. 26. 7. 12. 1; 27. 1. 6. 8, 19; 15. 17; 27. 8. 1. 8, 9; *Vat. Frag.* 141, 151, 222, 223, 235, 244.

[153] D. 1. 7. 32. 1; 3. 5. 3. 4; 4. 4. 45. 1; 13. 6. 3 pr.; 22. 1. 17. 2–3; 26. 4. 1. 3; 26. 5. 2; 26. 7. 2 pr.; 11; 26. 8. 1 pr.; 5 pr.; 26. 10. 3 pr.; 27. 1. 6. 2, 7, 8, 10, 19; 17. 1; 27. 3. 1. 13; *Vat. Frag.* 223; *Inst.* 1. 25. 8.

[154] See esp. Russo Ruggieri (1990a) 334–9, who inclines on no real evidence to the view that at least absence of opposition was required. On the other hand, Volterra (1966) 124–6, surveying the same evidence, insisted on the irrelevance of the adoptee's wishes, and this is the predominant view.

adoption procedure require that the adoptee, who must be present, does not oppose the adoption.[155] However, what this 'old rule of law' mentioned by Justinian may be is a mystery. A text attributed to the Hadrianic jurist Celsus says: 'In adoptions, enquiry is made as to the wishes only of those who are legally independent; but if they are being given in adoption by their *pater*, in these cases the will of both parties must be ascertained, by their consenting or not making objection.'[156]

Clearly, there is something wrong here. The second half of this passage does not make sense as it stands; it is implicit in the contrast with the first part that the wishes of the *filiusfamilias* being given in adoption are immaterial (and *utriusque* 'both parties' is otiose, since in the nature of things the consent of the *paterfamilias* is already evident). It is generally assumed that the text has been interpolated, although an attempt has been made to save something from Celsus' text by suggesting that classical law required, if not the positive consent of the son, at least the absence of express opposition.[157] Unfortunately, there are no other legal texts at all which can be used to support or undermine this idea. The only other text brought into discussions of the question is a passage from the *Controversiae* of the elder Seneca, *Contr.* 2. 1. 19–20 (justifiably dismissed as irrelevant by most scholars), where the fictitious situation posited as a basis for presentation of arguments is 'A rich man has repudiated (*abdicavit*) three sons. He asks a poor man for his one son in adoption. The poor man is willing; when his son refuses, he repudiates him.'

Seneca's text is not concerned, however, with the law as it stands. The passage is an exercise in rhetorical *divisio*, ways of constructing lines of argument, and the situation is unreal. *Abdicatio*, a Greek prac-

---

[155] *Cod. Iust.* 8. 47 (48). 10 pr.: 'Et contradicendi filio ex iure vetere datur licentia et invitus transire ad aliam familiam non cogitur.' Two months later Justinian, again writing to the praetorian prefect, this time about simplifications in the adoption procedure, specifies that all that is required is a declaration to the magistrate by the *pater*, in the presence of all three parties concerned, and 'eo qui adoptatur . . . non contradicente' (without opposition by the adoptee). For 'against his will', cf. Paul, *Sent.* 2. 25. 5: 'Filiusfamilias emancipari invitus non cogitur' (A son in power is not emancipated against his will); see 1.1 n. 2 above. Paul's statement, suspected of being post-classical, is confirmed only by a law of Anastasius (*Cod. Iust.* 8. 48. 5: AD 502).

[156] D. 1. 7. 5: 'In adoptionibus eorum dumtaxat qui suae potestatis sunt voluntas exploratur: sin autem a patre dantur in adoptionem in his utriusque arbitrium spectandum est vel consentiendo vel non contradicendo.'

[157] Russo Ruggeri (1990) 334–9.

tice, was not recognized as having any effect in Roman law.[158] The theme was evidently a stock fictional one from the rhetorical schools, and Seneca sets out two model treatments for the son's speech of protest, by the Augustan rhetoricians Arellius Fuscus and Pompeius Silo.

Fuscus' treatment is divided into arguments from law (*de iure*) and from duty (*de officio*). The former are not in fact legal arguments, but merely those of sophistic rhetoric; they are, with some abridgement, (i) 'If I am subject to my father because I am his son, it is doubtless in order that I may be his son . . . and I am responding to his repudiation, in order not to cease to be his son'; (ii) 'If I am losing my father, what difference does the method make? *If I cannot refuse* [my italics], why repudiate me instead of transferring me?' In (ii), it is taken for granted that the son's opposition is legally immaterial.

Silo starts with 'the hackneyed and derided ploy' (*vetere et explosa quaestione*) 'Is a father to be obeyed in everything? And even if in everything, yet is he nevertheless not to be obeyed when it is being brought about that he is not a father?' He continues: 'Can a son be given in adoption against his will? If not, then can he be repudiated for the reason that he is exercising his own judgement? Or, granting that he can [sc. be given in adoption against his will], then can he be repudiated, not when he is acting against his father's will, but when he is using his judgment badly?' (That is, can he be repudiated for making a bad decision, irrespective of whether or not it is going against his father's wishes?)[159]

The argument is contorted, but clearly Silo is not seriously questioning whether or not the father has the power to give his son in adoption against his will. An entirely artificial opposition is set up: giving in adoption and repudiation are treated as mutually exclusive alternatives—though the latter was not, for the Romans, a practice

---

[158] Quint. *Inst. Or.* 7. 4. 11; *Cod. Iust.* 8. 46 (47). 6 (Diocletian: 1539 Honoré); Saller (1994) 117–18.

[159] Sen. *Contr.* 2. 1. 19–20 (Fuscus): (i) 'Si ob hoc subicior patri quia filius sum, in hoc sine dubio, ut filius sim; et ad manum argumentum est: nempe abdicanti respondeo. Quid ita? Cum ei respondeo, scilicet id ago, ne desinam filius esse; atque idem ago, cum respondeo emancipanti.' (ii) 'Quid enim ad amittendum patrem interest, utrum eiiciar an transferar? Si non licet recusare, cur potius abdicas me quam tradis . . . (Silo) an in omnia patri parendum sit; etiamsi in omnia, an ibi tamen non sit parendum, quo efficitur ne pater sit; deinde quaesiit an invitus filius dari in adoptionem possit; si non potest, an ob id abdicari possit, quod arbitrio suo usus est; an ut possit, possit non cum contra voluntatem patris, sed cum male arbitrio suo utitur.'

with consequences recognized in law. Clearly, neither rhetorician is offering any serious challenge to the father's right to remove his son from the *familia*, whatever the son's wishes.[160]

Moreover, several legal texts make it clear that children *in potestate* had no power to control the actions of a *paterfamilias*, either to terminate or continue the *potestas*. According to Modestinus, infants could be given in adoption. Clearly, they were in no position to express an objection. Again, Marcianus states positively that a *filiusfamilias*, whether natural or adopted, could not compel his *pater* to emancipate him. He goes on to complete the text of a rescript of Antoninus, cited by Papinian in support of the statement that on occasion someone adopted when under the age of puberty could, on attaining adulthood, obtain a hearing before a magistrate to demand emancipation; but it is clear that only adrogation is in question. On balance, then, it appears that in classical law *filiifamilias*, of whatever age, could be given in adoption without their consent being sought.[161]

On the other hand, there is clear evidence that one particular kind of adoption could not be carried out without the consent of a *filius* particularly, though indirectly, affected by it. This, discussed further in 2.9 below, was the adoption of someone as a grandson, and his assignment to an existing *filiusfamilias*, as if born of the latter. The require-

---

[160] The value to be attached to this passage of Seneca is rather restrainedly summed up by Voci (1980) 45 n. 43: 'Dalla lunga controversia di Seneca è impossibile ricavare un dato sicuro: il metodo è, come sempre, quello di porre ipotesi contrarie e di dedurne i risultati possibili' (No certain conclusion can be drawn from Seneca's lengthy controversy; as always, the method is that of positing contrary hypotheses and deducing from them the possible results). More bluntly, Volterra (1966) 124 dismisses the text with the comment that a simple examination of the arguments of this theme for schoolboys shows that the procedure of adoption was quite independent of the wishes of the adoptee.

[161] D. 1. 7. 31 (Marcianus), 32 (Papinian), 33 (Marcianus); 1. 7. 42 (Modestinus). Against such evidence, Paul, *Sent.* 2. 25. 5 ('a son in power cannot be emancipated against his will'), already discussed, can carry little weight. As Buckland (1963) 124 n. 3 observes, if even tacit consent of a *filiusfamilias* were required, we should expect to find some mention of provision for *restitutio in integrum* ('going back to square one'), but there is none. Russo Ruggeri (1990a) 334–8, hedges; while recognizing the difficulties of alleged evidence to the contrary, she is nevertheless reluctant to accept that consent was not required, and suggests (338) that it was 'plausible' that in the classical period what was required was not explicit consent but the absence of a specific statement of opposition. This she justifies by a reference to Celsus' known interest in the problems of willingness ('fu particolarmente attento, come è noto, ai problemi della *voluntas*'); the relevance of the ethos of Hadrianic policy towards children of irregular unions, in which she accepts a modern view that Celsus had a determining role (references at 338 n. 62), is, at best, tenuous.

ment that the *filius* give his consent may have been existing practice by the first century AD, and incorporated by Julian in the edict. Paul, in his commentary on the edict, says, 'Julian also writes this', implying that Julian was not the first to take this view; Masurius Sabinus may have expressed himself on the legal consequences of such adoptions. A grandson so adopted, with the son's consent, was not recognized as a *suus heres*, since after the grandfather's death he did not become legally independent but fell into the *potestas* of the son who was his notional father; but if the son had not consented to the adoption, the grandson did not come under his *potestas* (and so presumably was counted as a *suus heres* with a claim to an entire separate share of the inheritance—a no-win situation for the son).[162]

This insistence on obtaining the consent of a *filius* to having an adoptive grandson foisted upon him in this way was doubtless well intentioned, but as just indicated, and explained further below (2.9), it was unlikely to be of much practical value to the *filius*. Here, as in other matters of adoption and emancipation, if it came to a clash of wills, grandfather, as *paterfamilias*, always had the whip-hand.

2.8 ADOPTION IN FREEDMAN FAMILIES

For ex-slaves, adoption might be expected to hold particular attractions. Conjugal relations between slaves were not recognized as marriages in law. Once a slave was freed, it was on occasion found desirable to take account of existing biological relationships for certain purposes, such as the avoidance of incest between natural parent and child, or, where *potestas* was irrelevant, the observance of the *pietas* due to a mother.[163] However, formation of a family which was recognized in law as such, i.e. a *familia*, with legitimate children born of a lawfully wedded wife, subject to *patria potestas* and with concomitant inheritance rights, became a possibility only after they had been released from slavery. For many, this might already be too late; the *lex Aelia Sentia*[164] of AD 4 made 30 the minimum age for manumission, except in certain special cases. For women slaves, the consequences were particularly serious, since it meant that a large part of their

---

[162] D. 1. 7. 6 (Paul 35 *ad edictum*), 10 (Paul 2 *ad Sabinum*), 11 (Paul 4 *ad Sabinum*).
[163] D. 2. 4. 4. 3, 5; 23. 2. 14. 2; 23. 2. 54.   [164] Gaius 1. 13–21, 25–6, 36–41.

child-bearing life was past before they could begin to bear freeborn children at all, legitimate or otherwise.

Children born in slavery and subsequently freed were, in the eyes of the law, fatherless, and belonged to different families from their parents. Many illegitimate children were also born to freedwomen. Despite their legal designation, *volgo concepti*, 'conceived at large', their conception did not necessarily result from promiscuity.[165] The father might be the mother's owner, who had set her free before the child's birth, but who was unable or unwilling to marry her. He might be a fellow slave, not freed in time to marry her before the child's birth—or not freed at all.[166]

Even if all three, father, mother, and child—or even father and child—achieved freedom, they might not all be citizens; slaves not properly freed according to the requirements of the *lex Aelia Sentia* had, under the *lex Junia*, merely the status of 'Junian Latins'. Not only did such mixed-status families have no access to the opportunities available to citizen freedmen and freedwomen of 'regularizing' their relationships in law, they had no way of providing for their children; patronal claims were paramount. Since, under the *lex Aelia Sentia*, slaves had to be at least 30 years old to become citizens on manumission, this imposed a serious delay—specially for the mother—in starting a freeborn family. Women could, however, become citizens under the age of 30 if they were freed in order to marry their patrons, and there are over thirty examples in the funerary inscriptions of *CIL* 6 (Rome) alone of the expressions 'patron and husband' and 'freedwoman and wife', perhaps intended to demonstrate that the mother was a citizen.[167]

Even for those ex-slaves who achieved freedom and citizen status for both children and parents, the difficulties did not stop there. How could they set about turning their fractured family into a *familia*? And would it necessarily be in their best interests to do so?[168]

---

[165] D. 1. 5. 23 (Modestinus) 'Volgo concepti dicuntur qui patrem demonstrare non possunt, vel qui possunt quidem, sed eum habent, quem habere non licet' ('Conceived at large' is what those people are called who cannot identify their father, or who can, but who have one whom it is not lawful to have).

[166] Traces of such family situations are sometimes detectable in inscriptions: Flory (1984) 216–24. See also 3.7 below.

[167] Sirks (1983) 211–92; Gardner (1986a) 225, (1989) 254 n. 42. Examples are Passienia Gemella and Julia Helpis cited in the text.

[168] These, and related problems and alternative possibilities are considered also in Gardner (1997).

Illegitimate children could be 'legitimated' by being taken into *potestas*; and this could be achieved by adoption.[169] This might seem straightforward—but not for ex-slaves and their families. In the first place, both father and child had to be Roman citizens.[170] If the child was Roman (of a Roman mother) and the father Junian Latin, there was a possibility, albeit a fairly slim one, that the father might become a Roman citizen and thereby acquire *potestas* over the child,[171] making adoption unnecessary, but not if things were the other way round, i.e. the father Roman and the mother and child Latin. Secondly, even if both father and child were Roman citizens, since the child was legally fatherless and therefore *sui iuris*, adoption would have to be carried out by adrogation. Female children therefore could not be adopted at all, until the comitial procedure was replaced by imperial rescript. Whether very many adoptions, even of sons, are likely to have been performed is doubtful; the practical difficulties of carrying though an adrogation have already been discussed. There are a very few possible—though not certain—examples in inscriptions.[172]

There could be additional legal problems in adrogating children who were themselves ex-slaves. If the child had been born in slavery and subsequently freed, he was the freedman of his former owner, who, if still alive, had normal patronal rights over him; these also[173]

---

[169] Legitimation by the subsequent marriage of the parents did not appear until Constantine, and then only for restricted categories of existing freeborn Romans, was temporarily given prospective application by Anastasius in AD 517, and was not generalized until Justinian: *Cod. Iust.* 5. 27. 5, 6, 7, 8, 10, 11; *Nov.* 12. 4, 18. 11, 78. 4; Buckland (1963) 129; van de Wiel (1978) 307–50 and (1992) 327–58; Arjava (1996) 212–13.

[170] Ulp. *Reg.* 10.3: 'Neque autem peregrinus civem Romanum, neque civis Romanus peregrinum in potestate habere potest' (An alien cannot hold a Roman citizen in power, nor a Roman citizen an alien).

[171] Gaius 1. 29, 66; this applied also if both parents were Latin: Weaver (1990), 275–305, esp. 275–81.

[172] Gardner (1991) 253–7; where the child is described as 'son and freedman' or the parent as 'patron and father', the latter could either have fathered the child on one of his own slaves, or have fathered him while still himself a slave, and bought and freed him after his own manumission—the designation as 'son', however, is not proof positive that an adoption had taken place. Salomies (1992) 16, 43–4 finds only eight examples of inscriptions in which adoption is explicitly referred to, and of these only one indicates that the adoptee was illegitimate: *CIL* 6. 33513 (=*ILS* 8556) 'M. Aurelius Sp. f. Secundus, quem sibi T. Sextius Hilarus adoptarat.' Enquiry is not helped by the ambiguity or inadequacy of clues to status in much epigraphic evidence: Gardner (1991) 244–5, with bibliography in nn. 21–2.

[173] Except for the right to *operae* (services), to which special conditions applied: *D.* 38. 1. 5, 22. 1; 50. 16. 70.

passed on the patron's death to his children. [174] If the freedman were brought under someone else's *potestas*, this produced a conflict of interest; therefore adopting someone else's freedman was one of the circumstances in which, according to Ulpian, one 'ought not' to adrogate without good grounds: 'Likewise one ought not to adrogate more than one person, save on good grounds (*iusta causa*); but neither ought one to adrogate someone else's freedman, or an older person a younger.' [175]

The implication is that in the absence of special factors permission to adrogate would not be granted. That the would-be adopter was the freedman's own biological father was likely to be accepted as 'good ground', at least under the Empire. [176] Ulpian says: 'A slave born to me while I was a slave can be brought into my *potestas* by special grant of the emperor.' [177] Since this remark comes from Ulpian's commentary on the *lex Julia et Papia* it is possible that the 'special grant' was instituted in one or other law as one of several ways in which ex-slaves were given encouragement by Augustan marriage legislation to form traditional Roman *familiae*, headed by a *paterfamilias*; special permission was needed, because, as the rest of Ulpian's text makes clear, the child also had been born in slavery and subsequently freed. There is perhaps the implication that such natural children, once legitimated by adoption, were allowed to count towards relief from the penalties of childlessness, or even the achievement of the *ius liberorum*.

Such special imperial permission would presumably not be needed when a freedman was adopting a natural child who was also his own freedman (i.e. bought and subsequently manumitted by him), or, indeed, when an owner manumitted and adopted a slave child fathered by him. Tolerance towards this practice, however, did not extend all

---

[174] Gaius 3. 45–7, 53–4, 58, 64; D. 37. 15. 5; Watson (1987) 39–40. Tryphoninus D. 38. 2. 50. 5 posits a case where a patron's son is also the freedman's *suus heres*, having been adopted by him, and is left by will a lesser portion than his due (whether as *filius* or as sole survivor of the patron's family is not clear); but as patron's son he can refrain from taking up the inheritance under the will and claim the lot on intestacy. This is fairly obviously a theoretical example.

[175] D. 1. 7. 15. 3: 'Item non debet quis plures adrogare nisi ex iusta causa, sed nec libertum alienum, nec minorem maior'; see also 1. 7. 15. 2. On the possible nature of the 'good ground' see Gardner (1991) 244–5.   [176] D. 1. 7. 17. 1 and 2.

[177] D. 1. 7. 46 (Ulpian, *lex Julia et Papia*, 4): 'In servitute mea quaesitum mihi filius in potestatem meam redigi beneficio principis potest.' 'Redigi ... potest suggests that the imperial grant did not directly put the child into the natural father's *potestas*, but gave consent to proceed with adrogation.

the way up the social scale. In the early Empire, senatorial Romans were unlikely—should they have wished to do so, though there is no evidence that any did—to be given permission to adopt their illegitimate children, whether freed or freeborn. Later, Constantine explicitly penalized not only senators, but local duumvirs or holders of priesthoods, who attempted to legitimize them (*in numero legitimorum habere*—this could cover both adoption and subsequent marriage to the mother), at least if the mothers were slaves, freedwomen, or women of the 'shameful' categories—i.e. actresses, innkeepers, prostitutes, procuresses—and their daughters.[178]

Although, as suggested above, Ulpian's remark (*D*. 1. 7. 46) may imply that adrogation by one ex-slave of another, his natural child, earned exemptions for the adopters, there is no indication that these benefits were extended to men adopting their own freedmen. It is unlikely that patrons wishing to adopt their own natural children were to be encouraged to propagate through their slaves as an alternative to marrying a free woman, while the ex-slave father who had already gone to the trouble of purchasing his own child was clearly in no need of an additional incentive.

Although no source directly says so, it is likely that adrogation of such natural children was permitted, against the normal rule, even when the freedman adopter had already acquired other children.[179] Contrast the rebuff offered in AD 286 to a patron wishing to adopt someone who is, he says, his own freedman, but who is apparently *not* claimed to be his natural child: 'Since you declare that the person whom you wish to adopt is your freedman, and you have not supplemented your pleas with any appropriate justification, such as that you have no children, you understand that the authority of law rejects your request.'[180]

If the child being adrogated by a third party was a freed slave, what

---

[178] *Cod. Iust.* 5. 27. 1; Arjava (1996) 211–12. In effect, Constantine was extending the field of application of Augustus' restrictions on senatorial marriages: Evans Grubbs (1995) 283–94; Arjava (1996) 213.

[179] As seen above, blood relationship could be a ground for making exceptions and allowing adrogations not normally permitted: *D*. 1. 7. 15. 2, 17. 1.

[180] *Cod. Iust.* 8. 47 (48). 3 (=1500 Honoré: Diocletian and Maximian, 16 June AD 286): 'Cum eum, quem adrogare vis, libertum tuum esse profiteris nec ullam idoneam causam precibus indideris, id est quod non liberos habes, intellegis iuris auctoritatem desiderio tuo refragari.' Being the petitioner's own natural child would surely have been *idonea causa*.

happened to the patron's rights? Previous contractual obligations were still actionable after adrogation,[181] so presumably if *operae* (services) had been contracted for as a condition of manumission, the patron could insist on their fulfilment. With regard to the patron's right to proper respect (including freedom from prosecution), and to inheritance from the former slave after the latter's death,[182] texts are not explicit, but it may perhaps be deduced that the patron's rights remained in existence, although he could not assert a claim to any property the freedman had had when adrogated, should he die while still in the *potestas* of his adopter.[183] This, although possibly to the financial advantage of the adopting father, was hardly an eventuality which he or his adopted son would wish to find realized.

While the adrogated freedman might acquire, these private obligations to his patron apart, all the private rights of a *filiusfamilias* within the *familia* of his adoption, to Roman society at large he was still a freedman, and subject to limitations on his public rights. That is, even the natural father could not alter the freedman status of a child fathered upon one of his own slaves, willing though he might be to acknowledge natural parentage. The same would apply both to fathers adopting (with the necessary permission) their natural sons, who were the freedmen of someone else, and also to fathers buying and manumitting their own children, born in slavery, so making them their own freedmen, then adopting them.

It is not clear, however, how such adoptions may be identified. In funerary inscriptions, there are a few examples of family groups in which the natural father is also patron, for instance *CIL* 6. 23848, where the dedicator commemorates his ex-slave wife and his (their?) ex-slave son, as well as a freeborn son who is given priority over his brother in the order of the inscription: 'To the gods of the dead. To

---

[181] Gaius 4. 38; *D.* 4. 5. 2. 1.

[182] For the nature of patrons' rights, see *D.* 38. 2. 1 (*operae*); Gaius 3. 41–2 (inheritance); Gaius 4. 46, *D.* 3. 1. 1. 11, 22. 5. 4, 37. 15, 48. 4. 7. 2 (respect); Gardner (1993) 22–32.

[183] I am no longer convinced by the argument put forward in Gardner (1989) 248 that it may be deduced from legal texts on clandestine or fraudulent adrogations (*per obreptionem*) that both those, and adoption by the natural father by imperial dispensation, left patrons' rights unaffected, while adrogations by other persons required patrons' consent which, when given, entailed loss of rights; the argument is essentially *ex silentio*, and does not explain why, if patronal consent were enough, satisfaction of certain special criteria was also required (*iusta causa*). The relevant texts are: *D.* 1. 7. 46; 2. 4. 10. 2; 37. 12. 1. 2 (a parallel situation involving an emancipated freeborn child); 38. 2. 49.

Passienia Gemella his dearest, most compliant wife and freedwoman and his most pure son L. Passienius Doryphorus, and son and freedman Sabinus.'

Similar is *CIL* 3. 2371: 'L. Julius Narcissus, freedman of Julius, made this in his lifetime for himself and his wife and freedwoman Julia Helpis and his son and freedman Lucius Julius Vestalis.'[184]

The dual designation of Sabinus and Vestalis reflects their status. Within the *familia*, they were not freedmen but *filiifamilias*, with the same legal rights and obligations as freeborn sons. Outside, they were not recognized as freeborn, but had the same public disabilities as other freedmen—mainly, ineligibility for public office and, after the Augustan marriage legislation, a ban on marrying into the senatorial class.

The double designation of both mother and child ('wife and freedwoman', 'son and freedman') may have been a way of indicating that they had been manumitted under the age limit of 30 laid down by the *lex Aelia Sentia*, but were nevertheless Roman citizens, because of their relationship to their patron (i.e. 'good cause' was shown). Vestalis' father, and former owner, is himself certainly a freedman and Sabinus' father may have been. Both fathers could originally have owned the mother, and had a child or children by her. Alternatively, the family group may have been formed when father, mother and child were all slaves in the same household. The father was manumitted at a due age to receive citizenship, and then managed to purchase (or received as a legacy in his owner's will) and set free his wife and son. Sabinus, the slave-born son, is distinguished from, and placed after, his freeborn brother.

Whether the two fathers then went on to adrogate their freed sons is less certain. There is no sure way of telling, and the terminology of commemorative inscriptions does not offer much help. One possibility is that, as well as establishing citizen status, the double designation as son and freedman might be a way of indicating that the son had been adopted.

In another inscription a son commemorates his 'patron and father'

---

[184] *CIL* 6. 23848: 'D. M. Passieniae Gemellae coniugi et lib. suae carissimae obsequentissimae et L. Passiennio Doryphoro filio et Passienio Sabino filio et lib. sanctissimis.' *CIL* 3. 2371: 'L. Julius l. lib(ertus) Narcissus v(ivus) f(ecit) sibi et Juliae Helpidi coniug(i) et l(ibertae) et L. Julio Vestali f(ilio) et l(iberto).' See also Gardner (1989) 253–7 and n. 41.

but describes himself merely as his 'freedman'.[185] 'Telegennia, freed-woman of Gaius, made this for herself and for C. Telegennius, freed-man of Gaius, her patron. Anthus, freedman, set up statues for his patron and father. Chryseis Maior [or simply 'the elder'], freed-woman, an altar.'

Does this mean that Anthus, who does not call himself 'son', had not been adrogated, whereas Sabinus and Vestalis had?[186] Not necessarily; 'son' and 'father' in all three may merely indicate the biological rela-tionship (or, as suggested above, entitlement to citizenship). Calling a freedman 'son' is not enough to show that he had been adrogated.

An inscription from Rome offers what is, allegedly, another form of double designation, used to indicate the adrogation of a freedman. Among the group of inscriptions in the tomb of a freedman bronze-smith found in the Via Flaminia in Rome is the following (as inter-preted by one of the editors, Panciera):[187]

Lucius Aufidius Aprilis, bronzesmith, from the theatre of Balbus, set this up for himself and for ?Gargilia Secunda, his most pure wife, and for Gargilia Venusta, of unknown father, the most devoted wife of M. Antonius Felix, son of Marcus, of the Papiria tribe, freedman of Flaccus, and for Marcus Anto-nius Felix.[188]

Gargilia Venusta was perhaps the illegitimate (but freeborn) daugh-ter of Aufidius' wife, and perhaps also of Aufidius himself, and Marcus Antonius Felix the son-in-law. Felix is, according to the editor, described as son of a M. Antonius (no *cognomen* supplied), and freedman of Flaccus (no *gentilicium* supplied), and it has been suggested that this does not mean that he is the manumitted natural son of a M. Antonius Flaccus, but that Antonius and Flaccus are two different people; he was freed by one, Flaccus and adrogated by the other, M. Antonius.

The principal basis of this suggestion is the tribal affiliation. The long and chequered history of the allocation of voting rights to freed-men ended in the late Republic with freedmen still assigned to the

---

CIL 6. 27137 'Telegennia C.l. Epiteuxis fecit sibi et C. Telegennio C.l. Dionysio patrono suo. Anthus l. statuas patrono et patr(i). Chryseis l. Maior aram.'

[186] As originally suggested in Gardner (1989) 254–5.

[187] Lissi Caronna and Panciera (1975) 224–8.

[188] 'L. Aufidio Aprilis c[or]inthiarius [de thea]tro Balbi [sibi] et [Gargili]ae Secundae [uxo]ri sanctissimae et [Gar]giliae Sp.f. Venustae, M. Antoni M.f(ilii) Pap(iriae tribus) Flacci liberti Felicis uxori piissimae, et M. Antonio Felici.'

four urban tribes,[189] whereas Papiria was a rustic tribe. Therefore, the argument runs, Felix, who was someone else's freedman, must have been adrogated, not manumitted, by a M. Antonius, who was not himself a freedman; either that or M. Antonius and Flaccus *were* the same person, and the whole curious form of expression (including the anomalous tribe) was 'an act of homage to the patron-adrogator' whose separate roles could thus be better distinguished—not a very convincing alternative.

It is not in itself impossible that a freeborn Roman, of the artisan class, should wish to adrogate someone else's freedman. He himself may have been of freedman descent, and reasons can be imagined, such as that he was related to Felix by blood in some way. However, none of this really follows; the whole construction is a mirage. The inscription need not be read in this way at all. Much more plausible is the reading: '(Marcus Antonius) Felix, freedman of Marcus Antonius Flaccus, son of Marcus, of the Papiria tribe.' In other words, it is the freeborn Flaccus who belongs to a rustic tribe, not his freedman Felix—and there is no statement at all to the effect that Felix is his son. This text does not help, therefore, in trying to detect adrogations by natural fathers of their freed sons.

The point that such adrogation does not change civil status is made, with emphasis, several times in the sources, and most strikingly by Ulpian. In a passage already partially quoted he says: 'A slave born to me while I was a slave can be brought into my *potestas* by special grant of the emperor; however it is undoubted that he remains of freedman status.' The same applied in the case of someone adopted by his own former owner: 'If someone admits himself to be a freedman, a patron cannot, even by adopting him, make him freeborn.'[190] The conflict of interest between paternal and patronal rights would not apply here, where the two persons were one and the same; Ulpian's point is merely that the adoption does not alter the freedman's civil status.

Two earlier jurists are cited on the same issue.[191] Marcellus, a member of the *consilium* of Antoninus Pius, remarks, in a commentary on the *lex Julia et Papia*, on one particular civil disability that was not removed from a freedman by adoption: 'Note should be taken that,

---

[189] Treggiari (1969) 37–51.

[190] 'Libertinum tamen eum manere non dubitatur': *D.* 1. 7. 46; *D.* 1. 5. 27 (Ulpian 5 *opinionum*) 'Eum, qui se libertinum esse fatetur, nec adoptando patronus ingenuum facere potuit.'   [191] See also Gardner (1989) 237–41.

although a freedman who has given himself for adrogation to a
freeborn man has acquired the rights of a freeborn person within his
[the adopter's] *familia,* as a freedman he is nevertheless to be barred
from marriage to someone of senatorial rank.'[192]

How early this view, that adoption did not alter freedman status,
had become accepted is not known. In the first century AD, according
to Gellius, 'Masurius Sabinus wrote that it was lawful for freedmen
to be adopted by freeborn men; but he thought it was not permitted,
nor should it ever be, that persons of freed status should by adoption
usurp the legal rights of the freeborn.'[193]

It is possible that Masurius Sabinus, who was active under Tiberius,
was also offering a juristic interpretation of the Augustan legislation
on marriage, and in particular the question of marriage with the senatorial class. However, as cited by Gellius, Sabinus goes on to apply
the point more widely. ' "Otherwise (i.e. if adopted freedmen did
acquire the rights of freeborn)," he says, "if this ancient regulation
were to be preserved, even a slave could be given for adoption by his
master through the praetor (sc. in the same way as a *filiusfamilias)*":
and this he says many authorities on ancient law wrote was possible.'

The reference to 'ancient authorities' has been assigned, on the basis
of Justinian *Inst.* I. II. I2, to a remark of the elder Cato, that slaves
adopted by their owner thereby are freed, something which was no
longer possible in classical law, but perhaps had once been. Sabinus,
dealing with the law of his own time, perhaps intends a *reductio ad absur-*
dum; someone adopted no longer acquires (whatever his own original
status) the status of his adopter.[194]

A slight puzzle remains. Both Sabinus and Marcellus specify adoption by *ingenui,* freeborn Romans. Why specify that the adopter is

[192] D. 23. 2. 32: Sciendum est libertinum, qui se ingenuo dedit adrogandum,
quamvis in eius familia ingenui iura sit consecutus, ut libertinum tamen a senatoriis
nuptiis repellendum esse.

[193] Gell. 5. 19. 11–12: Libertinos vero ab ingenuis adoptari quidem iure posse
Masurius Sabinus scripsit. Sed id neque permitti dicit neque permittendum esse
umquam putat, ut homines liberti ordinis per adoptiones in iura ingenuorum invadant.
Alioquin, inquit si iuris ista antiquitas servetur, etiam servus a domino per praetorem
dari in adoptionem potest. Idque ait plerosque iuris veteris auctores posse fieri scripsisse.

[194] This is the explanation of Watson (1967) 88–98, who suggests (94) that there had
been a change in the law: 'A *libertinus* adopted by an *ingenuus* became *ingenuus* only so
long as it was accepted that the position in the State of an adopted person was that of
the adopter . . . But once it was decided that status in the State was not altered by adoption . . . a slave could not be adopted.' Gardner (1989) 240-1 considers the possibility
of a shift in the meaning of *ingenuitas,* from membership of a class (the patriciate) to
free birth.

freeborn, when this is not relevant to Sabinus' main point? It is not relevant at all to that of Marcellus (who indeed may merely have taken it over from Sabinus). The status of the adopter is not what matters, but that of the person adopted. Similarly, sons born to citizens in lawful marriage were freeborn Romans, whatever the status of their fathers; being a freedman was a phenomenon that lasted only one generation. The likelihood is that this was exactly the point that Sabinus intended to make: no matter who the adopter was, even if he was freeborn, that made no difference to the adopted son, who remained legally *libertinus*, of freedman status.

If the father himself was a freed slave with a patron, or patron's children, still living, whatever the possible attractions of entitling his children to use filiation and patronymics, so disguising their origins, he could be doing them a disservice by adopting them; as already observed (1.8), in certain circumstances it could even be advantageous to emancipate his legitimate children. A child, whether freeborn or freed, who was *sui iuris* could possess property in his or her own right, and one who was freeborn did not have to worry about the claims of a former owner interfering with his own wishes for the disposal of his property after death. Once adopted, the child's property was absorbed in that of the adoptive *pater*, and was vulnerable to claims by patron and patron's family.

In the early Republic, adoption of illegitimate children was the ideal solution. When the freedman died, if he had not left a will, his *sui heredes*—i.e. his children, including adoptive children, and his wife, if she was *in manu*—inherited all his property and the patron was excluded. This was 'obviously unjust' (*aperte iniquum*) according to Gaius. The 'injustice' was probably perceived when Rome's increasing wealth, and the opening up of economic opportunities outside the ownership of land, meant that freedmen began to have property worth coveting. The law was therefore changed, and the praetor's edict guaranteed the patron at least half, even if there was a will, and the entire estate on intestacy, against any *sui heredes* other than legitimate natural children or grandchildren.[195] It is also possible that freedmen had begun to use adoption (even perhaps of outsiders) and to take their wives into *manus*[196] with the

---

[195] Gaius 3. 40–1; Gardner (1993) 21–3.

[196] Compare the manœuvre, thwarted by the *senatusconsultum Gaetulicianum*, to try to circumvent the Augustan restrictions on inheritance between husband and wife: *P. Berol.* 11753; *FIRA* ii. 427; Noy (1988) 299–304.

deliberate intention of controlling the disposal of their property and cutting out the patron.

This change in the law, which occurred during the Republic and probably before the end of the second century BC, greatly reduced the attraction of adrogating illegitimate children. The only freedmen unaffected were those whose patrons were not only already dead (which would include those freed by will), but had left no children. The *lex Fufia Caninia* of 2 BC may have been intended to restrict the numbers of such free-floating *liberti*.[197]

We have no way of telling whether it was in fact common for freedmen to adrogate their illegitimate children; there is little evidence and what there is is ambiguous. Everything depended upon the family's particular circumstances and the choice, to adrogate or not to adrogate (for those to whom it occurred at all) could involve as much gamble as calculation.

2.9 FAMILY FAVOURITES: ADOPTION WITHIN THE FAMILY

Adoption is normally understood to mean bringing someone from outside into the family group and making him or her legally part of it. However, some legal texts in the *Digest* seem to reveal Romans using a combination of emancipations and adoptions actually within the immediate family, usually, it seems, with the intention of adjusting inheritance rights so as to favour particular individuals within the family group.[198] Inevitably, these changes of status involve breaking apart the structure of the original *familia*, reshaping it and also forming new *familiae*.

These measures, radical from a legal point of view, are, from the family point of view, mere devices. Though presented hypothetically, situations such as those described could quite plausibly occur in real life. Jurists are concerned to analyse their effects within the system of rules of Roman law. We may observe, however, that these rules themselves have changed over time, so as to accommodate 'family' feelings and wishes, without sacrificing the basic structure of the *familia*; we also observe jurists, such as Ulpian, quoted below, contributing to the process of change by suggesting on grounds of equity appropriate

---

[197] Gardner (1991) 21–39.
[198] See also the comments in Gardner (forthcoming–*a*).

interpretations of the rules. These changes are a strong indication that the discussion is based on real-life occurrences, not merely the products of legal imagination.

One type of strategy involved transfer of grandchildren by adoption between the *familia* of their natural grandfather, in whose *potestas* they were, and that of their natural father, who had been emancipated. The intention, however, appears to have been not to create inheritance rights where none existed, but to modify those they already had; even without recourse to adoption, the legal boundaries between the two *familiae* became increasingly blurred over time, so far as concerned rights of inheritance between the two.

Already in the latter part of the first century BC, the clause *unde liberi* in the praetor's edict included a provision that not only *emancipati*, but also children born to them after emancipation, could make a claim for *bonorum possessio* of grandfather's estate in this category.[199] Children born before their father's emancipation and remaining in the *potestas* of their grandfather could of course succeed as *liberi* to their grandfather, sharing, as we have seen, after Julian's amendment to the edict, with their emancipated natural fathers.[200] They could also, however, succeed to these natural fathers, despite the fact that they were now in a different *familia*; this may have resulted from a later interpretation of the edict.[201] Whether this predated or postdated the Julianic amendment is impossible to say; in any case, once again civil law, based on the *familia*, was being set aside in favour of 'family', of the blood link.

By the time of the Severi, it is being debated whether or not children who remained in the power of their grandfather when their father was not just emancipated, but actually given in adoption to an outsider, are to be allowed to claim *bonorum possessio* of their father's property. Ulpian says cautiously, 'My view is that the following opinion is more humane, that this son, even though he is not in the same *familia* as his father, is nevertheless to be admitted to possession of his property.'[202] The appeal is to equity, and again the blood tie is

---

[199] D. 37. 6. 5 pr.; 38. 6. 5. 1.   [200] D. 37. 8. 3; 38. 6. 5. 1; 37. 4. 13. 3.

[201] D. 38. 6. 6: Ulpian's phrase 'rei aequitas et causa edicti' (both the equity of the situation and argument from (?) the edict) perhaps implies subsequent interpretation. If such children were still in their grandfather's *potestas*, he, as the immediate beneficiary, must be prepared to make *collatio* of his property, or else to emancipate them.

[202] D. 37. 4. 3. 9: 'et arbitror humaniorem esse hanc sententiam, ut filius hic, quamvis non sit in eadem familia, in qua pater, ad bonorum possessionem tamen eius admittatur.'

preferred to the legal bond of *familia*. It is a long time—not, indeed, until the legislation of Justinian—before the further step is taken of dissociating inheritance rights from *potestas* and creating a two-tier system of adoption, with 'full adoption' being reserved (except in the case of adrogation) to blood kin.[203] The development of inheritance rights, however, already has a long history behind it, not only in the ways just indicated, but in the increase of rights between mothers and children (see below, 3.3).

This is the background to Ulpian's comments on the legal consequences of some adoption practices. Apparently, for instance, it was not unknown for grandfathers to adopt children born to their sons after the latter had been emancipated. This need not have made any difference to the grandchildren's place of residence and lifestyle, nor to what either the natural or the adoptive parent chose to leave them in their wills, but it could make a difference to their prospects in the event of intestacy. In fact, it was a way of enabling that branch of the family, should a will fail, to claim *bonorum possessio* of twice as much as it could otherwise.

In what is at first sight a rather puzzling text, Ulpian says

If a man after being emancipated has acquired a son and given him in adoption to his own father as a son, it is most equitable that he [sc. the adopted son] should have the rights given any adrogated son, and therefore he is to be joined with his father (*idcircoque patri suo iungendus est*); but if this grandson is represented as having been emancipated after the adoption, then it will be most equitable for him to refrain from the estate (since he recovers his original status), and he ought not to be joined with his father.[204]

Something is evidently wrong with the first half of Ulpian's statement; the mention of *adrogatio*, in particular, conflicts with the apparent implications of 'joined with his father'. As we saw, a child born before his father's emancipation, and remaining in his grandfather's power, was protected by Julian's amendment to the edict; he shared with his emancipated father, if the latter chose to make a claim, the portion of the estate due to the single *stirps* which they jointly embodied. Someone adrogated, however, was, by definition, fatherless

[203] Kurylowicz (1979).

[204] *D.* 37. 4. 3. 4 'Si quis post emancipationem quaesitum sibi filium patri suo in adoptionem dederit in locum filii, aequissimum est ei praestari quod cuivis adrogato filio, idcircoque patri suo iungendus est. sed si emancipatus hic nepos post adoptionem proponatur, aequissimum erit eum abstinere (recipit enim locum suum) nec debet patri suo iungi.'

and acquired a claim in his own right which needed to be shared with no one. Mommsen therefore proposed the deletion of *idcircoque . . . iungendus est*; a simpler emendation, and more apt to the particular situation described, is to insert *non* before *iungendus*. He is *not* to be joined with his (natural) father. In the present case, the child is in the *potestas* of his grandfather not as his natural grandson but as his adopted son. His natural parentage has become irrelevant; it is *as if* he had been adopted when legally fatherless, and he and his natural father each represent a separate *stirps*. Therefore, between them, they can claim twice as much of the estate as the father alone, and presumably this was the whole point of the manœuvre. Grandfather intended to favour this branch of the family above others.

The disadvantage (not explained by Ulpian) is that, as a *filius* in an adoptive *familia*, the child lost his right to inherit from his natural father, should the latter die first. If there appeared a possibility that this might happen, it could provide a motive for grandfather, as his adoptive father, to emancipate him. On emancipation, the child lost the right to inherit from his adoptive father (and therefore, as Ulpian observes, ought not to be 'joined' with his natural father, if the grandfather should after all die first), but recovered his right to inherit as one of the *liberi* from his natural father (Gaius 2. 136–7). This presumably meant also that he could still, in due course, as one of the *liberi* of a deceased *emancipatus*, inherit from his natural grandfather. The family, therefore are covering all possible eventualities.

Ulpian goes on to consider another possible situation. A son is emancipated and his grandson, still in the grandfather's power, is given to him in adoption (D. 37. 4. 3. 7). His father then dies, before the grandfather, but the grandson, though technically in another *familia*, is allowed to claim *bonorum possessio* of his grandfather's property, 'because,' says Ulpian, 'he is in the *familia* of a person [sc. his adoptive, as well as natural, father] who himself could have claimed possession against the terms of a will'. As we have already seen, children of *emancipati*, whether born before or after their father's emancipation, could succeed under the edict to their natural grandfathers, and also (probably by interpretation of the edict, in the case of those born before their father's emancipation) to their natural fathers.

Ulpian seems merely to be explaining that, in the event, the changes of personal status involved have made no difference to the child's rights of inheritance from his grandfather. The point of this adoption is never shown, but—if a real instance—it may have been undertaken in the knowledge that the father was likely to die before the grandfather. Transferring the child allows him to succeed directly to his father's property, without its becoming merged in that of his grandfather, as it would if the latter, as his *paterfamilias*, had had to claim on his behalf; he still has a claim, through his father, to succeed to his grandfather.

The same is true, says Ulpian (*D.* 37. 4. 3. 8), in another instance, where the situation is the converse. An emancipated son has given his son, born after his emancipation, in adoption to his natural grandfather, and has then died. The child nevertheless ought to be admitted to his father's property, 'as though he were not part of another *familia*'. Again we are not told any details of the situation envisaged, but perhaps the grandfather has already died (otherwise the child could not have a claim on his own account) or else he is claiming on the child's behalf. In the former event the child will already have inherited as a *suus heres* from his grandfather.

There is more, however, to Ulpian's remark than meets the eye. In the previous case, the grandson 'is admitted' to his grandfather's property, because he qualifies under the edict. In this instance, however, he '*ought* to be admitted', *admitti debet*, to his father's property. That is, Ulpian is putting forward a legal opinion, on grounds of equity. Normally, a person given in adoption into another family, and still in that family after the death of the adoptive father, could claim possession against a will of the property of his natural father *only* if instituted an heir in his will, and if his father had left other children, one of whom had instituted proceedings against the will (*D.* 37. 4. 8. 11); we are not told that this was the case. Ulpian, aware of existing inheritance rights in the families of *emancipati*, is perhaps suggesting that in this instance, where the adoption is, as it were 'in the family', the legal demarcation lines ought to be ignored, and family relationships rather than *familia* should be allowed to prevail. The relaxation of the rules that he is suggesting is not very dramatic. Children born before their father's emancipation were already allowed to inherit from their natural fathers; now he is proposing that those born after his emancipation, and then transferred back into their grandfather's *familia*, should be allowed the same right.

Father and son might also, however, be in different *familiae* when, as in a text mentioned above (*D.* 37. 4. 3. 9), the father is not emancipated, but given in adoption to an external *familia*, in which he dies, while his son remains in the grandfather's *potestas*. This is even further removed from those situations so far admitted as providing a claim in law to inheritance. Even here, however, Ulpian is prepared to argue that decent feeling requires that the child be allowed access to his father's property; that is, *familia*, and the strict letter of the rules of civil law, should yield to 'family' ties.

Another type of strategy, mentioned in several texts, involves adoption—usually of a grandson—actually within a single *familia*. The purpose of this curious manœuvre appears to be to allow the *paterfamilias* to show favouritism to one branch of his descendants over another, by rearranging their legal relationships to each other and so altering their relative order of priority in inheritance on intestacy. Two stages are involved, since it is necessary for the *paterfamilias* first to emancipate the child, then to adopt, by adrogation, to bring the child back into the *familia*. A grandson by one of two sons might be transferred by this method to the other son; one of two grandsons might be adopted as a son, even as the father of another grandson; a grandson by a living son might be adopted as a son, so acquiring inheritance rights separately from his father (whether the latter was in power or emancipated).[205]

A variation is offered in a question raised by Marcellus. A man who had a son, and a grandson by that son, emancipated the son, then adopted him, as a grandson, then emancipated him again. Does the father impede the grandson's claim? Ulpian's answer is elliptical. Even, he says, if the son were emancipated (sc. without the re-adoption as grandson and subsequent emancipation), he would not exclude the grandson's claim, under the edict. Nor, Ulpian suggests surprisingly tentatively, does he do so either as grandson, or as emancipated a second time. He does not explain why, but the reason, again, is that the grandson does not, on the death of the *paterfamilias*, revert to the son's *potestas*;[206] he and his father now constitute two separate *stirpes* of the family, with a total of double the inheritance rights.

In the most elaborate example, a grandfather has two sons in power, and by one of these two grandsons. He emancipates the second son and adopts one of the two grandsons as a son, passing over the emanci-

---

[205] *D.* I. 7. 15. 1; 37. 4. 3. 1 and 3; 37. 8. 1. 9.

[206] *D.* 37. 4. 21. 7; cf. *D.* 1. 7. 41 (Modestinus). In *D.* 38. 6. 1. 7, where the same situation is described, Ulpian gives the reason that this is because he is in power (sc. after his re-adoption) as an adoptive son, not as a natural son; contrast the view of Papinian in *D.* 28. 2. 23 (below).

pated son in his will. The effect of this, whether or not the emancipated son chooses to make a claim for *bonorum possessio*, is that on intestacy the childless son comes in for only one third of the grandfather's property, while the other son's branch of the family comes in for two-thirds.[207] Grandfather, perhaps with the aid of good legal advice, has very successfully exploited the rules of *familia* to play the game of family favourites.

What has been going on, in all the situations described, is that advantage has been taken, both of the *familia*-oriented civil law rules of inheritance, and of modifications to the civil law rules originally introduced to protect 'family' interests, i.e. those both of emancipated sons and of their children left behind in their grandfathers' *potestas*, for quite a different purpose—namely in order to make as certain as possible that grandfather's particular pets will be the lion's share of the inheritance, even if his will should be upset.

Occasionally, it seems, a parent who gave way to moods or pettishness and regretted it might fail to undo the damage. A father emancipated his son, then disinherited him (a necessary precaution if he wished to leave him nothing, otherwise his will would be invalid), then adrogated him again. The disinheritance, says Papinian, holds good, even although normally adrogation breaks a will, because the son ought to be regarded not as 'transferred' into his father's *potestas*, but as 'returned'. The truth is not to be obscured by an imitation of nature.[208] We may perhaps detect in Papinian's comment a hint of disapprobation of such capricious tinkering with the *familia* structure, a disapprobation not apparently shared by Ulpian.[209]

A puzzle remains. Emancipation effects release from *patria potestas*. The same person can be brought back into *potestas* by adrogation, but for that the consent of the person being adrogated is required. Why, it has pertinently been asked, should an emancipated son (or, one may add, grandson) go along with this, specially where it appears not

[207] *D.* 37. 8. 1. 9. Details in Gardner (forthcoming –a).

[208] *D.* 28. 2. 23; cf. 37. 4. 8. 7 where Ulpian paraphrases Papinian as saying that the son's natural rights prevail. Disinheritance, *potestas* and adoption: Gaius 2. 123, 136–7.

[209] Cf. *D.* 38. 2. 42: an attempt to evade some of the legal effects of an emancipated brother's disinheritance is declared ineffectual, 'quoniam poena, quae legibus aut edicto inrogarentur, adoptionis remedio non obliteraretur' (since the penalty required by law or edict would not be wiped out by adoption). In contrast, Ulpian (*D.* 38. 6. 1. 7) refrains from comment, and bases his answer solely on the legal situation.

to be in his interests?[210] How could the *paterfamilias* who emancipated him compel him to participate voluntarily in the adrogation?

The answer to the second question is that he could not, at least in the case of an adult, and therefore there would be no point in undertaking the manœuvre unless the *emancipatus* was willing, and believed that he stood to gain overall. If the adrogation followed hard upon the heels of the emancipation (and as far as our evidence goes, this is likely to be the case with most of the examples, especially those where grandchildren's status is altered in this way: there is no mention of the kind of special circumstances that applied to Domitia Lucilla's adoption), then there would be no time for independent acquisition of property and nothing to lose. Where there was a time lapse, presumably some gain was intended—though the best-laid plans could go awry (as in the case of the father mentioned above who had a change of heart and adrogated the son he had disinherited).

If the emancipated son or grandson (the more commonly mentioned case) was under age he would not be legally capable of giving consent. A preliminary investigation was required, but no doubt his father or grandfather's status as a blood relative, as well as the inheritance benefits, of the kind discussed above, would carry weight, and presumably on coming of age he would have the same right as anyone else adrogated while *impubes* to have his condition reviewed, if he wished.[211]

How these goings-on were viewed by other persons in the power of the *paterfamilias* is another matter. It was apparently not in grandfather's power, at least under the Julianic edict, to adopt an outsider on the fiction of being born of a son in power; the *filiusfamilias* also, it

---

[210] Consent to adrogation: Gaius 1. 99: *D.* 1. 7. 2, 24; Volterra (1976) 219ff. It is against the sons's interests, for example, Volterra suggests, where the *patria potestas* will not terminate at his father's death, as when he is adopted by his own brother or cousin and loses the right to be admitted to *bonorum possessio* of the adrogator's property; the texts, however, present no example that fits. Adoption as a grandson need not necessarily imply adoption as (fictitiously) the son of an existing *filiusfamilias* (*D.* 1. 7. 37 pr., 43, 44). Ulpian's case (*D.* 37. 4. 3. 1) is the wrong way round: one of two grandsons has been emancipated, and then re-adopted as the father of the other grandson; the consent of the grandson kept in power is not required. Possibly Volterra has misinterpreted *D.* 38. 2. 42 (Papinian), mentioned above, where the situation is that one emancipated son, made heir to his father, has adrogated another, disinherited by his father, presumably to try to avoid the consequences of the disinheritance: in the view of Papinian, this ruse should not be allowed to succeed.

[211] *D.* 1. 7. 17. 1; 32; 33.

seems, had to consent to the adoption[212]—not unnaturally, since in due course the child would fall under his *potestas*, and become his *suus heres* (D. 1. 7. 10). This would be a sensible way of acting betimes to secure continuance in the male line if the son was childless and likely to remain so, or even to die before his father.

Such an adoption was not necessarily, however, to a son's advantage. If the son already had children of his own, his father's action introduced an additional person with whom the son's inheritance would eventually have to be shared. It was also open to grandfather to keep the adoptive grandson and emancipate his natural son, and the son could not do anything about it, despite the fact that he stood to lose. Since agnatic bonds created by adoption terminated when the relationship did, the emancipation of his adoptive father meant that the adoptive grandson, still in grandfather's *potestas*, would be entitled to a separate whole share on intestacy (whereas, if the son had any children of his own, they would have to share with him as their natural father, should he make a claim).[213] If the son refused his consent to the adoption, it was still open to father to go ahead and adopt the outsider as grandson, without assigning him any determinate father[214] (again entitling him to an entire separate share when his adopter died) and there was nothing at all that any children *in potestate* could do to prevent that.

It was possible for a man with sons to adopt someone as if he were a grandson born of a specific son. It was also, as just remarked, possible for him, with or without sons of his own, to appoint someone simply as a grandson, without assignation to a named son as father. The point of this—even as retaliation against a recalcitrant son—is not clear, since such a grandson might just as well, one might think, have been adopted as a son. Where there were already sons and grandsons in the family, Proculus is cited for the opinion that 'indeterminate' adoptive grandsons did not have consanguinity with the other grandsons. Children of brothers were one degree further apart in agna-

---

[212] D. 1. 7. 6, 10 and 11, all from Paul, citing Julian in 6; though Celsus (D. 1. 7. 7) appears to contradict, he may be referring only to agnates other than the recipient *filiusfamilias*; these texts could also apply to transfers of grandchildren born within the *familia*. For the adoption of an outsider as grandson by a son, see D. 28. 6. 2.

[213] D. 1. 7. 28; 37. 8. 6. On consent to emancipation, see above, 1.1, n. 4.

[214] D. 1. 7. 37 pr. (Paul), 43 (Pomponius), 44 (Proculus). The citation of Pomponius comes from his commentary on Scaevola's *ius civile*, and Paul may be glossing Pomponius: so Kurylowicz (1981) 29. On Proculus, see the text above.

tion than nephews/nieces and uncles; but without knowing the nature of the question Proculus was answering it would be risky to draw conclusions about possible grandfatherly concern about the relationships imposed on the next generation but one.

In sum, while sons in power could refuse to consent to have outsiders foisted upon them as their children, this power of refusal was not worth very much, since father had means of retaliation; nor is there any indication that anyone's consent (other than that of the *filius* who was recipient father) was required for transfers of grandsons born within the *familia*, either to assign them to different fathers, or to promote them to sons, or, indeed, to emancipate them. Father therefore, it seems, had a fairly free hand to play family favourites within the *familia*.

2.10 THE PURPOSES OF ADOPTION

Adoption was a legal device, operating within the frame of reference of a society structured on the *familia*. This determined its nature and effects, some of which have been examined above. It was only one of a number of possible devices which were used, separately or in combination, for various emotional or economic reasons—others included marriage, emancipation, so-called testamentary adoption, and the use of wills in general. Because of its legal effects, it was not something to be lightly undertaken, by any of the parties involved (at least, of those who had a say in the matter). From the circumstances in which adoption was, or in some instances was not, resorted to it is possible to some extent to guess at the particular reasons directing their choice, reasons in which both sentiment and practical calculation can be found, though not necessarily both at once.

A question not so far considered is the purpose for which the Romans devised adoption in the first place. Unfortunately, while a little is known about the mechanisms of adoption in early Rome, it is only a *very* little. The history of the early development of wills is similarly ambiguous and should also be examined more closely, since there are striking resemblances between early testamentary procedures and those of adoption. Almost nothing about the scanty evidence for the applicability of these procedures is agreed. Was adoption of persons *in potestate* possible before the Twelve Tables, or only adrogation of persons already *sui iuris*? Was the 'historical' form of will by bronze and balance (*per aes et libram*)—that is, by mancipation, formal conveyance—in use before the Twelve Tables, or not until later? Were wills originally made only in the absence of *sui heredes*, or even where these existed? There is little or no evidence, and sharp division of opinion among modern scholars.[215]

It appears that in early Rome both adrogation and (by a procedure obsolete in historical times) will-making were performed in a popular assembly. Wills were made either in the *comitia calata*, an assembly meeting summoned twice a year for that purpose, or, if war was imminent, *in procinctu*, i.e. the same popular assembly in a state of military readiness; adrogation was carried out before the *comitia curiata*. Despite the two names, the assemblies appear to have differed only in voting methods, not in composition.[216]

Use of the popular assemblies is some indication of the importance attached by the community to both types of procedure, and therefore to the institution of the *familia* itself, the basic social and economic unit of the society. Likewise, the procedures still in use in historical times (all forms of mancipation) for testation ('by bronze and balance'), for adoption of persons *in potestate*, and for emancipation, required, in the participation of magistrates and seven other Roman citizens, a vestigial assembly.[217]

Gaius' account (2. 102) represents the making of wills 'by bronze and balance' (the procedure in use in classical Rome) as originally a procedure intended for use in emergency only, when someone was in imminent danger of death (*si subita morte urguebatur*) and had not yet made a will either in the *comitia calata* or *in procinctu*. 'His estate, that is his patrimony' (*familiam suam, id est patrimonium suum*) is made over to

---

[215] On *adrogatio* and early wills Kaser and Watson, for example, represent opposing points of view. For Kaser (1971) 65–6, 105–6, only *adrogatio* of persons *sui iuris* was possible before the Twelve Tables; wills in the *comitia calata* and *in procinctu* were made only where there were no *sui heredes* on intestacy, and had the sole function of creating one. Watson (1975) 41–2, 65–6, inclines hesitantly to the views that these were true wills, for the institution of heirs, and available even if there were *sui heredes* (cf. Crawford (1996) 640), and that *adrogatio* could originally be used also for persons *in potestate*. Both believe that the will *per aes et libram* came into use before the Twelve Tables: Kaser (1971) 107–8, Watson (1975) 61. However, note the scepticism on the possibility of deciding this point expressed in Crawford (1996) 639–40 (with references to earlier discussion), summed up in the remark: 'The bibliography is enormous and there is no evidence.'

[216] Gaius 2. 101; Gellius 5. 19. 5–6, 15. 27. 2–4. According to Gellius 15. 27. 2, Labeo wrote of *calata* as the general term, *curiata* that for a sub-division.

[217] Gaius 1. 119, 132–4; 2. 104.

a 'friend' (*amico*)—i.e. not a *suus heres*, perhaps not even an agnate—with instructions for distribution to individuals according to the testator's wishes. The implication appears to be, not that wills were originally introduced merely in order to allow Romans to show favouritism among their *sui heredes*[218] (in Gaius' account, there evidently are none), but in order to provide for the transmission of patrimonies when there were no *sui heredes* and unlikely to be any, and perhaps even the prospects of agnate succession were poor. As for the other two procedures, *in procinctu* also is an emergency situation, since a man might well fail to return from war, and the infrequency of the special *comitia calata* points in the same direction—if heirs were lacking, one made a will in case something drastic happened before the next opportunity came round. The related problem of responsibility for the *sacra* of the *familia*, if there were no *sui heredes* to inherit them automatically, was the subject of pontifical regulation, attested from at least the middle of the third century BC (Cicero, *de legibus* 2. 48–53; see 3.2 below); the pontiffs decided that the *sacra* were to follow the property.

Gaius, then, appears in the passage cited to assume that the will *per aes et libram*, like the other two varieties, was originally instituted for use by persons without *sui heredes*. However, like later jurists, Pomponius, Paul, and Ulpian, he apparently also knew a text of the Twelve Tables which mentioned provision for *tutela* (absent from the versions of Twelve Tables 5. 3 in *Ad Herennium* 1. 13. 23 and Cicero, *De inv.* 2. 148), so implying the existence of *sui heredes*, i.e. children under age and/or adult daughters: 'By the law of the Twelve Tables, parents are allowed to appoint by will tutors to their children, whether male or female, provided that they are in their power.' The two texts are not necessarily incompatible. Just as the will *per aes et libram*, though predecemviral in origin, appears to be a later development than the other two (in so far as it involves taking up the time and attention of fewer fellow citizens), so the possibility of testamentary provision for *tutela* may have been a still later extension of its application, for the benefit of fathers leaving *sui heredes* but no agnates to be responsible for *tutela*.[219]

---

[218] As suggested by Voci (1982) 407 in a discussion of predecemviral and early post-decemviral developments.

[219] *D.* 26. 2. 1. pr.: 'lege duodecim tabularum permissum est parentibus liberis suis sive feminini sive masculini sexus, si modo in potestate sint, tutores testamento dare.' The possibility suggested above is not considered in Crawford (1996) 639–40.

Adoption appears to have had a similar origin,[220] as a device securing the continuance of the *familia*, its property and its *sacra*. Someone without any *sui heredes* could acquire one by *adrogatio*. Methods of adoption developed as procedures became available. The character of the procedure of *adrogatio* was quite different from the *mancipatio* later used for adoption of persons still in power. Someone legally independent offered voluntarily to submit himself to the *potestas* of another, i.e. to terminate his own *familia* and become part of another. This required a legislative act by (initially) the whole Roman people—understandably, since the *familia* of the person being adopted, with its religious cult, was itself terminated.

Adrogatio was used in the historical period only for adoption of persons legally independent. There is no sign that it was ever used in early Rome for transfer of a *filiusfamilias* out of the *potestas* of one *paterfamilias* into that of another, although this, as observed by Watson, would seem 'more acceptable both socially and sacrally' than terminating a *familia* by adrogation. The likely explanation is the obvious one, that no procedural mechanism yet existed whereby a *paterfamilias* could release a *filius* from his own *potestas*.[221] Whereas the basic procedure of mancipation was sufficient to allow the development of the will *per aes et libram*, it was probably only, as seen above (2.2), as a result of an interpretation of a rule in the Twelve Tables that it became possible to use the procedure also for removal of persons from a *familia*, either for release from *potestas* or for transfer of *potestas* to another head of *familia*, i.e. for emancipation or for giving in adoption. Adrogation preceded adoption.

The initial purpose of the institution of adoption therefore, like that of will-making, appears to have been to allow people without *sui heredes* of their own to acquire someone to inherit their patrimonies—and, initially at least, it was possible to adopt (sc. by adrogation) only someone capable of carrying on the *familia* in the sense of the agnatic line, i.e. only a male.

This consideration of perpetuating the line seems always to have retained great importance for the Romans. There are few instances of adoption of females, and, although there was no bar to adoption by persons with children of their own, there is, so far as the evidence permits one to judge, a dearth of examples outside the imperial house

---

[220] For a similar relationship between adoption and testation in early Athens, see Todd (1993) 221ff.   [221] Watson (1975) 41; *contra*, Kaser (1971) 66.

of someone with living sons adopting another.[222] Only in exceptional circumstances, as we have seen, was someone with children of his own permitted to adrogate.[223]

With most adoptions, then, by most people (that of Clodius being an obvious exception), the primary, though not the only, consideration was the destination of the property which they had to leave. For ex-slaves, achievement of citizen status and solidarity as a 'real' Roman family may have come first—specially as property, given patronal rights, could suffer from adoption. For those not encumbered by patrons, however, freedom to determine who should benefit from the property was the main attraction. Wills were one method, but wills could fail; inheritance rights were more secure.

Having an heir—any heir—was not enough; it mattered to have the heir of one's choice. Sentimental reasons might dictate the choice of beneficiary. We have observed women seeking replacements for lost children, as Syra, who chose her stepsons; and men with no sons looking for some male at least of their blood to whom to leave their estates. Among the latter, personal predilection (family favourites again) might determine the particular choice. What determined which of C. Claudius Pulcher's sons was adopted by his brother, or which Cornelius Scipio was 'adopted' in his grandfather's will (we do not know whether the regular adoption of his brother came before or after this)? Was Scipio Aemilianus his aunt's favourite among the four sons of L. Aemilius Paulus? Did fathers 'put forward' one son rather than another for consideration by a would-be adopter? For the most part, except for a Clodius or a Domitia Lucilla, we learn from the sources nothing more than the bare fact of the adoption.

We have already remarked on the extent to which, among the few attested examples, heirs are chosen from relatives on the mother's side. Even among the Roman senatorial élite of the late Republic, where modern academic fashion for a time wanted to see adoptions as a branch of political intriguing, there is some reason to believe that

---

[222] Obvious exceptions are Tiberius' adoption of Germanicus, and Claudius' adoption of Nero, both at the instance of others (sc. Augustus and Agrippina minor. Plural adoptions are attested ; for instance, Q. Fabius Maximus, praetor 181 BC, who had no sons of his own, adopted two from two different fathers, L. Aemilius Paulus and Cn. Servilius Caepio, and Domitius Afer adopted the two Curvii brothers (Pliny, *Ep.* 8. 18). Someone with only a daughter might wish to adopt a son—cf. Augustus' adoption of his grandsons.

[223] 2. 8 above; cf. D. 1. 7. 17. 3 (on the adrogation of *pupilli*) and, for the contrary, *Cod. Iust.* 8. 47 (48). 3 (=1500 Honoré).

not only was blood thicker than friendship (political or otherwise), but that the limits of the agnatic kinship were less important than 'family' through both male and female lines. As will be shown in Chapter 3, Roman law responds to these feelings in gradually altering the legal relations between the two sides of the family, at least as regards inheritance and *tutela*, so changing the character of the *familia* in these respects, though leaving virtually untouched the central principle of *patria potestas*, which is retained for its importance for social order.

Every usage, however, is open to abuse. *Patres* with living children began to use the rules for engineering the family structure, in order to play favourites with more guarantee of success than if they had relied only on their wills being implemented (see 2.9 above). In effect, for the purposes of transmission of property, the *familia* itself, regardless of its other functions, is being treated as just another legal device. Some legal disquiet is perhaps detectable in relation to such practices as emancipation of a son, followed by his adrogation.[224]

There is more overt disapproval when this treatment is applied to an adoptive son. Although serial adoption—that is, giving someone whom one has adopted in adoption to another person—is permissible and tolerated,[225] it is unacceptable for an adoptive son to be passed back and forth into and out of the *potestas* of the same person. 'One cannot', says Paul, 'adopt for a second time someone whom one has adopted and then emancipated or given in adoption.'[226]

Why not? The objection in some instances might be moral. The person giving an adoptive son in adoption to someone else may be presumed, like any responsible father, to be doing so for the benefit of the son, and the adopter's motives, in adopting someone *alieni iuris* and therefore without property of his own, can reasonably be regarded as honourable. If the second adopter then died, the adoptive son could inherit.

Re-adoption by adrogation of a natural son previously given in adoption (especially of one who had left behind children in his *familia*

---

[224] Papinian in *D*. 28. 2. 23; see 2.9 above.

[225] Gaius 1. 105: 'Si quis per populum sive apud praetorem vel apud praesidem provinciae adoptaverit, potest eundem alii in adoptionem dare' (If someone has adopted a person by means of the people, or before a praetor or provincial governor, he can give the same person in adoption to someone else).

[226] *D*. 1. 7. 37. 1: 'eum quem quis adoptavit, emancipatum vel in adoptionem datum iterum non potest adoptare'; cf. on *D*. 28. 2 .23 (Papinian) above.

of birth), along with his property, and perhaps after he had inherited from an adoptive father, could also be seen as for the benefit of the natural family as a whole.

However, re-adoption of an adoptive son who was now independent was perhaps suspect, although it is difficult to see why, since he would have to consent to his own adrogation. Is there perhaps a hint here of disapproval of something resembling the moral, though not legal, crime of *captatio* (inheritance-hunting), which nowhere appears directly in the *Digest*[227]—that is, a suspicion that a *pater* and his adoptive son, given in adoption to a third party, were cynically using adoption to secure that third party's inheritance? Re-adrogation would secure the second inheritance for the original adoptive father, and the son's reward for going along with the scheme would be recovery of the right to inherit from the first adoptive father. Refusal of permission to re-adrogate, however, while thwarting the original adoptive *pater*, would do nothing to prevent the son's keeping the inheritance (though he had no further claim on his original adoptive father's inheritance). If the adoptive son had simply been emancipated, the reason for the objection to re-adrogation is even less obvious; however, bearing in mind Papinian's remark that regarding a natural son as adoptive obscured the truth by an imitation of nature, it may be that the *repeated* use of the 'imitation of nature' (i.e. of adoption) towards someone originally an outsider seemed to involve a dangerous disrespect for the social values of the *familia*.

Collusion, this time between *patres*, underlies a situation mentioned by Paul in book 11 of his *Questions*. 'It has been asked', he says, 'whether there is a basis for an action, if you are given a son in adoption on the condition that after, say, three years you give the same person to me in adoption. Labeo thinks that there is no basis for action, for it is not in accordance with our ways to have a son on a temporary basis.'[228]

In other words, if there had been a collusive arrangement between the *patres* that the transfer from one *familia* into the other was to be no more than temporary, and the first adopting *pater* then refused to

---

[227] Champlin (1991) 87–102; *D.* 31. 77. 24 he suggests (94 n. 44) may contain a hint of *captatio*, though without the context it is not possible to be sure.

[228] *D.* 1. 7. 34 Paul, *xi quaestionum*. 'Quaesitum est, si tibi filius in adoptionem hac lege sit datus, ut post triennium puta eundem mihi in adoptionem des, an actio ulla sit. et Labeo putat nullam esse actionem: nec enim moribus nostris convenit filium temporalem habere.'

honour his side of the agreement, he could not be legally forced to do so; the praetor would simply reject an application.

This is introduced by Paul as a theoretical question. Labeo's interest, which predates the Neronian scandal recounted in Tacitus, *Ann.* 15. 19 (discussed above, in 1.7), may have been concerned with earlier attempts to circumvent Augustan legislation on marriage and children by temporary adoptions; the wording of the text would admit both the possibility of return by agreement to the original *pater*, and transmission to someone else for enjoyment of the same privileges of paternity (in AD 62, the adoptees were simply being emancipated once they had served their purpose). This much, however, is speculation, not knowledge. The purpose of the manœuvre is not explained, and what purposes it might have had after Nero closed the loophole in the Augustan legislation are not clear. They need not necessarily have been discreditable in themselves; for instance, temporary adoption might conceivably have been used as a form of labour-hire agreement.[229] This also, however, might have been seen as a misuse of the purpose for which adoption was originally intended, and of parental power.

Jurists have taken up Labeo's opinion that if the adopter fails to give up the adoptive son for re-adoption (or further adoption) he cannot be sued for fulfilment of the agreement. Though preserved in the title on adoptions and emancipations, it perhaps belongs more appropriately in *D.* 45. 1, on verbal contracts, since it could be regarded as a particular case of the general principle that dishonourable conditions are not to be honoured.[230] Although the purposes for which such temporary adoption was used may not in themselves have been dishonourable, it was, Labeo said, not in accordance with Roman values.

It cannot be said for certain that the Romans ever used serial adoption in such cynical ways, although clearly lawyers intended that such behaviour, if met with, should incur disapproval and not be allowed full legal effect. Adoption was a mechanism for altering the composition of the *familia*, the basic legal unit of society, primarily in the interests of perpetuation to the next generation; because of the social importance of paternal authority, too much tampering, for inappropriate purposes, with the *familia*-based structure of society was dangerous, and not to be encouraged.

---

[229] The early Roman institution of *mancipium*, giving sons into temporary bondage, which did not extinguish *potestas*, was long obsolete: Gardner (1993) 12–14.

[230] Cf. *D.* 45. 1. 121. 1, 123.

Similar concern is visible in Justinianic rules on adoption. It is noteworthy that much of the earlier legal writing relating to full-blown classical adoption survives as still appropriate in Justinianic law; the number of detectable interpolations in the *Digest* is small. The context of application of the rules, however, is different and perhaps also the rationale.[231]

Giving in serial adoption, for instance, is still possible, but now only when the person adopted or adrogated is not an outsider (*non extraneus*).[232] Since someone given in adoption comes under the *potestas* of the adopter only when the latter is a maternal or paternal ascendant, i.e. grandfather or great-grandfather (and therefore the adoptee is not *extraneus*), this naturally follows, and all that results from subsequent adoption is a certain readjustment of the individual's priority in right to inherit from various members of his family, both in the agnatic and cognatic line. This is no more than the kind of tinkering with lines of inheritance in which we have seen *patres* in an earlier period indulging, within the confines of their own immediate *familia*.

However, although all adrogations continue to give the adrogator *potestas*, he cannot now, unless he is also his blood ascendant, give his adoptive *filiusfamilias* in adoption to someone else. The reason is presumably that (by an extension of the rule by which a son given in adoption to an outsider by his natural father retains inheritance rights from the latter) when the adopting father is, though adoptive, also a blood ascendant, 'as both natural and legal right concur in this person',[233] this does not lose the *filius* all right to inherit from his adrogator. To allow an external adrogator, however, to pass on his adoptive son to someone else would make it too easy for him to denude the latter of his property and all acquisitions made while in *potestas*; even though in Justinianic law the *filius* must not actively object to being given in adoption, that in itself was not necessarily a guarantee of his willingness.

The strictures on re-adoption and temporary adoption (*D.* 1. 7. 34

[231] Kurylowicz (1984); he explicitly rejects (3310 n. 13) the view of Lavaggi (1946) 45–68, that the law of the *Digest* on adoption and adrogation has been extensively interpolated.

[232] *Inst.* 1. 11. 8 (cf. Gaius 1. 105). Note, however, that *non extraneus* in Justinian has a wider range of application than in the old civil law, according to which all heirs other than *sui heredes* (that is, those who had been actually in the *potestas* of the deceased) were 'extraneous': Gaius 2. 152–7.

[233] 'iure tam naturali quam legitimo in hanc personam concurrente': *Inst.* 3. 1. 14; cf. *Cod. Iust.* 8. 47 (48). 10.

and 37. 1) are also retained, although now they can apply only where the adopters are ascendants in the paternal or maternal line. Again, the reason is not immediately obvious, especially for the retention of *D*. 1. 7. 34 (since the inheritances involved were all now 'in the family'), but one possibility—I offer this as a tentative suggestion only—is that both practices could be used by relatives (both agnatic and cognatic) to pass *filii* around the various *familiae* comprised in the family, in order to avail themselves of their services and earning power through the exercise of paternal authority. This could be seen as an abuse of that authority, similar to the one which almost a thousand years before may have motivated the compilers of Rome's first legal 'code', the Twelve Tables, to deprive of his *potestas* a father who sold his son into bondage once too often—a measure which may have created the possibility of giving in adoption in the first place.

3

Outside the *Familia*: Mothers and Children

3.1 INTRODUCTION: THE MATERNAL RELATIONSHIP IN CIVIL LAW

In archaic Rome, because women at marriage were customarily placed *in manu*, that is, under the power of their husbands, virtually all married women were in the same *familia* as their children; by the end of the Republic, virtually none were. Although Ulpian's well-known definition of what constituted a *familia* in strict law (*iure proprio*) includes the mother, *materfamilias*, to mention her as a member of the *familia* is by his time (early third century AD) an anachronism.[1] It had long since ceased to be customary for married women to be taken into the power of their husbands, and the word *materfamilias* itself had changed its meaning in common usage to mean either a respectable married woman, or a woman whose status was defined not by being married, but by being legally independent, i.e. one whose *paterfamilias* had died.[2]

Seen from the viewpoint of civil law, the Roman mother, depending on whether she had been taken into *manus* or not, was either a subordinate in her husband's *familia*, like her children, or an outsider. In

---

[1] D. 50. 16. 195. 2: 'familiam dicimus plures personas, quae sunt sub unius potestate aut natura aut iure subiectae, ut puta patrem familias, matrem familias, filium familias, filiam familias quique deinceps vicem eorum sequuntur, ut puta nepotes et neptes et deinceps' (We call *familia* a number of persons who are by nature or by law subject to the control of one person, for example father of a *familia*, mother of a *familia*, son of a *familia*, daughter of a *familia*, and those who succeed them, for example grandsons and granddaughters, and so on).

[2] For these various meanings, see e.g. Gell. 18. 6. 4; D. 1. 6. 4; 3. 5. 14; 23. 2. 41; 24. 3. 30. 1; 24. 3. 34; 47. 10. 15. 15; 50. 16. 46. 1; Gardner (1995) 384–6. Cicero in *Top.* 3. 14 still restricts the use of *materfamilias* to a woman married with *manus*; the rest, he says, are termed *uxores* (wives).

neither case did she have any legal authority to control the actions of her own children; that was the prerogative of her husband.

A woman who had been taken into the *manus* of her husband, or of his *pater*, was juridically the equivalent of a daughter in the household (though in the latter case, she did not become independent, like her husband, when his father died, but came in turn into his *manus*). She had the same rights of intestate inheritance from her husband as her own children, any children he might have had by other marriages, and any adoptive children. After his death, all of these were legally her agnates. She could inherit from all of them (though the children of the males took precedence over her in inheriting from their fathers) and they had priority over all other heirs in inheriting from her. After her husband's death, one or more of the sons, as agnate, would exercise guardianship over her management of her finances and could control such activities as will-making and, should she want to remarry, constituting a dowry. She was a member of the *familia*, and disposal of her property could be controlled by, and for the ultimate benefit of, the members of the *familia* in the next generation—not unjustifiably, since some of the property at least will have come to her from the late *paterfamilias*.

This system, which prevailed in early Rome, worked to the benefit of the *familia* into which she married. It was gradually replaced by one which benefited the *familia* into which she had originally been born; she was not given into her husband's power, but retained in that of her father (for reasons discussed in 1.5.2 above). The chief difference, so far as she was concerned, was that she became legally independent sooner. She still had no legal control over her children. Her male agnates still controlled her disposal of property, but now they were members of her original *familia* (primarily, her brothers), and they, not her children, were her heirs. This system also worked well, to the benefit of her relatives by birth, so long as there were plenty of agnates in each generation (which is the same as to say, children born to the *patres* of each preceding generation, and surviving), who could inherit from the women and keep the money within the agnatic line of descent; otherwise, under the rules of civil law the property dispersed among the *gens* members.

However, as suggested above, a shortage of heirs in the male line was not uncommon, becoming acute by the latter part of the first century BC, and prompting modifications to the civil law in the praetor's edict in the late Republic. Some evidence of the problem may also be seen in earlier Republican legislation on inheritance, from as early, indeed, as the Twelve Tables. Later on under the Empire other social factors encourage the development of still closer rights of inheritance in the maternal line, which will be discussed further in 3.2 and 3.3 below.

These and other factors, considered in 3.4–7 below, also place increasing importance on the mother–child relationship. Whatever the strict legalities of the *familia*, there is evident in the classical period a strong social expectation of active concern and involvement by mothers in the welfare of their children, both during marriage and after its dissolution by divorce or the death of the *pater*; this applies also to some extent to other relations on the maternal side. The maternal relationship assumed particular importance in the absence of a father. The death of a father left the child an orphan and the mother a widow—an event which, since men tended to marry at a later age than women, was not uncommon—and responsibility for the physical care of the child tended to fall upon her. Widows might remarry; even if they did, the stepfather was not the legal *pater* of the child, and some arrangements had to be made for a legal guardian to look after his or her property.

In a large section of society outside the élite in which children were, for one reason or another, illegitimate, there was no legally recognized *pater*, and might also be no biological father on the scene. There the mother's role was particularly important. Unmarried mothers and their children might or might not be living as a family with the biological father—many were not. Among ex-slaves, in particular, biological families did not necessarily conform to the criteria of the legal *familia*;[3] the child, being illegitimate, had no legally recognized *pater*, nor, in strict law, any other relatives, other than blood relatives through his mother—and those only if she was freeborn. If the mother was an ex-slave, there might also in fact be a lack of kinsfolk, none of the kind of network of relatives and ascendants found in free society, no aunts, uncles, grandparents, and cousins—unless, that is, the mother had come from a household big enough to develop a 'family in *familia*' among the slaves. Even then, the difficulties of keeping in touch were manifold.[4]

[3] Bradley (1991a) chs. 6 and 7; Dixon (1988) chs. 2 and 3; B. Rawson (1989), 10–41; Saller (1991a) and (1994) ch. 8; Gardner (1996) 83–100 and (1997).
[4] Flory (1978); Bradley (1984) ch. 2.

3.2 DEATH AND RENEWAL: THE IMPORTANCE OF COGNATES

More than one demographic study has put forward the view that the Romans, and in particular the Roman élite, were failing to reproduce themselves, especially in the male line, during the Republic and early Empire—a perception of decline shared also, it appears, by the Romans themselves and one which Augustan marriage legislation attempted to remedy.[5] An examination of certain developments in the Roman law of inheritance during the Republic suggests that the problem may have been one of long standing, and present from a very early date, even before the Twelve Tables.

Will-making originated before the Twelve Tables (see 2.10 above) and although it could be used to favour sons rather than daughters, as was the tendency of wills also in classical Rome,[6] this may not have been its prime purpose. There was less risk in archaic Rome of dispersal through female heirs; property still consisted mainly of *res mancipi*, whose disposal required authorization from a woman's tutor, and agnate *tutela* was strong. A more basic reason for the original introduction of wills is lack of direct male heirs. It is implicit in Gaius' account (2. 101–3), both of the later will 'by bronze and balance' and the earlier procedures on the battlefield or at one of the twice-yearly meetings of the *comitia calata*, that wills were made in order to assign the property when a man had no *sui heredes* and seemed unlikely to have any, and when the security of the agnate succession was also uncertain. Intestate succession was reasonably safe, so long as a family continued to perpetuate itself in the male line, but not if there were no surviving sons (or their sons) or even agnates.[7] With or without females to inherit, the property could ultimately end up being dispersed among the *gentiles*.

There were religious implications also. By the mid-third century BC at latest the pontiffs find it necessary to make rulings about what is to

---

[5] Brunt (1971) chs. 8–9, on the late Republic (though perhaps exaggerating the extent of exposure of female infants), and Hopkins (1983) ch. 2 (with Graham Burton), with particular reference to males in the senatorial class in the 2nd and 3rd cent. BC. For factors affecting fertility, see also Saller (1987) 20–35 and Parkin (1992) 111–33.   [6] Champlin (1991) 114–20.

[7] Limiting the intestate inheritance to the nearest agnate, as Gaius (2. 11–13) says the Twelve Tables did, may have been intended to limit dispersal outside the direct male line, but, if agnates were in short supply, risked having the opposite effect.

happen to the family cults, the *sacra*,[8] when estates are left by will to persons other than the direct heirs. These direct heirs, *sui heredes*, were the children, or sons' children, of the (male) deceased; women did not have *sui heredes*, so even if the property went to a direct heir, if that direct heir was a woman, the problem of the *sacra* arose in the next generation. *Sui heredes* succeeded to the *sacra* automatically; other heirs did not.[9]

First, according to the 'older authorities' (*antiqui*), liability for the *sacra* is to fall on anyone made heir in the will, and second on those who receive the greater part of the property. This latter ruling, upheld according to Cicero by several pontiffs, of whom the earliest mentioned by name is Ti. Coruncanius, *pontifex maximus* from 254 BC, refers to persons who are not the designated heirs, but receive, as a legacy or gift at death, as much as all the heirs, i.e. at least half the estate. Third, and apparently associated by Cicero with P. Scaevola, *pontifex maximus* from 130 BC, liability falls on anyone who received as a legacy anything at all, if more than half of the estate was bequeathed in legacies—which is an interesting indication of how far testamentary practice had developed by then. It seems that it was already a well-established, and perhaps even socially incumbent, usage to disperse a large proportion of one's estate in bequests to outsiders.[10]

How large a proportion went this way doubtless varied with individual circumstances; those with sons to inherit their property were perhaps less likely to leave the bulk of the estate away from them.

If *sui heredes* did not inherit, the future of the *sacra* was in jeopardy, since other heirs could always refuse an inheritance; *sui heredes*, until probably the middle of the first century BC, could not (1.6 above, at n. 67). If the pontiffs are worried, then it seems fairly clear that by the mid-third century, and probably earlier, family property was commonly being left to heirs who may have been agnates, but who were certainly not the children of the deceased. It is hard to believe that a Roman father, if he had had sons, would not have made them his heirs. The implication is that a significant proportion of Roman men

---

[8] For a brief account of family cults and their relation to Roman public religion, see North (1989) 605–7 and bibliography there. For a detailed description, still fundamental is de Marchi (1896). [9] Cic. *De legibus* 2. 48–52.

[10] Champlin (1991) ch. 7, who regards this practice as an expression of 'a social (as distinct from 'natural'—my parenthesis) affection for those who had helped and supported the testator through life' (131).

have no sons to whom to leave their estates. There is also, it seems, not much concern to refrain from dispersing estates, merely in order to safeguard the interests of these other, external, heirs; if widespread, such indifference might tend to erode the wealthy Roman upper class. The *lex Cincia* of 204 BC[11] points in the same direction as the pontifical rulings. This law restrained gifts between the living, and is obviously directed at the wealthier sections of society. Valuable gifts (we do not know what, if any limits were fixed) were permitted only between blood relatives up to the sixth degree, i.e. up to second cousins, which could still permit dispersal among a wide range of persons.[12] That such a law was felt necessary indicates that Rome by the late third century BC was already very different from the archaic society of enclosed, agricultural *familiae*. This gift-giving behaviour belongs to a more open society, of social interchange, of (hopefully) reciprocity, of networking. Who has been getting the gifts? And how much would this in practice restrict the behaviour of the Roman élite? How much of the Roman élite, which was a relatively small society, was connected by intermarriage within the sixth degree, or even more remotely, either as cognates (i.e. blood-relatives), or as *adfines* (relatives by marriage)? The original law, however, excludes *adfines*, as well as other strangers.[13]

It is apparently felt that gift-giving is contributing to the dispersal of property to an extent that could endanger the social position of the next generation. It is interesting that under the *lex Cincia* gifts are permitted between blood-relatives. *cognati*, up to the sixth degree, since that includes relatives through the female line. This may be to some extent a recognition of a *de facto* situation—agnatic lines, through males, are failing, so 'family' connections are gaining in importance. The nearest degree of cognatic relationship, however, is that between parent and child. Husbands and wives and their respective cognates are merely *adfines* of each other, and there was a customary ban, of

---

[11] Crawford (1996) 741–4.

[12] The indefatigable calculations of the jurist Paul demonstrated that, in the unlikely event of each possible cognate relationship in a family being represented by a separate living individual, the sixth degree would amount to a total of 448 persons, the seventh degree to 1,024: *D.* 38. 10. 10. 17–18.

[13] By later interpretation, gifts between certain *adfines*, i.e. certain step-relatives and in-laws, were permitted: *Frag. Vat.* 302. An incidental effect of the law would be that a man whose daughter had married with *manus* would no longer be able to expend generosity upon her through gifts to her husband (since she was in his *potestas*, but he was merely an *adfinis*, not a cognate).

unknown but probably early origin, on gifts between them.[14] This meant that husband and wife could not validly make valuable gifts to each other, nor could the wife and her cognates make gifts to their children, who were in the husband's *potestas*; but once a father was dead, a mother and her relatives could be (and were) as generous to the children as they wished (see 3.4 below).

Behaviour similar to that provoking the *lex Cincia*, and similarly difficult to account for if there had been children, especially sons, to consider, appears to lie behind a series of laws, starting in the early part of the second century, which restricted testamentary freedom. The *lex Furia* forbade legacies or gifts at death[15] exceeding 1,000 asses, except to certain persons (i.e. close relatives up to the seventh degree); the *lex Voconia* (169 BC) said that no one must receive as legacy or gift at death more than the heir or heirs together took, and that testators in the highest census class were not to institute women as heirs;[16] finally a plebiscite of 40 BC, the *lex Falcidia*, specified that at least a quarter of the estate must go to the heir or heirs.[17]

The problem, according to Gaius, was that too many wills were failing as a result of the refusal of persons named as heirs to accept the inheritance, because what they got was not worth it—'nec quicquam praeter inane nomen heredis' (nothing but the empty title of heir); too much of the estate had to be paid out in legacies, leaving little to the heir. The first two laws were ineptly framed, since neither restricted the *number* of legacies, and so left the possibility of frittering away most of the estate. Evidently the social pressure to remember friends and associates in this way was strong; even the *lex Falcidia* allowed three-quarters of the estate to be dispersed (though that does not necessarily mean that everyone made wills of that nature).

These laws affect all heirs nominated in wills, whether they are relatives or not. However, the type of behaviour which they are intended to restrain, involving the splitting up of estates in innumerable small bequests, suggests that a significant number of people either have no

---

[14] D. 24. 1; Stein (1985).

[15] A 'gift at death' was effectively the same as a legacy. The actual handing over took place during the donor's lifetime, but the transfer of ownership did not take effect until his death.

[16] The purpose of the latter clause was presumably to keep wealth available for the use of aristocratic males with a public career to pursue; Gardner (1986a) 170–7.

[17] For all three laws, see Gaius 2. 224–7, and for the *lex Falcidia* also Crawford (1996) 779–80.

direct heirs in the male line to succeed them, or else that they are not nominating them as heirs in their wills. The latter alternative is much less likely, especially among the Roman élite. At the time of the *lex Furia* and the *lex Voconia*, and possibly still when the *lex Falcidia* was passed, *sui heredes* could not refuse an inheritance, whether nominated as heirs in a will, or on intestacy. This means that, since a political career was costly, a wealthy Roman who nominated his sons as heirs in a will which left the bulk of his property in bequests to other people would in effect be blighting their career prospects in public life by denying them their inheritance. The implication, therefore, is that a considerable number of people are dying without sons to succeed them, and making wills that dissipate the property.

An alternative strategy was, where possible, to choose heirs at least within the family, if not the *familia*. The effect of the shortage of direct heirs was to enhance the importance of family connections outside the agnatic line, that is, relatives through women. We have already observed (2.4) a certain fondness for adopting kinsfolk connected through female relatives; similar considerations might affect the choice of heir. A man with no sons, and looking for a suitable heir related to him by blood, might, like Vibius Capax (1.5.1 above) choose his sister's son, without necessarily adopting him, or his own half-brother by the same mother but a different father—so M. Porcius Cato was the joint heir of his stepbrother Q. Servilius Caepio, along with the latter's daughter (Plutarch, *Cato Min.* 11. 6); or if he had, like the old man in Catullus 68 (1.5.1 above), only a daughter, he would welcome the birth to her of a grandson, albeit in a different *familia*.

Choices like these are illustrated in the fine collection of examples of transmission of property through the female connection to be found in Cicero's account of a much intermarried group of families in the Italian town of Larinum (in the speech *Pro Cluentio*, delivered in 66 BC).[18] According to Cicero, Cn. Magius, the last surviving of the three sons of Dinaea, a twice-married widow, left his estate between his mother and young Oppianicus, the son of his dead sister Magia and Statius Albius Oppianicus; he himself had previously been the heir of his half-brother N. Aurius, son of Dinaea's first marriage. Presumably, though Cicero does not tell us this, Aurius and Magius had inherited from their respective fathers when they died. Magius

[18] Cic. *Pro Cluentio* 11, 13–14, 21–35.

made his will shortly before his death; at that time, his own wife had no child, but said she was pregnant. This expected child was designated heir in the will, with a legacy to his mother, Magius' wife; should he not be born, she got nothing, and Dinaea and young Oppianicus were to inherit, as they did. Magius' wife miscarried; Cicero alleges that it was an abortion, Oppianicus senior having bribed her with an amount equivalent to the legacy, to ensure that his own son would be heir, before marrying her himself.

Dinaea herself, when she approached death, made her grandson, young Oppianicus, her heir, but also left a large legacy to the other son of her first marriage, M. Aurius, who had disappeared during the Social War, but was rumoured to have been enslaved, and still to be alive.

'When', says Cicero, 'some hope was held out to this woman, who had lost her children, of recovering one son, she summoned together all her relatives (*propinquos*) and the friends of her son and begged them, with tears, to take up the matter, search for the young man, and restore to her that son, the only one of many whom Fortune had seen fit to leave to her.' Unfortunately, M. Aurius' death was confirmed; his relatives alleged that he had been murdered by Oppianicus senior.

The effect of this series of wills was to concentrate in one person, young Oppianicus, the property of three separate family lines, that of Dinaea's first husband, that of her second husband, and her own. We are not told how closely related Dinaea's *propinqui* were; they may even have been her agnates. However, Cicero treats it as right and natural that she would wish to leave her property not to them but to her own son and her daughter's child. This is not mere forensic rhetoric; he expects no less, in later years, of his own estranged wife Terentia (see below).

In sharp contrast to Dinaea's is the behaviour of the defendant Cluentius' wicked (in Cicero's version of events) mother Sassia. Instead of making Cluentius, son of her first marriage, her heir, she allegedly plotted his destruction and promised her estate to her stepson, the same young Oppianicus, son by Magia of Sassia's third husband, Statius Albius Oppianicus. Oppianicus senior had previously been married to Cluentia, the sister of Sassia's first husband Cluentius. Six times married in all, he had been unfortunate in the survival rate of his offspring. Two of his three children, by three different mothers, had died young (Cicero alleges dirty deeds), leaving only Oppianicus junior, the middle child. In due course Sassia married off young Oppianicus to Auria, her daughter by her second marriage, whose late father, Aulus Aurius Melinus, Sassia's second husband, was perhaps related to the other Aurii, and was an *adfinis* of Sassia herself. He was her nephew by marriage, being—probably—the son of her sister-in-law Cluentia by her second husband, another Aurius (otherwise unknown, but possibly a relative of Dinaea's first husband). He had previously been married to Sassia's daughter (and young Cluentius' sister) Cluentia, but Sassia had broken up the marriage (by, Cicero alleges, conducting a flagrant affair with Aurius) and married him herself.[19] Cicero concentrates throughout on Sassia's alleged iniquity, and there was—to say the least—an evident estrangement between her stepson and son-in-law Oppianicus, and her son Cluentius, which had now come to a head in Oppianicus' indictment, on charges of poisoning, of Cluentius, who had been responsible in 74 BC for Oppianicus senior having been convicted (unjustly, according to the present prosecution) of the same crime.

Sassia, according to Cicero, chose to take sides in the family quarrel by aligning herself with her stepson and son-in-law Oppianicus. It looks as though, Cluentius having been the only son, and probably also the principal heir, of his father, Sassia regarded him as provided for, and intended to concentrate the inheritances from her side of the family on her stepson,[20] and on her grandchildren, if any, through him and her daughter Auria. In these grandchildren would eventually vest the inheritances of at least six lines—Dinaea and both her husbands, the Aurius whom Sassia had married, Sassia herself and Oppianicus. To this should be added whatever Sassia's daughter Auria had had, via her father, from his mother Cluentia (senior), as well as whatever, if anything, Sassia had inherited from her three husbands, or Oppianicus senior from those of his five previous wives

---

[19] Moreau (1986) stemma I, p. 188, takes *consobrinus*, the term used of Aulus Aurius Melinus' relationship to his first wife, daughter of Sassia and her first husband Cluentius, to mean that he was son of a Cluentia, sister of Cluentius senior, rather than of a Sassia, sister of our Sassia; cf. D. 38. 10. 1. 6, where Gaius explains that though there are three different terms for agnatic cousins (children of two brothers), cross cousins (children of a brother and a sister) and parallel cousins (children of two sisters), the term *consobrinus*, which strictly means the third, is commonly used to mean all three. Aurius will then have been cousin both of his first wife and of Cluentius junior.

[20] So also Moreau (1986) 185. Whether Cluentius' sister Cluentia was still alive at the time of Cluentius' trial is unknown.

who predeceased him, and his childless brother (whose wife also had been an Auria).[21]

Attention is drawn by Bradley (1991*a*), chapters 6 and 7, to the effects on familial structure of serial remarriage, and especially the formation of complex networks of interconnections; deaths, early by modern standards, were also an influential factor. He discusses the Larinum set along with several of the better-known upper-class family groups from the late Republic—such as Sulla with his five wives and Mark Antony with his five (six if one counts Cleopatra), of whom one, Fulvia, was married three times and widowed twice; his second wife, Antonia, was also his cousin. His fifth wife, Octavia, lost her son by her first marriage, Marcellus, in his twenties. At least two of Antony's wives, and probably the children by the first, predeceased him; so did two of Pompey's five wives, both in childbirth. We may also remember that Cicero's daughter was married three times, predeceased her father, and had no children surviving beyond infancy. This particular group of families in Larinum was not unique in the number of marriages contracted by individuals, even by Oppianicus, nor does the death rate among its children and younger adults seem exceptional, despite the charges of murder made, on behalf of an interested party, by Cicero. Allegations of foul play apart, there was an evident lack of surviving agnates and of male heirs among the men of this group of families, but a network of cognate relationships, especially as a result of intermarriage and remarriage. It was therefore possible to leave property 'within the blood' while avoiding its dispersal.

The shortage of male heirs also had important effects on the role and function of the tutors of women. The unavailability of male agnates to be tutors and control a woman's disposal of family property that passed to her mattered less if there was a similar shortage of agnatic relatives to inherit from her. There was some incentive to enable women to bequeath property to their own children, rather than to leave it to be claimed by members of the *gens*. Already in the law of the Twelve Tables, it is said, fathers could appoint persons of their

[21] Whether Sassia could hope also, in the event of a conviction, to receive Cluentius' property is unclear. Under the Republic, someone condemned of murder was 'interdicted from fire and water' (i.e. exiled from Italy and effectively disfranchised) though what happened to their property is uncertain, i.e. whether it went to their relatives or not; under the Empire, it was confiscated by the state: *D.* 48. 8. 3. 5 (Marcianus—3rd cent. AD).

choice to be tutors to their children (above, 2.10), implying that some wished or needed to; from the late third or second century BC, in default of either testamentary or agnatic tutors, magistrates were empowered to appoint them.[22]

This marks a change in the function of tutors of women, many of whom are not now agnates. They are no longer there to protect their own interests, as agnates, by preventing women from making wills and leaving the property away from the immediate heirs, that is, themselves. Their function is rather to help women to preserve the value of their property in their lifetime, in the interests of those to whom they may wish to pass it on, and especially of their children.[23]

3.3 DEVELOPMENTS IN INHERITANCE LAW

So long as a woman left a valid will, then she could benefit her children by leaving her property to them. By the late Republic it is taken for granted that she will do so. In 58 BC, Cicero writes in some agitation from exile to his wife Terentia, who has told him that she is going to sell some of her own real estate to raise money. He begs her to think better of it, in case the attempt to restore him fails, and to try to get their friends to bear the costs instead. 'In the name of our [or possibly 'my'] wretched state, our boy is already ruined, let us not ruin him utterly!' In other words, she ought to preserve her fortune in the interests of young Marcus' future. No similar anxiety is expressed at this time about Marcus' older sister Tullia, who was already five years into her first marriage (though soon to be widowed), and, as a woman, was not destined for a public career. However, over a decade later, after Cicero's and Terentia's divorce, Cicero continues to expect that his ex-wife will make proper provision for both her children in her will, and later hints, after Tullia's death, that Terentia ought likewise to 'do the right thing' by Tullia's little son, as he himself has done in his own will.[24] That is, like Dinaea, Terentia has a son and, for a few months at least, a grandson by a dead daughter, and Cicero expects that they, and not any of her own relatives, will be the main beneficiaries under her will.

---

[22] *D.* 26. 1. 6. 2, 26. 2. 1 pr.; Buckland (1963) 147–8.

[23] Gardner (1986a) 14–22; (1993) 89–91.

[24] Dixon (1986). Cic. *Ad Fam.* 14. 1. 5: 'per fortunas miseras nostras, vide ne puerum perditum perdamus'. Terentia's will: *Ad Att.* 11. 23. 3, 25; 12. 18a.

If Terentia, or any other mother, had died without leaving a valid will, then her agnates, if she had any, would have had first claim, both in civil law and under the praetor's edict, to her property. If there were no agnates, then by this time the praetor's edict gave the succession to cognates (see 1.4), who included children and grandchildren. Young Marcus and little Lentulus[25] might not have been the only cognates, but they were closer than any others, and Marcus' claim would have been prior to that of Lentulus, since he stood in the first degree (i.e. closer than anybody), Lentulus in the second.[26] We do not know if Terentia had in fact any surviving brothers or sisters or other relatives. A half-sister Fabia, who was a Vestal virgin, was certainly alive in the 60s—Catiline prosecuted her unsuccessfully on a charge of incest, and Clodius, apparently before the tribunate of Cato (62 BC) slandered her as well as other priests and priestesses—but, as a half-sister, she was more remotely related than Terentia's own children.[27] Cicero's correspondence provides no further information. All the same, it was socially important, and even a matter of duty, to leave a 'good' will.[28]

A mother, unlike a father, was not required explicitly to mention her children in her will, either to institute them as heirs or expressly not to do so, in order for the will to be valid. However, by the middle of the first century BC there was evidently a strong feeling that parents had a moral obligation to make a fairly generous provision for all their children (unless the latter could be shown explicitly to have deserved to be cut off), and a praetorian remedy, the 'querela inofficiosi testamenti' (complaint of unduteous will) was available (see 1.5.2 above). Children, and certain other close relatives, who felt that they had been unfairly treated, could bring a suit challenging the will.

Interestingly, this social expectation that parents would do the decent thing by their children applied to both parents. In its implementation in the praetorian remedy of the *querela*, the blood tie was treated as being at least as important as *familia*. The breaking of the agnatic tie between father and child by emancipation or adoption made no difference; not only children *in potestate*, but those

---

[25] The short-lived son of Tullia and her third and last husband Cornelius Dolabella, who had himself acquired the *cognomen* on his adoption.   [26] *D.* 38. 10. 1. 3–4.

[27] Fabia: Ascon. 91C; Plut. *Cato Min.* 19. 3.

[28] For Roman attitudes to the matter, see Champlin (1991) 5–28.

emancipated, or even given in adoption, could challenge their fathers' wills. All children could challenge their mothers' wills. The obligation was reciprocal; children were expected to show proper appreciation towards their parents, and parents could challenge their children's wills.[29]

Cicero did his best to exploit such social attitudes, in the interests of his client Cluentius. He claimed that at the time of the court case in 74 BC, in which Cluentius appeared against his stepfather Oppianicus (see above), the former had not yet got round to making a will. The implication is that this was something unusual and unexpected and must have had a special reason, which Cicero duly supplies, managing in the same breath to cast a slur on Cluentius' mother Sassia and to praise Cluentius' sense of propriety. Cluentius, he says, was torn. Sassia was such an unnatural mother that he could not bring himself to leave her anything; on the other hand, he could not (sc. as one conscious of filial duty) completely omit her from his will.[30] We need not, however, read into this an allusion to the 'complaint of unduteous will' (which may not as yet have been introduced in 74 BC); Cicero is appealing to the customary moral values of his audience, shared, he implies, by Cluentius.

One of the earliest probable references to the *querela* concerns a mother's claim against a son's will. The case, which fell around the middle of the first century BC, was pleaded by Asinius Pollio on behalf of one Liburnia, whose son had left her nothing at all, making his heir a certain Novatius, in recognition of his past friendship. Asinius countered by sarcastically imagining a clause in which the son justified disinheriting his mother, on the grounds of her past behaviour towards him. But what sort of behaviour could he allege? 'My dearest, sweetest mother, who devoted her life to me, who gave birth twice on the same day', and so forth.[31]

From this and a couple of other references[32] we may gather that the feeling that, irrespective of *familia*, parents, of either sex, and their children had a moral, even if not a legal, right to inherit something substantial from each other had received formal acknowledgement in the

---

[29] For fathers, see the discussion in 1.5.1 and 1.5.2 above, of Val. Max. 7. 7. 2 and 5.

[30] Cic. *Pro Cluentio*. 45: 'neque legare eius modi matri poterat animum inducere, neque testamento nomen omnino praetermittere parentis' (he could neither bring himself to make a bequest to such a mother, nor in a will to pass over entirely the name of a parent).   [31] Quint. *Inst. Orat.* 9. 2. 9, cf. 9. 2. 34–5.

[32] Val. Max. 7. 7. 2 and 7. 8. 4; see 1.5.2 above.

institution of this legal procedure, the 'complaint of unduteous will' by the middle of the first century BC.

And there, for the time being, matters rested. Children of mothers who had been married with *manus* had been able to inherit from them on intestacy as agnates; with the decline of *manus*, few, if any, were left who came into that category. Otherwise, if there was no valid will, they could still inherit, but only as cognates, and only, it seems, if they were legitimate. If there was a will, children could bring the *querela* if they received less than a fourth of what they would have received on intestacy (by an interpretation derived from the *lex Falcidia*, which required only that heirs in a will receive one fourth of the estate between them).

Only a few certain examples of the use of the *querela* against a mother's will are attested for the later Republic and early Empire. In a rather self-congratulatory letter, the younger Pliny relates how he dissuaded a disgruntled son from bringing a complaint of unduteous will before the centumviral court. The story is not straightforward, however, and has political undertones, and Pliny's account may be suspected of being disingenuous.[33] A certain Pomponia Galla had disinherited her son, Asudius Curianus, and named as heirs Pliny himself, another senator and several knights. The son first tried to arrange a private deal with Pliny, asking him to give him his share, on the understanding that it would be returned to him eventually (presumably when Asudius died—we learn presently that he was rich and childless). This was to be a kind of *praeiudicium*—in other words, when Asudius brought a complaint in court, he could support his claim to have been unjustly disinherited by pointing to the apparent approval and sympathy shown him by so eminent a personage as Pliny.

This was rather shady, and Pliny, by his own account, took a high moral tone: 'respondebam non convenire moribus meis aliud palam, aliud agere secreto, praeterea non esse satis honestum donare et locupleti et orbo' (I told him that I was not the sort of person to do one thing openly and another in secret—besides, it was not very honourable to make a gift to someone both rich and childless). Pliny had evidently spotted the danger that he himself would subsequently get the reputation of being a *captator*, an inheritance-hunter. Instead, he offered to waive his claim to a share of the estate *if* he were satisfied

---

[33] D. 5. 2. 8. 8–9; Pliny, *Ep.* 5. 1; Gardner (1986*a*) 186; Buckland (1963) 328–9.

that Asudius had been unjustly disinherited, and he brought in two distinguished ex-consuls to the discussion (so much for Asudius' attempts at secrecy). This domestic tribunal decided that Pomponia's disinheritance of her son had been justified; nevertheless, Asudius went ahead and gave notice of a lawsuit, not against Pliny, but against the other heirs. This was an obvious feint, designed to intimidate them into settling out of court, since Asudius could blackmail them with their previous political associations with the 'Stoic opposition' under Domitian,[34] which might be brought up in court. Pliny then, at their request, negotiated a settlement with Asudius. As Pliny tells it, he pointed out to Asudius that he would have had no case if he had been left a fourth part of the estate. However, instead of simply advising him to accept the equivalent from the heirs, he volunteered to top it up himself, by doing as Asudius had asked in the first place and giving him an amount equivalent to his own share—despite the fact that, as he pointed out, Asudius, two years having elapsed, no longer had any possible legal claim against him. Why did Pliny do this? He would have us understand that he acted merely out of consideration for the others—though he too had a reason, in his past associations, to avoid a court action (he had been friendly with leading Stoics). Another interpretation might be that he was honouring the deal which he had in fact made with Asudius, the verdict of the two consulars having been merely an embarrassment, and they having been brought in merely to divert responsibility for a *praeiudicium* from Pliny himself.

The deal with the other heirs duly went through. Asudius later died, and left Pliny a legacy, which he describes as 'moderate' and claims was a tribute to his own staunch old-fashioned morality, and the reward of a good conscience and good reputation. Reading between the lines, Pliny's own conduct was not free from suspicion of self-interest.

Other unhappy families appear in the legal and literary sources. According to the jurist Paul, a mother with two daughters left three-quarters of the estate to outsiders, one-quarter to one daughter and passed over the other. This is possibly a theoretical example, but may derive from a real case in his own time (early third century AD); such maternal favouritism is not unknown. Valerius Maximus, writing in the reign of Tiberius, related the story of the apparently thrice-

---

[34] Cf. Pliny, *Ep.* 1. 5; 3. 11.

married Aebutia, wife of L. Menenius Agrippa, who made one daughter, Pletonia, her heir, while leaving only a small legacy to the children of the other daughter, Afronia. The latter, though Valerius perhaps implies she would have been justified in resorting to the *querela*, did not do so. She refrained from bringing suit against her sister, in the interests of family harmony.[35] In Paul's example, the daughter passed over brought a complaint of unduteous will and won, but apparently she had claimed the whole inheritance. The question of legal interest was, what was to happen to the other sister? She had not challenged the will, having been left a quarter of the estate, but she should not suffer on that account; her legal entitlement was unaffected. Paul's answer was that the complaining daughter should have half the estate, which is what she would have had on intestacy. It was not right to let her put in a claim for the whole estate, to the detriment of her sister (this implies that the magistrate who granted her an action in those terms was at fault).

During the reign of Augustus, on two occasions appeals were made on behalf of ill-used children—one against the will of a father, the other against that of a mother—directly to the emperor, who decided them by decree.[36] In one, Valerius Maximus represents the emperor as acting (unlike the complainant's father) in true fatherly spirit, as 'father of his country', in the other with all the justice and solemnity of personified Equity herself—though it is clear from Valerius' own account that the emperor's decision here was influenced by the belief that there had been an attempt to evade his laws on marriage and inheritance.

The first, successful, plea was on behalf of C. Tettius, disinherited by his father while still an infant; Valerius makes a point of mentioning that Tettius senior and the child's mother Petronia were still married at Tettius' death. Tettius had most iniquitously denied the paternal name to a child begotten in his own house (*in proprio lare*). It sounds very much as though Tettius had suspected his wife of infidelity and tried to disown the child; however, he had made no move to divorce her. This, perhaps, is why the matter was brought to Augustus—it touched upon his adultery law.

In the other case, a woman called Septicia disinherited her two sons by an earlier marriage, leaving a will in favour of her second husband, Publicius. Septicia did not need to marry, in order to

---

[35] Val. Max. 7. 8. 2; *D.* 5. 2. 19 (Paul).   [36] Val. Max. 7. 7. 3 and 4.

receive inheritances freely under the Julian laws, since she had already been married and had at least two children and was past the age of child-bearing (though if she outlived Publicius and he had no other heirs, as his wife she could hope to inherit, even on intestacy). Whether Publicius had ever married before is not stated, but he also was evidently beyond the age limits within which the Julian law penalised failure to remarry (he was 'fairly old', *senex admodum*). The dowry may have been an inducement; Augustus, however, recognizing that the marriage was not made for the procreation of children, refused to let him keep it. Evidently, the marriage was to some extent one of convenience on both sides; Valerius says Septicia acted out of spite towards her sons.

Both these disputes were settled directly by the emperor, and did not involve the bringing of a lawsuit under the *querela*. Later imperial rescripts, responding to enquiries from or on behalf of other disgruntled children, deal with the question of whether they have grounds for bringing the *querela*, against an allegedly unfair parental will. In AD 197, Septimius Severus laid down an important principle. As we saw above, in 2.5.2, failure by a man when making a will to provide for the possibility of children being born later might invalidate the will (because of the requirement that *sui heredes* must be instituted heirs or expressly disinherited). Women were not required specifically to institute or disinherit their children; but, said Severus, if a child was born after a woman made a will, and she did not get round to making another will, the child had obviously done nothing to justify being left out of the existing will, so ought to be allowed to bring the *querela*, the complaint of unduteous will. He went further. If the mother had died in childbirth and other children were heirs, the child should be allowed *virilis pars*—that is, the amount that would have been his share if the estate had been equally divided among all the children on intestacy (by this time, the *senatusconsultum Orphitianum* (see below) had given children priority over all other heirs on intestacy to a mother's estate, though a will was not invalidated if they were not instituted)—but if outsiders had been named as heirs, then he could bring the *querela*. This judgement establishes an important principle: possible *postumi* had to be taken into account by women as well as by men.[37] Failure to do so would not invalidate a

---

[37] *Cod. Iust.* 3. 28. 3 (45 Honoré).

will, but it provided adequate ground for a successful challenge to the will, using the *querela*.

Several relevant rescripts of Diocletian survive, revealing both the limits of maternal authority and the expectation of *pietas* from both children and parents (of either sex).[38] One appears to be a mother-in-law story. Faustina's mother, having originally approved of the man she married, changed her mind and cut Faustina out of her will. Diocletian says firmly that she has given her mother no justification to do so, since she has no obligation to conform to her mother's wishes in matters of marriage or divorce (whereas a father's authority was still required for marriage though, after Marcus Aurelius, he could not compel divorce).[39] In another response, children who tried to stop their mother from making a will are told that they deserved what they got (or rather did not get). Behind another rescript lies a story like the *cause célèbre*, in the younger Pliny's day, of Attia Viriola;[40] a disinherited daughter successfully challenged as undutiful, before the centumviral court, the will her father made in favour of his new wife. The right, Diocletian tells the stepmother who applies to him when her stepdaughter, totally disinherited, launches the *querela* against her father's will, is on the daughter's side. If she cannot be proved to have given her father any just cause of offence, she can claim the entire estate.

The first of these answers reminds us that *potestas* is still the father's exclusive right, the second that *pietas* is due from children towards mothers as well as fathers, and the third, not only that equity demands that blood relatives be preferred to outsiders, but also that the inheritance prospects of children may be threatened by the remarriage of a parent—as happened also to the sons of Septicia, and Afronia, daughter of the thrice-married Aebutia.

The 'complaint of unduteous will' could afford children some protection against unfair treatment in their parents' wills, although perhaps more effectively, to begin with, against the wills of fathers than of mothers. At the time when the *querela* was introduced, children, unless emancipated, had priority over all other heirs in intestate

---

[38] *Cod. Iust..* 3. 28. 20, 23, 22 (2128, 2365, 2198 Honoré). In a fourth instance (*Cod. Iust.* 3. 28. 25: 2714 Honoré), the parents are estranged, but the mother has had to take into consideration the effect of the *senatusconsultum Orphitianum* (see below).

[39] Gardner (1986a) 11; Treggiari (1991) 460–1.

[40] Pliny, *Ep.* 6. 33; Gardner (1986a) 184–5.

inheritance from their fathers, and emancipated children also were included by the beginning of the Empire. In inheriting on intestacy from their mothers, however, they ranked only as cognates, and her agnates took precedence over them. This situation did not change until the passing of a senatorial decree in AD 178, the *senatusconsultum Orphitianum* (see below), which gave a woman's children priority over all other heirs. However, the few attested instances of suits brought under the *querela* before then against a mother's will provide no examples where the beneficiaries under the will were her agnates, and so we cannot say for certain how courts decided in such cases— whether the claims of *familia* (i.e. the agnates) were upheld against the close tie of blood between mother and child (and if so, whether of all agnates, or only those in the closest degree, i.e. the mother's brothers and sisters), or whether the feeling was that equity demanded that the children receive their mother's property. Since the *senatusconsultum Orphitianum* so resoundingly and firmly put the children in first place, this may suggest that it reflected feelings which had previously found practical expression in earlier jurisprudence, that is, that courts had been tending to find in favour of the children.[41]

The civil law on intestate inheritance and the modifications to it in the praetor's edict during the late Republic were concerned only with persons of legitimate birth. Legitimate children could inherit as *sui heredes*, in civil law, or as *liberi*, under the edict, from fathers only, and as *cognati*, under the edict, from both fathers and mothers. In the final form of the praetor's edict, as consolidated under Hadrian, the clause *unde cognati* had been extended to allow illegitimate children to inherit from their mothers.[42] This, together with other developments affecting illegitimate children, will be discussed in 3.6 below.

The next major legislative change came under Hadrian. In the sad event of children dying before their mother, the *senatusconsultum Tertullianum*[43] enhanced the rights of certain mothers to inherit from them. In civil law, mothers had had no right at all of inheritance from their children. The praetor's edict had admitted them to inherit, but only as cognates. Under the *senatusconsultum* they could now

---

[41] Humbert (1972) 189–97.

[42] D. 38. 8. 2 (Gaius); 4 (Ulpian); 8 (Modestinus); this covered inheritance of child from mother and vice versa, and also inheritance between brothers and sisters born of the same mother.

[43] D. 38. 17; Paul. *Sent.* 4. 9; Ulp. *Reg.* 26. 8; *Inst.* 3. 3; Voci (1963) 18–21; Buckland (1963) 372–3; Meinhart (1967); Gardner (1986a) 196–8.

inherit ahead of other cognates, in the category of *legitimi* (that is, if the dead child was a daughter, or a son who had died leaving no children). They still came a considerable way down in the order of priority in that category. The child's father (if the child had been emancipated) came first. Next came brothers and sisters by the same father (*consanguinei*), including those adopted, or from his other marriages.[44] If there were no brothers, only sisters, the mother shared with them, though she came ahead of any other agnates there might be.

Only women with the *ius liberorum* could benefit under the *senatusconsultum Tertullianum*—that is, freeborn women who had had three children or freedwomen who had had four. Since the reign of Augustus, such women were not required to have tutors to control their disposal of property; however the risk of the child's patrimony leaving the family through the mother was not great. Few women, and especially few freedwomen, were likely both to have had enough freeborn children to obtain the *ius* and to have outlived all the children, natural (possibly by more than one marriage) or adopted, who had been in the same father's *potestas* as the deceased, as well as children who had been emancipated (for the application of the *senatusconsultum* to mothers of illegitimate children, see further in 3.6 below).

As we have already seen, the rules of inheritance had already undergone various extensions to accommodate inheritance between those inside the *familia* and those now outside—that is, where some members had been emancipated or given in adoption. These additional rights for mothers introduced further complications to calculating the order of precedence among the various claims to an estate which might arise. The jurists, as is their wont, discuss a number of possibilities, mainly in theoretical terms. One, however, is of interest both because it may derive from a real case—an imperial rescript is cited—and because of the ruling given.

According to Ulpian: 'If a man had died survived by a daughter, whom he had given in legal adoption, and also by his mother, the deified Pius has decreed that the *senatusconsultum Tertullianum* is not to be applied and that mother and daughter are to be admitted together to possession of the property as cognates in the first degree.'[45]

---

[44] Warning: Gardner (1986a) 197 is mistaken in saying that *consanguinei* did not include children from more than one marriage; it is clear from *D.* 38. 16. 1. 10–11 that it covered all those in the same *potestas*, including also adoptive children.

[45] *D.* 38. 17. 2. 9: 'Si quis decessisset relicta filia, quam in adoptionem legitime dederat, relicta et matre, divus Pius decrevit cessare senatusconsultum Tertullianum et

Even although, under the praetor's edict, children given in adoption could inherit only as cognates, the mother's right under the *senatusconsultum* brought her in only near the bottom of the category of *legitimi*. If the daughter had not been given in adoption (which was not something within her control), she would have come in the top category, *liberi*, and excluded her grandmother from the inheritance. Pius' decision therefore was that they should share, despite the *senatusconsultum*. His decision may have been made partly on grounds of equity, and the account in the *Digest* allows us to trace how the legal argument may have gone. The dead man's mother and daughter are both to succeed, as cognates in the first degree. If the *senatusconsultum* was set aside the mother, whom the *senatusconsultum* had promoted to the category of *legitimi*, went back to being a cognate in the first degree. The daughter was, and always had been, a cognate in that degree: adoption had not affected that relationship, but only the agnatic link. Therefore both ought to be allowed to inherit in the same degree.

It was also provided under the *senatusconsultum* that if a dead child was under age (*impubes*) and his mother had not applied for tutors to be appointed to his property, she was not to be admitted to the inheritance.[46] Ulpian has a good deal to say about various circumstances that ought to be taken into consideration. For the most part, he represents the mother as having been merely negligent or misinformed, rather than ill-intentioned, in not requesting that tutors be appointed (except for a possible underhand stratagem (§ 34–6) of suggesting bad characters as tutors, in the expectation that the praetor will reject them). Once or twice (§§ 25 and 46), he mentions the possibility that the child's father himself might have wished to leave the matters in the mother's hands, rather than those of tutors[47]—after all, it was open to fathers to make provision themselves, by appointing tutors in their wills. The law, however, did not permit women to act as tutors and handle the affairs of the heads of other *familiae*; this was one of the results of their lack of *potestas*.[48]

This chapter of the *Digest* as a whole highlights some of the ways in

simul esse admittendas ad bonorum possessionem unde proximi cognati matrem et filiam.'

[46] D. 38. 17. 2. 23; for its application, ibid. 24–46.
[47] Mothers administering their children's property: Chiusi (1994) 164–75, and see 3.5 below. [48] Gardner (1993) 85–9, 97–101; see also 3.5 below.

which the shape of Roman families was influenced by certain basic demographic events—later age at marriage for men than for women, high mortality, especially among children, and low life expectancy generally. The death of the *pater* was an event that came early in the life of many Romans; hence the concern with tutors and with widows.[49]

The *senatusconsultum Tertullianum*, in giving mothers some rights of inheritance from their children, did not do so at the expense of fathers or agnates; where there were any survivors in the male line, they had priority. The reverse became the case with inheritance *from* mothers. In AD 178, the *senatusconsultum Orphitianum*[50] put children (even, apparently, illegitimate children—see below) first in order of succession to their mothers, over *all* other heirs—which, in the case of a woman, means the *legitimi*, i.e. agnates, patron of a freedwoman and manumitting parent. This appears from Ulpian's gloss on a relevant clause from the *senatusconsultum*, which he quotes: 'If no one of the sons, or of those to whom at the same time the inheritance is offered as *legitimi*, is willing to claim the inheritance for himself let the old law operate.' 'Those to whom at the same time the inheritance is offered' means not only deceased sons' children, who 'represented' their fathers, but, after the *senatusconsultum Orphitianum*, daughters' children also.[51]

Ulpian explains that this means that if even one son is willing to accept the inheritance, the 'old law' does not operate—that is, no other heir at all is admitted. He gives an example: if there is a son and a patron (i.e. the dead woman was a freedwoman) and her son refuses the inheritance, the patron takes it; in other words, the patron takes it only if no son does.[52]

[49] Saller (1994) esp. chs. 1–3 (demographic analysis) and 8 (arrangements for guardianship). I have not been able to consult the four volumes of J. U. Krause, *Witwe und Waisen im römischen Reich* (Stuttgart, 1994–5).

[50] D. 38. 17; Paul. *Sent.* 4. 10; Ulp. *Reg.* 26. 7; *Inst.* 3. 4; Voci (1963) 22–3; Buckland (1963) 373–4; Meinhart (1967); Gardner (1986a) 198–200.

[51] 'No one of the sons', by the convention that in Roman law, in contexts where sex is irrelevant, male terms will be understood to include females, covers both sons and daughters: D. 31. 45 pr.; 32. 62, 50. 16. 1, 152, 195. Daughters' children: D. 38. 7. 2. 4.

[52] D. 38. 17. 1. 9: 'Si nemo filiorum eorumve quibus simul legitima hereditas defertur volet ad se hereditatem pertinere, ius antiquum esto.' Meinhart (1967) 69ff. argued that patrons were not originally excluded in the *senatusconsultum* by freedwomen's children, and that this practice developed only through juristic interpretation; Gardner (1986a) 200 followed hesitantly, suggesting that the interpretation was based on analogy with the exclusion of the manumitting parent of an emancipated freeborn woman by her children. However both parent and patron inherited, as *legitimi*, under

It did not matter if the children had undergone *capitis deminutio* (i.e. been emancipated or given in adoption), since that affected only the agnatic connection, that is, their inheritance rights from their father's side.[53] Nor did it make any difference if they were still in their father's power, though in practice this meant that the inheritance became his; steps to change the law to ensure its eventual transmission to the children do not begin until the fourth century AD. Before that, whether the property itself passed to the children was likely to depend upon the terms of the father's will; afterwards, the father's hold on the property is no longer absolute ownership, since it must be preserved for eventual handing on to the children; a similar situation had existed, with regard to the return of dowry to wives, since the Republic. In any case, as long as the father lived he himself had the benefit of the income from it.[54]

One effect of the *senatusconsultum* was that a condition of emancipation was no longer enough to ensure that a *pater* would not get his hands on property left by an estranged wife to their children; other devices were necessary, such as appointment of other heirs, charged with a trust (*fideicommissum*) to hand it on to the children once they were legally independent, or substitution of alternative heirs, to succeed if the condition of emancipation was not fulfilled. One father quite cleverly tried to bring a *querela* of unduteous will, arguing that the mother had unjustly disinherited her children by such a substitution. Diocletian would have none of it. The mother had taken that step because she did not trust the children's father, so she had been acting in their best interests.[55]

The *senatusconsultum Orphitianum* was important where for some reason or another the mother had not left a valid will, and especially important for those who had no other chance of intestate inheritance, that is, illegitimate children and the children of freed slaves. Illegitimate children did not have the support of a *paterfamilias* or inheritance expectations from one, and a freedwoman's children, before the *senatusconsultum*, might be ousted by a patron's claim.

'the old (praetorian) law' and patrons also inherited under civil law (Gaius 3. 43), so analogy was not needed.

[53] D. 38. 17. 1. 8 (Ulpian).
[54] D. 31. 77. 7, 19. Gardner (1993) 69ff; Evans Grubbs (1995) 114–7; Arjava (1996) 98–105.   [55] *Cod. Iust.* 3. 28. 25 (2714 Honoré); see also 1.13.

Those who were both illegitimate and born of a freed mother were doubly unfortunate.

After the *senatusconsultum*, all children had essentially the same level of priority in inheriting on intestacy from their mothers as from their fathers—that is, in the top category, as *liberi*, from fathers and as *legitimi*, at the top of that class, from mothers. The economic well-being of the next generation was safeguarded by making family as important as *familia* in inheritance.

In the fourth and subsequent centuries the process of assimilation between agnatic and cognatic inheritance rights, i.e. from the paternal and maternal side, continued. Specially noteworthy are the measures by which, from Constantine onwards, a father's control over property coming to children in his power from the mother's side was reduced to no more than usufruct, that is, deriving income from the property (see n. 54). The *tutela* of women, and with it much of the advantage for women of having *ius liberorum*, withered away. Eventually, the new system of inheritance introduced by Justinian did away with the distinction between male and female lines and with talk of agnates and cognates.[56] *Patria potestas* survived—it had a public purpose, extending beyond the family; inheritance was a private matter.

3.4 FAMILY FINANCES: MATERNAL INFLUENCES

The twin pillars of the position of *paterfamilias* were property and power. He had *potestas* over the members of the *familia*, and he owned all its property, to which they were the heirs in civil law. The property of his wife was, legally at least, completely separate from his, although in practice both might be drawn upon to supply the day-to-day needs of the household. For the use of the property of both husband and wife for domestic purposes, see e.g. in D. 24. 1, §§ 18 and 28 (use of slaves, clothing or a house belonging to one or other spouse), 29. 1–31. 1 (making of clothes for members of the household) and 31. 9 (supply of foodstuffs for slaves or horses). This was not incompatible with keeping account of the origin and ownership of such domestic resources; this is implicit in the chapters of the *Digest* (33. 9 and 10) which discuss legacies in wills of domestic items such as furniture and

---

[56] For a summary of developments in inheritance law, see e.g. Kaser (1975) 497–511; Buckland (1963) 374–6.

furnishings (*supellex*) and foodstuffs and store-cupboard supplies (*penus*), specifically defined as items for daily use, and distinguished from things intended for sale.[57]

Sometimes, it seems, particularly where home-grown produce was used and/or records were inadequate, confusion could arise: the implications of *D.* 29. 2. 87 and 32. 37 pr. are worth considering. In the former, the question is whether a son who took possession after his father's death of a field, thinking it was part of his mother's property (when in fact it belonged to his father) was to be regarded as having 'acted as heir' of his father, and therefore accepted the inheritance. Papinian apparently accepts the possibility that a son, heir to both father and mother, should be uncertain to which inheritance a specific piece of property belonged. In the latter example, Scaevola supposes that a dying man bequeaths to his mother a piece of land which in fact was already hers (*qui proprius matris erat*). Scaevola does not go into detail, but we may imagine that one source of such confusions could be the way in which dowry property changed owners. It belonged to a husband while the marriage lasted, but could be reclaimed by the wife at his death or if there was a divorce; the younger members of the family, however, may not have been privy to the details of parental financial arrangements. The implication of such vagueness about ownership is that property belonging to both parents had routinely been drawn upon to supply the daily needs of the household, regardless of which of them actually owned it; there are also perhaps implications about the availability—or rather its lack—of the kind of documentation, such as title deeds, which are requisite nowadays. If landed property had been bought by either parent, they might have preserved documents recording the witnessed conveyances of ownership by *mancipatio*; similarly, the text of a dowry agreement, or, if it had come by inheritance, of a detailed will might still exist, but such kinds of documentary evidence could not be counted upon—as in *Cod. Iust.* 8. 55. 2=1408 Honoré (n. 61 below), where a donor had burned the record of transfer of property.[58]

---

[57] *D.* 33. 9 and 10. Although both *penus* and *supellex* were defined by jurists in terms of ownership by the *paterfamilias* (33. 9. 3 pr.; 33. 10. 1, 7. 1), property ownership (unlike *potestas* over free persons) was not restricted to males, and in most of the actual legacies discussed, the testator and the recipients are not identified: Gardner (1996) 393–5.

[58] Gardner (1993) 182ff. discusses problems of proof, one of which is the loss or unavailability of documents. A land registration system was introduced by Augustus, but on its deficiencies, see Crook (1967c) 147–9.

In strict law, however, the property belonging to the wife was completely separate from that of her husband, and valuable gifts to him or (which in law amounted to the same thing) to the children in his *potestas* were not legally valid.[59] If either husband or wife was still in *potestas*, the ban extended to the *paterfamilias* in whose *potestas* they were, and to anyone else in the same *potestas*, and so, for example, uncles and aunts and grandfathers, and also paternal grandmothers (so long as they were still married to the grandfather) might have to restrain their generosity.[60]

Maternal grandmothers, on the other hand, being in a different *familia* from both parents, were free to spoil their young relatives to their hearts' content (as were paternal grandmothers, once widowed or divorced), and so in some third-century rescripts we find, for instance, one grandmother presenting a granddaughter with a gift of a slave, another giving a dowry for a great-granddaughter still *in potestate*. The dowry became the husband's property during the marriage; if the girl's *pater* had given it, he could have reclaimed it when the marriage ended, but, because this dowry had come from someone legally an outsider, and was classed as *adventicia*, it would only return to the donor if she had made a legal agreement with the bridegroom to that effect. In this instance she had, and a rescript from Maximinus' office patiently explains to her grandson Sulpicius (the old lady being now dead and the marriage also apparently over) that he cannot simply reclaim his daughter's dowry in the same way as one given by himself, but can bring a claim under the agreement as his grandmother's heir. Sulpicius was not alone in his puzzlement over legal niceties. One grandmother attempted to give her granddaughter her 'own' dowry property, despite the fact that her own husband was still alive and therefore—legally—owned it. Another, after some family quarrel, thought she could cancel a transfer of property simply by burning the deed of gift.[61]

The legal rule that gifts between husband and wife and certain of their relatives were invalid did not, of course, have the effect that in

---

[59] Treggiari (1991) 366–74.

[60] *D*. 24. 1. 3. A 'valuable' gift was one that was held to have 'enriched' the recipient (*D*. 24. 1 *passim*)—so certain gifts in kind, such as slaves or land, were not valid gifts, nor were sums of money, if used for the purchase of such things; birthday presents, however, and consumable items such as perfumes and luxury foods were allowable (*D*. 24. 1. 31. 8–9).

[61] *Cod. Iust.* 7. 60. 2, 5. 12. 6, 8. 53. 21, 8. 55. 2 (1799, 937, 2235, 1408 Honoré).

practice husbands and wives did not make such gifts to each other, or women and certain of their relatives to their children;[62] they did, and for the most part it did not matter. The rule meant merely that unless the donor confirmed the gift when the marriage relationship of the parents ended—that is, by divorce or the death of either partner—it legally continued to belong to the giver. It was as well to remember this when making a will, or sorting out the household belongings after a divorce—or even when selling something valuable—in case someone wanted to be awkward later. Only occasionally otherwise might legal problems arise. Parents might, for instance, put slaves at a son or daughter's disposal for his or her personal use, but legally ownership remained with themselves; so it is specified that if, say, a daughter was accused of adultery, those slaves might not be manumitted (to avoid their being handed over for torture to obtain evidence) by the father or mother to whom they belonged.[63]

Once the children were out of *potestas*, however, whether on their father's death or because they had been emancipated, or once their parents were no longer married, i.e. their mother had been widowed or divorced, there was nothing to prevent her (or indeed her relatives) from giving her generosity free rein, if she were so inclined. Benefactions came perhaps mainly from widows, rather than from divorcées. Although divorce from her husband would also remove the ban on a mother's making gifts to children still in his power, ex-wives, particularly if the split had not been amicable, were perhaps unlikely to want to make over property, when the ex-husband, not the children in his *potestas*, became the legal owner; as we have already seen (1.9 at n. 118), bequests in wills might sometimes be made dependent on a condition of emancipation. As far as emancipation is concerned, statistical estimates of how frequently this occurred are not possible. However, given the demographic possibility that 'just over one-third of Roman children lost their fathers before puberty, and another third then lost their fathers before age twenty-five' (Saller (1994) 189), and bearing in mind the earlier marriage pattern for

[62] In *D.* 24. 1. 3. 4 a gift by a mother to a son *in potestate* is held to be invalid unless he is a soldier, in which case it is part of his *peculium castrense* (Buckland (1963) 280) and held separate from his father's property.

[63] *D.* 40. 9. 12. 3 and 7. Contrast *D.* 40. 8. 8, where a mother has given some slaves to her daughter, already out of *potestas*, on condition that they be manumitted when she (apparently the mother) died; if they were released beforehand, the freedom held good *so long as the donor consented* (showing that the recipient of the gift had power of legal action and was not *in potestate*), and when the donor died, they must be freed.

Roman women than men, many children will have been fatherless, and many mothers will have been widowed, and in a position to contribute directly to their children's resources—or, indeed, those of their stepchildren. Augustus' consort Livia seems to have given her stepdaughter, the unfortunate Julia, after her father's death, two of a family group of three slaves whom she had previously put at her disposal to look after her in exile (and perhaps spy on her); some time after Augustus' death, Julia manumitted the father and son, and Livia the mother, whom she had retained in her own ownership.[64]

Not surprisingly, maternal gifts are documented in the legal sources only if there is some legal point to be made; the examples that occur, in which squabbling families are likely to be over-represented, may be taken as merely the tip of an iceberg of mainly unproblematical instances. There is also more than a hint that some mothers at least (like, as we have seen, some fathers) showed favouritism towards certain of their children, to the disadvantage of others—or at any rate, that dissatisfied and disgruntled children chose to believe this. In AD 245 the emperor Philip responded to an appeal from a brother and sister, Nicanor and Papiniana. Their mother, they alleged, had, first of all, deliberately tried to forestall a possible 'complaint of unduteous will', by giving away most of her property during her lifetime, both to other children and to outsiders. Then, however, she had made the error of making Nicanor and Papiniana heirs to only one-sixth instead of the accepted one-fourth (and required them to pay out most of that in legacies and *fideicommissa*). If that was so, replied the emperor, they could bring a claim 'under the form devised for unduteous will'—i.e. they could not only challenge the will but demand revocation of part of the gifts also. Diocletian makes similar responses to two people appealing against maternal favouritism towards their brothers and sisters.[65]

One favourite outlet for maternal generosity was the contribution of dowry for daughters. This was possible even if the daughter was still *in potestate*, since the dowry became legally the property of her husband, and was not a gift to the daughter herself. However, unlike dowry provided by a *pater*, it was classed as *adventicia* and was not reclaimable by the donor at the end of the marriage. It was as well to be aware of this legal fact before committing oneself. To meet the

---

[64] Shaw (1987); Saller (1987), developed in (1991*a*) 25–42 (age at marriage) and 189 (demographic consequences). Julia's freedmen: Gardner (1988).

[65] *Cod. Iust.* 3. 29. 1, 7, 8 (1251, 1491, 2366 Honoré). See also 1.10 above, at nn. 153–5.

difficulty, a premarital contract for the return of the dowry could be made with the husband. Another possibility was to have the dowry consist only in the usufruct of some property, whose ownership remained with the mother—two examples are found in the legal sources.[66] One rescript from the office of the emperor Valerian in AD 258 is worth quoting for the amusement value of what it implies:

If, with the intention of providing a dowry for your daughter, you pledged your property to your son-in-law, you are wrong in thinking that you can claim the benefit of the *senatusconsultum*; for men of good sense [or perhaps 'foresight'] have taken the view that this [type of] case is to be excluded from that benefit.[67]

This text is in the chapter concerned with the *senatusconsultum Velleianum*,[68] under which magistrates could refuse to allow a creditor to sue a woman who had stood guarantor for someone else's debt. It looks very much as though the woman, Sepiduca, having promised a dowry, had not kept her word. When her son-in-law tried to get her to pay up, and apparently things had gone so far as the threat of a court action, Sepiduca, acting on some rather shysterish legal advice, tried to represent the dowry as a debt owed not by herself but by her daughter to her husband, and herself as merely a guarantor on her daughter's behalf; then, as a woman, she invoked the protection of the *senatusconsultum Velleianum* to avoid being forced to pay, but made the mistake of approaching the emperor to get official backing for the line she was taking. She was perhaps unaware that long before this two emperors, Pius and Severus, had issued rescripts saying that women who attempted fraud were not to be allowed the benefit of the *senatusconsultum* (D. 16. 1. 3); their intervention was aimed at women who undertook an existing obligation on behalf of someone else, in full awareness of what they were doing, and with no intention of paying up. Sepiduca was trying to wriggle out of her own obligation by representing it as someone else's; however, such pettifogging (and the reference to *prudentes viri* suggests that this particular trick had been tried before) received short shrift.

The generosity of mothers and mothers-in-law could give rise to

---

[66] D. 23. 3. 5. 9; 34. 5. 16; *Cod. Iust.* 5. 12. 8, 17, 18 (1078, 2129, 2141 Honoré).

[67] *Cod. Iust.* 4. 29. 12 (1334 Honoré): 'Si dotare filiam volens genero res tuas obligasti, pertinere ad te beneficium senatus consulti falso putas: hanc enim causam ab eo beneficio esse removendam prudentes viri putaverunt.'

[68] D. 16. 1; Gardner (1986a) 75–6, 234–5, (1993) 97–9.

problems, specially when a marriage ended. It could be important to distinguish between anything given by way of dowry, and direct gifts. A certain Dionysia is reassured: 'If, during your marriage, your mother gave you a house, she made this part of your property.' Presumably Dionysia is now divorced or widowed, and her ex-husband or his heir is challenging the ownership of the house, suggesting that it was part of the dowry; in fact, it was given to her later, and not as part of the dowry arrangements. Elsewhere, two daughters-in-law are told that mother-in-law cannot take back a gift validly made. In one instance, mother-in-law has merely changed her mind; in the other (discussed below)she is apparently trying, by the threat of revoking the gift, to put pressure on her daughter-in-law not to divorce her husband.[69]

Another gift provoked a family row. According to Papinian, a mother not only contributed a dowry but at the same time gave her son-in-law some additional property, in her daughter's name, and in her daughter's presence. This, Papinian said, should be treated as a direct gift made to the daughter (who is already legally independent)[70] and passed on by her to her husband:

If the mother has taken offence, she has no right to recover the goods and cannot legally claim them, on the grounds that the husband had given a formal acknowledgement that they were handed over to him separately from the dowry, to be applied to the daughter's use, since that statement does not amount to a limitation on the gift, nor distinguish ownership from use, but merely distinguishes the girl's personal funds (*peculium*) from dowry.[71]

Although Papinian couches his reply in legal terminology, it is fairly clear what has happened, and what his advice is. The husband

[69] *Cod. Iust.* 5. 16. 19 (1925 Honoré: AD 294) 'Si constante matrimonio tibi mater domum tradidit, hanc in tuis fecit bonis'; *Cod. Iust.* 5. 16. 23 (2442 Honoré: AD 294); *Frag. Vat.* 284 (1509 Honoré: AD 286).

[70] Though *peculium* is usually used elsewhere to refer to funds made available by a *paterfamilias* for the personal expenditure of a son or daughter *in potestate*, the term is used here simply to distinguish the daughter's own personal property from the dowry property, which for the time being belongs to her husband. That the mother could be held to have made a direct gift to her daughter shows that the latter was no longer in her father's *potestas*.

[71] *D.* 39. 5. 31. 1: 'nec matrem offensam repetitionem habere vel eas recte vindicare, quod vir cavisset extra dotem usibus puellae sibi traditas, cum ea significatione non modus declarationis declaretur nec ab usu proprietas separetur, sed peculium a dote puellae distingueretur.'

has not in fact, as was intended, been making the goods, given separately from the dowry, available for his wife's needs. Mother-in-law, however, has to be told firmly that that is none of her business. She has made a gift to her daughter, but asking the husband to use it in a particular way does not give her the right to force him to do so. She cannot dictate what her son-in-law does with something that now legally belongs to her daughter.

Some mothers apparently thought that the power to confer some financial assistance gave them a right to interfere in the conduct of their children's lives, in ways that were the prerogative of the *paterfamilias.* In AD 286, a woman called Alexandria appealed to Diocletian. Her mother-in-law had previously made her a gift of some property, but now Alexandria is contemplating divorcing her husband, and mother-in-law has apparently threatened to sue her for the return of the gift if she does. Alexandria is told to invoke the aid of the provincial governor, who will see to it that her legal right to the property is not disturbed. On the matter of divorce, although the emperor is careful not to encourage her, he is firm that mother-in-law has no authority in the matter: 'As for keeping the marriage going, it is up to you to decide whether, even though your children are an obstacle, you want to persist in your intention.'[72]

Almost thirty years before, a daughter had given in to financial pressure from her own mother, who threatened to disinherit her if she did *not* divorce her husband. Such a condition, however, was morally unacceptable and unenforceable, and the emperor Valerian has some blunt words for her:

You are more to blame than your mother; for if [or, 'unless' with Mommsen's reading] she wanted you to be her heir, she would not order you to break off your marriage—a useless act. Moreover you complied with her wish by divorcing, but what you ought to have done, even faced with such a condition, was to prefer marital harmony to financial gain. For assuredly, since morality forbids compliance with such conditions, you could have kept your marriage, without any loss. Go back to your husband then, knowing that you will keep the inheritance from your mother, since you would have it, even if you had not divorced him at all.[73]

---

[72] *Frag. Vat.* 284 (1509 Honoré: AD 286): 'de matrimonio vero retinendo tui arbitrii est, an velis et filiis communibus intervenientibus in eodem proposito perseverare.'

[73] *Cod. Iust.* 6. 25. 5 (1332 Honoré): 'Reprehendenda tu magis es quam mater tua. illa enim si [*nisi* Momm.] heredem te sibi esse vellet, id quod est inutile, matrimonium te dirimere cum viro non iuberet. 1. Tu porro voluntatem eius divortio comprobasti:

The meaning is probably that, if she had defied her mother, and the latter then did go ahead and disinherit her for refusing to divorce, she would have had very good grounds for a complaint of 'unduteous will'.

Such maternal interference in the marriages of children had no foundation, then or previously, in any kind of legal authority. Only the *paterfamilias* had such a legal control over divorce—and then not if it was initiated by the other spouse, but only over the actions of his own children—and even that power had been curtailed in the previous century.[74] Although some mothers, it seems, may have considered that their generosity entitled them to interfere in their children's marriages, the law did not concur.

3.5 MOTHERS AND TUTORS

The appointment of guardians to look after the assets of young orphan children was, given the likely demographic situation, a matter of widespread concern among Romans. It has been estimated that about one-sixth of Roman independent property owners were children under the age of puberty, and therefore legally requiring a tutor for the administration of their property.[75] Conscientious fathers customarily made provision for this when drawing up their wills, choosing close friends or relatives in whom they felt they could place reliance to look after the interests of the ward (*pupillus*). The closest male relative would seem the most obvious choice, either, on the paternal side, the closest agnate (brother, or paternal uncle), or a maternal uncle.

Whether in practice such relatives were often available is not something on which any reliable statistics can be offered. Saller (1994) 197

oportuerat autem, etsi condicio huiusmodi admitteretur, praeferre lucro concordiam maritalem. enimvero cum boni mores haec observari vetent, sine ullo damno coniunctionem retinere potuisti. 2. Redi igitur ad maritum sciens hereditatem matris, etiamsi redieris, retenturam, quippe quam retineres, licet prorsus ab eo non recessisses.' Cf. *Cod. Iust.* 3. 28. 20 (2128 Honoré), discussed above (at n. 38).

[74] Treggiari (1991) 459–60.

[75] Saller (1994) 12–70, 190; he estimates that a further one-fifth were still under the age of 25. Since, though technically adult, they could claim incompetence and inexperience as grounds for cancelling transactions (*restitutio in integrum*), it was in the interests of those dealing with them, as well as of the young persons themselves, for them to have curators monitoring their transactions; this, however, was an informal and voluntary arrangement: Buckland (1963) 169–72.

estimates that perhaps 40 per cent of wards had a paternal uncle living at the time of their father's death, but only 1 or 2 per cent a brother old enough (over 25) to take full legal responsibility for being tutor. He also thinks that, because Roman women married at an earlier age than men (and therefore were likely not only to be younger themselves but to have younger siblings than their husbands), more maternal than paternal uncles were likely still to be alive, but fewer were likely to be old enough to be tutors. This argument, however, takes insufficient account of the possibility of maternal relatives (or indeed sons) from a previous marriage or marriages, who would, naturally, be older. Too much weight cannot be placed on such generalizations from computer-based statistics, especially as the composition of individual families could vary widely.

Although the safeguarding of the young person's patrimony might seem a matter requiring a tutor who belonged to the *familia* rather than the 'family', on the basis of such scrappy literary and juristic evidence as there is, it appears that Romans freely resorted to maternal as well as paternal male relatives, and also to friends outside the family altogether, for the office of *tutela*, and not only when no paternal relatives were available. Several tutors, from both inside and outside the family, were sometimes appointed. The group might be mixed, as in an instance in Cicero's *Verrines*: stepfather, paternal uncle, family friend, and an important senator (for patronage). A freedman might be included, to do the actual donkey-work of administration.[76]

The sense of 'family' is partly a matter of blood relationship, both inside and outside the *familia*, though it is apparently felt to extend also into some relationships by marriage. Cicero is an important source for Republican sentiments. He himself traces his personal connection, from an early age, with the great orator of a previous generation, L. Crassus, to the latter's close friendship with L. Visellius Aculeo, the husband of Cicero's maternal aunt, and so Cicero's uncle by marriage.[77] At a personal level, in his letters, he says little, other than to refer to himself once or twice with joking circumlocution as 'your sister's son's paternal uncle' (addressing Atticus, whose sister Pomponia was married to Cicero's brother Quintus), and to congratulate Atticus that his maternal uncle Caecilius has 'done his duty', by making Atticus his heir. A few years earlier, he had felt it necessary to

---

[76] Saller (1994) 195–8; Cic. *Verr.* 2. 1. 130–53; *D.* 26. 7. 58 pr.; 27. 3. 1. 6.

[77] Cic. *De Or.* 2. 1. 2; E. Rawson (1991) 16–33, esp. 26–7.

apologize to Atticus for refusing to undertake a prosecution on behalf of Caecilius—he was obligated to the defendant, who had helped him and his brother in their candidacies for office.[78]

Cicero also gives us some helpful indications of the value attached to 'family' in public contexts, among the Roman élite of his own time and a century or two before. Q. Tubero (1.9 above), who lost a praetorian election by projecting the wrong 'image', was related to the man he was supposed to be honouring, Scipio Africanus Minor, by blood, entirely through the female line. He was the son of Scipio's natural sister Aemilia. The man who was actually arranging the whole commemoration of the great man, Q. Fabius Maximus, was a blood relative of Scipio in the male line, but the agnatic connection had been broken—he was the son of Scipio's brother who, like Scipio himself, had been given in adoption. Because of that adoption, Fabius, like Tubero, was related to Scipio only as a fairly remote cognate; nevertheless, he was chief organizer of the commemoration and called upon Tubero, as 'family', to take a part in the ceremonies.

When it suits him (and presumably therefore, also, his audience), Cicero in political contexts (or semi-political, as in the choice of interlocutors for his philosophical treatises) happily exploits blood relationships in the maternal as well as the paternal line—irrespective of whether or not original agnatic legal ties have been severed, as by adoption—in order implicitly or explicitly to praise or blame by comparison or association the person who is his subject for the moment. Addressing M. Scaurus, he holds up to him, as an example to urge him to mend his ways, Q. Metellus, the paternal uncle of his mother.[79] Mark Antony, in the *Philippics*, is taunted with recollections both of the worthiness of his maternal uncle L. Caesar and the unworthiness of his paternal uncle, C. Antonius Hibrida (whom nevertheless he is reproached for not helping sufficiently in his exile).[80] The younger Cato's connections in particular are exploited. Caesar's assassins, Cicero says, were influenced not by Cicero himself, but by family history and tradition—such as L. Domitius Ahenobarbus, whose father and whose maternal uncle (Cato) died in the cause of freedom. Addressing Brutus (himself adopted into the Servilii), he makes a point of mentioning his *avunculus*—i.e. his mother Servilia's half-brother, the same Cato.[81]

[78] Cic. *Ad Att.* 5. 19. 3; 6. 8. 3; cf. 10. 4. 6. Caecilius: *Ad Att.* 3. 20. 1; 1. 1. 3
[79] Cic. *Pro Sestio* 101.   [80] Cic. *Phil.* 1. 27; 2. 14, 27, 56, 98; 8. 2.
[81] Cic. *Paradoxa Stoicorum* 1; cf. *De Fin.* 3. 6. 7; *Ad Att.* 5. 21. 13.

Brutus himself, in a letter written at the beginning of July 43, appeals to Cicero on behalf of his sister and his children, not to let the behaviour of her husband, their father, damage them. He begs Cicero, and through him the rest of the Senate, to attach weight to the fact that Brutus is their *avunculus*, rather than that M. Aemilius Lepidus (the later triumvir) is their father. Junia, Aemilius' wife, though bearing the same *nomen* as Brutus (before his adoption), was in fact only Brutus' half-sister; they had different fathers.

Whatever the legal constraints of *patria potestas*, or the rules of intestate sucession, it appears that in general the Roman élite of the late Republic attached as much importance to 'family' connections, whether paternal or maternal, as to *familia* alone. The letters of the younger Pliny give a similar impression of the society of the late first century AD; maternal uncles are several times referred to, as guarantors, by their own probity, of the worthiness and respectability of their younger male relatives, and perhaps with the implication that they themselves are regarded as morally influential in the family. The credentials of a bridegroom include a reference to the character of his maternal uncle; Sextus Erucius' maternal uncle C. Septicius (the dedicatee of Suetonius' *Lives*) is mentioned in a letter of support for the candidacy of Erucius, the first of his paternal line to attempt to enter the Senate; another *avunculus* is mentioned, as a personal friend both of Pliny's and of the addressee, in another letter of recommendation. The raffish Ummidia Quadratilla was the grandmother—whether maternal or paternal is not certain—of Ummidius Quadratus, who lived with her in his youth, and whom she tried to shelter from too close acquaintance with her taste for bawdy mime performances.[82]

A few rescripts from the second and third century also show maternal relatives involved in assisting each other with personal difficulties, on an informal basis. Nephews are found helping maternal uncles with their problems, one with a question of civil status, another against attempted extortion by a magistrate. A maternal aunt engaged a woman to escort her nephew to Rome to have a tutor appointed; this suggests that this child was doubly orphaned, and living with the only available relative.[83]

It is not surprising, then, to find that, when relatives are selected and

[82] *Ep.* 1. 14; 2. 9. 4; 4. 4; 7. 24 and Syme (1984) 1159–60, 1162–3, who inclines to the view that she was his paternal grandmother.
[83] *Cod. Iust.* 2. 11. 14, 5. 62. 14, 2. 18. 2 (948, 1051, 33 Honoré).

named in wills as tutors for young orphans, the selection is not confined only to the agnatic line.

Literary and legal texts do furnish a few examples of close male agnates, a brother or paternal uncle (*patruus*), as tutor.[84] One may perhaps add Junius Mauricus, who—though admittedly these are not functions required of a tutor—makes it his business to find a suitable husband for his brother's daughter and a teacher for his nephew. The financial implications of both, however—arranging a dowry, paying a teacher—would concern a tutor, as would the cost of rearing the child. Mothers and/or other relatives and tutors were expected to cooperate in such matters or, if they could not agree, to ask the praetor or provincial governor to decide.[85]

There was, however, no legal requirement that the *paterfamilias* should nominate a male agnate as tutor in his will. The social expectation that they would be nominated, if available, is likely to have been strong, although the *paterfamilias* was free to nominate anyone he liked (if of suitable character and financial solvency). If he appointed no one, and any *tutor legitimus*, that is, a male agnate (paternal uncle, brother, or a son of either) was available, then it was inappropriate for a magistrate to appoint any other tutor, and a person so appointed could refuse. This was natural, because the nearest agnate, besides being the person on whom, according to Roman civil law, the duty of *tutela* fell automatically, if the *paterfamilias* had made no other arrangements, was also the person first in line to inherit if the child (as yet too young to make a will) died. According to Scaevola this was extended by a praetorian decision also to appointments made in a will of external persons as tutors; if there was a *tutor legitimus* available, then the person appointed had good grounds for claiming exemption. Friends and remoter relatives might be encouraged to accept the burdensome duty of *tutela* by the reward of a legacy.[86]

Relatives through the female side also were a likely choice as tutors, not only mothers' brothers, but even aunts' husbands (though these

---

[84] Saller (1994) 196 n. 46. Junius Mauricus: Pliny, *Ep.* 1. 14, 2. 18.

[85] *D.* 26. 7. 47. 1; *Cod. Iust.*. 5. 4. 1, 46. 2, 49. 1 (63, 1271, 543 Honoré); see also Saller (1994) 193–5.

[86] *D.* 27. 1. 37 pr.; Gaius 1. 144, 155–7; *Cod. Iust.* 5. 30. 1, 5. 34. 9 (1565, 2160 Honoré: AD 290, 294). *Pace* Saller (1994) 196, it is perhaps an exaggeration to take the praetorian judgement cited by Scaevola (*D.* 27. 1. 37 pr.) as an index of the degree to which the paternal uncle or brother was 'the expected [sc. voluntary] choice'. On excuses and exemptions, see Buckland (1963) 149–52, Kaser (1971) 357–9. Legacy: *D.* 27. 1. 36 pr.

were, strictly, only *adfines*, relatives by marriage, not *cognati*, relatives by blood). Cicero (losing no chance to blacken the character of anyone associated with the prosecutor, young Oppianicus, in the eyes of the jurors—i.e. of right-thinking Romans), not content with accusing Oppianicus senior of having bribed the wife of his former brother-in-law Cn. Magius to procure an abortion, points out that, although Magius had made his sister Magia's son, Oppianicus junior. his secondary heir, should the expected posthumous child not be born, he nevertheless did not appoint Oppianicus senior, his late sister's husband and that nephew's father, to be tutor to the expected child. Magius' own half-brothers, the Aurii, it will be remembered, had perished; and Cicero provides no information about the family of his wife. The message seems to be that, if no agnates, or else maternal uncles, are available, then a sister's husband is a natural choice.

As always, however, we have to be wary of omissions and simplifications in our sources. Magius probably did appoint a tutor, or even tutors, for the expected child, though we do not know who they were.[87] Cicero chooses to concentrate on what presumably he expected his audience to regard as a significant omission, that is, that Magius did not nominate the nearest thing to a living male relative that he had—his late sister's ex-husband. Later, he accuses Oppianicus senior of having 'killed in chains and slavery his own son's maternal uncle' (*avunculum filii sui in servitute ac vinculis necaverit*)—the reference is to M. Aurius, one of Magia's half-brothers by his mother's first marriage. Oppianicus senior's relationship both to Magius and to M. Aurius was one in law only—he was an *adfinis*. His son was related to them by blood; he was a cognate, through his mother.

Maternal uncles were likely to be chosen as tutors, especially if no close relatives on the paternal side were available, although there is little direct evidence. As a child, the younger Cato was brought up, both his parents already being dead, along with his sister Porcia and Servilius Caepio and Servilia, his half-brother and half-sister by his mother's previous marriage, in the home of his mother's brother Livius Drusus (the tribune of 91 BC).[88] Although our sources do not say so, the likelihood is that Drusus was also tutor to the children.

---

[87] On the reasons for, and composition of, groups of multiple tutors, see Saller (1994) 195–8. These groups, especially in the Roman élite, were likely to include a 'big name' to be a friend in high places at need (as in Cic. *Verr.* 2. 1. 135, where the 'big name' is one of the consular Marcelli).

[88] Val. Max. 3. 1. 2; Plut. *Cato Min.* 1–2.

3.5 Mothers and Tutors

What arrangements were made for the *tutela* after Livius' death is not known; the detail about Cato's upbringing is mentioned only for the sake of the hagiographic story[89] of how, when Poppaedius Silo, leader of the Italian allies demanding citizenship, was staying with Drusus, the steadfast little boy (still only 4 when his uncle died) refused, even when threatened with being thrown out of a high window, to pipe up to urge his uncle to support the allied cause. Once or twice also in the legal sources maternal uncles are mentioned as tutors.[90] For the most part, however, family relationships are not mentioned.

If fathers had not nominated tutors, or if for some reasons existing tutors ceased to be available, a replacement had to be found. Though mothers, either in their own lifetimes, or in their wills, might make known their own wishes in the matter, which magistrates were sometimes disposed to take into account, they did not themselves have the power to appoint tutors for their children.[91] Appointment of a tutor had to be requested from the magistrate, and there are several references in legal texts to mothers, and occasionally other relatives, doing, or being expected or instructed to do this.[92] There was no legal compulsion on the mother to have the tutor replaced and no legal sanction that could be applied, until the passing of the *senatusconsultum Tertullianum* (above, 3.3), which allowed those mothers with the *ius liberorum* intestate succession to the property of their children. It was specified in the *senatusconsultum* that eligible mothers who did not apply to the praetor for tutors for their children would forfeit this right of inheritance, and this sanction was interpreted, according to Ulpian, as applying in the provinces also, where mothers should make application to local magistrates.

How effective an incentive this was likely to be in practice is doubtful. As we have seen, the odds were against many mothers—of

---

[89] With a passing resemblance to the story (told, if we may believe Aulus Gellius 1. 23, by Cato's ancestor, the censor) of the high-minded young Papirius Praetextatus, who, having attended Senate with his father, refused to reveal to his mother the secret matters he had heard discussed there.

[90] *Cod. Iust.* 5. 28. 6, 2. 21. 7 (2279, 2351 Honoré).

[91] *Cod. Iust.* 5. 47. 1 (36 Honoré)—request, possibly from a sibling now adult, to have a child's tutor replaced; 5. 29. 1, 5. 28. 4 (658, 677 Honoré).

[92] Mothers: *Cod. Iust.* 5. 31. 3, 32. 1, 5. 31. 6, 5. 46. 1, 5. 34. 6; 2. 12. 18 (410, 420, 701, 889, 1860, 2147 Honoré). Occasionally other relatives make application: a maternal aunt, a paternal great-uncle, a paternal aunt and once, in error, a maternal grandfather (presumably a testamentary appointment): *Cod. Iust.* 2. 18. 2, 5. 31. 10, 5. 31. 5, D. 27. 1. 13. 12 (33, 2331, 580, 192 Honoré).

legitimate children at least—being able to inherit under the *senatuscon-sultum*, since, partly owing to the very fecundity which qualified them to inherit under the *senatusconsultum*, there were likely to be too many other potential claimants among the relatives in the agnatic line; the situation with illegitimate children would be rather different (see 3.6 below). Mothers, however, might still succeed, irrespective of the *senatusconsultum*, though only as cognates, if there were no nearer relatives. They did not need to have the *ius liberorum*, nor to have applied (as the *senatusconsultum* required) for tutors. The emperor Septimius Severus probably cancelled this possibility also, by a letter addressed to Cuspius Rufinus (consul AD 197):

> I wish it to be clear to everyone that I use all possible means of assisting wards, since it is a matter of public concern; therefore any mother who does not seek suitable tutors for her sons, or who does not promptly supply other names if the earlier ones excuse themselves or are rejected, is not to have the right of applying for the property of her sons if they are intestate.[93]

The emperor's letter was not a mere restatement of the clause in the *senatusconsultum*. More mothers, including many not eligible to inherit under the *senatusconsultum*, now stood to lose if they did not obtain tutors for their children.

Ulpian's lengthy discussion[94] suggests that some attempt was to be made to apply these sanctions sensibly, nevertheless the criteria are strict. The woman is expected to make some effort to find out in advance whether her suggested nominees have grounds for exemption.[95] It is no excuse that her husband wished her to avoid tutors and manage the property herself;[96] on the other hand, if she herself has been made heir by her husband, with a *fideicommissum* to pass on the estate to her son when he reaches adulthood, it is unreasonable to penalize her for not requesting tutors for a son who did not yet have any property to manage.[97]

Answers survive to two enquiries made to the emperor Diocletian. Someone appears to have asked whether a mother was to be forbidden to inherit, when the application for tutors had been delayed because

---

[93] D. 38. 17. 2. 23; 26. 6. 2. 2 (Septimius' letter): 'Omnem me rationem adhibere subveniendis pupillis, cum ad curam publicam pertineat, liquere omnibus volo. et ideo quae mater vel non petierit tutores idoneos filiis suis vel prioribus excusatis reiectisve non confestim aliorum nomina dederit, ius non habeat vindicandorum sibi bonorum intestatorum filiorum.' [94] D. 38. 17. 2. 24–46, esp. 25, 46.
[95] D. 38. 17. 2. 32. [96] D. 38. 17. 2. 25; cf. D. 26. 2. 26 pr., 26. 7. 5. 8.
[97] D. 38. 17. 2. 46; cf. D. 35. 1. 77. 3; 36. 1. 59. 2; 36. 1. 80 pr., 14.

the procurator whom she had commissioned to make the application had been killed by robbers; the emperor replied that that would be harsh. A reply concerning a less exotic situation, but showing equal humanity, is given to a certain Procula—possibly the anxious mother herself:

Although in the case of civil offences (*delictis*) it is established law that no one is excused on grounds of age, nevertheless, it is quite inappropriate to deny the inheritance to a mother who does not apply for a tutor for her sons because of the thoughtlessness of youth (*aetatis lubrico lapsa*), since this applies only to more mature mothers.[98]

Procula, if she herself was the bereft mother, was still very young, and perhaps not old enough to have qualified for the *ius liberorum*; she may have been applying as a cognate. The restriction on the *senatusconsultum* to mothers with the *ius liberorum* was first relaxed under Constantine, though only to the extent of allowing the mother to inherit one-third as against paternal uncles of the deceased, or their descendants. Constantine also allowed mothers to inherit, even if they had not applied for tutors while the children were minors, if the children survived to adulthood. There is no evidence for previous legal practice in such instances.[99]

Whatever the law might say, some mothers did attempt—and even with the encouragement of their late husbands—to manage their children's property without having tutors appointed at all. Even when there were tutors, mothers might manage the children's affairs without resort to tutors. There was no question of punishing the mother (except that she might lose her right to inherit in the event of the children dying, if no tutors at all had been appointed), but her activity did create some legal problems, because, as a woman, she did not have the legal capacity to do certain things on behalf of another person who was (technically at least, even if still a child in age) a *paterfamilias*, a 'head of household'. As Papinian pointed out:

A mother, following the wishes of a father, and relying on her own sense of what is incumbent on her, may manage her son's affairs—but she will not have the right to appoint an agent at her own risk to conduct litigation, because she herself does not have the right to go to law in her son's name,

[98] *Cod. Iust.* 5. 31. 8; 2. 34. 2 (1675, 2219 Honoré).
[99] *Cod. Theod.* 5. 1. 1; *Cod. Iust.* 6. 56. 3.

nor to alienate items of his property, nor to discharge a debtor of the minor by accepting the money. [100]

One mother is said to have handled all her daughter's business for nine years, including selling goods at auction through financial agents (*argentarii*), arranging a marriage and delivering property (presumably as dowry) to the daughter's husband. The auctioneers were considered to be released from their liability to the daughter for the proceeds of the auction by the fact of having paid over the money to the mother (since the contract was with her), but not if they knew that the property was the daughter's and nevertheless paid over the money, knowing that the mother was insolvent. [101] This is perhaps a theoretical example, but the key point is that the mother did not have the right of administration of the girl's property.

When mothers did, nevertheless, engage in transactions concerning their children's property, it was in everyone's interests to find an appropriate procedure for making them accountable. Their administration could not be challenged in court, as that of tutors could when their office ended, by an *actio tutelae*. Instead, an action could be brought under the general heading of 'negotia gesta' (unauthorized administration), which in general was a way of making liable someone who had acted on behalf of another person without having a mandate to do so. Alternatively, there was, according to Ulpian, provision under the edict for an action *protutelae*, 'for unauthorized tutelage' (really a subdivision of the action for *negotia gesta*). This had been introduced, Ulpian explains, to cover both eventualities, when it was uncertain whether someone actually was tutor or was merely acting as if he were. [102] Obviously, there could be no mistake as to whether a woman was tutor or not, since women could not be tutors; but the action could conveniently be used against them concerning transactions that were properly the business of tutors.

If there were tutors, even if they were willing to acquiesce in the mother's handling of affairs, it was advisable for them to get some se-

---

[100] *D*. 3. 5. 30. 6: 'Quamquam mater filii negotia secundum patris voluntatem pietatis fiducia gerat, tamen ius actoris periculo suo litium causa constituendi non habebit, quia nec ipsa filii nomine recte agit aut res bonorum eius alienat vel debitorem impuberis accipiendo pecuniam liberat'; cf. Gardner (1993) ch. 4, esp. 100–1.

[101] *D*. 46. 3. 88.

[102] *Actio tutelae*: *D*. 27. 3; *Cod. Iust.* 5. 54. 3, 9. 51. 4 (309, 899 Honoré). *Actio negotiorum gestorum*: *D*. 3. 5; Paul. *Sent.* 1. 4. 4. *Actio protutelae* (sic): *D*. 27. 5. 1 pr. Buckland (1963) 163–4, 537–8, 545.

curity or undertaking from the mother that they themselves would be indemnified for what she did, since, though they could use an *actio negotiorum gestorum* against her, they themselves were still liable under an *actio tutelae*.[103]

Ulpian cites a particularly awkward situation discussed by Papinian, perhaps a real case, where the father in his will had specifically instructed the tutors to administer his sons' affairs in accordance with the advice of their mother, so apparently releasing the tutors from personal obligation. This sort of conflict of authorities is highly likely to lead to trouble. Were the tutors still liable, even if they acted entirely on the mother's advice? Or could they ignore her advice? Papinian's answer is delicately phrased: 'The tutors' office is not thereby impaired; but it will be fitting for good men to accept a mother's sound advice, despite the fact that neither the release of the tutors nor the father's wish nor the intervention of the mother detracts from the function of the tutor.'[104]

The tutors are still liable; but the insertion of the words 'good men' and 'sound' leaves tutors, in such a situation, free to ignore the mother. Their authority is thereby maintained. Of course, if they turned out to have been mistaken in rejecting her advice, their charges could sue them later, or she herself (though at her own expense[105]) could sue them, as 'suspect', and, if successful, have them removed from office.

The 'crimen suspecti tutoris' (charge of being an untrustworthy tutor), which was believed to go back to the Twelve Tables, was one which women were exceptionally permitted to bring on behalf of a third party, if they were near relatives—mother, grandmother, or (by a rescript of Septimius Severus) sister, and even nurse, or any other woman, so long as the praetor was satisfied that she was actuated by a strong sense of duty (*pietas*); there are seven imperial rescripts, dating between AD 196 and 241, concerning the bringing of this charge by women, two apparently by women against their own

---

[103] Paul. *Sent.* 21. 4. 4; *Cod. Iust.* 5. 46. 2 (where mother and paternal grandfather are both handling the children's affairs), 5. 51. 9 (1272, 2121 Honoré); a mother could not, however, subsequently use the *senatusconsultum Velleianum* to deny liability for obligations undertaken on behalf of the ward, unless the tutor had connived in order to evade liability himself; *Cod. Iust.* 4. 29. 6 (803 Honoré).

[104] D. 26. 7. 5. 8: 'non idcirco minus officium tutorum integrum erit, sed viris bonis conveniet salubre consilium matris admittere, tametsi neque liberatio tutoris neque voluntas patris aut intercessio matris tutoris officium infringat.'

[105] *Cod. Iust.* 2. 18. 1 (23 Honoré).

tutors, one (in view of the indications of age) possibly by a sister, the rest by mothers on behalf of their children.[106] The *crimen* provided an additional safeguard for *pupilli* against being cheated by the men set to look after their property.

Mothers, however, were not penalized if they failed to keep an eagle eye on tutorial activities. Although they risked losing inheritance rights if they did not ask for tutors to be appointed at all, they were not necessarily expected either to be capable of judging in advance who would be reliable, or to make a judgement on their performance while in office. 'It takes a male mind', commented Claudius Tryphoninus, a jurist roughly contemporary with Ulpian, 'to make judgements on activities of this kind and assess them, and a mother can be unaware even of misdemeanours, and it is enough if she asked for a tutor who seemed suitable at the praetor's initial investigation.'[107]

It is evident, however, that tutors contemplating malpractice could not safely rely on such a low estimation of maternal shrewdness; some tutors did find themselves facing prosecution.

3.6 ILLEGITIMATE CHILDREN

Illegitimate children belonged to no *familia*; they had no *paterfamilias*, and their natural brothers and sisters (and aunts and uncles), if they had any, were not their agnates. Under the Republic and for at least the first century of the Empire illegitimate children had no expectations of inheriting from anyone (unless someone might leave them something in a will). They had no legally recognized fathers,[108] and the clause in the praetor's edict allowing inheritance, in default of agnates, between *cognati* (blood relatives) being a modification of the

---

[106] *D.* 26. 10. 1. 2, 7; against own tutors: *Cod. Iust.* 5. 43. 4, 7 (816, 1079 Honoré); against brothers'/sisters' tutors and curators?: *Cod. Iust.* 5. 37. 12 (1156 Honoré); against children's tutors: *Cod. Iust.*. 2. 18. 1, 5. 43. 1, 5. 37. 4, 5. 43. 3 (23, 265, 353, 804 Honoré).

[107] *D.* 26. 6. 4. 4 (Tryphoninus): 'eiusmodi facta diiudicare et aestimare virilis animi est et potest etiam delicta ignorare mater, satisque est eam petisse talem, qui inquisitione per praetorem habita idoneus apparuit.' Cf. *Cod. Iust.* 5. 46. 1, 3 (889, 2038 Honoré).

[108] *D.* 1. 5. 19, 23; 2. 4. 4. 5; biological relationships were, however, to be taken into account for the avoidance of incest: *D.* 23. 2. 14. 2, 54. Illegitimate parentage also counted for those marriages forbidden to senators under the Augustan marriage legislation: *D.* 23. 2. 44. 3.

civil law of succession, applied initially only to legitimate kin. By the time of the final codification of the praetor's edict under Hadrian, however, the clause *unde cognati* was understood to apply to illegitimate children and their maternal kin;[109] this is known to legal writers from the middle of the second century AD.

When did this happen? It was argued above (1.5.2) that the second modification to the praetor's edict, the introduction of the clause *unde liberi*, allowing legitimate children who had left the *familia* (i.e. had been emancipated, or even given in adoption) a claim to inherit from their fathers in the same category as children still in power, probably did not occur until after the middle of the first century BC; it was only since the 60s that they had been able to inherit from either parent as *cognati*. It is highly unlikely, given the proclaimed moral purposes of Augustan legislation on marriage and inheritance, and the incentives it offered to procreation of legitimate offspring, that illegitimate relationships will have been recognized for any inheritance rights in his reign, or indeed for some time thereafter.

However, the same emperor's legislation on manumission of slaves had helped to increase the numbers of children who, through no fault of their parents, were born illegitimate.[110] This was caused perhaps to some extent by the limitations placed by the *lex Fufia Caninia* (2 BC) on the number of slaves an owner could manumit in his will (so increasing the likelihood of separation of slave 'partners', if only one could be manumitted), but even more so by the status differentials set up by the rules for manumission in the *lex Aelia Sentia* (AD 4). The minimum age requirement for manumission to admit the ex-slave to Roman citizenship was 30 years, unless special cause was shown (e.g. that the woman was being freed to marry her owner). Women slaves set free below the age limit had a better chance of motherhood, but at the cost of citizenship. Freed slaves whose manumission did not conform to the requirements were given a free, but non-citizen, status, as 'Junian' Latins; their illegitimate children would also be non-Roman.[111]

Even if both parents were free, difference of status could rule out the possibility of their marriage and the production of legitimate children.

---

[109] *D.* 38. 8. 2 (Gaius); 4 (Ulpian); 8 (Modestinus); this covered inheritance of child from mother and vice versa, and also inheritance between brothers and sisters born of the same mother.   [110] Cf. Gardner (1996) 88–93.

[111] Gaius 1. 17–19, 22–4; Ulp. *Reg.* 5. 9.

The father might be Roman but the mother only 'Junian' Latin (because manumitted below the minimum age), in which case marriage was impossible. If (which was less likely) the position was reversed, i.e. Roman mother and Latin father, or if both were Latins, then under the *lex Junia* access to citizenship (with the possibility also of legitimation of freeborn children of the union) was possible, but in practice difficult to achieve.[112]

An added complication was that a Republican law, the *lex Minicia*, had ruled that, while illegitimate children normally followed the status of their mothers, in those cases where the father's status was known and was 'inferior' to the mother's (i.e. she was Roman and he was free but non-Roman), the child took his status. Moreover, it seems that the status of children born of such unions between a Roman mother and a Latin father had not been resolved either in the *lex Aelia Sentia* or in the *lex Junia*.[113] Add to all this the unawareness and lack of record of personal status that seems not to have been uncommon in the lower classes of Roman society,[114] and it becomes evident that the problem was one that would grow in scale with each succeeding generation, as non-citizen illegitimate children were born and in turn made irregular unions which did not and could not have the legal character of *iustum matrimonium*, lawful marriage.

Hadrian did something to relieve the situation. He ruled that, whatever the circumstances, the child born of a Latin man and a Roman woman was to be Roman (so setting aside the *lex Minicia* in relation to these couples). As for quasi-marital unions that turned out to be irregular because of status differences (and the children therefore illegitimate and/or non-Roman), someone—and it seems likely that Hadrian was again the emperor responsible—in effect gave magistrates *carte blanche* to use their discretion and give couples the benefit of the doubt. If they were trying to live like decent Romans, and had started a family, then it would be accepted, without too much inquiry, that they had genuinely been mistaken about their status. Everyone would become a Roman citizen, the child would be brought under its father's *potestas*, and a regular Roman *familia* would be constituted.[115] Such a concession, if acted upon by couples to whom it applied, would do something to reduce the number of

---

[112] Gaius 1. 28–35; Weaver (1990) 275–305.
[113] Gaius 1. 78–80; Ulp. *Reg.* 5. 8.   [114] Gardner (1986*b*), 1–14.
[115] Gardner (1996) 93–9.

illegitimate children—though there is no way of knowing how many couples actually learned of, and took advantage of, this possibility.

Hadrian's reign therefore seems more likely than that of Augustus, or any of the intervening emperors (whose record on such matters is unimpressive), for the enlightened change, perhaps part of Julian's codification of the edict, giving illegitimate children (who previously had no claim to inherit from anyone at all)[116] the possibility of inheriting as cognates from their mothers, and also from their brothers and sisters by the same mother.

To allow illegitimate children to succeed as cognates was no great step. Legitimate children and their mothers already had mutual rights of inheritance from each other. This, however, did not depend upon the civil law, i.e. it was not because the children were legitimate and in the *familia* and under the *potestas* of their fathers (adoptive children, as we saw, had no such right of inheritance from the wives of their *patres*), but simply, as provided in the praetor's edict, in virtue of their blood connection as *cognati*. Gaius, in a commentary on the provincial edict, states the difference clearly, and incidentally shows that by his time illegitimate children were able to inherit as cognates:

In this section [of the edict] the proconsul, on grounds of natural equity, promises possession of property to all cognates, whom connection of blood calls to an inheritance, even if they fall short in civil law. Therefore, even illegitimate children can claim possession of a mother's property and she of theirs, and likewise brothers of each other's, under this clause.[117]

Ulpian (*Rules*, book 6) confirms: 'If a bastard dies intestate, his inheritance goes to no one on grounds either of consanguinity or agnation, since both derive from a father; but his mother or uterine brother can apply for possession under the edict.'[118]

All cognates were blood-relatives, in so far as they were connected by blood through either the male or female line. *Consanguinei* also

---

[116] Illegitimate children were not in the *potestas* of a *pater*, and had no legitimate brothers and sisters, so no agnates.

[117] D. 38. 8. 2: 'Gaius libro sexto decimo ad edictum provinciale. Hac parte proconsul naturali aequitate motus omnibus cognatis promittit bonorum possessionem, quos sanguinis ratio vocat ad hereditatem, licet iure civili deficiant. itaque etiam vulgo quaesiti liberi matris et mater talium liberorum, item ipsi fratres inter se ex hac parte bonorum possessionem petere possunt.'

[118] D. 38. 8. 4: 'Ulpianus libro sexto regularum. Si spurius intestato decesserit, iure consanguinitatis aut agnationis hereditas eius ad nullum pertinet, quia consanguinitatis, itemque adgnationis iure a patre oriuntur: proximitatis autem nomine mater eius aut frater eadem matre natus bonorum possessionem eius ex edicto petere possunt.'

literally means 'blood-relatives', but the term as used by jurists meant children of the same father only, and was extended to include adopted children; 'agnates' the wider term, included those descended from a common *pater* in an earlier generation, i.e. not only brothers and sisters but paternal uncles and their descendants.[119]

Both Gaius and Ulpian are saying, therefore, that illegitimate children could also succeed as cognates to brothers and sisters of the same mother. They would not inherit, though, if more than one legitimate child of the same mother survived, because the legitimate children would be agnates and take priority over their illegitimate brothers and sisters, who were only cognates, in inheriting from each other. The reason for this discrimination was presumably that since legitimate children were likely to have inherited some of their father's property, their agnates, that is, legitimate children of the same father, ought to have prior claim.

It was also under Hadrian that the *senatusconsultum Tertullianum* was passed. This was interpreted by Julian as applying also to inheritance from illegitimate children.[120]

Whether illegitimate children were included from the first in the *senatusconsultum Orphitianum*, and given the same priority in inheriting from their mother as her legitimate children, or whether this was extended to them only later by interpretation is not clear from the texts; by the time of Ulpian they certainly do benefit.[121] Illegitimate children, however, did not inherit from their fathers, except, by a special dispensation of Hadrian's, the children of serving soldiers and veterans.[122]

Among the families which stood especially to benefit from these changes were the families of Roman freed slaves (see 3.7 below). It was probably not a rare occurrence that an older child in a freedman family was illegitimate, and subsequent children were legitimate. The older child may either have been born to a mother who was herself freeborn, or who had been freed, but was unmarried (i.e. the father would not or could not marry her, being still a slave, or perhaps her patron but unwilling or ineligible because already married, or of senatorial rank), or may himself have been born a slave and only subse-

---

[119] D. 38. 16. 1. 9–11, 2 pr.–1.
[120] In the thirty-eighth book of his *Digest*: D. 38. 17. 2. 1.
[121] D. 38. 17. 1. 2; Meinhart (1967); Gardner (1986*a*) 198–200.
[122] Bruns[7], 196.

quently set free. Illegitimate children of freed and freeborn mothers are sometimes detectable in inscriptions, either by the designation *Spurii filius*, 'of unknown father', or if the mother and child have the same family name, and that of the mother's husband is different; the mother's status is not always indicated. Ascription of freedman status to the child himself indicates, however, that he was born in slavery.[123] The illegitimate children of freed slave-women benefited from these changes, to the extent that they could now at least inherit from their mothers. Illegitimate children of freeborn mothers were relatively fortunate; some might have inheritance rights going back over more than one generation, as shown by an opinion of Modestinus (third century AD): 'Modestinus gave the reply that grandchildren are admitted to possession of their maternal grandmother's property on intestacy none the less because they are stated to be illegitimate.'[124]

Although Modestinus speaks of grandmothers, the same could apply to inheritance, as a cognate, from the father of a mother who was herself legitimate but had no agnates. Implicit in Modestinus' statement is the same point already made by Ulpian. *Potestas*, consanguinity (in the technical sense of descent from the same *pater*) and agnatic descent are irrelevant to inheritance through females, which rests upon the blood connection only. Ulpian also remarks (*D.* 5. 2. 29. 1) that illegitimate children can bring a complaint of unduteous will, although we have no other evidence as to how soon this became accepted as law.

Illegitimate children were, by definition, legally fatherless, and therefore in need of tutors to administer their property, if they had any. Their natural fathers—supposing that they were known, and in touch—were under no obligation to nominate tutors for them in their wills, and indeed were no more legally able to do so than mothers: 'An appointment of a tutor made by a natural father has no effect, and it cannot be confirmed without an enquiry.' However, if they did, then, as when a mother nominated a tutor, the appointment might be confirmed, after investigation by the praetor.[125]

---

[123] Some indication of the variety, and vagueness, of methods of indicating status (including not doing so at all) found in inscriptions is provided, e.g. in the analysis of Weaver (1990) of 300 families from Rome (see his Table 1, p. 283); in over a third of his sample (36 per cent), status of the children is uncertain.

[124] *D.* 38. 8. 8. 'Modestinus respondit non ideo minus ad aviae maternae bona ab intestato nepotes admitti, quod vulgo quaesiti proponuntur.'

[125] *D.* 26. 3. 7 pr. 'Naturali filio ⟨cui nihil relictum est⟩ tutor frustra datur a patre nec sine inquisitione confirmatur'; cf. *D.* 26. 6 pr., on appointment by a mother. 'Cui

The pressure to find tutors for illegitimate children was perhaps less, however, in that fewer of them were likely to have anything worth administering. Most illegitimate children were likely to belong to the poorer levels of society, and in particular to be born from ex-slaves.[126] The illegitimate children of freedwomen, especially those born slaves and allowed to be freeborn Romans only because their mother's manumission had been unduly delayed by an heir charged with a *fideicommissum* to manumit her, had no paternal inheritance, and probably not much prospect of largesse from elsewhere. Ulpian (though not necessarily with freedwomen's children in mind) remarked that a mother should be pardoned who had failed to request a tutor for a child who was insolvent.[127]

It cannot be taken for granted, however, that all illegitimate children were financially badly off. Modestinus (above) wrote about an illegitimate grandchild as having a maternal grandmother with property; she herself could quite possibly have been a single mother, i.e. both mother and grandmother had produced illegitimate children. The children of Roman soldiers, likewise—and those of some gladiators—though illegitimate, were not necessarily poor. Illegitimate children could also be found, perhaps as *alumni* (fosterlings)[128] in the homes not only of the relatively prosperous lower classes, but also in those of the *honestiores*, the upper classes—such as the daughter of Rufina, the (freeborn) concubine of the Roman senator Cocceius Casseianus, whose name suggests a family connection with the historian Dio Cassius Cocceianus. The daughter, possibly Cocceius' own natural child, whom he called his *alumna*, suggesting that he maintained her, and perhaps had her reared in his household, was made joint heir with the senator's legitimate granddaughter—much to the latter's annoyance, though apparently she did not succeed in preventing her from claiming the inheritance.[129]

The illegitimate child, moreover, was not necessarily living in a single-parent household, or out of touch with his or her biological

nihil relictum est' (to whom nothing has been left [sc. in the will]) is surely interpolated; it was Justinian who first gave natural fathers permission to nominate tutors at all for their illegitimate children, though only for the administration of anything they left them in their wills: *Cod. Iust.* 5. 29. 4. For nomination of tutors by mothers, see *D.* 26. 3. 21; Gardner (1986a) 152.

[126] Those born as slaves, if freed while still under age, *impuberes,* were likely not to be Roman citizens at all, but Junian Latins.　　[127] *D.* 38. 17. 2. 45.
[128] B. Rawson (1986) 173–86; Weaver (1991) 167–9.　　[129] *D.* 34. 9. 16. 1.

father. Rufina's daughter is probably an example of an illegitimate child living with her mother and natural father. Owners, also, who had fathered children upon their female slaves (or freedwomen concubines) might well continue to have the children, and perhaps also their mothers, living in the household, *en famille*. For instance, in Herculaneum in the reign of Vespasian a witness gives evidence that 'the girl calling herself Petronia Justa' was brought up in the home of her mother's former owner, Petronius Stephanus—though, since we do not have the complete dossier, we do not know how her suit against Petronius' wife, to prove that she had been born after, not before, her mother's manumission turned out. Under Diocletian, a woman called Paulina seems to have been faced with a similar challenge to her claim to free birth; she is told that it is up to her to prove it. A Roman veteran C. Julius Diogenes, living in Egypt under Hadrian, did not manumit in his lifetime two slave women, probably his natural daughters, whom he made his heirs in his will, but he left legacies to the twins born to him by a manumitted slave, Julia Primilla—she was manumitted only shortly before their birth.[130]

Ex-slaves also, though sometimes separated by manumission or previous sale of family members, did sometimes succeed in keeping together, though relatively few certainly freed (i.e. slave-born) children are attested in inscriptions.[131] These children, however—since slave relationships were not recognized in law—would not have inheritance rights from their mothers.

There are traces also in the legal sources of fathers' involvement in the welfare of their illegitimate children. Though details such as the ages of the offspring, and whether or not they were still resident in their father's home, are lacking, it is clear that their father is aware of their existence and taking some steps to provide for them. Julian, for example, discussing fraud upon creditors, produces what is apparently a typical, and not merely imaginary, situation (though Titius is frequently employed in legal examples as a conventional name, like 'John Doe'): 'Lucius Titius, though he had creditors, handed over all his property to his freedmen, who were also his natural sons.'[132]

---

[130] 'Petronia Justa': *Tab. Herc.* 13–30; Paulina: *Cod. Iust.* 4. 19. 17 (2179 Honoré); Julia Primilla: *P. Lugd. Bat.* XIII.14; Gardner (1986a) 140.

[131] Treggiari (1969) 214; see also n. 123 above.

[132] D. 42. 8. 17. 1: 'Lucius Titius cum haberet creditores, libertis suis isdemque filiis naturalibus universas res suas tradidit.'

The point is that these were not sons *in potestate*; Titius had therefore, in law, made valid gifts, to outsiders—before the creditors pounced. The same effect could have been achieved by gifts to emancipated sons; that Julian chooses to specify natural children by slaves suggests that this was a real, and not rare, occurrence. Similar means were used (see 1.8 above) to keep property out of the hands of patrons.

Twice, Paul makes a point of mentioning that a child is illegitimate. He tells us[133] that L. Titius (who is extremely active in our legal texts) made a gift of a slave-woman, Concordia, to his natural daughter, Septicia, and then in his will made a legacy of Concordia and other slaves to his daughter, with a *fideicommissum* that she was to manumit her. The legal question was whether she could be compelled to do so; the answer was that she could not, since Concordia was already her property (i.e. since Septicia was not *in potestate*, the gift was valid). The argument would have been the same had Septicia been emancipated; however, Paul chose to specify that she was illegitimate. Again, he discusses an example of inheritance left between two sons, one legitimate (aged one year), one natural, with reciprocal substitution between them should either die (sc. before the father himself); when the legitimate child, still *impubes*, died *after* his father's death, his part of the inheritance, Paul said, should go to his mother.[134] Although again he uses the 'John Doe' name, L. Titius, in this instance the detail that one of the co-heirs was a natural child is not at all necessary for his argument, and makes no difference at all to the legal point.

All three examples are presented as theoretical, but in none of them was it necessary to specify that the child was a natural child. This suggests, not necessarily that the examples may possibly have been suggested by specific actual cases, but that Julian and Paul do not regard such family situations as uncommon.

Many of the lower-class families in Roman society, especially those including ex-slaves, will not have been able to constitute *familiae* in the legal sense. Concubinage also, especially with freeborn women, was always a delicate question for the Romans, and legitimation by subsequent matrimony never became fully accepted until Justinian.

[133] *D*. 40. 5. 40 pr.
[134] *D*. 28. 6. 45. The purpose of the substitution had been merely that at least one heir should be left to take the estate; Paul is dismissing a mistaken idea, that Titius had made a pupillary substitution in favour of the other son, i.e. in effect making a will in advance on behalf of his infant legitimate son.

Illegitimacy arising from certain causes, in particular certain 'unequal' unions, could, as we saw, in some instances be set aside, in others not; and it did not in itself necessarily entail a social stigma. [135]

3.7 MOTHERS AND CHILDREN IN FREEDMAN FAMILIES

The families of Roman freed slaves were among those which stood especially to benefit from the extension described above of inheritance rights between mothers and children, particularly illegitimate children. The composition of such family groups was infinitely variable. Families—even if all their members were of citizen status, which was not always the case—might include children who were freeborn and legitimate, freeborn and illegitimate, and perhaps some slave-born. As remarked above, it was probably not a rare occurrence that an older child in a freedman family was illegitimate, and subsequent children were legitimate. The older child may either have been born to a mother who had been freed, but was still unmarried, [136] or may have been born a slave and only subsequently set free. The latter was the case with the family of the freedman L. Julius Narcissus (2.8 above); his wife Julia Helpis was also his freedwoman, and L. Julius Vestalis is referred to as his son and freedman.

In ex-slave families, given the absence of status designations in many inscriptions, it is not always possible to distinguish between legitimate and illegitimate children. That a child was freeborn but illegitimate may be suspected where the mother and child have the same family name, and that of the mother's husband is different; this would not necessarily hold, however, where both parents had been slaves of the same owner, since both would then have the same family name. Only the freeborn child, whether legitimate or illegitimate, could inherit from his mother—slave relationships were not recognized in law for inheritance purposes, therefore the freed slave could not benefit either from the, possibly Hadrianic, extension of cognate inheritance or from the *senatusconsultum Orphitianum*.

---

[135] Rawson (1989); van de Wiel (1978) 307–50 and (1992) 327–58; Arjava (1996) 205–17.

[136] This also applied if the child was conceived before her manumission and born afterwards (Paul. *Sent.* 2. 24. 1). It applied even to children born before her manumission, if that had been unduly delayed: *D.* 1. 5. 22; Paul. *Sent.* 2. 24. 4. This is confirmed in several 3rd-cent. rescripts: *Cod. Iust.* 7. 4. 3, 4; 4. 57. 4 (497, 498, 1083 Honoré).

Finding actual cases, though, of such 'mixed' families is not easy. Important studies of the epigraphic evidence for freedmen families have been made by a number of scholars,[137] who frequently point out that reconstruction of family histories from epigraphic evidence must usually be imperfect and to a great extent reliant on guesswork. This is not only because of the unhelpful habit in many inscriptions of omitting indications of a person's status as freeborn or freed, but also because the picture is often incomplete and the evidence capable of more than one interpretation.

A rare example from the latter part of the first century AD[138] in which the same family is commemorated in two inscriptions illustrates, despite its ambiguities, the heterogeneous composition of many freedman families and the changes in status that might be undergone by individual members. The wording is capable of several interpretations, which carry a range of implications about the legal relationships of the members of the family, and even their economic prospects.

(i) *CIL* 6. 18398: 'Fl(aviae) Phronime, Phoenix Caes.n.ser(vi) coniugi et Fl. Cerealis et Phronimus et Celerina matri' (To Flavia Phronime. Phoenix, slave of Caesar, to his wife, and Flavius Cerealis and Phronimus and Celerina to their mother).

The deceased mother was apparently free, like many of the partners of imperial slaves,[139] but it is not clear whether she was freed or freeborn, and the father is still a slave. The son Cerealis has a *nomen* (the same as his mother's), Flavius, as well as a *cognomen* and so is free; but was he born free? It is not clear whether we are meant to understand 'Flavius' and 'Flavia' with the names of the other two children (in which case they too are free), or whether they like their father are slaves.

(ii) *CIL* 6. 8580 (=*ILS* 1497): 'T. Flavio Aug.lib. Cereali tabul. reg. Picen., Phoenix Caes.n.ser.filio pientissim(o), P. Junius Frontinus fratri dulcissim(o) et Celerina soror' (To T. Flavius Cerealis, freedman of Augustus, records officer for the Picenum region; Phoenix, slave of Caesar to a most dutiful son; P. Junius Frontinus, and Celerina his sister, to a dearest brother).

One matter at least has been cleared up in the second inscription.

---

[137] In particular B. Rawson (1966) 71–83 and (1989); Treggiari (1975) 393–402, (1981*a*) 59–81 and (1981b); Weaver (1972), ch. 8, (1986) and (1990).
[138] Discussed in Weaver (1972) 143 n. 1.   [139] Weaver (1972) 114ff.

Flavius Cerealis was born a slave. That could mean either that his mother was an imperial freedwoman, or that she had originally been free, but that he had been born a slave in consequence of the *senatus-consultum Claudianum* of AD 52 in relation to the offspring of free women who cohabited with slaves.[140] Phronimus is missing, although the mysterious brother P. Junius Frontinus (with no status indication) may be Phronimus in another guise. There are several possibilities. Phronimus could have been a manumitted slave, adopted by a P. Junius, or sold to Junius and manumitted by him; or Phronimus and Junius Frontinus may be two different people, Junius being the son of Phoenix's subsequent 'marriage' to a Junia; it is even possible that Flavia Phronime had at some stage been legally married to a P. Junius.

In the eyes of the law, this group of people includes four, five, or even six separate *familiae*—those of Flavia Phronime, Flavius Cerealis, Junius Frontinus, Celerina (if free), and Phronimus (if free and not the same person as Junius). The father, Phoenix, has no legally recognized relationship to any of them, nor does the freed brother, Cerealis. All the children are illegitimate—except, possibly, Junius. If Junius, Celerina, and Phronimus were all born free and children of Flavia, they all counted as cognates of each other, as well as of their mother, but Cerealis, being slave-born, did not. Nevertheless, that these people appear together in two inscriptions indicates that, whatever the law might say, they thought of themselves as a family.

Other implications of these inscriptions are worth exploring. Not only the mother's status, but the time in which a family group such as this lived, could affect the economic situation of the rest of the family. Since Flavia and Phoenix were not legally married and the children were not in his *potestas*, she could make gifts to all of them during her lifetime, so far as her means allowed (though, if she were subject to *tutela*, tutor's authority might be needed for disposing of some kinds of property).

After Hadrian, all Flavia's freeborn children, both legitimate and illegitimate, had the right to inherit from her if she died without a will, as cognates: that would exclude Cerealis. Since, however, the family name is Flavius, the probability is that this family belongs to a period before illegitimate children had this right: that would also exclude Celerina and Phronimus, though perhaps not Junius.

---

[140] Crook (1967b) 7–8; Weaver (1964) 137–9 and (1972) 164ff. The woman herself was enslaved unless the man's owner consented to the union; even if she were allowed to remain free the children might by agreement be slaves.

If Flavia was a freedwoman, however, none of them stood to inherit anything when she died, so long as her patron was alive, or had left children, since at that time patrons took precedence, as *legitimi*, over her children, who ranked only as cognates. Only after the *senatus-consultum Orphitianum* could children, legitimate or—by the early third century at latest—illegitimate, exclude the patron; before it, under the Augustan *lex Papia*, only legitimate children excluded him, and then only in part.[141]

If she herself was freeborn, then having three freeborn children gave her the *ius liberorum*, which meant that she could do what she liked with all her property while she lived, and make a will (supposing she had any property worth leaving) without reference to any tutor; that would allow her to benefit them all, Cerealis as well. If, however, she was a freedwoman, she did not qualify for the *ius* (four freeborn children, who at this stage probably still had to be legitimate, were needed); therefore she needed tutorial consent during her lifetime, and her patron could prevent her making a will.[142]

A good many of the legal difficulties which might affect families including ex-slaves have already been discussed (1.8, 2.8, and 3.6 above). One effect of the *senatusconsultum Orphitianum*, as noted above, was that, by the early third century, not only a freedwoman's legitimate children, but illegitimate children as well, could apparently exclude her patron's claim to her estate entirely. This seems extraordinary, yet Ulpian's exposition of the relevant clause in the *senatus-consultum*[143] is quite clear. 'So long as even one son wishes to claim the legitimate inheritance, the old law does not apply ... and if perhaps there is a son and a patron, then, if the son refuses the inheritance, it is offered to the patron.' A little earlier, he has stated: 'Illegitimate children also are admitted to the legitimate inheritance [i.e. to inheritance in the top category, as *legitimi*] of their mother.' (Presumably this also meant that the illegitimate, as well as the legitimate, children of an emancipated daughter now took precedence over

---

[141] Gaius 3. 44 (1.8 above); *D.* 38. 17. 1. 9 (3.3 above).

[142] The tutor of an imperial freedwoman would, strictly speaking, be the emperor who was her patron; but it is hard to believe that this was practicable. Freedwomen (other than those with women patrons) could not have replacement tutors (Gaius 1. 174); were imperial freedwomen perhaps given blanket authorization for day-to-day transactions (though possibly not for the making of wills)?

[143] *D.* 38. 17. 1. 9 (3.3 n. 52) with 38. 17. 1. 2 (3.6 n. 121).

her father, who as *parens manumissor* came lower down in the category of *legitimi*.)

It seems extraordinary that by the early third century Romans should be prepared to interpret the *senatusconsultum Orphitianum* in a way that set aside the rights of patrons to their freedwomen's estates, in favour of illegitimate as well as legitimate children. At a stroke this will have enormously increased the numbers of children eligible to benefit.

Why were the Romans willing to do this? Any answer must be speculative, but it must be borne in mind that this came after a long period of change and development of the law, during which more and more importance had been accorded to blood relationships, particularly that between mother and child, and eventually to the benefit of illegitimate as well as legitimate children. Development had followed two lines.

The inheritance rights of legitimate children to succeed to their mothers' property were progressively extended from the late Republic on; an important reason for the early changes to the rules of inheritance was, it was suggested above, failure of agnatic lines of succession. By the later Republic also a strong social expectation had arisen that mothers would make provision in wills for their children; they no longer had the automatic legal right to inherit, as their mothers' nearest agnates, that they had had when their mothers were commonly in the *manus* of their fathers, and so part of the same *familia*. The change to the praetorian edict, allowing legitimate children to inherit as cognates, was a response to both factors. Allowing children to make the 'complaint of undutious will' (though, as suggested above, not necessarily at first to the disadvantage of any agnates of the mother) was also a response to current social attitudes. The weakening of *tutela* over women under Augustus, Claudius, and Hadrian[144] further paved the way for the *senatusconsultum Orphitianum*.

For illegitimate children, there was at first no change, but later, by the time of Hadrian, probably to a large extent because of certain unintended effects of the operation of Augustan social legislation, especially the manumission laws,[145] there had been an explosive increase in the numbers of unmarried parents and illegitimate children. Hadrian apparently did something to curb this trend by making it possible for

---

[144] Dio 55. 2; Gaius 1. 115a, 145, 171, 194; Gardner (1986a) 19–21.
[145] Gardner (1996).

some previously ineligible couples to marry, but he also gave illegitimate children some right of inheritance from their mothers. By a time some years before the passing of the *senatusconsultum Orphitianum*, the birth of illegitimate children could be registered in the official records (such registration, instituted by the Augustan *lex Julia et Papia*, had previously been reserved for legitimate children). Marcus Aurelius is probably to be given the credit for this extension.[146] By the time of the *senatusconsultum*, therefore, the ground had already been well prepared for extending its provision, as happened by interpretation within at most a generation, to illegitimate children. The two lines came together.

The leap was not enormous. The agnatic tie between father and legitimate child was based in civil law, and was terminated by legal means, such as emancipation or giving in adoption. The cognatic tie between mother and child was based on 'natural law' not civil, i.e. purely on the blood relationship,[147] and therefore existed whether or not the parents were or ever had been married, and whether or not the child had—or ever had had—agnatic links with a lawful father and his *familia*.

Therefore there simply was not the same basis for discriminating—when the question eventually arose—between the patron's rights over the estates of mothers of legitimate and of illegitimate children. All were equally her own natural born children. A further point of some importance is that, as we saw above (3.3), the *senatusconsultum Tertullianum* was interpreted by Julian, soon after its passing, as applying also to mothers of illegitimate children. This probably means (though it is not a development for which we have independent evidence) that already by that time it was accepted that illegitimate children should count towards a mother acquiring the *ius liberorum*. The *ius liberorum* gave a freedwoman the right to make a will, without the consent of her patron, and if she now acquired the *ius* in virtue of illegitimate children, it would be all the harder to maintain, as was the case with freedmen, that despite a will, only legitimate children could serve to reduce or eliminate the patron's claim. Our only evidence is in Gaius, who says only *liberi*, 'children', without qualifying them as legitimate, in contrast to the detail he gives on patronal rights over the estates of freedmen.[148]

---

[146] *D.* 22. 3. 16 (Terentius Clemens on the *lex Julia et Papia*); 29. 1 (Scaevola); SHA *Marcus* 9.7; Schulz (1942–3).   [147] *D.* 38. 10. 4. 2.   [148] Gaius 3. 39–44.

The idea had gained firm acceptance that a mother's children, legitimate or not, had chief right to inherit from her, and this applied to the children of freedwomen as much as to those of the freeborn. In any case, there may seldom have been much for a patron to lose, since while freedmen might prosper in business by using craft skills in which they had received training as slaves, freedwomen, on the whole, were more likely to be fulfilling the roles of wife and mother, if they were lucky, or making such living as they could in retail selling, or the service industries.

The *Constitutio Antoniniana* (AD 212) had perhaps already been passed by the time Ulpian gave his interpretation of the clause in the *senatusconsultum*. The *constitutio* made all free persons within the Empire Roman citizens. Like Hadrian's intervention earlier, it may have done something in the first instance to keep down the production of illegitimate children by making it possible for previously ineligible couples to marry. It also may have created inheritance rights for many illegitimate children who did not previously have them, for example if they or their mothers had been Latins—and this would certainly have been to the disadvantage of the mother's patron. This, however, was a short-term effect, since only existing Latins were transformed into Roman citizens; the operation of the manumission laws would continue to produce Latins.

Illegitimate children might not have expectations of an inheritance from a *paterfamilias*, but from the early third century they, like their legitimate siblings, had a better title than anyone else to inherit from their mothers, whether that mother was freeborn or freed. For the freedwoman's child who was also illegitimate, this might be particularly important for his future prospects in life.

Conclusion

Since the intention was to explore the relationship between *familia* and family, to a great extent this book has been concerned with Roman family law—or at least, with certain aspects of it. Attention has been focused primarily upon property, its ownership and transmission, and upon property rights, in so far as these depend upon membership of a *familia*, or upon 'family' relationship. This is not only a matter of the availability of evidence (although much, or rather most, of surviving legal writings concern property), but also of its nature. Provision for economic welfare, whether one's own, or that of one's dependants and kin, is a necessary practical concern for most people. Roman legal writings on the topic are not only a source of information on the legal rules and mechanisms involved, but are also uniquely revelatory of social mores and social values—i.e. not only of how people actually behaved, but how they were expected to behave towards 'family'—and, most importantly, they reveal how Roman society was prepared to modify the legal rules of the *familia* in response to changes in the needs of society.

About *patria potestas*, on the other hand, in so far as that concerned control and discipline within the *familia*, little or nothing has been said above, since it is in the main irrelevant to the concerns of the present work (1.7, on paternal rights, under the Julian law on adultery, to take action against adulterous daughters, is an obvious exception). The legal powers of punishment and coercion possessed by the *paterfamilias*, many of them, especially the more extreme, seldom if ever likely to be invoked in practice, derived entirely from his legal status as head of a *familia*, not from family relationships—the latter gave him, at most, a certain moral authority.

Concerning internal control and discipline in the *familia*, a great deal has recently been written by social historians, whose explorations of emotional and moral relationships within the family group have challenged the authoritarian image of the *paterfamilias* presented by the

Conclusion

legal rules, while demographic studies have challenged the assumption that such paternal control was a social reality for much of the lifetime of many Romans.[1] Law and life—*patria potestas* in the *familia*, and fatherhood in the family—are distinguished. Overall, the tendency has been to minimize the impact in practice of paternal legal powers of discipline.

Such work may be seen as a corrective to the distorting effect of the concentration, in most studies of Roman law, on the purely legal content of such powers. Legal historians, being primarily interested in the formal institutions themselves and their legal effects, have tended to concentrate on describing changes in the legal content of *patria potestas*, and in particular on cataloguing successive limitations and restrictions on its components,[2] among which those relating to discipline are the most numerous group. This approach, unfortunately, gives both these disciplinary powers and their dilution more prominence than they are likely to have held in the experience of most Romans; severe punishments, specially of adult children, let alone exercise of the 'ius vitae necisque' (power of life and death), were hardly likely to have been an everyday event in the lives of most Roman households; that is why rare (real or alleged) instances are the stuff of legends and moral treatises.[3] In daily life, members of the *familia* were much more likely to encounter the consequences of the other principal aspects of *patria potestas*, i.e. ownership of the property of the *familia* and legal liability of the *paterfamilias* for the actions (and especially, in terms of the impact on ordinary life, the contractual obligations) of its members.

Implicitly or explicitly, some legal historians have deplored the erosion and decline of *patria potestas* which they believe successive alterations and restrictions to represent, along with the supposed similar fate of the 'family' (identified with the agnatic *familia*). Theories on the reasons have been proposed—such as the change from peasantry to a monetary economy (which, at least, arguably

---

[1] On the emotional climate of family life, see the works referred to in the Introduction, at nn. 4–8; on paternal mortality, Saller (1987) and (1994) chs. 2 and 3.

[2] See esp. Buckland (1963) 102–4 and Schulz (1951) 150–5. Schulz is inclined to dismiss the whole institution as an archaic and pointless survival of a harsh patriarchy.

[3] As remarked above (Introd. n. 2), customary restraints on the exercise in practice of such disciplinary powers are discussed by Rabello (1979), Voci (1980), and Harris (1986). It is noteworthy that the Roman moralist Valerius Maximus treats as showing exceptional severity the actual exercise of the ultimate power of life and death: 5. 8 (all instances with overt political importance), and 6. 1. 2–6.

bears some relation to otherwise attested developments), the influence of Hellenistic thought, and, later, influences from Greek and other eastern systems of law, and from Christianity.[4] This alleged influence of external ideas, however, lacks the support of positive evidence, and such theories are now generally disregarded by social historians, who examine legal change not as a separate phenomenon but as part of the evidence for the social history of the Roman world, and prefer to look for reasons in the historical context.

Moreover, such paternal power of punishment, although potentially dramatic, is arguably less important for the functioning of families within Roman society at large than other aspects of the legal status of being a *paterfamilias*. What, after all, is meant by *patria potestas*? The term is often loosely used to refer to a whole range of powers, but also of responsibilities and obligations. Does it refer to the coercive and punitive power of the *paterfamilias* over such persons as may be *in potestate* in his *familia*? or to his right (and responsibility) to act at law on behalf of the *familia*? or to his sole ownership and control, at least in his lifetime, of all the property of the *familia*?[5] The second and third of these are directly concerned, as the first is not, not only with the basic legal structure of the Roman *familia* but with its function in Roman society as a whole. The *paterfamilias* is, for any act with legal consequences, *the* point of contact of each legal unit, *familia*, with the rest of Roman society, which is also made up of such units. Paternal discipline, though important for the orderliness of society in general, is internal to the *familia*, whereas property ownership and legal liability involve interaction with outsiders. Note that these outsiders may also involve family members not in the *familia* (to whom the *patria potestas* of the head of the *familia* does not apply).

Although much appears to change in Roman family law—to the extent that one legal historian[6] can write dramatically of the *familia* as

---

[4] See e.g. Kaser (1971) 268–70, (1975) 72–5, 141–6, (1980) 77–8 (Kaser (1980) is the English version of his student textbook abridged from the main (1971/5) handbook); cf. the suggestion of Voci (1982), discussed in 1.1 above, on the reasons for the introduction of emancipation. On Greco-oriental law, Mitteis (1891), and for Christian influence Biondi (1952–4) were fundamental but both have subsequently been much criticized; see Jolowicz (1965) 542–7, Arjava (1996) 3–6. Arjava (1996) also on several points exposes the inadequacies of the evidence to support Mitteis's thesis: 48–50, 54–8, 65.

[5] See e.g. the list of 'chief elements'; of *patria potestas* in Buckland (1963) 102–3. For the distinctions, see Voci (1980) 96ff.

[6] Kaser (1975) 72–5, (1980) 77–8; he links the changes particularly with the introduction of cognate inheritance.

'disintegrating' (verflüchtigt)—these changes are not fundamental to the constitution of the *familia* in civil law, a great deal of which does not change at all. The basic legal structure of the *familia* remains intact, over the thousand and more years from predecemviral Rome to the *Digest* of Justinian, undergoing only minor changes.[7] The legally defined membership of the *familia* under the headship of a *paterfamilias* remains the same (even although in practice one position, that of the *materfamilias*, or wife *in manu*, ceases to be filled). The *paterfamilias* continues to be the sole person who has legal authority to act on behalf of members of the *familia*, and who is legally responsible for the actions of those under his control. He continues to be sole owner of its property during his lifetime, and the members of the *familia* continue to be equally entitled—in default of his having made other arrangements—to inherit on his death, as they were in the beginning (before the possibility existed of making alternative arrangements, i.e. of making wills).

The most significant legal changes are those concerned with the law of inheritance on intestacy, i.e. with those entitled to inherit the property of the *familia* once the *paterfamilias*[8] is dead and the original *familia* has ceased to exist, and especially with the extension of inheritance rights to blood relatives (cognates) who are no longer, or never have been, members of the same *familia*. These changes, which have been discussed above in considerable detail, show especially clearly how in law (albeit more slowly and sometimes belatedly) as in life the claims of legal kinship, *familia*, were subordinated to those of natural relationships, of 'family'.

Legal historians, however, are not always careful to distinguish between *familia* and the natural 'family',[9] and in consequence may represent such changes in inheritance law as evidence for a change in

---

[7] Principally, the introduction of some minor praetorian actions available directly to a *filiusfamilias*, the introduction of the *peculium castrense*, some protection of the inheritance rights of children, and, after Constantine, a requirement that maternal property eventually be passed on to children: Gardner (1993) 62–3, 74–5; and, on inheritance, 1.3–7 above.

[8] Bearing in mind always that an independent woman is also, in legal terms, a *paterfamilias*, even though her *familia* consists only of herself: *D.* 50. 16. 195. 5.

[9] Fayer (1994) 284 appears to confuse the two. Buckland (1963) avoids the term 'family', as does, on the whole, Schulz (1951), though he speaks once or twice of 'family property', but Nicholas (1962) 66 and Jolowicz (1965) 122 use 'family' when discussing inheritance in the *familia*. Kaser (see text below) identifies *familia*, the legal unit ('Rechtsverband') and family ('Familie').

the nature of the family itself. It may be said, for example, that 'the Roman family' was originally agnatic but that this conception was replaced by increasing recognition of cognatic (i.e. blood) relationships—although some writers are more careful than others to express themselves accurately, or at least to distinguish this purely legal recognition from emotional ties based in blood kinship. An extreme example of the consequences of lack of distinction between the two is to be found in the influential legal historian, Kaser, who explicitly identifies the Roman family (Familie) with the legal unit (Rechtsverband), the *familia*. For him, the internal autonomy of the *familia* and the absoluteness of the power of the *paterfamilias* within it represent the institution in its purest form. His emphasis throughout is on the power of control embodied in *patria potestas*, and on its erosion (rather over-stressed), without discussion of the purposes both of the original institution and of the modifications made to it. The consequences of the changes in Roman family law, and in particular of the recognition of cognate inheritance, are in his view dramatic—no less than the disintegration of the 'family unit'—and he therefore sees the cause of the changes as a growing individualism, and desire to break away to independence (sc. on the part of those *in potestate*). [10]

On such a view, the alternative to the *familia*, and to paternal autocracy, it seems, is rejection of family ties. However this, as shown in some detail in Chapter 1, was by no means the case in Roman life—emancipation clearly did not entail isolation from one's nearest and dearest. On the contrary, it appears to have served as an alternative to *familia* in fulfilling some of the main economic functions of the *familia*. In Chapters 2 and 3 also, attention was drawn to evidence for the importance attached by the Romans to blood ties with persons outside the *familia* (both originally, and also by departure through emancipation or giving in adoption).

The dependence of such an interpretation as Kaser's on the twin errors of taking the theoretical legal powers of the *paterfamilias* as describing social reality, and of equating the legal concept of *familia* with actual families, is obvious. As already pointed out, much of the work of Roman social historians in recent years has received its initial impetus from awareness of this error of equating 'family' and *familia*. Cognate relationships—ties of blood—were, and appear always to

[10] Kaser (1971) 50–1, 268, 669; (1975) 72, 142; (1980) 77, 333.

have been, of great importance in Roman society, and for a variety of reasons, some of which this study has attempted to explore. That 'family' economic welfare was regarded as more important than retaining unaltered the composition of the individual *familia* is shown by such practices as emancipation and adoption—not only *taking* in adoption, which is more often studied, but *giving* in adoption as well; the motives of the donor are as relevant as those of the recipient. The importance attached to the blood link, even when the original agnatic legal bond has been dissolved, is demonstrated not only by surviving anecdotal evidence, both in literary and legal sources, of family-spirited behaviour (such as that of Scipio Aemilianus) but by the ways in which the legal rules of inheritance are altered, and new rules developed, in order to take account of extra-legal factors such as *pietas* between blood relatives. On cognate inheritance, see especially 1.5, and also, in 1.12, some of the ways in which the developed law may be exploited to show favouritism within families.

For the influence of family affections across *familia* boundaries, there is ample literary evidence. One may think for example of the behaviour of relatives whose agnatic links have been severed by adoptions, as for instance in the families of Scipio Aemilianus and Q. Fabius, or where serial marriages have created numerous cognate relationships—as with the younger Cato and his half-siblings, with Brutus, or in the whole tangled family trees of Dinaea and Sassia. Above all, there are the links between children and their mothers and maternal relatives, shown both directly and in such ways as in the choice of persons for adoption.

In Roman legal sources, these family feelings are displayed both anecdotally, as for instance in various situations prompting replies in imperial rescripts, and also more generally, in the assumptions and expectations, underlying these replies, as to what constitutes appropriate family-spirited behaviour. Such assumptions and expectations may also be detected underlying the juristic opinions preserved in the *Digest* and other legal writings, both in the choice of situations (whether hypothetical or with a basis in fact) on which to comment, and in the factors which are held relevant to influencing interpretations of the law. This is especially evident where reasons of ethics, rather than strict law, are invoked.

Similar considerations appear to underlie various changes in the law, not only that relating to intestate inheritance, about which a good deal has been written in the foregoing chapters, but also to inheritance by will. A good example is the introduction of a legal remedy, the 'complaint of unduteous will', for those who felt that insufficient attention had been paid in a close relative's will to the claims of family affection. This legal remedy was accessible, as we saw, not only to *familia* and agnates but also to those no longer in the *familia*, i.e. to emancipated children and to those given in adoption. On intestate inheritance, note especially the comment of Gaius, on succession by cognates under the provincial (and, so also, it may be assumed, the praetorian) edict: 'The proconsul, prompted by natural equity, promises possession of property to all cognate relatives, whom a claim of blood calls to the inheritance, though they may fail at civil law.'[11] That is, they would have no claim at all under civil law, even if there were no agnates surviving; but if their blood connection 'calls them to the inheritance' (that is, if there are no agnates), the edict recognizes the moral justice of allowing them to inherit.

Readers will hardly have failed to notice that a good deal of the family law with which this book is concerned is that relating to intestate inheritance. For this there are a number of reasons, the main ones (apart from the obvious, that the making of wills is, precisely, a way of exercising individual choices and *avoiding* circumscription by the rules of civil law)[12] being, first, that changes in the law of inheritance, and especially of intestate inheritance, are particularly revelatory of Roman attitudes towards family and kinship (such as those just discussed), and, secondly, that they also offer some pointers towards the nature of the social conditions which prompt these attitudes. Among social factors particularly emphasized above were the apparent shortage of direct male heirs, and the effects of manumission of slaves.

Some legal historians would disagree about the importance of this area of Roman law. Buckland (1963) 365 revealingly dismisses intestacy as of minor importance, on two grounds. One is that long before classical times intestacy had become unusual. Certainly, it was probably unusual for anyone with any substantial amount of property not to make a will; but, as repeatedly observed above, and also emphasized recently by Saller,[13] wills could easily fail on technicalities, so produc-

---

[11] *D.* 38. 8. 2: 'Proconsul naturali aequitate motus omnibus cognatis promittit bonorum possessionem, quos sanguinis ratio vocat ad hereditatem, licet iure civili deficiant.'

[12] A point often stressed (see e.g. Corbier (1985) 520, Saller (1991*a*) 29–30, and Champlin (1991) 8–13), although such freedom, as these authors observe, was itself nevertheless subject to certain social and legal restraints.

[13] Saller (1991*a*) 30–3; (1994) 164–6.

ing unintended intestacy—and keeping lawyers busy assessing, in theory, the merits of various claims, and magistrates in doing the same in actuality. It was therefore just as important for a Roman father to make what advance provision he could for the possibility of intestacy as he did, in framing his will, to anticipate as many other eventualities as possible. This, for instance, is what the rather bizarre manœuvres of emancipations and re-adoptions within the *familia* described above are about—they are the activities of a *paterfamilias* trying to restructure the lines of intestate succession, just in case his will fails, so that his favourite heir will still get the lion's share.[14]

Buckland's second ground for dismissal is that intestacy is of little juristic value—'Apart from a few main principles, it is a mass of detail, throwing little light on other parts of the law.' The law of intestacy, it is true, is virtually a self-contained system, distinct from inheritance by will. Buckland's remark is true, however, only if one is concerned, as legal historians tend to be, to do no more than to describe the rules, their successive alterations, and their legal effects; the idea breaks down completely as soon as one becomes interested in exploring the reasons for changes in the rules. Buckland is able to adopt such a point of view not only because in the study of Roman law by legal historians little attention is paid to extra-legal developments, but especially because Roman law is conventionally treated by them in an artificially compartmentalized way.

This follows either the traditional tripartite division of Roman law (perhaps not invented by Gaius, but canonized for later ages by his manual, the *Institutes*) into the Law of Persons (status, and legal capacity of the individual), the Law of Things (property, inheritance, and contracts), and the Law of Actions (procedure), or a variant, the 'Pandecten-System' developed in nineteenth-century Germany.[15] As a result, areas of law concerning the family are arbitrarily divided off from each other and separately presented, and relevant connections are obscured. This is particularly clear in relation to the kinds of topics discussed in this book. Matters of personal status (emancipation, adoption, illegitimacy) are part of the Law of Persons. They have effects, however on property rights, especially inheritance entitlements, which belong to the Law of Things. Moreover, within the

---

[14] Saller (1991*a*) on heirship strategies; also e.g. 2.9 above on intra-familial adoption.
[15] Buckland (1963) 56–61; Schulz (1951) 10–11. The 'Pandecten-System' includes dowry and separate property in marriage under the law of persons, or 'family law'.

Law of Things, to take the most striking example, inheritance by will and inheritance on intestacy are usually separately treated in legal textbooks.

This compartmentalization of Roman law, which may be accounted for by lawyers' concern with expounding the rules, rather than analysing their social effects, tends to distract from observation that, within a self-coherent system such as that of Roman law, internal connections proliferate, and that the consequences of applying a given rule are unlikely to fall entirely within only one of the conventional main divisions. Social historians, not feeling themselves bound by these divisions, and alert also to extra-legal factors, are better placed to discern the overall picture.

Particular attention has been paid above, therefore, to considering how changes in the law are prompted both in response to historical developments in Roman society, and also in consequence of the effects in practice of previous changes in diverse areas of the law itself.[16] Connections are explored, for example, between developments in these two areas, the law of intestacy and the law of wills. In the praetorian law of intestacy, a special position is accorded not only (as in civil law) to *sui heredes*, i.e. to children and grandchildren still *in potestate*—but also, taking into account the effects of emancipation, to *liberi*; therefore in the praetorian law of wills there is a requirement that *liberi*, even if not *in potestate*, be expressly inherited or disinherited. The attitude underlying, in the law of intestacy, the development of cognate succession in the praetor's edict and especially, later, the increasing provision made by legislation for direct inheritance between mother and child, is reflected in the development of the 'complaint of unduteous will'. These changes are also related to developments in other parts of the Law of Things (e.g. on dowry and gifts) and of Persons (especially the law of adoption, and recognition, for the determination of status, of certain illegitimate relationships), as well as to social factors such as demographic trends, and the manumission of slaves.

One of the most pressing reasons for modifying the civil law of inheritance was the increasingly evident disparity between the demographic situation assumed by the *familia*-system, and the social realities of reproduction in Roman society. As already mentioned,

---

[16] e.g. as suggested above (3.6; see also Gardner 1996), Hadrianic remedies for certain undesirable social and legal effects of the implementation of changes made under Augustus.

modern demographic studies, based not only on statistical analysis of literary and, especially, epigraphic evidence but on the use of modern computer techniques to simulate probable or possible Roman family and kinship patterns, have tended to support the view that Roman families had difficulty in maintaining direct succession in the male line. Unfortunately, the assumption of such succession was basic to the idea of the *familia*. I have suggested above that many of the changes in Roman law to accommodate 'family' rather than *familia* are attributable to a situation such as that also indicated by such demographic analysis.

The Roman system of civil law, based upon the *familia*, was designed to secure certain ends and rested upon certain assumptions about Roman society. In respect of certain of these ends, however, the system was excessively simple and rigid, and proved less appropriate and less capable of securing the desired outcome, as the assumptions were falsified in practice. This desired outcome, one of the principal aims for which the system was devised, was to secure the economic well-being of successive generations of families by tightly controlling the possibilities of dispersal of their property, using the *familia* system to do so. The initial assumption was that each generation of men would be succeeded either by their children or by their own siblings in the male line (women, by being customarily taken into *manus*, were simply transferred into membership of the family group in which they would become mothers of the next generation), and the civil law of succession was formulated with that in mind. From an early date, however, it was found necessary to take account of situations in which these assumptions had failed to be fulfilled—hence, it was suggested above, the early development of will-making and the pontifical concern, in the middle Republic, for the fate of the family *sacra*. The situation is also implied in successive pieces of Republican legislation intended to limit dispersal of estates by legacies outside the family, or by gifts between the living. Hence especially the evolution of the praetorian law of inheritance, and other developments in inheritance law discussed above (particularly in 1.4–6 and 3.2–3).

Some devices were counter-productive. In a situation where direct heirs were lacking, the use of wills might tend only to encourage dispersal of family properties; as we saw, successive attempts were made, culminating in the *lex Falcidia*, to impose some restraint on excessive fragmentation of inheritances. For a time, also, the civil law system of intestate inheritance continued to work against itself—i.e. so long as women were commonly transferred into *manus* at marriage. This meant, since they did not become independent until widowhood, that they were likely to be retained for a greater part—or even the whole—of their life-span *in potestate* (whereas, if they were not transferred into *manus*, their independence was delayed only until a father's demise), so postponing the time when they might become available as heirs, and making dispersal among *gentiles* more likely. As *manus* declined, so inheritance by females, and through the female line, became both more practicable and more acceptable. Chapter 3 in particular, on changes in family law relating to mother and child, examines these developments.

Adoption, examined in Chapter 2, also underwent changes. In essence it was merely a mechanism utilizing a legal fiction of kinship, and the rules of the Law of Persons, in order to control transmission of family property, by artificial creation of direct heirs. As such, it was a clumsy device, with legal effects irrelevant to its purpose, since it involved subjecting an outsider to an alien *potestas*. This carried risks for someone giving in adoption, who might, like L. Aemilius Paulus, find himself left, by the death of his remaining sons *in potestate*, without direct heirs. It was also hazardous for those adopted, who might lose their natal inheritance, in the event of their father's intestacy. Its importance, for would-be adopters, as a means of creating direct (and, secondarily, agnatic) heirs to family property necessarily diminished with developments in inheritance law which established property claims for relatives even in the absence of agnatic links. Its function of altering the composition of the *familia* came to be used merely as a means of manipulating the order of priority among existing future claimants to family property. Finally, in Justinianic law, the property claim was separated from the unnecessary *familia* membership, in cases where there was no blood kinship by descent which could give it a semblance of relevance.

Emancipation, discussed in Chapter 1, appears, so far as we have evidence for motives, to have been resorted to mainly for economic reasons. Material benefit from sources outside the *familia* could not, however, be guaranteed, and there were also risks involving the inheritance, similar to those possibly arising from adoption. Safeguards were introduced, and most of the risks had been removed by a much earlier date than the completion of either of the processes of change referred to above. There was no alien *potestas* to complicate matters, as with adoption. Recognition of inheritance rights initially as a cognate, and soon after also of quasi-agnatic rights (the praetorian category of *liberi*), should the emancipated person wish to exercise them, was easier where there had originally been an agnatic connection with the father (rather than merely a blood connection with a mother). Danger of dispersal of property (i.e. should there be no direct heirs) was also countered both by the development of these inheritance rights for the *emancipatus* in his original *familia*, and rights of inheritance from him for children left in his original *familia*. In effect, the dividing line between family and *familia* was ignored for the purposes of inheritance between male parent and child; and, as with adoption, emancipation came to be used also as a procedural device for adjusting priority of inheritance claims within the family.

In addition, a large and important section of Roman society of the later Republic and the imperial period consisted of people for whom the hereditary, agnatic *familia* system had not been designed and for whom it was in many instances inapplicable, namely ex-slaves and their offspring. In all three parts of this study, detailed attention has been given to ways in which particular circumstances, such as civil status, illegitimacy and obligations to patrons, might affect such people. In particular, their existence gave an added boost, it was suggested above, to social pressures in favour of opening up inheritance between mother and child (3.6–7). In the families of first-generation ex-slaves, attention to the rules of the *familia* was often a matter of evasion (1.8 on possible uses of emancipation), or avoidance (2.8—sc. by refraining from adoption) rather than manipulation, and necessarily so, if the economic prosperity of the family group was to be protected.

Both in freedmen and freeborn families, however, the same principle applies. The civil law rules of the *familia* will be complied with when it suits them—but not if they are counter-productive, and some alternative means can be found which serves their purposes better. The Roman *familia* was not an end in itself but a means to an end. It was merely one among a number of legal mechanisms devised in order to serve the real end, i.e. the promotion of the welfare and contentment of the families, of whatever composition, of which Roman society was constituted, and through that the harmony of the society as a whole.

Bibliography

ARJAVA, A. (1996) *Women and Law in Late Antiquity*, Oxford.

AUBERT, J.-J. (1994) *Business Managers in Ancient Rome*, Leiden.

BAGNALL, R. S., and FRIER, B. W. (1994) *The Demography of Roman Egypt*, Cambridge.

BIONDI, B. (1952–4) *Il Diritto Romano Cristiano*, 3 vols. (Milan).

BORKOWSKI, A. (1994) *Textbook on Roman Law*, London.

BRADLEY, K. R. (1984) *Slaves and Masters in the Roman Empire*, Oxford.

——(1991a) *Discovering the Roman Family*, Oxford.

——(1991b) 'Remarriage and the Structure of the Upper-Class Roman Family', in B. Rawson (ed.), *Marriage, Divorce and Children in Ancient Rome*, London, 79–98.

——(1994) *Slavery and Society at Rome*, Cambridge.

BROUGHTON, T. R. S. (1951, 1952, 1986) *The Magistrates of the Roman Republic*, i–iii, New York.

BRUNT, P. A. (1971) *Italian Manpower 225 BC–AD 14*, Oxford.

——(1988) *The Fall of the Roman Republic*, Oxford.

BUCKLAND, W. W. (1908) *The Roman Law of Slavery*, Cambridge.

——(1963) *A Text-Book of Roman Law*, Cambridge.

CAMODECA, G. (1992) *L'Archivio Puteolano dei Sulpicii I*, Naples.

CASTRÉN, P. (1975) *Ordo Populusque Pompeianus, Polity and Society in Roman Pompeii*, Rome.

CHAMPLIN, E. (1991) *Final Judgments: Duty and Emotion in Roman Wills 200 BC–AD 250*, Berkeley.

CHIUSI, T. (1994) 'Zur Vormundschaft der Mutter', *ZSS* 111: 155–96.

CORBETT, P. E. (1930) *The Roman Law of Marriage*, Oxford.

CORBIER, M. (1985) 'Idéologie et pratique de l'héritage (Ier s. av. J.-C.–IIe s. ap. J.-C.)', *Index*, 13: 501–28.

——(1994) 'La Maison des Césars', in P. Bonté (ed.), *Épouser au plus proche. Inceste, prohibitions et stratégies matrimoniales autour de la Méditerranée*, Paris, 243–91.

——(1995) 'Male Power and Legitimacy through Women: The *domus Augusta* under the Julio-Claudians', in R. Hawley and B. Levick (edd.), *Women in Antiquity: New Assessments*, London, 178–93.

Bibliography

CORNELL, T. J. (1995) *The Beginnings of Rome*, London.

CRAWFORD, M. H. (ed.) (1996) *Roman Statutes*, vols. i and ii, London.

CROOK, J. A. (1967*a*) '*Patria Potestas*', *CQ* 17: 113–22.

——(1967*b*) 'Gaius 1.84–86', *CR* 81: 7–8.

——(1967*c*) *Law and Life of Rome*, London.

DALLA, D. (1978) *L'incapacità sessuale in diritto romano*, Milan.

DE MARCHI, A. (1896) *Il culto privato di Roma antica*, I, Milan.

DIXON, S. (1986) 'Family Finances: Terentia and Tullia', in B. Rawson (ed.), *The Family in Ancient Rome*, London, 93–120.

——(1988) *The Roman Mother*, London.

——(1991) 'The Sentimental Ideal of the Roman Family', in B. Rawson (ed.), *Marriage, Divorce and Children in Ancient Rome*, London, 99–113.

——(1992) *The Roman Family*, Baltimore.

DONATUTI, G. (1961) 'Contributi allo studio dell'*adrogatio impuberis*', *BIDR* 64: 127–98.

D'ORS, A. (1986) 'Una nueva lista de acciones infamantes', *Sodalitas* (Scritti Guarino), 6: 2575–90.

DUFF, A. M. (1958) *Freedmen in the Early Roman Empire*, Cambridge.

EVANS GRUBBS, J. (1995) *Law and Family in Late Antiquity*, Oxford.

FAYER, C. (1994) *La familia Romana: aspetti giuridici ed antiquari*, Rome.

FLORY, M. B. (1978) 'Family in *familia*: Kinship and Community in Slavery', *AJAH* 3: 78–95.

——(1984) 'Where Women Precede Men: Factors Influencing the Order of Names in Roman Epitaphs', *CJ* 79: 216–24.

GARDNER, J. F. (1986*a*) *Women in Roman Law and Society*, Beckenham.

——(1986*b*) 'Proofs of Status in the Roman World', *BICS* 33: 1–14.

——(1987) 'Another Family and an Inheritance: Claudius Brasidas and his Ex-Wife's Will', *LCM* 12.4: 52–4.

——(1988) 'Julia's Freedmen; Questions of Law and Status', *BICS* 35: 94–100.

——(1989) 'The Adoption of Roman Freedmen', *Phoenix*, 43: 236–57.

——(1991) 'The Purpose of the *Lex Fufia Caninia*', *EMC/Classical Views*, 34 (NS 10): 21–39.

——(1993) *Being a Roman Citizen*, London.

——(1995) 'Gender-Role Assumptions in Roman Law', *EMC/Classical Views*, 39 (NS 14): 377–400.

——(1996) 'Hadrian and the Social Legacy of Augustus', *Labeo*, 42: 83–100.

——(1997) 'Legal Stumbling-Blocks for Lower-Class Families in Rome', in B. Rawson and P. Weaver (edd.), *The Roman Family, Status, Sentiment and Space*, Oxford, 35–53.

——(forthcoming–*a*) 'Status, Sentiment and Strategy in Roman Adoption', in M. Corbier (ed.), *Adoption et 'Fosterage'*, papers of conference organized by the CNRS, Paris, 4–5 June 1993.

Bibliography

GARDNER, J. F. (forthcoming–*b*) 'Women in Business Life: Some Evidence from Puteoli', in P. Setälä (ed.), papers of colloquium held at the Institutum Romanum Finlandiae, Rome, 28–29 September 1995.

——(forthcoming–*c*) 'Sexing a Roman: Imperfect Men in Roman Law', in L. Foxhall and J. Salmon (edd.), *When Men were Men: Masculinity, Power and Identity in Classical Antiquity* (London).

GARNSEY, P. (1975) 'Descendants of Freedmen in Local Politics: Some Criteria', in B. Levick (ed.), *The Ancient Historian and his Materials*, Farnborough, 167–80.

GIRARD, P. F. (1911) *Manuel Élémentaire de Droit Romain*, 5th edn., Paris.

GONZALEZ, J. (1986) 'The *Lex Irnitana*: A New Copy of the Flavian Municipal Law', *JRS* 76: 147– 243.

GORDON, M. L. (1931) 'The Freedman's Son in Municipal Life', *JRS* 21: 65–77.

HARRIS, W. V. (1983) 'Literacy and Epigraphy', *ZPE* 52: 87–111.

——(1986) 'The Roman Father's Power of Life and Death', in R. S. Bagnall and W. V. Harris (edd.), *Studies in Roman Law in Memory of A. Arthur Schiller*, Leiden, 81–95.

——(1989) *Ancient Literacy*, Cambridge, Mass., and London.

HOLFORD-STREVENS, L. (1988) *Aulus Gellius*, London.

HONORÉ, T. (1982) *Ulpian*, Oxford.

——(1994) *Emperors and Lawyers*, 2nd edn., Oxford.

HOPKINS, K. M. (1983) *Death and Renewal*, Cambridge.

HUMBERT, M. (1972) *Le Remariage à Rome*, Milan.

IMPALLOMENI, G. (1963) *Le Manomissioni Mortis Causa*, Padova.

JOHNSTON, D. (1985) 'Prohibitions and perpetuities; family settlements in Roman law', *ZSS* 102: 220–90.

——(1988) *The Roman Law of Trusts*, Oxford.

JOLOWICZ, H. F. (1965) *Historical Introduction to the Study of Roman Law*, 2nd edn., repr., Cambridge.

KASER, M. (1971, 1975) *Das Römische Privatrecht*, i, ii, 2nd edn., Munich.

KNAPP, R. C. (1992) *Latin Inscriptions from Central Spain*, Berkeley.

KELLY, J. M. (1976) *Studies in the Civil Judicature of the Roman Republic*, Oxford.

KIRSCHENBAUM, A. (1993) *Sons, Slaves and Freedmen in Roman Commerce*, Jerusalem and Washington.

KUNST, CHR. (1996) 'Adoption und Testamentadoption in der späten Republik', *Klio*, 78: 87–104.

KURYLOWICZ, M. (1979) '*Adoptio plena* und *minus plena*', *Labeo*, 25: 163–82.

——(1981) *Die Adoption im klassischen römischen Recht*, Warsaw.

——(1984) 'Die justinianische Adoption', *Sodalitas*, 7: 3305–35.

——(1993) 'Zur nachklassischen Adoption', in M. J. Schermeier and Z. Vegh (edd.), *Ars Boni et Aequi: Festschrift für Wolfgang Waldstein*, Stuttgart, 187–201.

Bibliography

LAVAGGI, G. (1946) 'Una riforma ignorata di Giustiniano: *Adrogatio plena e minus plena*', *SHDI* 12: 45–68.

LENEL, O. (1927) *Das Edictum Perpetuum*, Leipzig.

LISSI CARONNA, E., and PANCIERA, S. (1975) 'Roma, via Flaminia 122. Grande tomba circolare, ara funeraria su basamento ara-ossuario e stele sepolcrali', *NSA* 29: 199–232.

MEINHART, M. (1967) *Die Senatusconsulta Tertullianum unde Orfitianum in ihrer Bedeutung für das klassische römische Recht*, Graz.

METTE-DITTMANN, A. (1991) *Die Ehegesetze des Augustus*, Stuttgart.

MILLAR, F. G. B. (1977) *The Emperor in the Roman World*, London.

MINIERI, L. (1982) 'L'adozione del genero', *Labeo*, 28: 278–84.

MITTEIS, L. (1891) *Reichsrecht und Volksrecht in den östlichen Provinzen des römischen Kaiserreichs*, Leipzig.

MOMMSEN, TH. (1877) 'Die pompeianischen Quittungstafeln des L. Caecilius Iucundus', *Hermes*, 12: 88–141.

MOREAU, PH. (1983) 'Structures du parenté et de l'alliance à Larinum d'après le *pro Cluentio*', in M. Cébeillac-Gervasoni (ed.), *Les 'bourgeoisies' municipales italiennes aux IIe et Ier siècles av. J.-C.*, Paris, 99–123.

——(1986) 'Patrimoines et successions à Larinum au Ier siècle av. J.-C.', *RHDFE* 64: 169–89.

MOURITSEN, H. (1988) *Elections, Magistrates and Municipal Élite—Studies in Pompeian Epigraphy*, Rome.

MRATSCHEK-HALFMANN, S. (1993) *Divites et Praepotentes: Reichtum und soziale Stellung in der Literatur der Prinzipatszeit*, Stuttgart.

NICHOLAS, B. (1962) *An Introduction to Roman Law*, Oxford.

NIELSEN, H. S. (1987) '*Alumnus*: A Term of Relation Denoting Quasi-Adoption', *Classica et Mediaevalia*, 37: 141–88.

NORTH, J. A. (1989) 'Religion in Republican Rome', in F. W. Walbank et al., *Cambridge Ancient History*, 2nd edn., vol. vii. 2: 573–624.

NOY, D. (1988) 'The *Senatusconsultum Gaetulicianum: manus* and Inheritance', *TRG* 56: 299–304.

OLIVER, J. H. (1970) *Marcus Aurelius: Aspects of Civic and Cultural Policy in the East*, Hesperia, Supplement 13, Princeton.

PARKIN, T. G. (1992) *Demography and Roman Society*, Baltimore and London.

PRÉVOST, M. (1949) *Les Adoptions politiques à Rome*, Paris.

RABELLO, A. M. (1979) *Effetti Personali della 'Patria Potestas'*, Milan.

RAWSON, B. (1966) 'Family Life among the Lower Classes at Rome in the First Two Centuries of the Empire', *CP* 61: 71–83.

——(1986) 'Children in the Roman *Familia*', in B. Rawson (ed.), *The Family in Ancient Rome*, London, 170–200.

——(1989) '*Spurii* and the Roman View of Illegitimacy', *Antichthon*, 23: 10–41.

Bibliography

RAWSON, B. (1991) 'Adult-Child Relationships in the Roman Family', in B. Rawson (ed.), *Marriage, Divorce and Children in Ancient Rome*, London, 7–30.

RAWSON, E. (1991) *Roman Culture and Society*, Oxford.

RENIER, E. (1942) *Étude sur l'histoire de la 'Querela inofficiosi' en droit romain*, Liège.

RUSSO RUGGERI, C. (1990a) *La Datio in Adoptionem I*, Milan.

——(1990b) 'Ancora sulla donna adottante', *Labeo*, 36: 57–75.

SALLER, R. P. (1984) '*Familia, domus* and the Roman Conception of the Family', *Phoenix*, 38: 336–55.

——(1986) '*Pietas*, Obligation and Authority in the Roman Family', in P. von Kneissl (ed.), *Alte Geschichte und Wissenschaftsgeschichte. Festschrift für Karl Christ zum 65. Geburtstag*, Darmstadt, 393–410.

——(1987) 'Men's Age at Marriage and its Consequences in the Roman Family', *CP* 82, 20–35.

——(1991a) 'Roman Heirship Strategies in Principle and in Practice', in D. L. Kertzer and R. P. Saller (edd.), *The Family in Italy from Antiquity to the Present*, London, 26–47.

——(1991b) 'Corporal Punishment, Authority and Obedience in the Roman Household', in B. Rawson (ed.), *Marriage, Divorce and Children in Ancient Rome*, London, 144–65.

——(1994) *Patriarchy, Property and Death in the Roman Family*, Cambridge.

SALLER, R.P., and SHAW, B. (1984a) 'Tombstones and Roman Family Relations in the Principate: Civilians, Soldiers and Slaves', *JRS* 74: 124–56.

——(1984b) 'Close-Kin Marriage in Roman Society', *Man*, 19: 432–44.

SALOMIES, O. (1992) *Adoptive and Polyonymous Nomenclature in the Roman Empire*, Helsinki.

SALWAY, B. (1994) 'What's in a Name? A Survey of Roman Onomastic Practice from c. 700 B.C. to A.D. 700', *JRS* 84: 124–45.

SCHULZ, F. (1942–3) 'Roman Registers of Birth and Birth-Certificates', *JRS* 32: 79–91 and 33: 155–64.

——(1946) *History of Roman Legal Science*, Oxford.

——(1951) *Classical Roman Law*, Oxford.

SHACKLETON-BAILEY, D. R. (1976) *Two Studies in Roman Nomenclature*, Cambridge.

SHAW, B. D. (1987) 'The Age of Roman Girls at Marriage: Some Reconsiderations', *JRS* 77: 30–46.

SIRKS, A. J. B. (1983) 'The *lex Junia* and the Effects of Informal Manumission and Iteration', *RIDA* 30: 211–92.

STEIN, P. (1985) 'Lex Cincia', *Athenaeum*, 73 (NS 63): 145–53.

SYME, R. (1984) 'Ummidius Quadratus', *Roman Papers*, iii, ed. A. R. Birley, Oxford, 1158–78 (=*HSCP* 82 (1979), 287–310).

——(1986) *The Augustan Aristocracy*, Oxford.

Bibliography

——(1988) 'Clues to Testamentary Adoption', *Roman Papers*, iv, ed. A. R. Birley, Oxford, no. 9, 159–73 (=*Titulus 4: Atti del colloquio internazionale dell'AIEGL su epigrafia e ordine senatorio, Roma 14–20 maggio 1981* I (1982 [1984]), 397–410).

TALBERT, R. J. A (1984) *The Senate of Imperial Rome*, Princeton.

THOMAS, J. A. C. (1967) 'Some Notes on *adrogatio per rescriptum principis*', *RIDA* 14: 413–27.

THOMAS, Y. (1980) 'Mariages endogamiques à Rome. Patrimoine, pouvoir et parenté depuis l'époque archaique', *RHDFE* 58: 345–82.

——(1982) 'Droit domestique et droit politique à Rome', *MEFRA* 94: 527–80.

TODD, S. C. (1993) *The Shape of Athenian Law*, Oxford.

TREGGIARI, S. (1969) *Roman Freedmen During the Late Republic*, Oxford.

——(1975) 'Family Life among the Staff of the Volusii', *TAPhA* 105: 393–402.

——(1981*a*) '*Concubinae*', *PBSR* 49: 59–81.

——(1981*b*) '*Contubernales* in CIL 6', *Phoenix*, 35: 42–69.

——(1991) *Roman Marriage: Iusti Coniuges from the Time of Cicero to the Time of Ulpian*, Oxford.

VAN DE WIEL, C. (1978) 'La Légitimation par mariage subséquent, de Constantin à Justinien. Sa réception sporadique dans le droit byzantin', *RIDA* 25: 307–50.

——(1992) 'Les Différentes Formes de cohabitation hors justes noces et les dénominations diverses des enfants qui en sont nés dans le droit romain, canonique, civil et byzantin jusqu'au treizième siècle', *RIDA* 39: 327–358.

VOCI, P. (1963) *Diritto Ereditario Romano, II: parte speciale*, Milan.

——(1980) 'Storia della *patria potestas* da Augusto a Diocleziano', *Iura*, 31: 37–100.

——(1982) 'Linee storiche del diritto ereditario romano. 1. Dalle origini ai Severi', in *Aufstieg und Niedergang der römischen Welt*, 2.14: 392–448.

VOLTERRA, E. (1966) 'La nozione dell'adoptio e dell'arrogatio secondo i giuristi romani del II e del III secolo d.C.', *BIDR* 69: 109–53.

——(1976) 'L'acquisto della *patria potestas* alla morte del *paterfamilias*', *BIDR* 79: 193–250.

WALDSTEIN, W. (1986) *Operae Libertorum: Untersuchungen zur Dienstpflicht freigelassener Sklaven*, Stuttgart.

WALLACE-HADRILL, A. F. (1981) 'Family and Inheritance in the Augustan Marriage Laws', *PCPhS* 27: 58–80.

WATSON, A. (1967) *The Law of Persons in the Later Roman Republic*, Oxford.

——(1971*a*) *The Law of Succession in the Later Roman Republic*, Oxford.

——(1971*b*) *Roman Private Law around 200 BC*, Edinburgh.

——(1975) *Rome of the Twelve Tables*, Princeton.

——(1977) *Law and Social Change*, Edinburgh.

Bibliography

WATSON, A. (1987) *Roman Slave Law*, Baltimore.

WEAVER, P. (1964) 'Gaius 1.84 and the *Sc. Claudianum*', *CR* 14: 137–9.

——(1972) *Familia Caesaris*, Cambridge.

——(1986) 'The Status of Children in Mixed Marriages', in B. Rawson (ed.), *The Family in Ancient Rome*, London, 145–69.

——(1990) 'Where Have All the Junian Latins Gone? Nomenclature and Status in the Roman Empire,' *Chiron*, 20: 275–305.

——(1991) 'Children of Freedmen (and Freedwomen)', in Rawson, B. (ed.), *Marriage, Divorce and Children in Ancient Rome*, Oxford, 166–90.

WIEDEMANN, T. E. J. (1989) *Adults and Children in the Roman Empire*, London.

WISEMAN, T. P. (1971) *New Men in the Roman Senate 139 BC–AD 14*, Oxford.

Index of Sources

287

288

Index of Sources

Index of Sources

General Index

General Index

Lightning Source UK Ltd.
Milton Keynes UK
UKHW012359270223
417775UK00001B/39